BALLS
and STRIKES

BALLS
and STRIKES
The Money Game in
Professional Baseball

KENNETH M. JENNINGS

PRAEGER

New York
Westport, Connecticut
London

Library of Congress Cataloging-in-Publication Data

Jennings, Kenneth M.
    Balls and strikes : the money game in professional
baseball / Kenneth M. Jennings.
        p.   cm.
   Includes bibliographical references.
   ISBN 0-275-93441-1 (alk. paper)
   1. Collective bargaining—Baseball—United States—History.
I. Title.
GV880.15.J46   1990
331.89′041796357′0973—dc20   89–38009

Library of Congress Catalog Card Number: 89-38009
ISBN: 0-275-93441-1

First published in 1990

Praeger Publishers, One Madison Avenue, New York, NY 10010
A division of Greenwood Press, Inc.

Printed in the United States of America

The paper used in this book complies with the
Permanent Paper Standard issued by the National
Information Standards Organization (Z39.48-1984).

10 9 8 7 6 5 4 3 2 1

Contents

Tables and Exhibit

TABLES

EXHIBIT

Preface

I believe baseball remains one of the few things that rewards individual effort in our country, . . . and I want it to remain that way. I don't want it to become unionized.

Tom Seaver, 1969

We voted unanimously to take a stand. We're not going to give another god-damn cent. And if they want to strike, let them strike.

Gussie Busch, 1972

We plan absentee ownership as far as running the Yankees is concerned. . . . We're not going to pretend [to be] something we aren't. I'll stick to building ships.

George Steinbrenner, 1973

Player-management relationships in baseball are dynamic multidimensional phenomena. This book focuses on confrontations and relationships between players and management from the perspective of several hundred collective bargaining participants—those union and management officials who negotiate the labor agreement, and the union members who must approve and live with the labor agreement.

This perspective is derived from a variety of media sources, related biographies, autobiographies, and academic articles. No attempt was made to compartmentalize the information: Don't be surprised to encounter an insight obtained from the *American Economic Review* combined with a quote from Sparky Lyle's *The Bronx Zoo*, to make a particular point. Sometimes related insights either reflect somewhat earthy situations and/or are described by the participants in obscene terms. These inclusions are not intended to sensationalize the book. Instead, they should offer some insight into the "common law of the shop" as well as participants' attitudes and behaviors, which in turn can shape various industrial relations activities and issues.

Balls and Strikes is divided into three parts. The first part reviews collective bargaining efforts from the time of the first professional baseball team in 1869 to the present. Key participants in the industrial relations process—owners, agents, the media, managers, and players—are discussed in the second part. The book then concludes with a discussion of contemporary industrial relations issues: drug and alcohol abuse, racial discrimination, and the relationship between pay and performance.

I hope that the reader will obtain additional insights into this fascinating sport/business, as well as an appreciation for baseball's off-field excitement and controversies.

Thanks go to many people for the contents herein. Betty Geitz made this book possible: Without her continued ability to read and process my notes and to encourage—maybe prod—my efforts, this book would not have been completed. Others who have directly or indirectly contributed include Ron Adams, Dave Augspurger, Tom Bradley, Kathy Cohen, Jay Coleman, Robert Craemer, Milton Derber, Jim Dunton, Mary Fischer, F. X. Flinn, Bruce Fortado, Penny Gaffney, Steve Hatem, Joan Hoffman, Maggie Jarpey, Bill Johnson, Dick Kip, Paul Kwartler, Grann Lloyd, Frank McLaughlin, Patricia Merrill, Marvin Miller, Kitty Moore, Ed Moses, LeAnna Payne, Lauren Pera, Jane Perkins, Peggy Pruett, Jim Renfroe, Carole Russo, Art Schack, Michelle Scott, Steve Shapiro, Scotty Smathers, John Taylor, John Thorn, Leslie Wager, George Warren, Steve Williamson, and Said Yari.

Finally, much credit goes to Jackie, Ali, and Bret who remained hopeful and cheerful in spite of my behavior while writing this book at home.

Part One

Collective Bargaining Efforts

One

Early Collective Bargaining

Baseball players have always been paid better than the average U.S. citizen. Players on the Cincinnati Redstockings, the first completely professional team, averaged $930—more than five times the per capita income ($170 a year) at that time (Table 1.1). Players' earnings in 1989 averaged $512,804—a figure more than 26 times that of the general population. Therefore, baseball players' already high salaries increased at an even higher rate than could be reasonably expected by a historical comparison.

Some attribute this situation to the Major League Baseball Players' Association (MLBPA), led by Marvin Miller. Indeed, under Miller the MLBPA has represented a very significant influence. Yet previous union leaders and organizations also formulated, approached, and partially resolved many bargaining issues—even as early as 1885.

EARLY COLLECTIVE BARGAINING EFFORTS: 1885–1923

Brotherhood of Professional Base Ball Players

There were three major players' collective bargaining efforts during the era 1885–1923. The first—the Brotherhood of Professional Base Ball Players—started eight years after the National League of Professional Base Ball Clubs was formed in 1876. The constitution of the league itself established rules for member clubs and players alike. One such player rule—clearly not applicable nowadays—stated that "each player must pay thirty dollars ($30)

Table 1.1
The Payroll of the First Professional Baseball Team

Name	Age	Occupation	Position	Salary	Salary as related to 1985 per capita income*
Harry Wright	35	Jeweler	Center Field	$1,200	$118,304
Asa Brainard	25	Insurance	Pitcher	1,100	108,418
Douglas Allison	22	Marble Cutter	Catcher	800	78,925
Charles Gould	21	Bookkeeper	First Base	800	78,925
Charles Sweasey	21	Hatter	Second Base	800	78,925
Fred Waterman	23	Insurance	Third Base	1,000	98,531
George Wright	22	Engraver	Short Stop	1,400	137,910
Andrew Leonard	23	Hatter	Left Field	800	78,925
Calvin McVey	20	Piano Maker	Right Field	800	78,925
Richard Hurley	20	Piano Maker	Substitute	600	59,152
		Total Team Payroll		9,300	916,940

Source: Lee Allen, *The Cincinnati Reds* (1948), pp.4–5, cited in Peter S. Craig, "Organized Baseball," Bachelor of Arts Thesis, Oberlin College, 1950, p. 17. The per capita income in 1869 was $170. Thus, Harry Wright's salary was 7.06 times the per capita income. Multiplying the 1985 per capita income—$16,757—by 7.06 gives the comparable 1985 salary figure.

for the uniform furnished him by the club for the season of 1877, and must, at his own expense, keep the same clean, and in good repair."[1]

A more significant rule that is also inapplicable today allowed National League players to enter into contract with other clubs for the players' future services. Apparently owners did not at first care whether players left their jobs and became employed with another team.

This situation changed in 1879. The owners realized that under this arrangement, certain teams would hire all the best players and increase their team's victories. The improved win-loss record would then result in increased fan attendance—the major source of team revenues in those days. Therefore, each of the eight National League baseball clubs pledged not to employ any player reserved by another team, and player mobility was effectively eliminated.

The reserve rule has been a major, long-standing obstacle to baseball player unions' achievement of gold-collar status. Further attention will be given to the reserve rule's first appearance in the collective bargaining agreement some 100 years later in Chapter Two; various reserve rule modifications are discussed in Chapter Eight. Players have objected to the rule all along.

John Ward, an accomplished baseball player of the early days, realized the reserve rule's obstructive nature in 1887, and urged its removal through collection action.

> There is now no escape for the player. If he attempts to elude the operation of the rule, he becomes at once a professional outlaw, and the hand of every club is against him. He may be willing to play elsewhere for less salary, he may be unable to play, or, for other reasons, may retire for a season or more, but if ever he reappears as a professional ball-player it must be at the disposition of his former club. Like a fugitive-slave law, the reserve-rule denies him a harbor or a livelihood, and carries him back, bound and shackled, to the club from which he attempted to escape. We have, then, the curious result of a contract which on its face is for seven months being binding for life . . .
>
> On the other hand, what reciprocal claim has the player? Absolutely none: For services rendered he draws his salary; but for a continuance of that service he has no claim whatever. . . . The club may hold the player as long as it pleases, and may release him at any time, with or without cause, by a simple ten days' notice; while the player is bound for life, and, no matter what his interests or wishes may be, cannot terminate the contract, even by ten years' notice.[2]

Ward also objected to three other unilaterally implemented rules:

1. Salary caps—the majority of players were kept under $2,500 a year;
2. A pay classification system that relegated the lowest paid players (Class E) to a maximum of $1,500 a year along with other job duties such as collecting admission tickets and sweeping up the ballpark after the game;
3. Selling players to other teams—for example, superstar Mike "King" Kelly was sold to Boston for $10,000 in 1886—without the affected players receiving any portion of the revenues.

In 1885, Ward formed the Brotherhood of Professional Base Ball Players to counter the aforementioned owner rules. The Brotherhood was constituted with the following charter:

> We, the undersigned, professional base ball players, recognizing the importance of united effort and impressed with its necessity in our behalf, do form ourselves this day into an organization to be known as the "Brotherhood of Professional Base Ball Players." The objects we seek to accomplish are:
>
> > To protect and benefit ourselves collectively and individually.
> >
> > To promote a high standard of professional conduct.
> >
> > To foster and encourage the interest of . . . . Base Ball.[3]

By 1887, this organization had an estimated membership of 90 players, and it sought formal recognition with the owners. The Brotherhood did negotiate with the owners, although real progress had not yet been made by 1888. Some players wanted to strike or use the courts to resolve the impasse. Ward discouraged these actions since he believed that the "gravest offense" a player could make was to break his contract. Many players had already signed their contracts for the 1888 season. Therefore, Ward headed off the strike action and discouraged two of the players from testing the reserve rule in court.

The Brotherhood League, and the Players' Protective Association

Player resentment against the club owners grew so much during this time period that the Brotherhood formed a rival league—the National Brotherhood League—in 1889. Financial backers provided initial support for the teams, which were then run as corporations—with the players sharing in the profits. Each game's receipts were shared fifty-fifty between the home and visiting clubs, but the home club could keep profits from the concessions. Players were now part-owners, and they began to adopt some practices against which they had previously protested. For one thing, the players realized that competitive, evenly watched games would increase fan attendance and revenues. They therefore allowed for the compulsory transfer of players to other teams in the league to equalize the teams' playing strengths.

The Players' (Brotherhood) League attracted players by offering three-year contracts that could be raised but not lowered from the salary structure in 1889. Still, not all players jumped the National League for the Brotherhood. The fans were the ones who benefited the most from the 1890 season. They were actively courted by both the leagues, and saw good baseball at cheaper ticket prices. The Player's League did score more fan attendance (980,887 for 532 games) than the National League (813,678 for 540 games).[4] However, with their greater financial reserves, the owners of the National League put an end to the Brotherhood League after only one season. Connie Mack, who had joined the Brotherhood before becoming a successful manager and owner in the major leagues for several decades, noted that the National League owners spent about $4 million dollars to bankrupt the Players League. But by the time the Brotherhood players returned to their former National League teams, the owners had at least realized that "ballplayers are human and must be given a fair deal or they will rebel."[5]

Ward blamed the Brotherhood League's defeat on its backers' "stupidity, avarice, and treachery." Against Ward's advice, these individuals had insisted on playing the same season schedule as the National League, and they were quick to remove their financial support at the first sign that they might lose some money.[6] Also, a majority of the press appeared to be against the Brotherhood. For example, one reporter wrote that players who transferred to the new league were "drunken knaves who would be idling on the street corners but for the opportunity the National League owners opened for them."[7] In any case, after the Brotherhood League collapsed, collective player actions were virtually nonexistent for the next ten years.

The Players' Protective Association was formed in 1900 by Clark Griffith and some other players. Nearly 100 players joined this organization, although none believed in striking for its demands. The Association unsuccessfully pressed for a $3,000 salary minimum and free uniforms. Its bargaining power was enhanced at least when many players moved to the rival American League—which was also formed in 1900, by Ban Johnson. However, this second union faded into obscurity when the National and American Leagues merged and held their first World Series in 1903.[8]

During the next ten years, baseball offered mixed returns to the various team owners. Some teams saw a tremendous growth in value and therefore in the franchise price paid by subsequent owners. Other teams realized only a narrow distinction between financial profits and losses.[9]

The Ty Cobb Strike and the Baseball Players' Fraternity

During a baseball game in the summer of 1912, Ty Cobb—a future Hall of Famer for the Detroit Tigers—was continually being heckled by a New York reporter named Lueker.

Cobb, sitting on the bench during the Detroit half of the inning, heard still another tirade from Lueker, "Hey Cobb, you're nothin but a yellow-bellied bastard!"

When the Detroit side was retired and Cobb started back out toward his position, manager Jennings, glancing at him, could tell what was going to happen. "I knew he was going to do it," Hughie said later. "Once I saw the look in his eyes, I was sure of it. But there was no way of stopping him."

Ty trotted down the left-field line. As he turned to go out into center field, Lueker cut loose with another stream of blue sparks. Cobb suddenly swung around and charged. He advanced on the bleachers in the direction of the voice, vaulted over the rail, and shoved his way through the mass of spectators until he reached Lueker. Then he began punching the daylights out of him.

"He hit me in the face with his fist, knocked me down, jumped on me and kicked me in the ear," Lueker told police later.

The New York fans were so amazed and startled that nobody moved a muscle until Cobb had finished with Lueker. Nobody could believe what they had just seen. No ballplayer had ever dared hop into the stands that way. As Cobb finished, they began to rise in rage. Ty had to fight his way back down to the playing field. All his teammates, led by Wahoo Sam Crawford, stood along the field brandishing bats. They were certain the fans would storm on the field and mob Cobb. They almost did.[10]

Cobb was suspended indefinitely for his actions, and his teammates presented the following strike agreement to the president of the American League, Ban Johnson.

B. B. Johnson, Fisher Building, Chicago

Feeling that Mr. Cobb is being done an injustice by your action in suspending him we, the undersigned, refuse to play in another game after to-day until such action is adjusted to our satisfaction. He was fully justified in his action, as no one could stand such personal abuse from any one. We want him reinstated for to-morrow's game, May 18, or there will be no game. If the players cannot have protection we must protect ourselves.[11]

Manager Hughie Jennings sympathized with his players. However, the owner of the Tigers indicated that games not played would be forfeited. Cobb reacted angrily to the suspension, believing he was justified in his actions and that an investigation should have been made before the discipline was imposed.

The Detroit players' strike action did not happen out of affection for Cobb. Few—if any—players liked Cobb. However, they realized that his .400 batting average was necessary to the team's success. Management responded somewhat frantically by hiring player replacements off the street. They took anyone "who could stop a grapefruit from rolling uphill." The Tigers lost the first game they played with replacements, 24–2. The second game was cancelled, with the striking players given a $100 fine and threatened with permanent removal from baseball. Cobb encouraged the players to return for the next game; and eventually Cobb himself received a $50 fine plus a ten-day suspension for his behavior.

It was this incident that must have led David Fultz to form the Baseball Players' Fraternity in 1912. Like its two predecessors, the Fraternity was concerned with raising players' salaries, and its members were given the option of jumping to a new rival baseball organization—in this case, the Federal League, which was formed in 1911. The league raided players and doubled the average player salary by inciting a bidding war. Star players really benefited from the increased possibilities for employment. Connie Mack, owner of a National League team at the time, recalled his initial anger when players jumped his team for more money. His perspective changed over the years, however, when he realized that he could hardly blame players for making a good business decision. Ty Cobb went through very hard salary negotiations for $10,000 in 1910. Yet in 1915, he was paid $20,000 ($839,476 in 1985 dollars) to remain with his team instead of jump over to the rival league.

The Federal League failed in 1915. In his memoirs, John J. McGraw—a very successful player, manager, and owner during that era—contended that the failure was due to lack of baseball experience among the Federal League executives. McGraw also felt that there were not enough good players in the country for three leagues (the National, American, and Federal). "Consequently, the Federal League, being the newcomer, could not get enough talent to offer serious competition."[12] By 1918 the Fraternity also faded out of existence, largely because its leader—Fultz—lacked the necessary leadership qualities.

He had a dour personality and was a poor social mixer. He often would lecture to the players about profligate habits. In his *Baseball* magazine columns, he regularly warned the players not to buy automobiles because they could not afford them. He wanted to expel players from the Fraternity for not hustling. He even allowed some players to organize a Prohibition campaign within the Fraternity.

How a no-drinking pledge might have advanced the interests of all the players in professional baseball is hard to imagine.[13]

Collective bargaining floundered for a long time after the demise of the Baseball Players' Fraternity. Players did threaten to strike in 1918, but the issue was increased World Series compensation—not union organization. In 1922 the National Baseball Players' Association of the United States was formed by lawyer Ray Cannon. Although it claimed a membership of 225 players in 1923, the union soon collapsed because players were not interested in its objectives.

John McGraw wrote that unions were unsuccessful during this time period because they failed to address players' real concerns. McGraw maintained that good players never did have any problem in obtaining good salaries; and that other players' salaries increased steadily with the progress of the game. Thus "players grow tired of seeing their dues go to pay the salaries of [union officers] who either sit in the offices looking important or travel about the country at the expense of the contributors."[14] McGraw felt that a union would be more successful if it addressed the retirement concerns of veteran players, since few players prepare themselves for this situation.

THE MEXICAN LEAGUE, AND ROBERT MURPHY'S GUILD

The Rival Mexican League

Two parallel developments—the rival Mexican League, and Robert Murphy's American Baseball Guild—stimulated collective bargaining interests in 1946. The Mexican League was formed by the five Pasquel brothers, who attempted to lure big-time U.S. players to Mexico. One of the brothers allegedly put five certified $10,000 checks on Stan Musial's hotel bed (Musial was earning $13,000 a year at the time) in an unsuccessful attempt to get Musial to switch leagues.

The Mexican League was more initially successful with two other stars: shortstop Vern Stephens of the Saint Louis Browns, and catcher Mickey Owen of the Dodgers. However, after signing a contract (five years at $15,000 a year) to play in Mexico, Stephens quickly returned—with the angry Pasquels threatening him and U.S. baseball management—when offered a higher contract in the States.

Mickey Owen suffered a rougher fate. He transferred to the Mexican League after the U.S. commissioner of baseball, Happy Chandler, had pronounced that any player who jumped his contract would be barred in the United States for at least five years. At first, Owen was unconcerned about the threatened suspension. He was pleased with his salary and believed that the surplus of U.S. players would improve the quality and magnitude of baseball in Mexico. The situation changed a few months later, however, when Owen returned to the United States to help the Dodgers during the 1946 pennant race. Owen considered his contract in Mexico to be terminated because he had been fired as manager.

Dodger management was very interested in having Owen back. However, many of the players wanted the jumped-contract suspension to apply to Owen. Marty Marion, a star player who was involved in resolving several collective bargaining issues in 1946, expressed a common player sentiment. "Owen jumped his team to go down there for that big money; now let him stay there."[15] Owen wound up sitting out a suspension; he eventually returned to play the 1949 season.

The Mexican League failed in 1946 for several reasons, such as lack of fans, inadequate playing fields, the costly investment in establishing stadiums similar to those found in the United States, and serious climate and atmosphere differences—problems that would not permit a long, smooth-playing season.[16] However, the league did at least make owners realize that competition for their ballplayers could occur.

Robert Murphy's American Baseball Guild

On the domestic front, there was a flurry of collective-bargaining activities during this time period. In early 1946 Robert C. Murphy, a lawyer and former examiner of the National Labor Relations Board, became concerned about the economic condition of baseball players. Murphy realized that certain stars—like Hall of Famer Jimmy Foxx (.325 batting average for 20 seasons)—had very inadequate retirement incomes. Also, some players were making below $3,500 a year at the time.

Murphy registered his American Baseball Guild as an independent union in Suffolk County, Massachusetts, on April 14, 1946. His union's program consisted of the following major points:

1. Freedom of contract should be established so a player would not be forced to join a particular club against his will.
2. Players sold or traded should receive a percentage of the purchase price (similar to the Brotherhood's earlier bargaining proposal).

3. Disputes between players and management regarding salary and other conditions of employment should be settled by collective bargaining.
4. Provisions should be made for security, insurance, bonuses, and other matters.[17]

Murphy claimed to have several star players as members. He also had the endorsement of the two major national labor organizations, the American Federation of Labor (AFL), and the Congress of Industrial Organizations (CIO).

One owner—Clark Griffith of the Washington Senators—considered this union to be doomed from the start since players were already well paid and negotiations had been accepted by owners and players as being on a basis of every man for himself. In Griffith's opinion, few—if any—$40,000-a-year players would strike simply because less qualified players were seeking $10,000.[18]

Griffith was correct in tieing the potential of collective bargaining to the contentment of star players with their wages and other working conditions. Many people in baseball believed at the time that fan attendance depended on the stars—on outstanding contributions and personalities. Dissatisfied "mediocre" players could always be replaced by minor leaguers. This was the situation until 1966 when Marvin Miller became head of the Major League Baseball Players' Association. Miller eventually convinced the players that every one of them was essential to game revenues, and he bargained for issues (minimum wages, pensions, salary arbitration, and so forth) that pertained to most—if not all—players.

Back in 1946, though, Robert Murphy wanted the National Labor Relations Board (NLRB)—an independent government agency originated by the National Labor Relations Act of 1935—to determine if the Guild should represent the players in collective bargaining activities for all major-league teams. The NLRB refused to hold this election, without giving a formal reason. The agency probably declined because it felt that professional baseball did not fall under its charge to oversee labor management relations in interstate commerce.

Murphy then decided to focus his attention on one team, the Pittsburgh Pirates, where—he claimed—a majority of players desired union recognition. He also selected the Pirates because Pennsylvania had a State Labor Relations Act and a related agency to administer it. A confrontation occurred with Pirate ownership on June 5, 1946. Murphy wanted management to recognize the Guild that afternoon. Management stalled, saying that they needed more time to study the situation. The Pirate players must have been impressed when the team's owner made his first visit to the clubhouse in 12 years to address them about the situation. Yet many of the players resented being talked down to and would have struck that day if Murphy had not dissuaded them.

Months later, he admitted that he had made a tactical error in not supporting the militant players. Murphy thought that management would eventually accept the Guild and that a strike would be unfair to the 26,000 fans who were waiting for the game to begin. He quickly followed up that blunder with another, by saying that the players would strike June 7 if management did not agree to hold a consent election to determine whether the Guild represented a majority of the Pirates. Some feel that Murphy—an outsider—should have let the players speak for themselves and in so doing persuade other players to join the Guild.

The vote was 20–16 in favor of striking—an impressive total, since trainers and coaches could vote under Guild rules. However, the strike did not take place because the Guild had previously established a two-thirds vote as being necessary to authorize a strike. Murphy figured that the majority of players voting to strike would also vote for union representation if another election were held. However, a representation election conducted by the Pennsylvania Labor Relations Board on August 21, 1946, proved him wrong. Only 19 of the 31 eligible team members voted in this election, with 15 voting against the Guild and 3 voting for (one of the votes was challenged and did not count in the total). Rip Sewell, the player credited with preventing the team from striking on June 5[19]—considered this vote a reflection of players' belief that they could make more money in a nonunion situation. It also reflected public opinion against players joining unions. Perhaps the first related public-opinion poll was conducted in July 1946—a month before the representation vote. Only 12 percent of the public responded yes to the question, "Would you like to see baseball players join labor unions?"[20]

AFTER MURPHY AND BEFORE MILLER

The MacPhail Report

Murphy realized that even the threat of players' collective action might generate better working conditions. The National and American League presidents and several owners met several times between the "negative" strike vote and August's representation election, to thwart player unionization. One outcome of these meetings was a managerial mission statement—the MacPhail Report—which stated: "A healthier relationship between club and player will be effective in resisting attempts at unionization by outsiders."[21]

More tangible management concessions did occur shortly after the MacPhail Report was circulated. Owners invited 26 players representing all teams to meet and formulate working condition reforms. Management modified and/or accepted some of these suggestions, such as a $5,000 salary minimum, increased severance pay, a spring training allowance of $25 a week, and a player pension plan. Formal player representation was also established, through the Major League Executive Council. This group would include players who were elected each year "for consideration of all matters which concern the standard form of player contract or its provisions and regulations, or other matters of club-player relationship."[22]

The player pension plan represented the biggest financial outcome of the reform meeting, and the plan was approved in February 1947. All players, trainers, and coaches on the opening day of spring training would be eligible for the following payouts: "A player, after serving five seasons in the major leagues, shall receive, on reaching 50, an income of $50 a month for the rest of his life. Each additional year of service will increase the pension amount $10 a month until a maximum of $100 a month is reached for ten-year men and over."[23] An annual funding pool of $675,000 was obtained from the receipts of the All-Star Game and from the $150,000 that sponsors paid for World Series radio broadcasting rights. Owners had to contribute a flat payment of $250 for every team player subscribing to the plan. Players' contributions varied depending on length of service.[24] A player who did not make the five seasons necessary for eligibility would have his contribution returned to him. If a player should die before receiving the benefits, his beneficiaries would receive his annuity for 120 months.

Although this plan did place about 80 percent of the burden on the owners, there were still some problems encountered by the players, as well. For example, less than 8 percent of the players on major league rosters in 1949 and 1950 were classified as ten-year veterans.

The 1950s and Early 1960s

Baseball's ruling body—the Executive Council—had been dominated by Commissioner K. M. Landis, but by 1946, during Commissioner Happy Chandler's regime, its character had changed. This new seven-member board reflected the influences of Murphy's unionization attempts and the Mexican League; it consisted of the commissioner, the two league presidents, one club owner from each league, and one player representative from each league. The first league player representatives were Fred "Dixie" Walker of the Dodgers and John Murphy of the Yankees. These representatives had no vote and could only discuss matters that involved players' welfare. The council also honored one team player representative for each team. The team representatives discussed team-specific problems with the particular team's owners. When a problem involved an entire league or both leagues, each team representative conferred with the league representative, who in turn presented the problem before league officials.[25]

Using this fixed system of representation, the players continued to press for bargaining issues even when their proposals were refused. Pension plan design and implementation was a most significant bargaining issue affecting all players. The issue came to the forefront with the death of a ten-year veteran—36-year-old Ernie Bonhaur—in 1949. Available pension revenues could not provide for Bonhaur's widow, and Commissioner Chandler hastily obtained additional revenues by selling the TV-radio rights for the World Series and the All-Star Game to the Gillette Safety Razor Company at a price of $1 million a year for the next six years.

Yet management did not give the players a detailed accounting of their pension plan. The next league player representatives (Ralph Kiner for the National League, and Allie Reynolds for the American League)—after consulting with the team player representatives—hired a lawyer, Jonas Norman Lewis, to serve as liaison between the players and the owners on this and possibly other issues. Lewis was not hired to be a union leader; his job was to represent the players before management. Kiner and Reynolds maintained that this action was not an attack on then Commissioner Ford C. Frick, nor on the owners. Indeed, the players were in such need of legal representation because of their poor business skills, that Lewis's hiring was intended to improve their relationship with the owners.

Lewis's salary was paid out of a central fund created by television revenues. The player representatives wanted Lewis to attend the summer 1953 meetings with management, but he was denied admittance to the meetings. Reynolds and Kiner did attend, probably due to their holding a philosophy of labor relations that stressed collective discussion rather than strikes or other union-type protests. Reynolds indicated, "I would be as much opposed to a labor boss in baseball as would the owners. We can only hope for the best and rely upon the fairness of the men who run baseball." This attitude was shared by Ralph Kiner. "All we want from Lewis is legal advice. We don't want a players' union. Lewis isn't interested in one, and the first hint that he is, out he goes."[26]

As it happened, Reynolds and Kiner did not receive much satisfaction on their pension concerns. However, they did reach agreement with management on the following three working-condition changes:

1. The allowance for moving was increased. A player traded from one eastern club to another eastern club or from one western club to another western club would receive a flat sum of $300 to cover moving expenses. A player traded from an eastern club to a western club, or vice versa, would receive a flat sum of $600 for expenses.

2. During spring training, if a player should elect to live outside the hotel at which the club was staying (with permission of the club), he would be reimbursed the full hotel rate.

3. If a player should require surgery for illness or injury suffered outside the line of baseball duty, he would not be required to undergo such surgery at his own expense.

4. Each player would receive $8 per day for meal money on the road.[27]

In 1954, former Commissioner Chandler accused management of possibly removing some of the pension funds reserved for the players. He also accused the current commissioner, Ford Frick, of being negligent by not representing players' pension interests.

Two days after Chandler's remarks, Commissioner Frick presented the media with a printed report of the pension plan. Frick disagreed with Chandler's contention that all radio-television revenues from the World Series and the All-Star Games should go to the players.

These receipts have always belonged to the clubs, according to their idea that, of the employer-employee relationship—which has been established in courts in other cases—they pay their players salaries to produce and the receipts from such production belong to the employer.[28]

All of the radio and television proceeds from the two events went into a central fund ($598,400 in 1954) that covered: (1) pension plan costs; (2) expenses of the commissioner's office not met by its share of the World Series gate receipts; (3) funds to enable each club to meet income taxes on its share of proceeds paid into the central fund; and (4) other purposes that the Executive Council might designate. The pension plan, which was funded by the players as well as the owners, would pay players with five years' service $50 a month at age 50 and ten-year players $100 a month at age 50.

The players' attorney, Lewis, was not pleased with Frick's remarks and stated that, under the present arrangement, management could unilaterally alter or cancel the plan at whim. Lewis felt that the players should have an active role in negotiating television contracts and that the increased revenues could generate a pension payout of $300–$400 a month.[29]

The players did get to have to a say on the pension plan shortly thereafter. In 1956 the old plan expired; and the new pension plan was funded with 60 percent of All-Star Game receipts and all radio and television profits from the game, along with radio and television receipts from the World Series. Also, the administration of the fund was to be handled by two selected major-league owners and two selected player representatives, with no fifth man or arbitrator involved. A joint statement made by the owners and players attending the meeting indicated that the new findings and administration procedures resolved any previous player-owner pension plan concerns.[30]

According to Ralph Kiner, who was at the meeting, the players did obtain a major concession from management. The owners had pressed for a flat $1-million-a-year contribution to the pension plan. But Kiner believed that the future looked bright for television and that therefore, 60 percent of TV revenues would be better for the players. Yet the players were not involved in negotiating for television contracts, in the first place. Commissioner Frick had the main—if not sole—responsibility for this revenue-generating effort, which resulted in $16,250,000 for the 1947–61 time period.

In any case, the new pension plan went into effect on April 1, 1957. Up to and through the 1961 season, a player would receive $88 a month at age

50 for five years of service, $175 a month for ten years of service, $225 a month for 15 years, and $275 a month for 20 years. Adjusting for inflation, these amounts would be $432, $858, $1,103, and $1,348, respectively, in 1986 dollars.

The pension plan was also extended to all players active, inactive, and retired since 1947, when the original plan was conceived. Another new provision under the plan provided the widow of an eligible player with pension payouts for life or until remarriage. And any player who paid $344 a year was also eligible for the following benefits: life insurance of $6,000–$20,000 (depending on length of service), individual/family hospitalization coverage, and disability payments of $450 a month for life or until recovery.

Due to these improvements, the players did not press for an involvement in negotiating the television contracts that expired in 1961. League player representatives Robin Roberts and Harvey Kuenn expressed "complete confidence in the commissioner making the best possible deal for us."[31]

Notwithstanding their progress in the area of pensions, players were less successful in raising their minimum salary of $6,000 a year. Various suggestions were made in the 1950s for raising the minimum to $7,000, $7,200, and $7,500. In 1958 the players proposed that the salary budget of each club should equal 20 percent of all its gross receipts. They justified their position by citing the following data:

—During the years 1952–56 the total income of the major league clubs increased about $10 million; players' salaries increased only $300,000 during this time period.

—In 1950 the percentage of salaries against gross income was 21.6; in 1956 the figure had dropped to 12.9.[32]

The owners rejected all of the salary increase proposals, and the minimum remained at $6,000.

The system of player representation did help to improve some working conditions during the 1950s and early 1960s. Lewis was fired by the MLBPA in 1959: For one thing, he had refused to tour spring training camps and obtain player insights regarding possible working-condition problems. Yet Lewis's replacement by Robert Cannon did not signal a desire on the part of the players to assume the traditional collective-bargaining stance. Player representative Bob Feller, a superstar much like the other player representatives at the time, reinforced Clark Griffith's remarks noted earlier. The star players realized that their salaries were large, and saw this as a reward for performance. Feller believed that players should promote baseball and that collective bargaining would only hurt: The public would neither understand nor sympathize with the concerns of comparatively high-paid baseball players. Bob Friend, another active players' representative and superstar, expressed similar thoughts some years later:

I firmly believe a union, in the fullest sense of the word, simply would not fit the situation in baseball. . . . Baseball is different than the ordinary business or industry. Players and management work closely together. If we begin operating a union, we immediately will begin antagonizing the owners. If union negotiators don't have something to argue about, they'll create something. They're always looking for trouble.

If the structure of our players' association was changed to a union, I believe it would result in ill will for the players. It would tend to destroy the image of the baseball star for the youngsters because of the haggling between the players and the owners. . . . We have made tremendous strides with our organization. We have improved the lot of the players financially with a minimum salary, $10 daily for meals, moving expenses when traded, etc. We have improved his working conditions with finer clubhouses, better batting backgrounds, etc. And is there a union that has as lucrative a pension plan as ours?[33]

Stan Musial agreed with Friend. Musial thought that player-management relationships definitely improved in the 20-year time period from 1938 to 1958.[34]

Also, not all teams were enjoying consistent financial success during the 1950s and early 1960s. In 1963—for example—National League attendance was at a record high, but total major-league attendance fell 4.3 percent because some American League teams had experienced attendance drops.[35] Perhaps there were some players who, like Robin Roberts, felt that a focus on traditional bargaining issues equally applicable to all clubs would put certain teams at a financial disadvantage. Roberts believed that the owners were more knowledgeable than the players in most financial matters. In any case, three of the four joint player-management meetings each year tended to focus on relatively inexpensive issues that were unique to particular teams.

The player representative system including the MLBPA also did not act like a union during this time period: The player representatives had no vote. Their role was to communicate possibilities for the owners to consider.[36]

The player "negotiation" minutes during this period reveal that players would sit next to the owners of their teams and discuss issues. High turnover among player representatives was a major problem. Agreed-upon issues were not always remembered over the years. Indeed, some time was spent in negotiating issues which had been previously resolved.[37]

This situation changed with the appointment of Marvin Miller in 1966.

Two

Marvin Miller and the MLBPA

EARLY EXPERIENCES

Selection and Orientation

The players did not carry Marvin Miller into the MLBPA on their shoulders. They wanted his successor—Robert Cannon—to be president, but Cannon refused. A four-man player committee (Robin Roberts, Bob Friend, Harvey Kuenn, and Jim Bunning) went to a prominent labor-relations professor, George Taylor, and obtained a list of six qualified candidates. The players' association then received Commissioner William Eckert's assurance that all the candidates were fine men. In April 1966 Miller was approved by the players, with a convincing margin of the vote (489 for; 136 against). This figure was even more impressive since some classes of management (trainers, coaches, and managers) could also vote.[1]

Miller had extensive labor relations experience with the War Labor Board; the Department of Labor, where he had trained mediators; and the United Steelworkers Union, where he served as chief economist. He appeared to be bringing to the job a different labor-management philosophy than his predecessor Cannon, who in 1964 had said, "We have it so good we don't know what to ask for next." Cannon believed that players had "the finest pension program in existence" and a "magnificent" relationship with the owners—who accepted player requests "99 percent of the time."[2]

Some baseball executives tried to inculcate in Miller a sense of owner permanence as well as benevolence. As Joe Cronin explained to Miller,

"Young man . . . I've been in this game a long time now and I've learned something that I want you to think about. Players come and go, but owners will be here forever, and don't you forget it."[3] Cronin was basically correct for his time: When Miller first came into office, owners represented a small continuous group that seemed unified on player-management issues, at least on the surface.

Yet the accumulation of player gains under and after Miller has been due in large part to subsequent owner turnover and dissension. Major disagreements among owners have occurred over collective bargaining strategies (strike, for example) and issues (free agent salaries for example). These disagreements discussed throughout this book were in large part stimulated by Miller, who—unlike Cannon—was accustomed to adversarial relationships.

Commissioner Bowie Kuhn—writing in his autobiography, *Hardball*—remembers being impressed at first by Miller's "low-key charm" which did not generate threats toward management. Kuhn contends that Miller was more occupied with securing his position with union members and heading off any challenges from other unions. Kuhn changed his assessment of Miller shortly thereafter. "As the months went by . . . I began to realize that we had before us an old-fashioned, nineteenth-century trade unionist who hated management generally and the management of baseball specifically."

Initially, Miller did not have a program or bargaining agenda. Unlike the earlier union organizers—Ward, Fultz, and Murphy—Miller placed much attention on finding out what the players wanted. "I'm very anxious to get the views of the players and find out what they would like this association to become. I'll have to feel my way and I'll be dependent on what they think."[4] He visited the spring training camps in 1966 and successfully convinced players that he was no "union goon," but—rather—a person who was genuinely interested in their working concerns. By their reactions during these meetings, the owners solidified Miller's position with the players even more. Miller indicated that the owners "have been my biggest allies. When some of them tried to talk their players out of hiring me in 1966, the men simply concluded: Anybody the owners hate that much can't be all bad!"[5] Bill Veeck said the same thing—that his fellow owners gave Miller the advantage. "Whenever Marvin needed help . . . these dunderheads seemed to do or say something that rallied his players behind him. Miller reminds me of a successful funeral director; he just sits back, wearing that sympathetic little smile of his, and waits for people to fall into his hands. And they always do."[6]

Another significant player-management development also occurred during the 1966 spring training season. Dodger pitchers Sandy Koufax and Don Drysdale held out as a "team": Neither one would sign his contract for the 1966 season until both were satisfied with their salary terms. This increased their bargaining power, thereby obliging Dodger management to approach them as co-equal parties to the contracts. According to Koufax, the action allowed each player to give the other moral support, too—and, more importantly, he would have a golf partner during the long stretches of negotiation silence.

While management might have tolerated one holdout, Koufax and Drysdale's combined record (49 wins and 20 losses) in 1965 would have been too much for the Dodger organization to lose. The holdout lasted until ten days before the opening day game in 1966. Terms of the settlement were not specifically revealed, but one estimate placed the contracts at $130,000 for Koufax and $115,000 for Drysdale. Sandy Koufax never even gave the figures in his autobiography, but he did write: "There is little doubt that we got two of the biggest raises in baseball history." If the estimates are correct, then so are his comments since he earned $80,000 the previous year.

Koufax and Drysdale had made a point that was not likely to be lost on other baseball players and Marvin Miller. Baseball players might indeed have the bargaining power to alter working condition terms imposed unilaterally by management but the players would have to make risky sacrifices in order to achieve their ends. Eventually, this message did come through, even if it was not explicitly delivered by Koufax and Drysdale. Subsequent bargaining gains (free agency and salary arbitration) have resulted in many players receiving far higher yearly salary raises than Koufax received in 1966.

Miller was concerned with populist bargaining issues—ones that affected the majority of the players he met during his spring training visits, not the stars. One such issue was the minimum yearly salary. He knew that the public would not be sympathetic to a raise, but contended that the players represented the top 500 in their profession and yet were making only $7,000. "In other fields if he climbed that high, he'd make more. Baseball should be like any other business."[7] Other player bargaining concerns pertained to scheduling of games, pensions, and insurance. Miller also found out that individual player contracts did not represent a bargaining issue as the players preferred to negotiate their own.

Was the MLBPA a union in 1966? Who knows? The issue was never resolved in the courts. An employee organization becomes a union either through voluntary recognition by the employer or through a representation election supervised by the National Labor Relations Board. When Miller was elected president of the MLBPA, the owners overruled their own Executive Council's recommendations and withheld approval of a $150,000 annual appropriation out of the pension plan's central fund for Miller's $50,000 annual salary and office expenses. The owners felt that they should not pay Miller to represent the players on any issue other than the pension plan.

Baseball owners were probably right in their interpretation of labor relations legislation. Dominating, financing, and supporting a labor union are all activities prohibited to management under federal labor law. Yet the owners' decision was not likely based on legal considerations: They appear to have had a similar situation with Robert Cannon, while yet paying his salary. The owners could have told Miller and the MPBLA that its new approach was, in reality, a labor organization; then they could have sought an NLRB representation election to determine whether the organization was supported by a majority of the players. This strategy might have been successful since, previously, the National Labor Relations Board had felt that professional baseball was outside its jurisdiction.[8]

Perhaps the owners were testing Miller's strength with the players. They decided that it was no longer necessary for each player to make his annual contribution of $344 to the pension plan. Instead, this amount could go to the MLBPA's operation, including Miller's salary. The owners may have felt that few players would agree to this arrangement and that most would want the allotment placed back in their paycheck. In retrospect, it is clear that management made a serious blunder—perhaps more serious than their behavior during the 1966 spring training season. They seemed to be giving voluntary recognition to the union and then making it easy—even free—for players to join the union by remitting their $344 yearly pension contributions. All the players received this payment; and the MLBPA probably received credit for obtaining this populist issue, without formal collective bargaining ever having taken place.

The First MLBPA Pension Settlement

In December 1966, the MLBPA and management negotiated a three-year settlement whereby the pension plan was increased $1.5 million a year making the total contribution $4.1 million. Miller agreed to accept a flat-sum contribution for pensions instead of the previous percentage of receipts, and received what was probably the first public criticism of his bargaining efforts. Bowie Kuhn, Allie Reynolds, and Bob Feller were among the critics: They thought that Miller had made a serious mistake since television revenues were only likely to increase over time, and a percentage of that increase would ensure more dollars for the pension plan.[9]

Yet Miller's arrangement nearly doubled the previous pension-plan payouts for those completing ten years in the majors and retiring at age 50 ($500 a month); five-year veterans would receive $250 in monthly payments at age 50; and 20-year men would receive $600 monthly at age 50. If a player waited until he was 65 to start collecting benefits, a five-year man would receive a monthly $644; a ten-year veteran, $1,288 monthly; and a 20-year player, $1,488 a month. The disability benefit was doubled to $500 per month, and widows' benefits were increased from 50 percent of the players' fixed retirement benefit to 100 percent. Also included was a voluntary dues checkoff, whereby the players' previous $344 pension contribution would go directly to the MLBPA. More than 99 percent of the players signed up.[10]

The First MLBPA Negotiated Labor Agreement

In December 1966 players presented their first collective bargaining offer under Miller to management. This included the following proposals:

—A raise in the minumum salary ($7,000 a year, which had been established in 1958) to $10,000. The median salary in baseball was estimated at $17,000 with approximately 25 percent of the players making $10,000 or less, and 6 percent making the $7,000 minimum.[11]

—Scheduling changes to soften the burdens of coast-to-coast flying and night baseball. The number of regular season games (162) was not likely to be changed. But other inconveniences such as day-night doubleheaders and flying from one game to another after "getaway" night games might be eliminated.[12]

—Wholesale revisions in the player contract to spell out specific obligations, reduce the amount that a player could be cut in salary from one year to the next, and increase various spring-training and travel allowances.

—Inclusion of some representative of the players in negotiations for World Series and Game of the Week television programs.

—A grievance procedure for resolving disputes which would ultimately go to "an impartial arbitrator, to be selected jointly by the parties, for binding decision."

—Thorough review of the reserve clause to seek ways of giving players more bargaining power in their salary negotiations.[13]

Baseball management established its collective bargaining committee: the Major League Clubs' Player Relations Committee. John J. Gaherin, president of the New York City Newspaper Publishers Association and an experienced industrial-relations executive, was hired as chief negotiator. The other eight members included the two league presidents and three owners from each league.

The first labor agreement (covering two years) between management and the MLBPA was established in February 1968. Minimum salaries were raised to $10,000 a year for any player on the roster between opening day and August, and $8,500 a year for players called up in September. Meal money during the season was increased from $12 a day to $15 a day. The training-camp weekly allowance was raised from $25 to $40 a week. The agreement also established a formal grievance procedure, including arbitration. This represented a significant gain for the players even though a man hired by the owners—the commissioner—would be the arbitrator. The agreement also provided for a joint labor-management study of the reserve clause.

During these negotiations, Marvin Miller was evasive regarding the players' militancy or the possibility of a strike if their bargaining goals were not reached. He informed one reporter that whatever negotiation tactics might be selected—including a strike—would depend on how strongly the players felt about the particular bargaining issue. Miller also acknowledged that a major objective of any tactic would be to convince players of their inherent bargaining power. "I never before have seen a group of people who are so irreplaceable in relation to their work. Once this is realized, they can have anything within reason."[14]

This attitude was not exactly echoed by George Meany, president of the largest labor federation in the United States—the AFL-CIO. Meany did not give the MLBPA his unionized blessing because he felt that baseball players were "independent contractors who don't need a good union but a good lawyer. . . . They are doing well enough by themselves without union help."[15]

Pension Plan Negotiations in 1969

Notwithstanding Meany's rebuff, all but one of the players on the major league rosters were dues-paying members of the MLBPA. This shared interest was particularly significant because both the pension plan and labor agreements expired in 1969—on March 31 and December 31, respectively.

Early in the year, players were worried about the possibility of a longer season caused by expansion of each of the big leagues from 10 teams to 12. Miller admitted that the owners were basically free to arrange their particular scheduling since the labor agreement would expire after the 1969 season.

Again, Miller was concerned with populist major bargaining issues. He realized that under the five-year eligibility requirement, about 59 percent of all players never did qualify for even the minimum pension payment; and fewer than 20 percent ever qualified for the ten years' service pension payment.

In 1969, management offered—at first—a pension funding increase to $5.1 million a year. Miller called this proposal "totally inadequate." He contended that the owners would receive $16.5 million a year from NBC for the Game of the Week, All-Star Game, and World Series television package—compared to $12.3 million in 1968. Thus the owners were receiving at least $4.2 million more but were offering only a $1-million increase to the players. When reminded that he was the one who had given up the direct percentage of television revenues, Miller responded (somewhat weakly) that the sum he negotiated in 1966 represented a pension-funding revenue allocation similar to that found in the past. Miller insisted that the players now required an annual pension-fund contribution of $5.9 million to break even, since $400,000 of that figure would be needed to meet the increased demand of the expanded leagues and, also, other monies were needed to retire the plan's debt at a maximum rate.

In January 1969 Miller prompted the first collective action since the MLBPA was formed. He urged players not to sign their individual contracts until an agreement was reached on the benefit plan. Miller contended, "If the players sign individual contracts, we will be forced to accept any meager [pension plan] offer the owners' representatives care to make. If, on the other hand, the players continue to stand together, we are confident that an equitable agreement can be achieved."[16]

About 125 of the 600 players in the National and American Leagues attended a meeting in New York (with the MLBPA picking up the tab on their travel expenses of $30,000) to determine how to proceed in the negotiations stalemate. The meeting was held on February 4—the night before the owners selected a new commissioner to replace William Eckert, who had been forced out in December. The players formulated a resolution reiterating their support of the policy that players should not sign individual salary contracts and should not report to spring training sites until the negotiations were satisfactorily concluded.

The owners claimed that their second pension offer of $5.3 million was more than generous, particularly since their operational costs—including player salaries—had increased dramatically. Management rejected the players' proposal that the impasse be turned over to arbitration. The chief management negotiator, John Gaherin, believed that the current negotiation teams had enough bargaining expertise and determination to successfully reach a settlement without third party intervention. One management official—apparently convinced that the players had received more than their share for the past several years—commented, "I hope the players do strike. . . . Maybe if they do, it will get the guys who don't want to play the game and give jobs to those who appreciate the big leagues."[17] Leo Durocher, who was manager of the Chicago Cubs at the time, boasted of telling his players that Cub owner William Wrigley would eat better than they would during a strike.

Miller accused management of bargaining in bad faith and claimed that their only goal was to test the players' resolve (which would not be, per se, a violation of federal labor relations law). Miller further indicated that 391 players had not signed their contracts, nor reported to spring training—a figure that showed players had some mixed sentiments over the issue.

Many players were uncomfortable with both collective actions. Cleon Jones noted in his autobiography that he sympathized with the MLBPA. However, he had received a contract from the Mets in January 1969, which made him reluctant to comply with the collective-action requests. "A player starts getting paid by a team from the day he signs, and there were things we needed the money for. [Jones's contract from the Mets included] a good increase, and I hadn't been making the kind of cash that allowed me to sit back from September to March without a penny coming in." Pete Richert showed up at camp because "I can't buy a house and strike at the same time." Russ Nixon did likewise as "you got to keep busy when you have four kids."[18] Some of the star players had their own reasons for not appreciating the job action. Carl Yastrzemski tried unsuccessfully to bypass the MLBPA by organizing with other superstars to negotiate an appropriate settlement. Tom Seaver said that he would not honor the players' referendum forever because "I believe baseball remains one of the few things that rewards individual effort in our country, . . . and I want it to remain that way. I don't want it to become unionized."[19]

A standoff occurred. Neither side knew if the other one would stick to its position. There was no past history to help the management as well as the union negotiators determine whether the players would continue their job actions into the actual baseball season.

Pension differences were settled nine days before the start of the 1969 spring training season. The owners would pay $5.45 million a year into the fund, instead of the $4.1 million paid in 1967 and also in 1968. Players were now pension eligible after four years, instead of the previous five years' service requirement. This provision was retroactive to the 1959 season: Anyone who played during the 1959 season or later and had four years' playing service would be eligible. The scale of retirement benefits was also increased:

For those retiring at 50, the rate will be $60 a month for each year of service up to 10 years and an additional $20 a month for each year from the 11th through the 20th. That means a four-year man will get $240 a month; a 10-year man $600; a 15-year man $700; a 20-year man $800. Payments can be made larger if the player waits longer to be collecting.[20]

The players also retained the right to 33 percent of television income. As with the labor agreement negotiations in February 1968, the majority of MLBPA members regarded the pension-plan bargaining gains to be a victory for the MLBPA. Players also realized that threatened—let alone effected—collective action could move management off its initial bargaining position.

In the last month of the 1969 negotiations, Bowie Kuhn was hired as commissioner. Marvin Miller publicly acknowledged Kuhn's past diligent service on the side of management, and hoped that he would bring a needed new vision and vitality to his position. Kuhn did not really influence the pension plan negotiations. He is much more identified with labor management negotiations in the 1970s and 1980s. Miller's attitude toward Commissioner Kuhn would change dramatically during this time period.

BARGAINING IN THE 1970s

The 1970 Labor Agreement

Negotiations between the union and management (represented by the Player Relations Committee (PRC) and its chief negotiator John Gaherin) over the 1970 labor agreement were the least publicized contemporary labor relations activities in major league baseball. After 35 bargaining sessions, the owners offered a proposal on May 1, 1970, that was rejected by the players in a 505–89 vote. The players wanted:

—A reduction of the 162-game playing schedule;

—An increase in termination pay, particularly for a player who makes it through spring training but is dropped before opening day; and

—A larger share of playoff revenues than that received in 1969—the first year the National and American League pennants were decided by divisional playoffs.

The settlement on a three-year labor agreement (1970–73) occurred some two weeks after the contract rejection vote, and represented a major player/ union victory. There was no reduction from the 162-game schedule. However, appealing as this issue was to all players, it appears to have been a throwaway issue that the MLBPA used for other bargaining concessions. The playoff revenues pool was increased $250,000 over 1969. The union also received a termination-pay contract provision. Players released during spring training would receive one-sixth (that is, 30 days) of their annual salary; they would get one-third (60 days) of their salary if released after opening day. Starting in 1972, players would receive full pay if they were released on or after May 15. The minimum pay was also increased from the $10,000 figure in 1969—to $12,000 in 1970, $12,750 in 1971, and $13,500 in 1972.

Another major union gain was the addition of an arbitrator to the grievance procedure on all issues that did not involve the "integrity of the game." The first labor agreement signed in 1968 had contained a grievance procedure (Schedule C), but the final step—"arbitration"—involved the commissioner. This situation was probably better for the players than the earlier representation plan (discussed in Chapter One). However, the commissioner is employed by the owners and cannot be regarded as an objective outsider or third party neutral. Richard Moss, counsel to the MLBPA, explained why the union had not pressed strongly for third party arbitration in its first labor agreement.

I don't know what, if any, issues would have been strike issues in 1968, but impartial arbitration clearly was not one of them. Other matters, as to which we did make significant progress in the negotiations, were considered much more important, for there was, even so recently, still a general lack of appreciation of how basic the issue was. We rationalized our defeat by deciding we would process grievances to arbitration, and we were confident that the record of that experience would conclusively demonstrate the importance of impartiality.[21]

Perhaps management was sincerely oblivious to the eventual cost of this "noneconomic" issue. In any case, the arbitration of grievances by third party neutrals eventually raised serious challenges to management's ability in disciplining players—as examined in Chapters Five and Six. Chapter Eight explores the major impact that one arbitrator's decision had on player mobility, by establishing free agency. And the extension of arbitration into

Table 2.1

Estimated Profits and Potential Profits (franchise value change) for Baseball
Teams in 1970

American League	Profit or (Loss) 1970	Franchise Value Changes Since Acquisition (Millions)
Baltimore Orioles	$345,160	$ 2.4 to $12
Boston Red Sox	$200,000	$ 0 to $10
California Angels	$100,000	$ 5.5 to $ 9
Chicago White Sox	(Loss)	$10 to $12
Cleveland Indians	($2 million)	$ 8 to $ 9
Detroit Tigers	Profit	$ 5.5 to $ 8
New York Yankees	($150,000)	$14 to $16
Kansas City Royals	($2 million)	$ 6 to $ 7.5
Minnesota Twins	$ 50,000	$ 9 to $12
Oakland Athletics	(Loss)	$ 3 to $ 8
Milwaukee Brewers	($1 million)	$10.8 to $11
Washington Senators	($1 million)	$ 9 to $ 7

National League		
Atlanta Braves	$120,000	$6.2 to $10
Chicago Cubs	$380,000	$ 0 to $11
Cincinnati Reds	$500,000	$ 8 to $10
Houston Astros	$100,000	$ 5 to $12
Los Angeles Dodgers	$1 million	$ 9 to $28
Montreal Expos	($1 million)	$10 to $14
New York Mets	$2 million	$3.8 to $20
Philadelphia Phillies	($1 million)	$ 9 to $10
Pittsburgh Pirates	$150,000	$ 0 to $12
St. Louis Cardinals	Profit	$3.5 to $14
San Diego Padres	($1 million)	$10 to $ 9
San Francisco Giants	($926,413)	$ 0 to $10

Source: "Who Says Baseball Is like Ballet?" *Forbes* 107 (April 1, 1971), p. 27.

resolving the salary disputes of individual players—discussed in Chapters
Eight and Nine—has had an undeniable economic impact on the game.

As for 1970, the season was probably not a profitable one for most owners.[22]
Estimates of the various teams' profits and losses are presented in Table 2.1.
The figures can be disputed, but it does seem as though most club owners
would have realized a better profit through selling the club than through
operational revenues. Then again, owners could realize tax write-offs on
their player contracts, and—as further discussed in Chapter Four—enjoy
certain noneconomic returns in the form of social prestige, as well.

A man who runs a $100-million-a-year business is usually anonymous to the general
public; a man who owns even a piece of a ball club that grosses $5-million a year is
a celebrity. His picture and comments are repeatedly published in newspapers, his

identity known in every corner of his community and beyond, and his ego is constantly massaged.[23]

Yet even the wealthiest club owner wants to see money coming in rather than going out. Owners do not view baseball as a charity and will try to eliminate or at least minimize their losses. Thus, many owners were in a cautious—if not belligerent—mood when negotiations over the pension plan occurred in 1972. Perhaps many players and/or union officials were displaying some militancy at this time to set the stage for the labor agreement negotiations coming up in 1973. Whatever the explanation, the 1972 negotiations resulted in the first general labor strike in professional sports.

The 1972 Pension Plan Strike

A four-year $70-million television contract negotiated in 1971 between major league baseball and NBC for the World Series, All-Star Game, and Game of the Week prompted the MLBPA to seek an increase in their $5.5 million-a-year share, to support their pension and insurance plans. Baseball club owners initially voted to keep the health and medical benefits up-to-date with a $400,000 increase, but voted not to increase the pension fund. Gussie Busch, owner of the Saint Louis Cardinals, explained, "We voted unanimously to take a stand. We're not going to give another god-damn cent. And if they want to strike, let them strike."[24] Paul Richards, vice-president of the Atlanta Braves, said that a stand must be taken against Miller or "there isn't going to be any baseball for a long, long time. The owners . . . simply aren't going to let Marvin Miller run over them any more."[25]

The MLBPA had two major contentions: (1) The pension fund contribution should be increased by 17 percent (to approximately $6.5 million a year) to offset the 17 percent cost-of-living increase since the last pension plan agreement in 1969; and (2) the increase would cost each club only $11,000, which would be supplemented by the $817,000 that was already in the pension plan surplus. At the time of this dispute, the pension fund had $60 million in revenues ($44 million in fixed investments, and $16 million in variable investments—stocks and other items that fluctuate in value). Higher than anticipated fixed interest rates had been creating a surplus of some $660,000 a year for many years. The surplus was also due to an overestimation of the number of players who would be receiving total disability payments out of the fund.

The players voted 663–10 to authorize a strike; and on March 31, 1972, the player representatives voted 47–0 (with one abstention) to strike the next day unless an appropriate settlement were reached or management submitted the impasse to binding arbitration by any prominent person not associated with either of the parties. Miller felt that management's position had shifted from economic costs to principle when it refused to let players determine how their own earned funds would be spent. He knew that the owners had previously used the surplus funds to increase pensions in 1967 and 1969, and figured that they were now simply testing the union's solidarity.

The owners were, and are, intent on making the players eat dirt. . . . I will let the players know that the owners are insistent that the players bend down and kiss the shoes of the owners. The owners have now taken on the full responsibility for prolonging the strike right into the season. I think the owners have miscalculated grievously.[26]

John Gaherin denied Miller's union-busting scenario, insisting that management had deposited $5.4 million into the pension fund and now planned to add another $400,000.

The strike on April 1, 1972, did not represent a consensual statement on the part of either the owners or the players. Bob Short, owner of the Washington Senators, suggested binding arbitration as a solution to the impasse, but "I almost got drummed out of baseball for saying it. There are owners who are adamant in their desire to break the Players Association and crack Marvin Miller, their group's counsel."[27]

William Bartholomay, president of the Atlanta Braves, thought that the season could be maintained with strike replacements from the minor leagues, although other managers would not accept this tactic (which was eventually used by professional football owners in 1987). Some owners—like Stu Holcomb of the Chicago White Sox and Calvin Griffith of the Minnesota Twins—believed that the players were blindly following Miller, and that management would simply close down the shop if the situation continued. Owner Joe Brown of the Pittsburgh Pirates echoed these sentiments: "I doubt very much that the owners will back down from their present stand. Never in my years in baseball have I seen the owners so solidified on any issue."[28]

Charles Finley, owner of the Oakland A's, exercised his prerogative to change his mind over the bargaining issue. One day after the strike began, he commented that players had forgotten two things: "First, they don't contribute one red cent to their own pension plan and, second, they already have the best pension plan in America." Finley's opinion changed, however, ten days into the strike when he maintained, "Very few owners knew there was any surplus in the pension fund. That was the main problem. . . . The owners didn't understand what it was all about."[29]

The players were also in some disagreement. Boston Red Sox pitcher Bill Lee noted in his autobiography, *The Wrong Stuff*, that Marvin Miller was "an intelligent and compassionate man who cared about the game *and* the players." He also wrote that some Red Sox players such as Carl "Yaz" Yastrzemski were opposed to this labor relations issue and action.

The day we went on strike [Miller] voluntarily gave up all claims on his salary, feeling that if we were going to be made to walk the financial plank, then it was only right that he walk with us. He did this without fanfare, and it won him a lot of respect. However, not all the players were solidly behind the walkout. Reggie Smith stood up the day we took the vote, announcing that he was voting no because every week out was going to cost him four thousand dollars, while it would cost most of the other players less than eight hundred. I looked at him and said, "Reggie, you didn't say that, did you? That didn't come out of your mouth?" But it had. Yaz and Petrocelli were also against the strike. They had been treated well by management and were close to Mr. Yawkey [the owner] so this stance was consistent with their honestly held beliefs. . . . The rest of the club voted strike and the brief discussion between Smith and me was forgotten. By everybody but Reggie. From that day on I was *numero uno* on his shit list. (emphasis in original)

The owners did revise their offer on April 11 by adding $500,000 surplus to the pension funds. Then, however, the owners disagreed over whether the games lost during the strike should be played. American League owners were in favor of not making up the games missed, while National League owners wanted to make up all the games. The impasse could have been settled with a simple majority (13 out of 24) vote, but *PRC* rules required at least five pro votes from each league, to avert league-versus-league politics.

The strike ended April 13 with the understanding that none of the 26 games missed during the 13 days would be made up. Each major-league player lost nine days' salary, for an estimated total loss of some $600,000. Players at the $13,500 minimum lost $675; those making more than the minimum lost more money. Hank Aaron—for example—lost $9,800. In announcing the settlement, Marvin Miller indicated that nobody ever really wins in a strike situation—a sentiment echoed by Bowie Kuhn. Miller also said he was disappointed that the public never knew the players had struck over "human dignity" rather than pensions or money.

The players may have won on principle, but their wage losses were higher than the $500,000 they gained from the strike. The owners took a far more serious economic beating. The $500,000 they saved by not agreeing with the MLBPA's initial proposal was offset by an estimated $5.2-million revenue loss.

Some blamed Commissioner Kuhn for not using his powers more forcefully to prevent the strike from ever taking place. Kuhn answered that he had performed his role as well as any commissioner who must represent both workers and management. The timing for his intervention had not been right—he said—and his involvement would likely have "inflamed" passions, thereby only perpetuating the dispute.

Many wondered how the strike would influence negotiations over the collective bargaining agreement that was due to expire on December 31, 1972, and the pension benefits agreement that would expire March 31, 1973. Miller was optimistic. He maintained that the 1972 strike would likely result in "a greater understanding by the owners of collective bargaining and the need to treat players as equals."[30] Kuhn, too, thought the strike would exert a positive influence on the 1973 negotiations. "We in baseball learned two important lessons: First, none of us wants to go this route again—we have gained wisdom from history. Secondly, we have learned the value of communication."[31]

Kuhn's forecast was seconded by some of the owners and players alike. Robert Howsam, a general manager, hoped Miller realized that his labor relations experience in the steel industry would not be applicable in future baseball negotiations. Mickey Stanley, outfielder of the Detroit Tigers, said that the players would be reluctant to strike again—a sentiment strongly shared by Pete Rose: "If there's another strike . . . the players' association will not get my support. . . . Last year's strike cost me $7,000 and a chance for 200 hits."[32]

The 1973 Labor Agreement Negotiations

After the 1972 negotiations, management reduced the number of members on its Player Relations Committee (PRC) from ten to six. Also, the voting rule for labor relations matters was changed to a simple majority of all major league clubs, without a minimum pro vote required for each league. Bowie Kuhn thought that the appointment of Milwaukee's Ed Fitzgerald as PRC chairman would greatly help Gaherin negotiate the labor agreement because Fitzgerald had good interpersonal skills and a flexible attitude.

Negotiation activities received little publicity until three weeks before the contract expiration date, when Bowie Kuhn publicly announced management's collective bargaining position on the player reserve issue. John Gaherin had called Miller and said that in ten minutes Kuhn would open a news conference and disclose the offer that the players had rejected. Miller's private response was not pleasant. "Why . . . that pompous, puffed-up-that-that phony—he's not asking, he's not consulting us, but on 10 minutes' notice he's violating our agreement! Is this what he considers integrity? Well, it's not my definition of integrity."[33] Miller's public response was no better. He felt that Kuhn's announcement represented amateurish, bad-faith bargaining that was in violation of a union-management agreement to resolve problems in private.

The major bargaining issues in 1973, along with the early union and management positions, are presented in Table 2.2. Bowie Kuhn announced two weeks before the contract expiration date that management was not likely to alter its positions on two of these issues: free agency, and binding arbitration. Kuhn maintained that any management concessions would adversely affect the game's balanced competition and therefore its integrity and economics. Negotiations continued without publicity although on January 5 the MLBPA did propose that the reserve issue be studied—but not

Table 2.2
Major Bargaining Issues in 1973 Negotiations with Early Owner/Player Positions

Reserve Clause

OWNERS: A player with five years in the major leagues becomes a free agent if not offered $30,000 for the sixth; or if not offered $40,000 after eight years.

PLAYERS: After five years as a professional (three in the majors), a player would become a free agent if earning less than the average salary (The owners estimate this at $35,000; the players at $32,000). After seven years as a pro (five in the majors), he would become a free agent if not earning 1 1/2 times the average; after nine years, if below twice the average.

The players also propose that a man become a free agent after seven years in the majors regardless of his pay, then again after 12 years and 17. If he sells himself to another team, the club that gets him pays half his salary as indemnity to the team that loses him.

Trades

OWNERS: After ten seasons in the big leagues, if the last five were with one team, a player could not be traded without his consent.

PLAYERS: After eight seasons, he could not be traded without his consent. Also, whenever a man is traded, he may ask his new club to reopen his contract; if they fail to agree on terms, it goes to binding arbitration.

Rosters

OWNERS: The number of players under control of each of the 24 teams would be cut from 40 to 38, and those on the varsity roster from 25 to 23. In addition, three players on each club must be made available for selection by other clubs in the league at $35,000 apiece.

PLAYERS: Rosters would stay at 40 men and 25 for the parent club. Each year, 10 players from the 40-man list would be freed from "protection" and offered to other teams. But a player would have to be notified he was being offered for such a draft and could remove himself from the list.

Minimum Pay

OWNERS: It would be raised from $13,500 now to $14,000 next year, $14,500 in 1974, and $15,000 in 1975.

PLAYERS: To $15,500 next year, to $16,500 in 1974, and to $17,500 in 1975.

Arbitration

OWNERS: No binding arbitration of pay disputes.

PLAYERS: If player and club cannot agree to contract by February 1 of any year, it goes to binding arbitration.

Source: New York Times, December 8, 1972, p. 58.

acted on—for a year. The players also dropped their request for a reduction in the 162-game playing schedule.

On February 9, 1973, the owners attempted to force the players' hands with a two-pronged announcement.

1. A proposed three-year labor agreement that would ignore the reserve rule, but would include salary arbitration; and

2. An order indicating that no spring training camp could be opened before March 1—the last date that all players have traditionally been scheduled to report for pre-season games.

Miller labeled this announcement "worthless," and objected to several aspects of management's salary arbitration proposals: Namely, management had made the following stipulations:

—Any player after three years' service could request salary arbitration, but the player could not then use arbitration the following year. Also, the maximum salary-cut limitations for the subsequent playing season would not apply to any player eligible to seek arbitration. Miller felt that this would enable the owners to remove the arbitration gains in their salary offer the following year.

—Arbitrators should consider—among other criteria—the club's league standing and attendance, but not its financial position or salary structure. Miller feared that a club's low attendance might reduce its players' salaries even though the club had significant revenues from television rights and other sources. Also, a pitcher who wins 27 games in a season might be paid less just because he was pitching for a last-place club.

Miller also said (probably with little conviction) that management's decision to close spring training camps—if continued after March 1—would be illegal under the Taft-Hartley Act and would prompt the MLBPA to take legal action. A comment made by Baltimore third baseman Brooks Robinson places the negotiation impasse in perspective: "I hate to see it. The players have not made a strike threat, have not taken a strike vote and don't intend to. We've expressed our willingness to continue bargaining, if necessary, without disruption to spring training or the regular season."[34] Miller, too, felt that the bargaining differences were negotiable—and that bargaining should not be conducted in public.

Negotiation sessions between union and management officials were resumed on an almost daily basis, with very little in the way of publicized results. When a tentative settlement was reached, it reflected some compromise. Management actually emerged with a stronger position on the reserve clause than it had initially proposed (see Table 2.2). The issue was to be excluded from union-management discussions during the three years of the labor agreement.[35] The owners' position on player trades was also accepted. However, the union's position that player rosters remain at 25 was maintained. Minimum salary levels—$15,000 for the 1973 and 1974 seasons, and $16,000 during the 1975 season—represented a compromise between union's and management's initial bargaining positions.

The biggest player victory involved binding arbitration for salaries. Most of Miller's objections seemed to have been met in the final settlement. After two years' service, a player could submit to salary arbitration in every year that he deemed it appropriate. The maximum salary reductions (not in excess of 20 percent of the previous year's salary or in excess of 30 percent of the salary two years previous) remained in force.

Players' past compensation and a comparison with the salaries of other baseball players were included as criteria for the arbitrator's decision, however. The performance of the club (team finish and attendance figures) was also included. The financial position of the player and the club were specifically excluded from arbitral review.

The labor agreement settlement also included a pension plan agreement in advance of the March 31, 1973, expiration date. Pensions had been the strike issue in 1972 and had received extensive media coverage, with every related nuance being covered. In 1973, however, *The New York Times* gave maybe three paragraphs' attention to the issue. Thus—notwithstanding their power and influence—the media are very much dependent on the willingness of labor-relations participants to supply them with pertinent information.

For the record, 1973 pension contributions were increased $610,000 over 1972—making the annual payment $6,150,000. This figure was the same for 1974 and was increased to $6,450,000 in 1975. A 50-year-old player with ten years' service would see his pension increase from $642 a month to $710, or from $7,704 a year to $8,520.

The 1976 Negotiations

Like the previous ones, negotiations in 1976 did not get off to an early start. A week after the labor contract had expired, Marvin Miller reported little progress, and considered the owners' bargaining manner or pace to be not "constructive." Kuhn retorted that Miller might not be thinking of the long-range adverse effects on the fans of baseball, who typically feel that players are well treated and would be turned off if players pushed too hard for additional gains. Kuhn's attitude was echoed by at least one baseball executive, who maintained that players have "never lived in the real world. . . . And they had better learn quick that if you like scrambled eggs for breakfast, it's not a good idea to eat the chicken."[36]

Initial bargaining issues reflected the players' desire to shorten the 162-game season, and management's desire to reduce the playing roster from 25 to 23 and have a four-year labor agreement. One major issue—modification of the player's reserve system—was unresolved. This issue was stimulated by arbitrator Peter Seitz's decision making players Andy Messersmith and Dave McNally (who had played the previous season without signing contracts) "free agents." Both the National and American League presidents knew that collective bargaining had to address this issue because some 200–

300 players could decide to play out their options and then become free agents. Lee MacPhail, president of the American League, commented, "We are suddenly without the reserve system which has served baseball so successfully for decades, [and] are now undergoing a restructuring of our entire organization. We don't want to jump into anything. We are looking for a reserve system we feel is workable and one the clubs can live with."[37] MacPhail felt that the MLBPA's position ran counter to the necessary elements of fan loyalty and competitive balance.

The arbitrator's decision was upheld in court, and the owners filed an appeal. This prompted Miller to remark, "The owners can't do two things at the same time—physically spend their time in litigation and still go on with negotiations."[38]

Again the owners attempted to put pressure on the MLBPA by not opening the training camps on March 1. Not all owners agreed with this decision. Bill Veeck of the White Sox claimed it "unfair and unreasonable," and wrong. Clark Griffith of the Twins remarked of Veeck's denunciation, "If we thought this was the act of a rational person, we'd worry about it."[39] Interestingly, Marvin Miller did not pursue his contention used in the prior negotiations that the lockout was illegal under the Taft-Hartley Act.

On March 10 the owners changed their original reserve offer of eight and one, by which an eight-year player would play out his option in the ninth year and become a free agent for his tenth year. With the revision, a six-year veteran could be a free agent if he did not receive a guaranteed contract for the next one or two years. An option year could follow that. The union found this offer to be a thinly disguised version of the original eight-and-one proposal.

The stalemate did produce some very descriptive rhetoric. Chub Feeney, president of the National League and a member of the *PRC*, commented, "They felt they had our swords and now they want our horses." Miller responded, "They want us to slit our throats, ear to ear, and then they say, 'We'll help you wipe up the blood.' "[40]

Players again supported the MLBPA—a situation that proved Miller's "proudest boast." Unlike most (if not all) other U.S. unions, the MLBPA enjoys 100-percent membership while having no compulsory membership clause in its labor agreement. However, the closed training camps and the possibility of an ended season did generate some player concern over collective bargaining's efficacy and direction.

Johnny Bench, for example—while he recognized Miller's past bargaining gains—believed that progress might be made this time only if the players bargained directly with the owners. Bench was not a player representative, but he and some 50 other players met with the PRC face-to-face in a five-hour meeting. No tangible results occurred. Perhaps there were some owners who thought this action weakened the players' bargaining position. However, the owners' bargaining resolve was also weakened, when a federal court of appeals upheld arbitrator Seitz's reserve rule decision that favored the players.

On March 14, the MLBPA counterproposed that any player under contract be able to play out his option year and then become a free agent (the one-and-one reserve clause). To minimize the owners' fear of their salary costs skyrocketing in their attempt to keep players from jumping teams, Miller suggested that the agreement be for just one year so the cost of the plan could be assessed.

The owners quickly responded with a proposal of their own. Each player whose 1975 major league contract was renewed for 1976 could play out his option in 1976 and then become a free agent. Any player who signed a contract in 1976 could play out his option in 1977 and then become a free agent. It was also proposed that players become eligible for free agency after seven years' service and playing out a one-year option. Further, a free agent would be eligible to negotiate with a maximum of eight teams, with the selection of clubs being in inverse order of the previous season's. A club losing a player would be compensated twice the player's salary, with a maximum compensation of $150,000. AL President MacPhail commented on this offer, "In order to get the spring camps open and the baseball season under way we have agreed to accept the one-and-one. . . . We bit the bullet. We are also reluctantly willing to face whatever consequences may come of this. Now it's up to the players to accept it. This is our final offer."[41]

Miller believed that this proposal would only cause liability problems for the union. Under the Seitz decision, players were free to negotiate with all 24 clubs. If the union accepted limiting a free agent's negotiation to eight clubs, then players could sue on the basis that their rights were being violated. He recommended rejecting the proposal and felt that the players were with him on this.

Some of the players, however, placed the opening of the baseball season above specific bargaining issues. Willie Stargell of the Pittsburgh Pirates—for example—stated, "My main concern is the start of the season. This is our lives. This is a totally destructive situation."[42] In any case, the players and their representatives seem to have softened Miller's initial response, as evidenced in this players' resolution that he read to the press. "We considered the owners' proposal carefully and found they reflect considerable progress. But additional work is required by negotiation. . . . In the interim, there is no justification for the training-camp lockout. . . . The lockout could be ended immediately."[43]

Bowie Kuhn may have been answering Miller when he ended the 17-day lockout on March 17 reasoning that the fans wanted the camps opened and that their interests should be "paramount." Kuhn's decision involved possibly $1 billion worth of business in terms of club and player revenues and related

Table 2.3

Major League Baseball Players Benefit Plan—Monthly Retirement Benefits[1]
(combined fixed and assumed variable[2] amounts)

Age of Retirement[3]	Years of major league service[3]	1962-66	1967-69	1969-72	1972-73	1973-76	1976-80
45	4	0	0	$174	$187.34	$206	$267.80
	5	0	0	218	233.18	258	335.40
	10	0	0	436	467.36	515	669.50
	15	0	0	509	550.36	601	781.30
	20	0	0	582	633.36	687	893.10
50	4	0	0	240	257.00	286	371.80
	5	125	250	300	321.00	358	464.75
	10	250	500	600	642.00	715	929.50
	15	300	550	700	756.00	835	1035.50
	20	350	600	800	870.00	955	1241.50
65	4	0	0	618	652.04	735	955.50
	5	262	644	773	814.56	919	1194.70
	10	523	1288	1545	1629.11	1838	2389.40
	15	623	1388	1745	1857.11	2078	2701.40
	20	723	1488	1945	2085.11	2318	3013.40

[1]The benefit plan, in addition to retirement benefits, covers such matters as widow's benefits, disability benefits, life insurance, health care benefits, dental, and severance allowance.

[2]Variable benefits are funded through securities investments. The variable benefits assume a growth of 4.5 percent a year.

[3]Examples at selected ages and selected years of major league service completed. Members may begin to draw retirement benefits at age 45 or thereafter, as long as they have completed four or more years of major league service. The monthly amount payable is based on age when retirement begins and years of major league service completed.

Source: U.S. Congress, House Select Committee on Professional Sports, "Inquiry into Professional Sports," Hearings, 94th Cong., 2nd sess., pt. 1, p. 381.

dollars from businesses such as airlines, concessions, and hotels, along with U.S. and state government receipts of taxes. Yet it did not end the bargaining impasse.

About three days after Kuhn's announcement, the owners withdrew their "final offer" from the bargaining table. Miller was nonplussed by the action, and the regular playing season began with both sides agreeing to disagree and to continue collective bargaining efforts. As reporter Dick Young wrote, the situation was being swept under the rug—with nothing solved, but only postponed.

In mid-June the owners informed the MLBPA that the regular deposit of $890,000 would be made into the players' benefit plan on August 1, provided that there was no interference with the All-Star Game to be played on July 15. There had been no strike threats by the union although there were some rumors that a boycott of the All-Star Game was a possibility. This would very likely have been a no-win situation for the players. The All-Star break is not a significant game from the fans' standpoint. Therefore, the owners would probably not grant large concessions in order to have it played. Yet at the same time, such a player boycott would generate negative public opinion, with some even considering the action unpatriotic.

A settlement was finally reached on July 12, with both union and management giving ground. No changes were made in the 162-game schedule, and management was successful in obtaining a four-year labor agreement and reducing the maximum number of players on its roster to 24. Yet the union did achieve some significant modifications to management's last reserve-rule proposal. A team receiving a free agent would compensate another team with draft choices, instead of dollars. Also—under a somewhat complicated procedure—a free agent could now deal with 12 teams, instead of eight as in management's previous proposal. This improvement suggests that the MLBPA was not so totally concerned that it could or would be sued for restricting the full number of teams (24) accessible to free agents under Seitz's arbitration decision. Indeed, Miller might have been using this concern as a negotiation ploy. According to the wife of Mike Marshall (of the Minnesota Twins), Miller informed Marshall that he needed a "hammer," or one of the players to say he would sue the association if it negotiated away any right to free agency. Marshall agreed to "sue"—a message that many papers took seriously and published, erroneously.[44]

The minimum wage was to be increased $1,000 for each year of the labor agreement. The players' minimum would be $18,000 in 1976 and $21,000 in 1979. The labor agreement also called for owners to increase the pension fund from $6.85 million to $8.3 million.[45] Table 2.3 indicates the large pension payment growth that resulted from collective bargaining efforts in the 1970s.

— Three —

Collective Bargaining in the 1980s

NEGOTIATIONS IN 1980

Preparations

Under Marvin Miller, MLBPA bargaining efforts had notched rather clear and substantial gains from 1966 to 1973. Negotiations in 1973 and 1976 represented a minor compromise from the original MLBPA bargaining position, but not a concession from previously obtained bargaining gains/labor agreement provisions. Many baseball owners probably realized that their "bargaining victory" only preserved the status quo—something they had had already, in years past.

Even more owners realized the dollar amounts that collective bargaining cost them. Players' average salaries for the years 1970 ($22,000) to 1980 ($130,000) rose an impressive 600-plus percent. The 1976 four-year labor agreement generated a $30.8-million management contribution to the pension fund and a 191-percent salary increase.[1]

In assessing their collective bargaining score, the owners also had to consider their chief union adversary, Marvin Miller, who was skilled in industrial bargaining tactics such as legal bluffs to gain union recognition and who knew the value of collective bargaining gains. Management's chief negotiator, John Gaherin, left in 1978 and was replaced by Ray Grebey, a labor relations executive with General Electric—a firm long experienced with collective bargaining laws and strategies.

Grebey was quick to realize that baseball's collective bargaining activities receive a disproportionate amount of media coverage. Most organizations with less than 1,000 employees would not even have such activities covered in the local newspaper. The extensive media coverage prompted Grebey to adopt the following strategy: "In dealing with unions, we have to stop pissing at each other in public. I'm not going to get into that even if one of my owners goes off on a toot and says the wrong thing."[2] To make sure that owners would not "shoot off their mouths"—as occurred during in the 1976 negotiations—the Player Relations Committee established a sub-disciplinary committee to determine an owner's guilt and penalty (reaching a maximum $500,000 fine) for public bargaining statements. Grebey publicly stated that Miller was not an adversary, but a "delightful, . . . thorough professional." "[Miller is] a tough SOB, but I like the guy and I would have a drink with him after our negotiation sessions."[3]

Grebey's media avoidance and his "friendship" with Miller were strained, however, when he publicly reflected management's economic concerns.

It is not our intent to poor-mouth baseball. The ability of individual clubs to pay is not the current issue. The important thing for Major League Baseball and everybody connected with it is how this rapid rate of [salary] escalation will affect baseball as an industry. And right now baseball as an industry [26 clubs, by that time] is not turning a profit. . . . With nearly three-fourths of increased revenues going to players' salaries, it seems apparent that the rapidly rising trend in salaries should be slowed down.[4]

If Grebey or a management negotiator were to indicate directly to the union an inability to pay, then management would be legally obligated under the National Labor Relations Act to disclose its financial books to the union. This situation happened in 1985, but did not occur in the 1980 negotiations. Miller was irked that management's economic rhetoric enabled the owners to have their cake and eat it too.

In every negotiation that I've been in in 13 years, at the opening session the owners' chief spokesman makes a speech, in which he says, "we have not, we do not, and we will not claim any financial hardship"—thereby removing the issue from the table, prevents us from asking for any data, and—and takes it out of the negotiations. That doesn't stop the owners' committee right after that meeting from walking out in the hall, cornering the first newspaperman and saying, "it's terrible, we are all losing money." The newspaperman has no statutory authority to ask for the data and simply prints what they say.[5]

Unlike in previous negotiations, this time both the management and union organizations gathered funds to offset possible strike costs. The owners reportedly established a $3.5-million strike fund made up of 2 percent of their 1979 gate receipts. According to Miller, management also had a strike insurance policy that would pay $1 million per day to the 26 clubs after the first two weeks of any strike. Each club would therefore receive $40,000 a day to help offset the loss of gate and television receipts. If a strike should last for the entire season, then each club would receive nearly $6 million from the insurance fund—plus have an average payroll savings of $3 million.[6] The union also established an emergency fund, which it began in 1978. Funds were derived from the players' licensing program (fees for players' photos on baseball cards, for example) and were estimated as capable of providing the players with $1 million in case of a strike.[7]

Bargaining Proposals and Activities in Spring Training

Union and management negotiators each had several bargaining issues/ proposals that remained basically intact through February 1980.[8] The union stuck with these five basic proposals:

1. A reduction of the current 162-game regular season schedule (very likely a throw-away issue by now, since no union member or officer had publicly stressed this issue for many years).

2. Trade on demand after eight years in the majors, when the last three years or more have been with the same club. In 1979 a player demanding a trade needed ten years in the majors, the last five years or more with the same club.

3. Free agency for players after four years, instead of the six years' eligibility in 1979.

4. A nearly 100-percent increase in the minimum salary (from $21,000 in 1979 to $40,000 in 1980), with subsequent salary minimums in a multiyear contract being tied to inflation.

5. A substantial increase in the owners' pension-plan contribution to include some retired players who had previously been excluded from the pension-plan average figures.

Management proposed a minimum salary of $25,000 for the first two years of a four-year labor agreement, and a minimum salary of $28,500 for the remaining two years. They also suggested three proposals in areas that were different from previous negotiations: (1) time restrictions on players' contracts; (2) a salary scale; and (3) major-league player compensation for some teams that lose free agents.

Under management's contract restriction proposal, players with four years of major league experience or less could not receive more than a one-year contract. The salary scale proposal applied to players with six years of experience or less—with minimums established for each year of performance, and corresponding maximums that would include incentive bonuses.

| First year player | $25,000 minimum to $25,200 maximum |
| Second year | $53,500 to $55,400 |

Third year	$69,200 to $75,200
Fourth year	$90,300 to $102,000
Fifth year	$117,000 to $138,400
Sixth year	$153,600 to $187,900[9]

Miller objected to both the time restriction on player contracts and the salary scale for the same reason: Management was wanting the union to do management's job. Under previous labor agreements and the union's proposed 1980 agreement, each owner had full discretion to determine the length and (with the notable exception of salary arbitration) the dollar amount of a player's contract. Yet the owners knew full well that each of them would not act in an independent but similar manner in negotiating individual player contracts. For example, one owner of the Philadelphia Phillies indicated why he would bid up salaries offered by the other owners: "We do it because we want to stay in contention and if I don't do it, maybe the players will go on the open market and some other owner might give them more."[10] Further, owners would be guilty of collusion (a situation that did occur in 1986 and is discussed in Chapter Eight) and possible antitrust violations if they agreed to similar player-salary contract limitations outside of those found in the labor agreement. Miller contended that, if these proposals were—as they seemed to be—based on owners' distrust of each other, then there would be every reason to think that the arrangements would only cause under-the-table deals between owners and certain players. The union would thus be placed in the impossible position of policing and possibly blowing the whistle on its own members.

The owners realized that they had made a mistake in their 1976 negotiations when they agreed to compensate a team for the loss of a free agent player by allowing it to make an amateur-player draft choice. More specifically, a team desiring a free agent would not mind bidding up salary offers because it would only be losing its draft rights to a basically unknown and unproven amateur player. Nine out of 48 first-and second-round amateur draft choices in 1975 were still playing in the majors in 1979. Eight of the 48 draftees in 1976 played in 1979; and three out of 52 amateurs selected in 1977 were still around two years later.

Ray Grebey therefore proposed that a team signing a "quality" free agent (one selected by eight or more teams in the reentry draft) would be entitled to freeze 15 of the players on its 40-player roster but would also be required to offer any one of the remaining 25 players to the team that lost the free agent, by way of compensation. The player selected as compensation must then remain on his new team's active roster for the next year through the All-Star break. The union realized that this proposal would provide some job security for the selected player. However, it could also result in fewer free agents signed, and lower salaries. The superstars would likely be unaffected, but many other players shared White Sox first baseman Mike Squires's attitude: "[The free-agent compensation proposal] would kill the chances for a guy like me if I ever got to the point where I was eligible for free agency and decided I wanted to go that route. . . . Who's going to be interested in me if they have to give up a Terry Forster or an Oscar Gamble to get me."[11]

On March 4, 1980—after some 23 negotiation sessions—the executive board (26 player representatives) of the Major League Baseball Players' Association voted unanimously to recommend that its members authorize a baseball strike on or after April 1. Miller realized that, in provoking this action and even a strike vote, it was not costing management anything at this time to test the union's solidarity. Some owners probably figured that the higher paid players—fearing large salary losses during a strike—would influence others to accept the owners' proposals. The MLBPA—for its part—believed that the owners were taking the union to the very brink to see if the players would show up on opening day of the regular season. Miller stated,

The owners ought to know from experience that if we call a strike on April 2 or April 3, there's not going to be an opening day on April 9. We're not going to go back in and politely give them a full 162-game schedule if they force us to the last extremity of a strike just as a test. If we go out, it will cost.[12]

Three other significant bargaining events also occurred during March. The owners proposed a pension-benefit plan that would feature a 40-percent increase in benefits for all current players and any player who had been active at some time in the past ten years. Lesser increases would go to ex–big leaguers who had not been active during the past ten years. Miller did not express enthusiasm for the plan; he said that it would only enable present players to keep up with past inflation.[13]

The owners also withdrew their salary scale proposal, and Grebey hailed the move as a "major breakthrough." However, Miller responded, "It's a little like you've been beating your wife and children for years. Then you stop, and now you want a medal because you stopped."[14]

Finally, near the end of March, the owners asked for mediation. The mediator, Ken Moffett, was deputy director of the Federal Mediation and Conciliation Service. He—or any mediator, for that matter—possessed no authority either to compel or to structure a particular bargaining settlement. Drawing on personal experiences and capabilities, the mediator can only try to help union and management reach a settlement. Yet the mediator is an invited guest who can also be asked by the union and/or management negotiator to leave at any time. Miller did not object to the mediation. However, he did think that this activity represented a stalling mechanism on the part of management.

On April 1 the MLBPA voted to cancel the remaining 92 exhibition–spring training games, return to play the opening day of the regular season, and consider a possible strike around May 22—close to Memorial Day—if a settlement had not been reached by that time. The players voted 967–1 for the strike. The lone dissenter was Jerry Terrell, who said that his vote was based on religious convictions. The 26 player representatives also voted for the strike position.

The MLBPA explained its return to start the opening season, with the possibility of a later strike date, in terms of owners' revenues. Owners do not lose so much money when games at the start of the season are cancelled, as poor weather and poor attendance often characterize these games. As Twins' player Mike Marshall put it, a strike on May 22 would be desirable for the union because the timing would inflict the most financial damage on the owners.

Yet it is still difficult to determine the precise reasons behind this action. Players do receive some expense money (but not their salaries) during spring training. Many of them would appreciate a week's vacation before the regular season begins, and their striking at this time does not represent a major sacrifice in the traditional labor-action sense. While owners would lose some revenues on account of cancelled exhibition games, they would likely lose more during the first week of the regular season. Therefore, the owners probably did not view this action in April 1980 as an expression of player solidarity. Indeed, some of the owners must have assumed that the players would not strike during the regular season because salary losses occur then.

Others perhaps agreed with California Angels owner Gene Autry, who preferred to write off the entire 1980 season because he considered the union's bargaining tactics and goals to be excessive.

I've been a member of unions almost all my life and I know that once they get their foot in the door, they're never happy. They keep wanting more with no consideration for the other side. There's only so far you can go, only so much water in the well, and for an owner who is trying to do the right things it's all very frustrating.

You bring your club to spring training to get it ready to play a championship season and then it walks away from the competition it needs and the fans who pay the bills.[15]

Autry's remarks are significant in two respects. First, his statement could presumably have been in violation of Grebey's media blackout, and Autry might therefore have received a $500,000 fine. However, there is no evidence that he was even investigated by the Player Relations Committee, let alone fined. Second, Autry had long been regarded as a "players' owner"— one who is respectful of the differences between players and has a concern for their welfare. Indeed, Don Baylor—player representative for the Angels—sent Autry a letter indicating that the players' action was not directed personally at Autry, whom they appreciated; instead, it was part of an overall union response to owners in general. In any case, Autry's response did indicate the widening owner militancy and resolve that characterized this and subsequent labor-agreement negotiations.

Many fans supported Autry: They believed that the players were "greedy" or "thoughtless," and the owners were "innocent victims."[16] In a poll conducted by the *Cleveland Plain Dealer*, 67 percent of the fans believed that the owners should not have backed off in their position on salary scales.[17] Player representative Mike Marshall expressed his disappointment over the fans' reaction, particularly since so many of these fans were also union members.

When the United Auto Workers union is in negotiations with General Motors, I don't pretend to understand the issues as well as the UAW members, but I support them. . . . The players know what the baseball industry needs, and the people should give our union the same respect we give to theirs. . . .

If we were another union, and we had been insulted like the owners have insulted us at the bargaining table, we would be out bombing cars by now.[18]

The players themselves strongly supported both the spring training cancellation and the possible subsequent strike action, likely agreeing with MLBPA member Greg Gross's attitude: "We are backing Marvin in any demands he makes. . . . He's the boss."[19] George Foster of the Mets extended Gross's remarks by stating that money was not the issue so much as protecting the free agent rights that had been obtained in previous negotiations.

Bargaining Efforts from Opening Day until the Strike Deadline

The players' spring training boycott resulted in no immediate change in their labor negotiations. Bargaining discussions were either unproductive or else nonexistent for over a month. The same thing applied to Commissioner Bowie Kuhn, who had been silent basically throughout this labor dispute. Kuhn felt that his silence was productive since he was being quickly informed about bargaining developments and had confidence in the union and management negotiators to avoid a long bargaining impasse. Kuhn did believe, however, that management was justified in its free-agent compensation proposal.

Both the owners and the players agreed to a lengthy bargaining recess from April 16 to May 6. Mediator Ken Moffett believed that the recess would not hurt anything since only one issue—free agent compensation—was really involved, and "we have too much time on our hands. We're far away from our deadline."[20]

Speculation then turned to the possibility of a strike on May 23. Grebey wondered in the press why players who were making so much money would even consider a strike, given the current economic situation in the country.[21] Some baseball executives such as Padres president Ballard Smith believed that the players were unrealistic because they only cared about themselves instead of the fans or the game, and because they underestimated management's capability—and maybe even desire—to take on a strike.

However, other executives such as Harry Dalton of the Brewers were more sympathetic to player concerns: "I hope that we are not about to witness another macho test of wills. From what I hear, the players association is genuinely looking for a compromise if we'll just give them something that they can accept without losing too much face."[22]

Dalton—who was fined $50,000 by the PRC for these remarks—must have agreed with the owner who admitted (anonymously) that he and other owners "created this [salary escalation problem] ourselves."[23] There were some owners and fans, then, who could see why players would not be all too likely to bail the owners out of such a self-imposed mess, particularly when the arbitrator and the courts were arguing against management's free agency stance.

Around May 16, management and the unions exchanged rather unpublicized bargaining proposals. Less than one week before the strike expiration date, there were four key issues still remaining. First, on free agent compensation, Miller wanted the status quo—turning the problem over to a study group in the meantime. Second, the owners offered an annual $14.4 million to the pension-benefit package; players were asking for $16.5 million. Third, the union wanted free agent eligibility after five years' service; management wanted the status quo: free agent eligibility after six years' service. And fourth, the owners proposed a $27,000 salary minimum in 1980, while the MLBPA proposed a $35,000 salary minimum.

All in all, there was no substantial bargaining progress before May 22. Moffett informed the press that "we're headed pell-mell toward a strike" and Miller, too, believed that a "small miracle" would be needed to stop the strike now. Yet Miller and Grebey met for off-the-record talks after the first bargaining session adjourned on May 22, and they returned again later with Moffett for some last-ditch bargaining. Around the same time, two owners—Edward Williams of the Orioles, and John McMullen of the Astros—exerted an influence on their fellow owners, while Bowie Kuhn assisted in bringing other owners in, too, on a settlement.[24] Moffett assessed this bargaining situation from the mediator's perspective: "Any negotiations in which management wants to take away something that the workers have, you've got the likelihood of a strike. . . . When they realized the players were serious about striking, the owners relented and made an acceptable proposal."[25]

In the end, the four-year labor agreement that emerged was both a partial compromise and a temporary truce. Most of the terms of the agreement remained in effect for the full four years, however. The minimum salary was increased to $30,000 in 1980 and then to $32,500, $33,500, and $35,000 for the next three years; also, management would contribute $15.5 million a year to the pension-benefit fund. Players again lost their proposal for a reduction in the number of regular games (which was no surprise, by now); and the eligibility requirement for free agency remained at six years' experience, rather than Miller's original proposal of four years. The union was successful in reducing the eligibility for salary arbitration from three baseball seasons to two.[26]

The biggest issue—free agent compensation—was basically placed on hold. Management's last offer on free agent compensation could be implemented after the 1980 labor agreement. This proposal created two levels of "premier free agents," which would include the top 50 percent of all major leaguers according to various performance statistics who were being sought by eight or more clubs. A team signing a free agent in the top 34 percent to 50 percent could protect 18 players. The team losing the free agent could then select any unprotected player.[27]

But this plan did not pertain to the 1980 reentry draft of free agents, which was conducted the same as the 1976–79 major league player drafts; and the new plan could be modified before it was implemented. The 1980 agreement called for a joint committee composed of two players and two club officials who must begin to study the issue no later than August 1, 1980. A report of two conflicting opinions must then have been issued by January 1, 1981, whereupon 30 days of bargaining could occur. If no agreement had been reached by that time, then the owners could implement their free-agent compensation plan described above or one of a less restrictive nature. The players could respond to this in one of three ways: (1) fully accept management's draft compensation proposal; (2) accept it only for the 1981 draft, if the owners would give them the right to strike in 1982; or (3) strike by June 1, 1981, if they had announced their objections by March 1, 1981.[28]

Both sides showed some dissension over the 1980 settlement. The owners voted 21–5 to ratify the 1980 Basic Agreement—which differed from previous contract ratification efforts, where a unanimous vote had always been sought and discovered.[29] Perhaps there were owners who thought that their bargaining brinkmanship could have gone on, particularly since some of the players were pressing for a secret ballot vote on strike actions. One player—who requested anonymity—said, "I know one thing. . . . If we ever do have a secret ballot vote on our team, Marvin is going to be in for a surprise."[30] The players ratified the Basic Agreement by a 619–22 vote, and the benefit plan by a 749–11 margin. Nevertheless, Miller said that he would postpone his long-planned retirement in 1981 if there appeared to be the possibility of a strike.

On the surface, only the one issue of free agent compensation could be renegotiated in 1981; and many people thought that the already resolved issues would ensure four years of labor peace. However, some owners were

not satisfied with the settlement, which again represented a one-way reduction in their discretion and an increase in their costs. They—like many
other management officials across the country during this time period—
expected the union to give up bargaining concessions as well. A few of the
owners believed that the players would agree to free agent modifications,
particularly since this was the only bargainable issue and since it was not
directly related to salary. Yet the negotiations in 1981 would show that very
few issues could still prompt and sustain labor conflict.

1981: HIGH STAKES UNION-MANAGEMENT CONFRONTATION

Bargaining until the Strike Deadline

A committee of two players (Bob Boone and Sal Bando) and two owner
representatives (Harry Dalton and Frank Cashen) was formed to study free
agent compensation, according to the provisions of the 1980 labor agreement.
No progress was made, however, and in February 1981 management exercised its right to issue the proposal made in 1980. Jerry Terrell, the lone
dissenter in the 1980 player strike vote, was now angry because management
wanted a major union concession over free agency without offering financial
justification.

Yankee owner George Steinbrenner threw management's bargaining challenge: "I have never seen the owners more unified and prepared for a strike
. . . Unless he handles this right, it could the Waterloo for Marvin Miller.
Marvin always waits for three or four owners to bolt. It won't happen this
time."[31]

Steinbrenner could afford to be so sure, considering the owners' financial
assistance plans that would operate in case of a strike. The owners had raised
a $15-million strike fund by each contributing 2 percent of their team's gross
revenues for the previous two years. Also a $50-million insurance policy
with Lloyds of London was to kick into effect, should the strike cancel 153
games. This policy would pay about $100,000 for every cancelled game up
to 500 games, or about 40 struck days. Although many teams were used to
earning more than $100,000 for every home date, they would all be saving
from payroll and operating expenditures during a strike.[32]

The players again indicated that they would support a strike—some of
them likely sharing the opinion of the New York Yankees' player representative, Rudy May:

Any time [union leader] Marvin Miller whispers, Strike, every major league player
is going to scream it at the top of his voice.
  Man, don't the owners know that there's going to be a whole generation of ballplayers' sons who grow up with the middle name Marvin? After all that this man

has done for us, who's going to be ungrateful enough not to lose some paychecks if we have to? The owners think that our salaries will make us selfish. Don't they understand that this is the first labor generation in baseball? The majority of guys on every team remembers how it used to be. Just seven years ago, having a BIG season got you a $5,000 raise . . . if you fought real hard.[33]

Even Pete Rose, who in 1976 had indicated that he would not strike again, seemed unperturbed that a strike would delay his passing Stan Musial's 3,630 career hits. Rose said that the game would eventually be played again, and so his breaking the record was just a matter of time. (Rose broke the record on September 11, 1985). Rose's strike nonchalance might have also been due to his guaranteed contract that paid him regardless of any games lost to the strike. This arrangement, shared by only a few other players including Tommy John and Steve Garvey, resurfaced as a major player-management wage concern in the 1989 negotiations.

The media now tended to blame the situation on the owners at least as much as on the players. The argument raised by Miller in the 1980 negotiations was repeated again—namely, that the owners wanted the union to solve problems that they themselves had created. At this time more than a third (nine) of the teams had owners with less than five years' experience in baseball management. In their eagerness to win, they and others were bidding players' salaries way up. For example, the sum of the salaries paid by the Houston Astros in 1981 to only five of their pitchers (Nolan Ryan, J. R. Richard, Don Sutton, Joe Niekro, and Joe Sambito) exceeded the entire team salaries paid by 18 major league clubs in 1980. Management seemed hypocritical at best to be asking the players' help—even considering that its free-agent compensation plan was not so directly limiting as the salary caps proposed in 1980.

One columnist noted that Ray Grebey was pursuing a double standard. After all, his former employer—General Electric—had not received compensation when Grebey left to become baseball management's chief negotiator. And another management negotiator, Harry Dalton, had switched teams in a general manager capacity, without compensation to his former team being involved.[34] Perhaps the strongest media sentiments against management were expressed by Edwin Pope of the *Miami Herald*, who stated, "The public understands that this baseball strike brands owners with the same stamp so long borne by players—money-grubbing fascists who would climb Sequoias to shout lies."[35] Commissioner Kuhn contended, however, that the situation was caused by Miller's "ego gratification" and the "outdated" trade union philosophy of never giving up an item obtained in previous negotiations.

For the first time, the NLRB became a rather direct participant in the negotiations. Its general council, William Lubbers, upheld the players' claim that management had not been bargaining in good faith when it failed to provide financial data to prove the necessity for free agent compensation. As previously noted, Marvin Miller was frustrated that management would repeatedly indicate at the bargaining table its ability to pay but then plead economic hardship in the media. Miller felt that management had crossed over the line—pleading actual inability to pay—and was therefore obligated to show in its bargaining position its financial records. As related evidence, consider the following comments made by the management officials:

Bowie Kuhn (at his "state of the game address" in 1980): "The fabulous gains in player compensation are not a figment of my imagination. . . . The prospect of staggering losses for our clubs is an emphatically real prospect."

Charles Bronfman (Expos executive): warned that the owners could not give in on compensation, because "as an industry, baseball is not healthy."

Calvin Griffith (Twins owner): "Some teams are going to go broke—it's bound to happen."

Bob Lurie (San Francisco Giants executive): "Just wait until one or two teams go under."[36]

With just over 24 hours to go before a strike deadline, the NLRB agreed to seek a restraining order so that a district court judge could hear and decide its injunction request. The injunction asked for a one-year extension of the 1980 bargaining settlement. It would rescind the free-agent compensation proposal unilaterally implemented by the owners in February 1981, and allow them the option of adopting the clause in February 1982, instead. The injunction would also allow the union to reopen the Basic Agreement on this issue and call a strike by June 1, 1982. Also, the full merits of the union's unfair-labor-practice charge would be heard by an NLRB administrative law judge at a later date. Grebey protested the NLRB's move as an "intrusion" into the collective bargaining process, yet both sides agreed to extend the June 1 strike deadline until the judge could hear the NLRB's injunction request.

Some baseball people thought that the owners would drop their bargaining proposal to avoid the injunction and/or the NLRB hearings. Either route could provide the owners with two major problems. First, they might be required to disclose their financial records to the union—a situation that most owners wished to avoid. Second, the owners could be found guilty of violating labor law (the duty to bargain in good faith), and a subsequent players' work stoppage would then become an unfair-labor-practice strike. This situation could result in players being legally entitled to recover pay lost during the strike; also, such a violation might cancel the $50-million insurance coverage.[37]

On June 10, Judge Henry Werker did not find cause for an unfair-labor-practice charge since no specific enough remarks about financial inability had been made at the bargaining table. Without an appeal action by the NLRB forthcoming, the union was free to strike 48 hours after receiving the decision. Some changes had actually been made to the original free-agent bargaining proposals before the strike deadline.[38] But these changes were not enough, and a strike began on June 12, 1981.

Strike Two in Professional Baseball

Players' salary losses for each day of the strike ranged from $181 for a player making the major league minimum to $7,777 for Dave Winfield (who had a $1.4-million annual salary). Yet player representative Rusty Staub believed that the players would be united for a long time over this strike: "This is the easiest issue we've ever had to vote on. We recognize the gravity of the situation, but we know we're right and what they are asking is so easy to say no to."[39]

In the opinion of Kuhn—and probably some of the owners agreed—this strike could have been prevented had Miller spent more time on serious bargaining than on filing charges with the NLRB. Kuhn noted that the players had never been given an opportunity to cast a strike vote by secret ballot, pro or con.

To illustrate player unity and allay the owners' concern that he was a destructive influence, Marvin Miller removed himself from the bargaining table before the contract expiration date and during the early days of the strike. The union was then represented by four players—Doug DeCinces, Mark Belanger, Bob Boone, and Steve Rogers—who were assisted by Don Fehr, MLBPA legal counsel. Any other player could attend the bargaining sessions—an option not given to the baseball owners by their Player Relations Committee.

Press accounts continued to hold management officials accountable for the strike. For example, one cover of *Sports Illustrated* carried the headline "*STRIKE!* The Walkout the Owners Provoked." The cover story blasted the owners and Commissioner Kuhn.

This is a struggle in which the workers fought to preserve the status quo and avoid a strike, while the bosses sought radical change and courted a walkout.... The commissioner of baseball all but told the world that his words were meaningless, his authority a joke.[40]

Interestingly, what *Sports Illustrated* considered the "status quo" represented the culmination of successful union challenges/labor agreement provisions that recently disrupted management's previously established status quo which had been the norm for decades.

In earlier negotiations, Commissioner Kuhn had been an active participant. In 1969 he helped the parties to resolve a pension dispute; in 1976 he reopened the spring training camps when owners had locked the players out; and in 1980 he had held several eleventh-hour discussions with Miller that resulted in the bargaining settlement and in the tabling of the compensation issue. Miller believed that Kuhn's inaction in the present conflict was due to the injunction hearings: "In order to defeat the injunction, they all had to perjure themselves by saying he had nothing to do with labor situations. It's as if he doesn't speak for anybody and he's stuck with the testimony."[41] Kuhn retorted that Miller's previous union experience—as an economist—had not prepared him to be good at the bargaining table since he had little sense of timing, no ability to close a deal, and a destructive hatred of Grebey and the PRC.

Three owners—George Steinbrenner of the Yankees, Eddie Chiles of the Rangers, and Edward Bennett Williams of the Orioles—allegedly met with the commissioner shortly after the strike began and asked Kuhn to replace Grebey and allow them to participate at the bargaining table. When Kuhn refused both these requests, Chiles reportedly threatened to fire him. Kuhn then informed Chiles that he was a "lame-brained old fool" who was embarassing everyone in the room because he knew nothing about the commissioner's office or labor relations.

Kuhn believed that free agent compensation was a most important issue, which could not be abandoned just to shorten the strike. He also believed it unfair to "hurl orders" at the 26 owners—telling them to avoid a strike at all costs—when he had no power to order the union to do the same.

There were only three negotiation sessions during the first eight days of the strike. When Ken Moffett was criticized for not calling more sessions, he responded that you do not have a meeting when there is nothing to talk about. Moffett viewed the situation as "a long waiting game"—one in which neither party gave any hint of possibly moving.

The Threat of a Cancelled Season

The bargaining impasse remained through June, and speculation turned to a likely settlement date. Some thought that the July 14 All-Star Game would prompt a settlement because the players would want to ensure that the television revenues for the game would be contributed to their pension-benefits plan.

The early days of July introduced and reintroduced several participants to the bargaining table. Marvin Miller returned, for the first time since the strike began. He did not think a settlement was near, but wanted to diffuse management's turning his absence into a "phony issue." According to Miller, the very same owners who had felt he was a bargaining impediment were now saying that he was necessary for a negotiated settlement. His perception may have been exaggerated; but it is true that the players did not get along with Grebey, neither on a bargaining nor on a personal basis. Player Rusty

Staub—a frequent bargaining participant—said, "There were a lot of us who would have liked five minutes alone in a padded room with him."[42] Owners Steinbrenner and Williams agreed that "deep-rooted animosity, pride and greed" at the bargaining table was preventing an early settlement.

Steinbrenner also indicated that he was standing behind Grebey and the Player Relations Committee,[43] even though PRC bylaws stated that a minimum of three National or American League owners could request a meeting between the bargaining committee and all owners. Eddie Einhorn, co-owner of the White Sox, acknowledged that such a move would be a sign of division and desperation, but he saw no alternative. Eight owners requested the meeting that was held on July 9. While viewpoints were exchanged, there apparently was no specific bargaining solution given. Mediator Moffett had presented to Miller and Grebey his own proposal for ending the dispute, timed so that Grebey could present it to the owners' meeting. Grebey did not present it, claiming that the proposal had been confidential. This continued the impasse even though the MLBPA indicated that it would accept Moffett's plan.

As a rule, mediators do not publicly present proposals unless they have assurances that both sides will at least use the proposal as a basis for further bargaining. Perhaps Grebey or a few of the owners—who may have gone around Grebey—promised Moffett something that could not be delivered. Or perhaps Moffett's proposal differed from Grebey's expectations. At one point, Grebey suggested that Moffett's proposal had been written by the union.

Also during this time, the National Labor Relations Board conducted hearings to determine whether management had indeed violated its good-faith bargaining obligation. The NLRB's decision on the union's complaint was postponed.

By July 12 the strike had cancelled 392 games and the All-Star Game, as well. Speculation then shifted to whether the entire season would be cancelled. Many saw August 1 as the next deadline: It would take about three weeks to train after settlement, and any season without at least 100 played games would be regarded a farce.

Two alternative approaches presented themselves in mid-July. First the MLBPA proposed that the free-agent compensation issue be submitted to final and binding arbitration. When this proposal was rejected, Don Fehr speculated that management might be only interested in prolonging the strike since they were not convinced that a third party neutral would accept their free agent position.

Second, Raymond Donovan—the U.S. Secretary of Labor—made an unprecedented visit to the baseball negotiators. After the meeting, Donovan cautioned that failure to resolve the strike would harm the American people. The *Washington Post* pointed out that this action ran counter to the Labor secretary's previously consistent stance of not "interjecting" himself or the

Labor Department into union-management negotiations. The *Post* also wondered why Donovan had selected baseball for his visit at a time when coal operators, air traffic controllers, and postal employees were approaching possible strike actions.[44]

Grebey and Miller agreed to move their negotiations from New York to Washington, D.C. Donovan also invited the Player Relations Committee. Management's negotiation team at the time consisted of Grebey, the American and National League presidents—Lee MacPhail and Chub Feeney—and three lawyers. The PRC consisted of MacPhail, Feeney, and Grebey plus six owners who had never attended formal negotiations. Miller said that these owners might get a different perspective if they were to attend the meetings, and then might even drop their former bargaining philosophy. "There are six hardliners who tell the others when to sit up, when to heel, and when to beg." When informed of Miller's remarks, Lee MacPhail said, "He should worry about his committee and we'll worry about ours."[45]

MacPhail's remarks may have been prophetic. The players were having to make considerable personal and economic adjustments because of the strike, and yet there was very little in the way of player dissension—at least in public—or challenging of Miller or the collective bargaining process. Bob Boone explained how it was for most players: "A lot of it is the nature of the animal. . . . In order to become a major league baseball player, you have to be tremendously competitive. These guys may go further for a principle than the average person."[46] Some maintain that Boone, a negotiation team member, and other well paid/performing players strengthened union members' strike resolve. Don Baylor, for example, notes in his autobiography, "I believe the fact that baseball 'superstars' have always been out front separates the MLBPA from the NFL Players Association, a union that has consistently struggled to make gains."

This situation may have been shifting slightly as August 1 approached. Davey Lopes called the contract negotiations a "circus."

Each side has handled it poorly. What the hell is the players' executive board doing in negotiations? I don't think they have credentials to be in a labor meeting. Do Doug DeCinces and Bob Boone have legal backgrounds? . . . I didn't see any postal clerks going into their negotiations. As an entity, we have become the laughing stock of the United States. Everybody's laughing at us. We are not to be respected as a union. . . .

The last thing I want to do is pick up a paper and read Doug DeCinces' synopsis about the players' feelings because he is not qualified and he doesn't know what he's talking about. This forget-the-season attitude really eats at me. Before we do that, brother, we better stop and take a vote.

We all better stop and think about that before we get so deep in this strike that we can't dig ourselves out. We've got to get back to the field. It's my life, it's my livelihood.

The only thing I've seen is what I've read in the newspapers. . . . Who's Jerry Reuss? [Player representative for the Dodgers] Is he still our player rep?[47]

Less than a week after Lopes's remarks, the MLBPA decided to hold a series of regional meetings with players to update them on the 47-day-old strike situation. The first regional meeting was held in Los Angeles (July 27) and was attended by 75 players—including Davey Lopes, who clarified his earlier position:

[I] think there was some misconception that myself and some other players who spoke up were not behind the players association. . . . That's not true. When you've been out of work for a long time, your natural reaction is to question why there hasn't been a settlement.

We are strong collectively as a unit. We have tremendous confidence in Marvin Miller. . . . He would never do anything detrimental to the players.[48]

Some say that management finally realized the union was solidified after hearing reports of the Los Angeles meeting and Davey Lopes's remarks.

On July 29, the owners held separate league meetings before coming together as an entire group (for the second time since the strike began on June 12). According to Lee MacPhail, these meetings were successful since everybody got to speak and no shouting took place. MacPhail also implied that there was a somewhat new and unified bargaining position on the part of management, but was not sure that an agreement could be reached with the union.

Terms and Implications of the Strike Settlement

These general meetings on both sides plus some private meetings that involved Miller, Fehr, Grebey, and MacPhail resulted in a settlement on July 31. The All-Star Game would be played on August 9, and regular season play would begin the next day. The strike had cancelled 706 regular season games—more than a third of the season—and there was much speculation as to whether anyone "won": the owners, the players, or the fans.

The owners received a one-year extension of the 1980 Basic Agreement. The new labor agreement would expire at the end of the 1984 season, with minimum salaries raised from $35,000 in 1983 to $40,000 in 1984. Meal allowances would also increase in 1984, as well as owner contributions to the players' pension plans.

Marvin Miller agreed to drop the MLBPA's complaint filed with the NLRB. This complaint alleged that an unfair labor practice had been committed by management; and it is conceivable that the administrative law judge's decision scheduled for August 3 would eventually have resulted in back pay for the striking players. Perhaps Miller was concerned that the reasoning expressed by Judge Werker in June might influence the NLRB's decision and/or subsequent decisions of the courts. In any case, he did receive—in exchange for dropping the complaint—players' service credit (applicable for benefit, free-agent, and salary-arbitration eligibility) for the games missed during the strike.

Management—for its part—received a certain degree of professional player compensation in the instance of free agents leaving one club for another. The details of this free-agent compensation plan are more fully discussed in Chapter Eight. Suffice it to say here that there can be no more than nine premium (or Type A) free agents who require player compensation, that the compensation is then taken from a "player pool," and that a team signing a free agent can protect 24 roster players from the pool while a team not signing a free agent can protect 26 roster players from the pool. However, no club can lose more than one player a year through compensation.[49]

Dennis Leonard, pitcher for the Royals, said that this situation amounted to an owners' collective bargaining victory, since they would now have the chance to obtain a professional instead of an amateur draft pick. Yet the owners were not claiming victory. An unusually subdued George Steinbrenner—for example—said, "In my 25 years in labor negotiations I learned that nobody ever wins, not the owners, not the players . . . only the lawyers."[50] While the owners collected a reported $44 million in strike insurance, they lost an estimated $72 million in ticket, concession, and broadcast revenues forfeited for the cancelled games. Estimated owner losses ranged from $1.6 million for the Twins to $7.6 million for the Dodgers.

Yet as a group, the players fared worse from the strike. While a few individual contracts guaranteed players their salaries during the strike, the total salary strike loss was $28 million. Losses ranged from $11,000 for those earning the $32,500 salary minimum to $388,500 for Dave Winfield.[51] The new player gain from this strike—in addition to pension and minimum salary increases for 1984—was in principle and in exhibiting unity in the face of lost wages. This unity was again expressed in the players' 627–37 ratification vote of the 1981 labor agreement.

Commissioner Kuhn believed that both sides had realized tremendous losses from the lengthy strike—which was likely to discourage them from using this option again in the near future. Apparently agreeing with Kuhn's assessment, Marvin Miller said that the 1981 strike was "an exercise in terminal stupidity. I don't wanna hear about who won. Nobody won nothin'. Baseball just lost. What's so disgusting is that there's no significant difference between what either side finally got and what they could have settled for by splitting the difference at midnight on June 11th."[52]

After the settlement, attention turned to the remaining season. The MLBPA allowed the owners to determine how the remaining games would count toward post-season playoffs. The owners then looked to maximize fan interest and related revenues, by implementing a "split season." Under this arrangement, the four teams with the best records in the American League East (the Yankees) and West (the Athletics) and the National League East (the Phillies) and West (the Dodgers) were declared the "winners" of the first part of the 1981 season. These teams would play the division winners of the remaining season in mini-playoffs. A team winning both season's halves would play the division team with the second-best overall season record.[53]

Some—like Pete Axthelm—noted that this arrangement could affect the game's integrity. Assume, for example, that the Orioles have the second-best overall divisional record and they happen to play the Yankees on the final day of the second season half. The Yankees were given the first divisional half, and are—say—tied with the Indians for the second half. If the Orioles win, the Yankees would nevertheless meet the Indians in the mini-playoffs. But by beating the Orioles, the Yankees might win both season halves and then face the Orioles in the mini-playoffs. This would encourage the Orioles to throw the game. Kuhn—eventually realizing the situation—modified the split-season format: If a team won both halves of the split season in its division, it would play the divisional runner-up in the post-strike season.

Yet Kuhn's change did not prevent the first-half winners from resting up their men for the playoffs and treating the remaining season as a series of exhibition games. Cardinals' manager Whitey Herzog believed that his division's first-half winners—the Phillies—wanted the Cardinals to win the second half because their premier pitcher, Steve Carlton, would likely beat the Cardinals in the mini-playoffs. According to Herzog, the Phillies figured that "all Steve Carlton had to do was throw his glove out on the mound and the Cardinals would surrender."[54] The Phillies pitched neither Carlton nor any of their other top pitchers against the Cardinals late in the season. Yet the Cardinals lost every one of those games, and the second-half division winner—the Montreal Expos—beat the Phillies in the playoffs. For the record, the Cardinals and the Cincinnati Reds both had the best overall playing records in their National League divisions, but did not win either half of the split seasons and were denied the playoffs.

Both owners and players were concerned about the effect of the 1981 strike and split season on fans' attitudes and attendance. For instance, Larry Bowa and George Brett said that they could hardly hold it against the public for not returning after the strike. Nationwide polls found that fans blamed owners and players about equally for the disruption of games.[55]

Baseball attendance did not increase during the split season in 1981, although it did not drop dramatically. Attendance actually set a record in 1982, which was surpassed in 1983. If they have to, fans can ignore baseball when it is not played, but they still want the game's missing aspects to return to their lives. During the 1981 strike, columnist-fan Bob Rubin predicted that the fans would indeed return to the games—transcending "the idiots" who operate it. Rubin admitted that he missed the box scores, the outrageous outbursts from players and owners, and all the variety of on-field action.

THE 1984–1985 NEGOTIATIONS

Pre-negotiation Changes and Influences

The two years of labor peace between union and management officials during the negotiated labor agreement did not carry over into their respective organizations. On January 1, 1982, Ken Moffett succeeded Marvin Miller as executive director of the MLBPA. Having received a 30–0 approval vote from the player representatives, Moffett was hoping that he could generate respect and some sort of accommodation from management.

The noted baseball writer Thomas Boswell shared Moffett's optimism, believing that the strike's lessons and events would prompt a subsequent labor peace.

Now, both owners and players know what serious business it is to push the other into a corner and force a real fight. In negotiations, mutual respect and, thus, mutual fear speed settlements. In baseball, that respect has never existed before.

The feud between Grebey and Miller—one so personal it tainted and damaged negotiations—has been removed. Said one of the parties closest to the table, they're both so straight out of the politics of the Great Depression that it's scary—romantic left-wing steel worker organizer against brilliant, tough capitalist. Each one thinks the other just might be the devil.[56]

Moffett did not really get a chance to test his mettle on the union side of the table. About a month into office, Moffett prevented Miller from sending a letter to the player representatives in which Miller sought their clarification of his role as consultant to the MLBPA. Then, just before leaving on a tour of the baseball training camps, Moffett changed the lock on the office door and departed without giving Miller a new key.

Moffett also seemed to disagree with Don Fehr and others over the MLBPA's role in player drug-abuse programs. Management disciplined several players for drug use during 1980–83 (see Chapter Six for more details), only to have arbitrators overturn the decisions; Commissioner Kuhn wanted the MLBPA to cooperate in establishing a joint drug-abuse program instead of filing grievances over the issue. Moffett leaned toward this approach. Fehr and some other MLBPA members, however, believed that the grievance procedure should remain a strong option. Moffett was fired in November 1983. About three months later he suggested to the press that some of the player representatives—believing there were four or five cocaine users within their clubs—had dismissed him because of his desire to work with management to end the problem.

In fact, some of the players had been wanting Moffett replaced because they heard owners say how easy negotiations would be in 1985 if Moffett were leading the MLBPA. Miller replaced Moffett on an interim basis, and in turn was replaced by Don Fehr.

Moffett believed that Miller was involved in his ouster. "He's been involved ever since we had that little flap last spring. He's saying there's no animosity, but he's ripped me to enough people, and it's gotten back to me. His fine hand has been involved. For him to say otherwise, he's a liar."[57] Miller contended that there had been no written correspondence, phone calls, or meetings with players in which he had discussed the Moffett situation, although he did attend a meeting at some players' request the night before Moffett was fired. Don Fehr—whom Moffett accused of plotting his demise—said that Moffett had been fired for "incompetence," such as not attending grievance and arbitration meetings. "As for that stuff about a kangaroo court, he was hired by the executive board and he was fired by the executive board."[58]

On management's side, new changes were occurring as well. Lee MacPhail had become director of the Player Relations Committee and Peter Ueberroth had replaced Commissioner Bowie Kuhn before the negotiations began in 1984 and 1985.

The labor agreement modifications on free agent compensation did not seem to be reducing player salaries or improving teams' financial positions. The 1982 average player salary was estimated at $235,000—or $50,000 higher than the 1981 average player salary. The president of the California Angels noted that management had not obtained anything from the strike since the partial compensation plan for free agents did not benefit management at all. Clubs lost in excess of $80 million in 1982, and owners contended that they lost $66 million in 1983.[59] As will be discussed later in this chapter, revenue losses in 1984 were the subject of extensive bargaining concern and controversy.

Early Bargaining Proposals and Activities

Thus, management entered negotiations in 1984 with the goal of holding down player expenses, while the players—viewing their recent salary increases—saw no essential reason to deny themselves more. Three issues emerged approximately eight months before the December 31, 1984, contract expiration date.

1. Pension contributions: Players received a $15.5-million contribution to its pension plan in 1984, or about one-third of television revenues. Baseball's new television package with NBC and ABC would generate $1,125,000,000 over the next six years. Fehr wanted one-third of that total, or a $62.5-million annual contribution.

2. Free agent compensation: Players wanted to eliminate the contract provisions over this issue that were formed in the 1981 settlement.

3. Salary arbitration: The clubs wanted some change in this procedure to stop sharp salary increases.[60]

Players were likely optimistic about collective bargaining after Peter Ueberroth became commissioner on October 1, 1984. Ueberroth quickly installed himself as the sole mediator in a labor-management dispute affecting umpires who were threatening to strike the 1984 post-season games. The settlement of this dispute showed that Ueberroth could take an active and possibly compromising role in the players' negotiations. In early December, Ueberroth met with the owners and urged them to become involved in a new labor-management cooperation, and then spent an unprecedented 80 minutes in a closed-session introductory meeting with the MLBPA officers and player representatives.

Yet negotiations in 1984 followed a similar course when they extended past the contract expiration date into 1985—apparently to no one's surprise. At the end of February, Ueberroth did indicate that he would order management to open its books if the chief union and management negotiators believed that this would significantly aid such collective bargaining efforts by facilitating trust between the parties.

The players were not overly enthusiastic about this development, particularly since negotiations could then shift away from specific bargaining issues to the types of financial measures and audit methods necessary to assess the financial records. Yet Fehr realized that the players would want demonstrable financial proof before making any concessions on economic issues.

On May 14 the Player Relations Committee proposed that—with financial understanding in progress—the MLBPA accept a freeze in benefits, salaries, and pensions. The union did not like this proposal, with at least one official terming it "pathetic." The owners indicated that they would provide a comprehensive proposal on May 22. Before the proposal was even made, however, the owners indicated that they had lost $42 million in 1984 and projected the following future losses: $58 million in 1985, $94 million in 1986, $113 million in 1987, and $155 million in 1988.[61]

When the owners did open their books to the union for the first time on May 17, Don Fehr was not impressed. In his opinion, the action was a deceptive public-relations tactic because the figures were "meaningless" and an "example of voodoo economics." One baseball executive with the Toronto Blue Jays agreed, saying "Anyone who quotes profits of a baseball club is missing the point. Under generally accepted accounting principles, I can turn a $4 million profit into a $1 million loss, and can get every national accounting firm to agree with me."[62] Fehr also gave two examples of how team losses can be manipulated:

1. A team recently bought for $50 million could show $9 million in depreciation losses each year.
2. An owner who has both a team and a cable television network might keep most of the money with the television operation, and then show the MLBPA the "empty pocket."

In any case, the MLBPA could not understand how owners faced with such dollar "losses" would continue to spend themselves into the poorhouse by bidding and paying exorbitant salaries.

The proposals made by the owners after opening the books and before July 15 included a $60,000 minimum player salary, permission for free agents to negotiate with all clubs and for teams to hire free agents without having to offer professional players as compensation, an annual contribution of $15.5 million to the benefits fund, an increase in eligibility for salary arbitration from two years to three years, and a salary maximum for arbitrators (according to which players could at most double their previous salary).[63] Ueberroth appeared to take a hands-off bargaining posture—similar to Bowie Kuhn in the previous negotiation—stating, "I have no power to stop a strike. If I had it, I wouldn't use it, because that would be unfair to the collective bargaining between labor and management."[64] Fehr believed that the owners were taking a hands-off bargaining approach as well, since management finally made its first offer (one that they knew would be rejected) six months after negotiations had begun.

On July 15 the MLBPA voted to strike on August 6 if no settlement were reached by that date. This strike date differed from previous negotiations in that the players would have received most of their paychecks by then, while the clubs would lose August and September's revenues. Ueberroth continued his noninvolvement in the dispute although by July 26 when there still seemed no settlement likely, he had changed his stance. "I just really can't allow there to be a strike that shuts down America's national pastime. It's been shut down too many times in the past. It's just not the right thing."[65]

One week before the August 6 strike deadline, management offered a $25-million annual contribution to the pension fund, but tied this figure inversely to annual salary increases of more than $13 million. For example, if annual salaries increased by $14 million—$1 million over the limit—then the annual pension would decrease $1 million to $24 million. Since salaries for 1985–88 were expected to increase by $34 million a year, the actual pension-fund contribution of $4 million a year would be a drastic reduction from previous agreements. Fehr responded angrily to the proposal, which represented a thinly disguised salary cap. "That's how you move the ball along? You [the owners] get four times the money from the national TV package and the pension contribution goes down?"[66]

Approximately 50 percent of the current players had experienced the previous strike and its severe salary losses in 1981. Management may have been testing the players' solidarity and resolve to take another—possibly equally long—strike in 1985. Most players realized that this latest proposal placed them in a no-win situation. They could either give up their own pension-plan proposal, which they believed to be reasonable, or risk taking a strike that might alienate the fans.

Ueberroth was no doubt aware of a poll[67] indicating that fans were basically against a strike when he entered negotiations four days before the deadline. Stating that he represented the fans, the commissioner made the following proposals to resolve negotiations before the strike date:

—The owners should drop all salary caps and accept the players' changes in free agency.

—The pension plan contribution should be raised, going from $23 million to $31 million over a five-year period. The difference between $23 million and the players' last request—$45 million—would be placed in escrow, and the players would finish the season. There would then be a 45-day bargaining period with a $1-million-a-day penalty for each day the talks dragged on. The penalty money would go to amateur baseball in the United States and Canada or to charity.

—Players should accept the owners' salary arbitration demands: raising eligibility from two years to three years; and limiting salary increases to 100 percent. There would be a "superstar" designation where by some players could receive an un-limited increase; also, the conditions would not apply to current major league players.[68]

Ueberroth's proposals were basically ignored by the negotiators. Indeed, management negotiator Lee MacPhail indicated that the PRC was the responsible party negotiating for the owners and that Ueberroth was not operating on management's behalf. Marvin Miller, who appears to have had an active consultant role during these negotiations, was also not enthusiastic about the commissioner's proposals. Miller believed that Ueberroth had "proceeded like an amateur," because he made his ideas public instead of relaying them to the management and union negotiators in private.

Management and the union exchanged pension-plan contribution proposals on August 4. The owners agreed to a $15.5-million guaranteed annual contribution; the MLBPA said that it would accept this lesser amount for the pension fund if the owners directed their savings from the players' original offer of $60 million to help financially troubled teams.

Strike Three

A day before the strike deadline, Ueberroth indicated that he might invoke Major League Section Rule 12-A, which says the commissioner can make any decision that he deems to be in the interest of the game. This provision had been invoked twice by Commissioner Kuhn to nullify player trades between teams. However, it had never been used in collective bargaining. The players struck on August 6, largely because of wide differences over salary arbitration. Some players immediately expressed their concern. For example, one day into the strike, ten Detroit players met in pitcher Milt Wilcox's room to discuss the issues. Wilcox then informed MLBPA negotiators of their thoughts.

What we're worried about is that they will get hung up on some things that really weren't in the best interests of the majority of the players. We want them to know that we don't want to have a long strike and lose a lot of money over something like the arbitration thing that would only affect a few players.[69]

Ueberroth decided not to use his Section 12-A "interest of the game" powers to prevent the strike, maintaining instead that the parties must be given free play to resolve their own differences. Yet John McMullen, owner of the Houston Astros and a member of the Player Relations Committee—when asked if the owners would compromise on the salary arbitration issue—replied, "No, no way."

McMullen and Fehr were both proven wrong when the strike ended after two days of missed games, and a five-year settlement had been reached. (The missed games were rescheduled and played.)[70] Management did obtain an increase in salary arbitration eligibility: Players would have to wait three years, instead of two, before using this alternative. Management also obtained a modification in the arbitration process (discussed in Chapter Nine), whereby players could only compare their salaries with others of equal value, comparable age, and similar experience—instead of with the large salaries paid to free agents. However, arbitrators were not given a salary cap or limitation to use in their decisions.

The union appeared to have obtained its free agent proposals. Any number of clubs could now try to sign a free agent, and teams would be compensated with amateur draft picks (as in the previous labor agreement), instead of with professional players.

The minimum salary was increased from $40,000 to $60,000 in 1985 and 1986, with a cost-of-living adjustment made prior to the 1987 season. The 1988 salary minimum would be the same as the 1987 salary minimum, and a subsequent cost-of-living adjustment would be made prior to the 1989 season. A retroactive pension-plan contribution of $25 million would apply to the 1984 season. In subsequent years, the pension plan contribution would be $33 million in 1985, 1986, 1987, and 1988, and $39 million in 1989. Under the new pension plan, a player with ten years of major league experience would receive an annual pension of $91,000 at age 62. The previous plan paid a player with 20 years' service $57,000 a year at age 65.

The players also received an increase in their World Series share. Previously they had received 60 percent of the gate receipts for the first four games after the commissioner took 15 percent off the top. Now the players would get 60 percent off the top. That would have given the previous year's world champion Detroit Tigers an extra $5,000 for each player and the San Diego Padres players an extra $3,500 each.

This agreement also provided a form of revenue sharing for the teams. Some $20 million in network television revenues would be set aside annually for those franchises losing the most money.[71] The "spirit of compromise" and a "sense of urgency" among the management and union negotiators had prompted the quick settlement after the strike action was taken. MacPhail noted,

It was really the last two meetings on Tuesday that got us there . . . We just had to compromise. We had to come to the end of the road and both parties had to compromise. We dropped the salary cap, or 100 percent limit, they dropped their opposition to three-year eligibility and the criteria for salary arbitration was a compromise.[72]

Ueberroth indicated that he had taken no role in facilitating the settlement—an attitude shared by Fehr and some of the player representatives. Yet Ueberroth may have influenced both compromise and urgency through some of his actions. Both in public and in private, he had told the owners that the players were doing their job on the field and that they—the owners—should not be asking the players to solve their own money problems. At the very least, he had helped keep the parties talking. He may also have turned up the pressure to settle on Wednesday when he joined the negotiations for the first time 75 minutes before announcing the tentative settlement to the public.

It would be simplistic, however, to compare Ueberroth directly with Kuhn in their collective bargaining roles. Ueberroth cannot be regarded as more effective than Kuhn simply because the strike under his involvement was 48 days shorter than the 1981 strike. Events and influences apart from the change in commissioners likely influenced the outcome. For example, since 1981 there had been major ownership changes or shifts on six clubs, as well as some changes on management's negotiating team, which may have created a more flexible bargaining atmosphere. And owners must have realized that the player unity established during the 1981 strike might again be provoked and prolonged in the 1985 strike. Also, management did not have any strike insurance, as it had in 1981. Therefore, a strike in 1985 would have increased the cost of disagreeing with the union's position.

From the union's perspective, players seemed to be more eager to resolve the bargaining impasse quickly in 1985. In previous labor disputes, the press had typically to wait a long time before they could find a concerned or dissenting player viewpoint to report. This was not the case in 1985. Perhaps the players who had experienced large strike costs in 1981 were now experienced with labor relations activities and issues, and realized that it would cost more to disagree than to agree.

WILL THE GOLD ERODE? COLLECTIVE BARGAINING AND 1990

The MLBPA's previous bargaining gains are likely to be tested strongly by the owners in the 1989 contract negotiations. Baseball owners emerged from the 1985 negotiations with the realization that the MLBPA could be made to yield some concessions. For example, the union's pension benefit share of television revenues was 18 percent in 1985, instead of 33 percent or higher in previous years.

Another realization occurred when the owners opened their financial books. Ueberroth claimed that this move stimulated owner awareness as each soon realized that he or she was not the only one losing money. Perhaps this educational lesson is what prompted owners to drop with little fanfare their free agent's compensation issue in 1985. The issue had been a major factor in the 50-day strike in 1981.

Players' bargaining resolve in 1989 is even more difficult to predict. Marvin Miller has always believed that professional baseball players are more militant then professional football players because minor-league working conditions are far worse than the college-campus training grounds. It is true enough that young major-league players do want to avoid returning to the minors. Dave Collins—after being called up from the Cincinnati Reds—observed, "I'd rather go out to lunch with my ex-wife's attorney than play in the minors."[73] In his book, *The Jock's Itch*, Tom House recalled his minor league introduction. The team's general manager picked him up at the airport in a driving rainstorm and said:

Just throw your bags and yourself in the back of the pickup truck. Jump on in and pull that tarp over your head.

I'm thinking, "Wow, okay, I guess I can put up with this," except for the fact that his fucking dog is riding up front in the cab.

In any case, both players and management have accumulated strike funds to increase their resolve and ability to take a strike in 1990. The owners agreed among themselves to give up their expected increases in national broadcasting revenues for the 1988 and 1989 seasons. These amounts (approximately $3.5 million per club) will generate a $100-million strike fund that can be used to purchase strike insurance and/or a line of credit. Some of these funds may also go to clubs in need of money should there be a strike.[74]

Yet the players may even be nullifying management's strike fund with one of their own. The product licensing agreement (including baseball cards) that Marvin Miller initiated in 1966 will generate approximately $50 million in 1988 and 1989. Players have agreed to add this figure to its already accumulated $20-million strike fund. Miller believes that this $70-million figure gives the unionized players "... a nice feeling. For the first time, the players are independent and will be at a point where they can weather a lockout or a strike better than the owners."[75]

Players might also benefit from a rival 8–12 team league playing 154 games from April through September 1990. The average net worth of the proposed league's principal owners appears higher than the average net worth of the principal owners of the 26 major league clubs. The league would initially seek 10–20 name players with comparable salaries plus revenue sharing arrangements. Clearly, this rival league alternative would benefit the union in its negotiations over the labor agreement in 1990. Some—perhaps many— players could augment their strike funds with employment in the rival league should a strike occur.

In the meantime, management has implemented a "lockout clause" in many player contracts. These clauses either free the club of any obligation to pay the player during any type of lockout or else let an arbitrator determine whether the player should be paid for that time. In either case, players would not receive their pay at the time of the lockout. Therefore, players strongly prefer that there be no lockout clause. Pitcher Bruce Hurst, for example, moved from the Boston Red Sox to the San Diego Padres in 1989 just because the Red Sox insisted on a lockout clause. Lacking any other option, players prefer a "defensive lockout clause": The only way players would not then get paid during a lockout is if the owners took this action in response to a players' strike.[76]

However, the lockout clauses may not be so effective a management tactic, after all, as they may actually be in violation of the labor agreement and therefore be unenforceable. Marvin Miller maintains that the lockout clause violates Article II, which states that special covenants may be included in individual player contracts "which actually or potentially provide additional benefits to the players."[77] Clearly, the lockout clause does not represent a player benefit. A grievance has not yet been filed over the clause, but players and/or the union will likely take such action if the clause is even implemented.

The MLBPA and management have apparently neutralized each other's bargaining strengths—a situation favoring no strike settlement in 1990. Also, the number of populist strike issues applying to a majority of union members may now be seriously curtailed. Previously obtained pension funding is now approaching the legal maximums—if not the members' nearly complete satisfaction.

The union may be on even shakier grounds with the minimum salary issue. *Sports Illustrated* reported all players' salaries for the 1987 season, when the minimum was $62,500. Since 1968, the largest percentage increase in minimum salary over preceding year has been 50 percent (from $40,000 to $60,000 in 1985). If this proportion were applied to the 1987 salary minimum, the union would be seeking $93,750. This figure would not generate too much negative public opinion, since fans are now used to baseball players striking over a salary much higher than their own. Also, public opinion never has appeared to influence the union or management negotiators. More significantly, however, a proposal for $93,750 minimum salary will not carry much weight with the MLBPA membership. In 1987, only 26 percent of the membership made less than this figure—a proportion that has declined further by 1989.

Two other issues—salary-level arbitration, and free agency—will be tougher to resolve, and require the MLBPA and management to alter previously established bargaining approaches. As discussed in Chapter Nine, research on player's pay and performance statistics in 1987 found no statistically significant relationship between pay and batting averages or pitchers' win-loss percentages. The inconclusive relationship between pay and performance also currently extends to the team level.

The MLBPA will justifiably claim little responsibility for this situation, as the union does not bargain for individual player salaries. Therefore, the union will not even consider direct salary-reduction mechanisms such as salary caps. However, it might need to explore salary arbitration and perhaps agree to modifications in this procedure. Few would argue the arbitrators' skills or knowledge, although no one other than the arbitrators themselves knows how these abilities are used. New bargaining provisions might require the arbitrators to explain their decisions and/or more clearly operationalize their decision-making framework criteria.

Free agency may emerge as a bargaining issue if one or both parties seek to incorporate or modify related arbitration decisions into the labor agreement. Chapter Eight discusses how this situation happened in 1976 (the Catfish Hunter case) and describes the subsequent free-agent collusion grievances heard by arbitrators Roberts and Nicolau that might prompt bargaining in 1990.

Management could also wind up assessing its issue formulation and bargaining stance in some different manner from its previous internal bickering and truculence. For example, management could attempt to increase the number of playing seasons necessary to become eligible for salary arbitration and/or free agency to atone for its past bargaining losses and/or to test union solidarity. But a more reasonable bargaining approach may be encouraged by the $1.1-billion television contract negotiated with CBS in 1988 (discussed more in Chapter Four).

It is easier to predict the timing of a strike lockout in 1990 than to predict its occurrence. Barry Rona, executive director of the PRC, suggests that management will either settle, absorb a strike, or have a lockout before the start of the 1990 season:

The players association has always struck the clubs during the course of a season and hit us at a point in time when we were at our peak drawing capacity. . . . This led to a cessation at the heart of the season—split seasons and all the other crazy things. Frankly, we're not prepared to let that happen to us again.[78]

The 1988 television contract with CBS may also prompt either an early settlement or an early impasse. The bulk of these funds are for the end-of-the-season events: the League Championship Series and the World Series. Players will have 80 percent of their salaries by August; the owners will have only about 20 percent of their revenues at this time. The owners will not let the players work without an agreement for most of the season, collecting most of their salaries, and then strike when management is most vulnerable.

Management and union officials have already taken an unprecedented move: meeting a year before the labor agreement expires. Both representatives have discussed revenue sharing, a method that apparently has benefited both labor and management interests in professional basketball. Yet Don Fehr of the MLBPA has viewed this bargaining issue and situation in cautious terms. Fehr views the definition of revenue and the amount to be shared as potential obstacles. He further contends: "You keep hoping it [the atmosphere between the two sides] will change . . . but there are no indications that will happen. You have to go by their [the owners'] past record."[79]

Part Two

Collective Bargaining Participants

Four

Owners, Commissioners, Media, and Agents

Previous chapters have related baseball owners, commissioners, and the media to selected player-management incidents, such as the labor agreement negotiations that occur every several years. These off-field participants in the game of baseball actually exert a more pervasive influence than just at bargaining time. They affect the daily implementation of the labor agreement and other player-management concerns (drug abuse, for example) that occur between collective bargaining efforts.

This chapter discusses the owners, the commissioners, and the media in more detail and suggests how their various backgrounds or other general differences can affect player-management relationships. Agents—the final participant category discussed here—are not at all involved with negotiating collective bargaining agreements, although they often implement labor agreement provisions (free agency and salary arbitration, discussed in Chapter Eight) when they represent an individual player.

OWNERS AND OWNER DIFFERENCES

Some 65 years ago, Ring Lardner wrote that the baseball owner is burdened with high payrolls (as much as $65,000 per team in 1912) and other expenses and headaches. He concluded that the owner is "not going to the poorhouse. No, but the asylum is not so far away."[1] Lardner's comment suggests many of the problems that owners face and/or bring on themselves.

The previous three chapters have illustrated that the owners are not always unified. This has contributed to the union's ability to achieve large bargaining gains at the owners' expense. In some cases, a team has more than one owner. Limited partnerships and their related tensions can be found on the Red Sox, the Yankees, and the Reds.[2]

Owners' distrust can initially occur in determining whether a prospective owner may join the league. In 1980, the American League owners—by an 11-against and 3-for vote (10 positive votes were needed)—denied Edward DeBartolo ownership of the White Sox. The reasons for this negative vote— that DeBartolo did not live in the team's city, and that he owned racetracks— were dubious since other owners had one or both of these characteristics. One of the League owners commented, "The American League unfairly and unthinkingly turned down a fine offer from a fine man. I am embarrassed."[3]

Existing owners have been known to knock each other in the media. Marge Schott (the Reds) once noted that George Steinbrenner (the Yankees) is "ruining baseball," while Calvin Griffith (the Twins) believes that the Red Sox "screwed things up for everyone else the way they pay."[4] Bill Veeck (the White Sox) used to insult owners with compliments:

[Charley Finley of the A's] at least is willing to try something. But he usually manages to louse up whatever he tries. He just does things without class.

It's not just that [Calvin Griffith] marches to his own drum; I don't even think he hears anyone else's. He doesn't identify with the fans—never has. He doesn't do things because they're good p.r. or politically smart. It's a strange thing to say, with that big fat belly of his, but in a perverse way I find him gallant.[5]

In his autobiography, Bowie Kuhn recalls a name-calling contest between George Steinbrenner and two owners of the White Sox—Jerry Reinsdorf and Eddie Einhorn—and the fines administered because of these insults, which were made in 1982 and 1983. Reinsdorf, angered because Steinbrenner signed one of his players, called the Yankee owner "totally irresponsible." Yet when the White Sox signed a free agent that Steinbrenner wanted, co-owner Reinsdorf crowed, "We beat fat George out of that one." Steinbrenner countered that the two White Sox owners could never agree on anything, and referred to them as "Abbott and Costello." Kuhn fined Steinbrenner $5,000 and the White Sox owners $2,500 for the remarks. Kuhn also ended up fining the Sox owners' for saying, "Do you know how to tell when George Steinbrenner is lying? It's when his lips move."

Many times, owners' verbal insults toward each other represent more fundamental underlying differences about the very basic business of running a club. Consider—for example—the remarks of Padres' owner, the late Ray Kroc.

I think baseball has to allow a couple of the weaker clubs that can't survive without help to fold. I know that sounds hard, but that's what happens in other businesses.

And once the threat of that possibility comes into focus, it might scare some owners out of paying these outrageous salaries. . . .

Marvin Miller knows what is going on. He is aware that the latest figures show our attendance is up, our total revenue is up in baseball. He also is armed with something even more important to him.

He knows there never has been a team in baseball that has gone bankrupt. And until some clubs go bankrupt, until some owners go out of business, there is nothing to prove we can't stand the gaff.[6]

In 1984, National League owners (prompted by the Saint Louis Cardinals) voted to censure Ted Turner of the Atlanta Braves for his signing of pitcher Bruce Sutter to a contract estimated between $9 million and $10 million. The censure motion—believed to be the first of its kind in major league baseball—dramatizes ownership differences, which can be grouped into the following five categories: (1) work experience, financial success, and baseball background; (2) attitudes toward players and the union; (3) team development methods: revenues and direction; (4) reliance on innovative promotional techniques; and (5) influence with other owners and/or the commissioner.

Work Experience, Financial Success, and Baseball Background

At least two surveys of owners' backgrounds have been made: one in 1968, and the other in 1981.[7] Both found that the vast majority of owners are very wealthy individuals who have amassed fortunes in other businesses (hamburgers, jeans, shipbuilding, radio and television, chemicals, real estate, lumber, and beer, for example), and regard their baseball venture as a hobby. Legendary Yankee owner Jacob Rupert's brewery interests made him worth about $75 million at a time when "a dime bought a decent meal and a nickel rolling across the floor attracted some real attention."[8] Two such wealthy owners—Ewing Kauffman of the Kansas City Royals, and George Steinbrenner of the New York Yankees—believe that they and all other owners are "egomaniacs." Marvin Davis—a Denver oilman who purchased the Oakland A's for around $12 million—observed, "As men get older, the toys get more expensive."[9] Ray Kroc, who founded McDonald's, indicates why he purchased the San Diego Padres:

I just wanted a hobby. It's an extravagant hobby, for sure. I could make more money out of one hamburger stand than I can out of baseball. But I love baseball and I have no interest in money. The only enjoyment I get out of making money is from the knowledge that people always say, If you're so smart, why aren't you rich? Well, I'm rich, so I guess you could say I'm smart. Money doesn't have anything to do with it.[10]

A related finding is that most owners (23 out of 26 in 1981) do not devote full time to baseball; they pursue their other business interests, as well.

George Steinbrenner, for example, spends only 25 percent of his time with the Yankees. Yet he says that he bought the team for the visibility it gives him: "No one pays attention to a shipbuilder."[11]

Walter O'Malley, owner of the Dodgers, was one of the few who devote full attention to baseball. Some feel that this situation helped contribute to the team's success. Yet a "part-time" owner can be effective, particularly if he or she delegates the operational—and perhaps business—end to others. Some owners, however, do not delegate much authority at all. A sportscaster once bluntly explained why Charley Finley leaves so few decisions to others: "He doesn't treat people like human beings."[12] One report on the San Diego Padres found a similar lack of delegation:

After nearly 12 years of floundering and drift, the Padres are where they are today because they've never had a sensible plan to get them anyplace but. They've had as many rings as Barnum & Bailey, with sometimes three people cracking whips at the same time. For example, just a few weeks ago, G. M. Bob Fontaine was fired, not by Kroc himself, nor by his son-in-law, Padre President Ballard Smith, but by Joan Kroc, Ray's wife and a director of the club. She insisted on it. So who's in charge? Lord knows.[13]

In 1987, five general managers were either fired or resigned, suggesting that owners do frequently give some thought to delegation or at least to their delegation choices. Perhaps the most controversial general-manager dismissal occurred when the Pirates recently fired Syd Thrift. He was hired by the team at the end of the 1985 season, when the Pirates had lost 104 games and were carrying a payroll that exceeded $12 million. Thrift was fired after the 1988 season when the Pirates won 85 games and had a payroll of $6.5 million (about $1.5 million less than the Dodgers' starting rotation, and nearly $4 million less than any other team in the National League East).

Pirates' President Carl Barger claimed that Thrift was dismissed because of communication and cooperation problems. Some maintain that Thrift was fired because he received too much publicity for the team's success.

Owners like Tom Monaghan of the Tigers, Walter Hass, Jr., of the Athletics, and Bob Howsam (former owner) of the Reds believe in delegation. Howsam's general manager, Dick Wagner, allegedly operated as a hatchet man—removing personnel such as Pete Rose and Sparky Anderson. Some general managers (Al Rosen of the San Francisco Giants, Bill Bergesch of the Cincinnati Reds, and Maurry Cook of the Montreal Expos) say that they have complete autonomy in their decisions, but they still inform the owners before making any moves.[14]

A related consideration is the extent to which owners participate in the operational aspects of the business. Although Walter O'Malley devoted full attention to his baseball business, he spent little—if any—time on playing field decisions (who should bat where in the lineup, for example). O'Malley confessed that he did not know the playing end of the game—an attitude shared by Gene Autry, owner of the Angels, and Jerold Hoffberger, who owned the Orioles.[15]

Another owner—Philip Wrigley of the Cubs—seldom attended baseball games. His successor-son William Wrigley also believed "that there's really nothing you can do while the game's going on, unless you want to interfere, or meddle. . . . When the game's going on, you can't hit, field, or steal bases for them—and as far as being an expert, while I've watched a lot of games and been closely associated with baseball people for a long time, obviously, I don't pretend to be any expert."[16]

A recent interview in the *Cincinnati Post* illustrates why Marge Schott, current owner of the Reds, defers to lower organizational officials on the team who know something about the game.

Q: Who do you see as your toughest competition?

A: [Schott] Well, I hope it's St. Louis.

Q: I mean in the division.

A: Let me see. I don't know. Maybe the Kansas City Royals.

Q: I mean your division.

A: Well, Pittsburgh's got some young men coming, and Los Angeles is going to come back.[17]

On the other hand, George Steinbrenner and Charley Finley—owners of the Yankees and the A's, respectively—have often been involved with the playing aspects of the game. Steinbrenner justifies his involvement by stating, "I mean when a guy driving a cab or working on a building in New York yells 'Attaboy!' or tells me to do this or do that, that's important to me, and I want them to know that I'm involved because I'm like they are. I die when we lose, just like they do."[18] Finley's daily involvement in game activities was probably understood, but certainly not appreciated, by the players. Pitcher Vida Blue agreed that Finley or any owner has a right to protect his or her multimillion-dollar operation, but also felt that Finley went too far in his attempt to control every team facet.

Attitudes toward Players and the Union

Involved—or even uninvolved—owners can sometimes have a relationship with the players that cuts across field managers and other organizational officials. Consider, for example, the relationship between Atlanta Braves' third baseman Bob Horner and owner Ted Turner. Horner was Rookie of the Year when hired by Turner in 1978, and hit .314 in 1979 with 33 home runs and 98 runs batted in. However, in 1980 the Braves got off to an awful start (one win; nine losses), and Horner was no different (two hits in 34 at-bats). Horner had a no-trade clause in his contract, but he could be optioned to the minors—which Turner attempted in April 1980.

Horner refused the minor league assignment and filed a grievance, contending that the action was the vindictive response of an "absolute jerk." Turner disclaimed Horner's assessment, indicating that a vindictive person would not have given Horner a three-year $1-million contract in the first place. Turner also countered that he and the other Atlanta Braves members were being punished for "Mr." Horner's "terrible" play, and that Horner's personal strike could extend through his multiyear contract for all anyone cared.

Commissioner Kuhn supported Turner's action. Marvin Miller, however, said Turner had acted like a "petty dictator" who was determined to strut his authority. Horner claimed that he went to bed every night praying he would be traded to avoid such "humiliation." To which Turner replied, "The only time I would consider trading him would be when I'm happy with Bob Horner as a person."[19] Yet the confrontation ended temporarily when Turner reinstated Horner before he had spent any time in the minors.

In 1987, Horner's multiyear $5.5-million ($1.8 million for the 1986 season) contract had expired; and, according to the Braves management, he was offered a three-year contract at $4.5 million or a two-year contract at $3.9 million. Horner denied that this ever happened, saying he was asked to take a 40-percent cut in salary after one of his best years (27 home runs and more than 500 at-bats for the first time in his nine years with Atlanta). He tested the free agent market, received only one offer (from the San Diego Padres, at approximately $700,000 for one year), and then played on a Japanese baseball team (at an estimated salary of $2 million for one season) where he hit 34 home runs in 89 games. During that same year Ted Turner signed Atlanta Brave outfielder Dale Murphy to a three-year $6-million contract, in part because of Murphy's demonstrated team loyalty. Turner also offered Bob Horner $900,000 for the 1988 season; the Japanese team offered Horner $10 million for a three-year contract. Horner refused both offers, signing instead a one-year contract for the 1988 season with the Cardinals. His signing and salary ($950,000 base, with various incentives possibly earning him another $500,000) did not immediately impress Whitey Herzog—manager of the Cardinals—who said, "I don't like Horner. . . . He never could hit in St. Louis."[20] Herzog may have been right: Horner left the 1988 season early after injuring his shoulder and hitting three home runs in 206 at-bats. Before the 1989 regular season began, Bob Horner had retired.

In 1988, George Steinbrenner publicly disputed stars Don Mattingly (for alleged lack of performance) and Dave Winfield—the latter over Steinbrenner's contractually required contribution to Winfield Enterprises, a nonprofit charitable foundation. Winfield has sued Steinbrenner three times in seven years, and contended that Steinbrenner owed $450,000 in 1988. Steinbrenner countersued, saying that Winfield has not paid his contractually required

$400,000 a year to his own organization. Steinbrenner's publicist further charges Winfield with fiscal irresponsibility: "If a politician or even a television evangelist conducted their financial affairs like the Winfield Foundation there would certainly be an investigation."[21] The suit was eventually settled out of court with both Steinbrenner and Winfield making additional contributions to the foundation.

There is probably no direct association between owner-player interactions and subsequent team performance. When Tom Yawkey owned the Red Sox, for example, everyone knew that he was very liberal and generous with his players. Critics would view this style as overindulgent—"spoiling the players"—when the team was losing. But when the Red Sox won, their success was attributed in part to the players' loyalty to such a generous boss.[22] On the other hand, Charley Finley's abrasive style of motivating players (described below) always somehow managed to produce a few positive team results.

Yet some characteristics do differentiate owner-player relations across teams. Some owners seem to be more approachable by players than others. This may be due to an optimistic, upbeat attitude and/or to a genuine interest in the players as individuals. Bill Giles, owner of the Phillies, says that his team's social gatherings with players and their wives has generated a "family" instead of an "employee-employer relationship."

Many players regard Gene Autry as one of the more approachable owners. Reggie Jackson—for example—was most impressed with Autry's concern for individual players, irrespective of their abilities. Fellow player Lyman Bostock agreed with Jackson's assessment after Autry offered to do anything he could for Bostock's wife when she was in the hospital. In fact, Bostock went so far as to back up his appreciation with action. He worried that he was not living up to his annual salary of $450,000 with his two hits in 39 at-bats at the start of the 1978 season. "If I don't do well the rest of April, I'm going to ask Mr. Autry not to pay me for the month. I want to give him his money's worth . . . If he [Autry] won't keep the money, I'll ask him to give it to some kind of organization that can use the money."[23]

Intimidation can represent another dimension of player-owner relationships. Mike Epstein, who played for the Oakland A's, claimed that owner Charley Finley would generate so much hatred among the players that they would perform better just to prove him wrong. Finley once threatened to send Reggie Jackson to the minors—which resulted in Jackson's referring to Finley as "that big asshole." Yet Jackson also indicated, "I took crap from him I wouldn't take from any other man."[24]

George Steinbrenner has also used intimidation on occasion. Dick Schaap describes this clubhouse meeting after a team loss:

He struck familiar notes. The players were lacking in dedication. They weren't earning their huge salaries. They were letting down the people of New York. They were a disgrace to their pinstriped uniforms. The players, already angry with themselves, turned their anger toward the boss. The tension was so great Reggie Jackson anticipated a fistfight.

"Fuck you, George," said Rick Cerone. "We don't need to hear this."

"I pay the bills around here," Steinbrenner shouted. "I'll say whatever I want. And we'll see where you're playing next year."

"Fuck you," Cerone said again.[25]

After this exchange, Steinbrenner asked Reggie Jackson to carry his "last word" note to Rick Cerone. It read:

Your strikeout to end the game with a man on third carries little weight with me. Stupid mental errors like rounding first too far does. Your vulgarities to me in the clubhouse afterward is water off a duck's back. It was said out of frustration, just as my answer to you was said out of anger. It has no bearing at all, and I want you to know that.

Maury Allen's book, *After the Miracle,* describes "the most extraordinary public player flogging by an owner that any member of the press had seen." This situation concerned Cleon Jones, who was spotted with a woman in a van and was charged with indecent exposure. Jones was never prosecuted for the charge because the Mets took care of the fine. However, the team's owners ordered Jones

to stand up at Shea Stadium and apologize for his actions to Mets fans. His wife, Angela, stood by his side. Mets board chairman M. Donald Grant stood by while Jones read his prepared apology. Members of the press who had to sit still for this humiliating charade were as embarrassed as Jones. Angela Jones's stoic face was the most significantly lasting memory of this episode.

Players can intimidate management officials, as well, when they express their concerns in the media. For example, pitcher John Candelaria told the Pittsburgh press that his general manager was a "bozo" because he was "scared" to trade for needed players.

Another pitcher, Goose Goosage—angered over a ban on beer in the team clubhouse—informed the press that the Padres' president, Ballard Smith, was uninformed and unconcerned about baseball. He also accused the team owner, Joan Kroc—who assumed this position after her husband Ray died— of "poisoning the world" with food served at McDonald's restaurants, and called both club officials "spineless and gutless." Gossage received a 20-day suspension and a loss of $25,000, to be donated to the San Diego Ronald McDonald House. This settlement was agreed on by Gossage, management, and the Major League Baseball Players' Association. Gossage also publicly apologized to the club officials and to McDonald's for making his remarks.

Owners' attitudes toward the MLBPA can also influence one or more collective bargaining negotiations, labor agreement administration, and related player-management relationships. Calvin Griffith and other owners may be of the opinion that a sports union eliminates player initiative. Yet Griffith, along with Finley and other owners, have proposed good-faith bargaining efforts with the MLBPA. Charles Bronfman of the Montreal Expos may have gone one step further when he suggested that negotiation disputes involve a third-party neutral arbitration panel, although he did not indicate whether the panel should issue binding decisions.[26]

Team Development Methods: Revenues and Direction

Owners differ over the amount and direction of money spent on player salaries and team development. They also differ as to where they spend this money—for example, on developing a scouting system for minor league players or on obtaining experienced players from other teams.

The amount of money an owner is willing to spend on a team is potentially related to the owner's and/or the team's financial resources. Cal Griffith, one of the more publicized "low rollers" of baseball, contended that his rather modest payroll reflects comparatively low revenues and revenue potential.

Listen, there aren't 26 major league cities. There are only so many Chicagos, Bostons, New Yorks and Los Angeleses where they gross $25–50 million each year. If we do $9 million we've had a great year.

There are, for example, 15 million people within 100 miles of Cincinnati. I doubt if there are that many people in all of Minnesota, the Dakotas and Iowa . . . That's why we have to watch our cash flow.[27]

In 1982, Griffith demonstrated his convictions by trading many of his stars to other teams. His team payroll ($1.7 million) was slightly more than that paid to just one player—Dave Winfield—on the Yankees.

Yet some owners will not spend money even though they have the available resources. Owners who possibly fall into this category have included George Argyros of the Seattle Mariners and P. K. Wrigley of the Cubs. Wrigley once traded Bill Madlock over a salary dispute in 1977. He did not think that fans come out to watch the superstars, and also felt that Madlock's trade would improve team morale.

Most of the players resent very much the kind of player who comes in and bleeds the company hollow and doesn't leave anything for them. . . .

[Madlock] was National League batting champion two years ago and he was the National League batting champion last year, but what's he going to do this year? That's the question.[28]

In 1986 the Dodgers were making the most money in all baseball. Yet, actually, their 1986 profits had fallen from an estimated $8 million in 1985 to $5 million in 1986. The team began taking commercial non–first class flights for the first time. Steinbrenner's Yankees, on the other hand, have spent money for such nonsalary expenses as three masseurs in spring training and left- and right-handed batting practice pitchers to travel with the team during the season to pitch for players who do not play regularly.

A team can spend money to develop potential and current players, or for player replacements. Charley Finley, Bill Veeck, and Calvin Griffith preferred to be in the first category, and successfully developed/recruited players through the "farm system" (minor league teams associated with their major league team's organization). More recently, the World Series teams in 1988—the Athletics and the Dodgers—have placed great importance on developing minor league players (Jose Canseco and Mark McGwire, for example). Current Dodger President Peter O'Malley explains,

If you want to compete, and if the farm system can't give you the commodity, the position player, then you look at trades . . . Then you look at free agency. But the farm system will continue to be the cornerstone of the organization.[29]

Free agency (discussed in more detail in Chapter Eight) and player trades are two sources for replacements. George Steinbrenner, who is probably the most expensive user of the free agent route, started slow by buying only one—"Catfish" Hunter—for his 1976 pennant-winning club; but by April 1989 he had spent $70,421,000 on 23 more free agents.

As previously noted, owners like Cal Griffith and P. K. Wrigley have used the trade route to remove some of their players. Bill Veeck probably established the modern-day record for trades when he moved 12 players in one hour and 15 minutes. Yet he subsequently acknowledged that the trading route has become more difficult these days. Owners on the receiving end of a trade have to be careful, as the player might come with complicated deferred and/or guaranteed payments as well as other restrictions in his contract.

Sometimes owners shift directions during their career, and sometimes this shift is all part of the plan. For example, Jerry Reinsdorf said that he first needed to build a solid team before looking for a free agent. He felt that a clearly established superstar and free agent such as Dave Winfield would have only 50 RBI's in a season with his team (the White Sox) as it was, because Winfield would never have a chance to hit with men on base.

Reliance on Innovative Promotional Techniques

Owners such as Horace Stoneham of the Giants[30] and P. K. Wrigley of the Cubs have been regarded as baseball traditionalists in that they wanted to preserve so many aspects of the original game. Wrigley, for example, prohibited the use of lights for night games—a situation that has several labor agreement implications under Article IV–Scheduling of the current labor agreement.

Charlie Finley had a far different approach to changes. He maintained that owners were lazy and stupid in not trying to counter declining attendance by implementing rule changes that would bring more action back into baseball. The "designated hitter" rule was one such change that was adopted by the American League owners (by an 8–4 vote) before the 1973 season. The rule allowed one batter to bat for another throughout the game without playing defense in the field. Significant performance changes can be noted when the 1972 and 1973 seasons are compared. In 1972, pitchers—who were typically the ones replaced under the subsequent designated-hitter system— had 1,705 strikeouts and a .145 batting average. The designated hitters' batting average was .257 in 1973. Also, an average of one and a half more runs per game were scored in the American League in 1973. These figures might be associated with the new attendance record of 13,433,605 set in 1973—up almost 2 million from 1972.[31]

This innovation has labor relations implications, too. Without the rule, owners had felt it necessary to carry more pinch hitters on their rosters since these players could be used only once during a game. Also, the starting pitcher can now remain in a close game if there is a designated hitter, since the pitcher does not have to be lifted as for a pinch hitter. These situations were a cause of concern to the union because management could now reduce their playing roster from 25 to 24 players.

Influence with Other Owners and/or the Commissioner

The differences among owners in power over their peers and the commissioner of baseball is a very subjective category since influence is so often exerted in private. Walter O'Malley received much publicity as being the owner who had the most sway with the commissioner. Ted Turner (and probably other owners) were sure that this influence was occurring, although Turner could not personally substantiate his impressions.

Another likely influential individual is Bud Selig, who owns the Milwaukee Brewers. Selig's 17 years of baseball experience make him the fourth-senior owner (behind August Busch, Jr., of the Saint Louis Cardinals, Charles Bronfman of the Montreal Expos, and Gene Autry of the California Angels). Selig has also been on several important committees—such as the one that selected Peter Ueberroth as commissioner, and another that negotiated the labor agreement in 1985. The relationship between the owners and the commissioner is further explored in the next section.

THE COMMISSIONER OF BASEBALL

Judge Landis

Owners first realized the need for a baseball commissioner in 1919, when eight members of the Chicago White Sox were accused of accepting money to throw the World Series. One of these players—"Shoeless" Joe Jackson— was perhaps baseball's greatest player. Babe Ruth admitted to copying Jackson's swing (Jackson hit .408 his first full season), and his glove was called "the place triples go to die." In 1920 the owners employed Judge Kenesaw Mountain Landis as commissioner to remove any negative impact of the scandal. Before the players went to trial, Landis said, "There is absolutely no chance for any of [the charged players] to creep back into Organized Baseball. They will be and remain outlaws. . . . It is sure that the guilt of some of them at least will be proved."[32] The players were found innocent of all charges. Yet Landis continued to prohibit their playing.

The owners were placing total faith in Landis when they wrote the following clause applicable to the commissioner's position:

We the club owners pledge ourselves to loyally support the commissioner in his important and difficult task, and we assure him that each of us will acquiesce in his decisions even when we believe they are mistaken, and that we will not discredit the sport by criticism of him or one another.[33]

This clause agreement gave Landis complete authority to investigate any practice suspected to be "detrimental to the best interests of the national game of baseball," and all power to take punitive action against leagues, clubs, officers, or players found guilty of such detrimental conduct. A fine could not be more than $5,000 for a major league or club. The penalty for a major league employee (player or administrator) might be suspension or even expulsion.[34] The commissioner also served as final judge in all disputes involving leagues, clubs, and players. Moreover, the major leagues and their clubs waived all right to recourse in the courts, so as to protect the commissioner's actions. Landis also handled player-management relations—a situation that forestalled players' collective actions bargaining during his tenure.

Landis was a tyrant, and the player's best friend. He told the men who paid his salary how they must behave and he threw the book at any who tried to cheat. When he decided a player had been kept down on the farm too long or otherwise treated unfairly, he declared him a free agent entitled to sell his services to the highest bidder. In a single ruling he would free as many as 100 farmhands of the Detroit Tigers or St. Louis Cardinals. Players felt no need of a union or a lawyer or agent because the commissioner's door was always open and they were confident he would give them a square shake.[35]

However, the clubs did receive the right to determine rules regulating the game. Landis could only interpret the rules and cast the deciding vote if the two major leagues disagreed.

Landis quickly set about enforcing the regulations and ran up against the most prolific rule breaker of them all: Babe Ruth. After the 1921 World Series—in which the Yankees participated—Ruth headed a traveling or "barnstorming" team that played baseball exhibitions around the country. This practice violated a rule that specifically prohibited barnstorming—postseason games by World Series participants. Landis fined Ruth and another player (Bob Meusel) their full World Series shares ($3,500 a piece) and suspended them for the first six weeks of the 1922 season. And Landis made both penalties stick.

Chandler, Frick, and Eckert

Early in 1944 the Judge was given another seven-year extension on his contract. He died the same year, however. One informed baseball observer maintained that "Landis put the fear of God into weak characters who otherwise might have been inclined to violate their trust."[36] Baseball owners carefully considered Landis's replacement: They wanted a new commissioner who was more of a figurehead, with political connections in Washington to keep Congress in a hands-off mood. In 1945 Albert "Happy" Chandler became the second baseball commissioner. He had the same sweeping powers as Landis, but did not seem to implement them. And as noted in Chapter One, Chandler was not averse to having collective discussions—if not collective bargaining—with the players. Perhaps his relatively short five-year tenure was due to the fact that he forgot the owners were signing his checks.[37]

The owners modified their deference to the previously cited commissioner clause initiated under Landis's regime by exempting joint rules and actions of the two major leagues from the commissioner's control. They also dropped their waiver of legal action (court cases) against the commissioner.[38]

Chandler's replacement, Ford Frick, was the only commissioner—to this day—who had experience as a newspaper and radio reporter. Frick's tenure (1952–65) did not influence the owners or player-management relations much. However, in his retirement speech in 1965 he predicted the conditions that would eventually contribute to the union's gold-collar status. Frick noted that satisfactory player-management solutions could not exist so long as clubs and individuals pursued public headlines by criticizing their associates, and let expediency replace sound judgment.[39]

Owners responded by cancelling their own right to sue the commissioner and their previous insistence that anything voted by the clubs was, ipso facto, in the best interests of baseball and therefore immune from the commissioner's challenge.[40] Yet the owners basically retained unilateral decision-making capability in fundamental issues such as expansion, television money, operational rules, pensions, and player relations.

Frick's replacement, William Eckert, quickly realized this situation when he was dismissed in 1968 with four years remaining on his contract. There were owners—like Mike Burke of the Yankees—who contended that Eckert had been fired because more clout was needed in the commissioner's office. Other baseball observers believed that Eckert, who could claim no previous baseball knowledge, had been set up to be powerless.

Bowie Kuhn

Controversy extended on into the matter of Eckert's replacement. Owners argued heatedly over the selection, with possible candidates ranging from Stan Musial to Hubert Humphrey. A compromise was reached in February 1969, when they hired Bowie Kuhn. Unlike Eckert, Kuhn had a thorough knowledge of the game; indeed, he had been legal counsel to management since 1950. Thus many owners must have felt confident that they could predict Kuhn's thoughts and actions through his previous legal advice.

Kuhn believed that he had as much power as the original commissioner—Landis—and that effective use of this power depended on leadership capabilities. He, too, professed self-confidence and promised that he would never act out of fear of losing his job.

During his first seven-year term, Kuhn made several decisions that affected player-management relations (concerning discipline, player mobility, and player eligibility, for example). Owners soon realized that the MLBPA and the labor agreement were not the only limits to their discretion. In 1974, Kuhn suspended owner George Steinbrenner, who had pled guilty in federal court to making illegal campaign contributions to former President Nixon, because Kuhn felt that Steinbrenner's action undermined the public's confidence in the game. Steinbrenner disagreed with the suspension but did not contest it in the courts.[41]

Kuhn also affected owner Charley Finley many times during his first term in office. Finley's star player, Reggie Jackson—after hitting 47 home runs in 1969—wanted his salary increased from $20,000 to $75,000. Finley held firm to his $40,000 offer and ordered Jackson sent to the minors when he started slowly in 1970. Kuhn prohibited the move, contending that it was an arbitrary and capricious abuse of the reserve system.

Kuhn fined Finley three times for alleged misbehaviors during the 1973 World Series—the most significant infraction concerning Finley's actions toward second baseman Mike Andrews. Finley had a doctor check Mike Andrews's shoulder after Andrews committed two errors in a game. Finley then removed Andrews from further World Series participation, claiming that the team doctor thought continued play would likely damage the player's career. Andrews, however, indicated that Finley had persuaded him to agree with the action so that another player could be added to the roster. Kuhn ordered Finley to place Andrews back on the team and pay a $5,000 fine.

There was a strong chance that Kuhn's employment contract would not be renewed in 1975. At least three-quarters of the teams in each league had to vote in favor of the commissioner to continue his employment. Conversely, four owners in either league could get the commissioner removed. There were four likely negative votes in the American League: Finley's Oakland A's, the Baltimore Orioles, the New York Yankees, and the Texas Rangers. However, the latter two teams voted in favor of Kuhn—leaving the final vote 22–2 in the commissioner's favor. This vote prompted the Orioles' owner to indicate, "The strength and conviction of New York last night was so strong you wonder how it just could have disappeared overnight. It would be interesting to find out."[42]

In March 1976, Kuhn ended George Steinbrenner's suspension nine months ahead of schedule. Charley Finley had a much less pleasant experience with the commissioner a month later when he sold three of his star players: Joe Rudi and Rollie Fingers ($1 million each) to the Boston Red Sox, and Vida Blue ($1.5 million) to the New York Yankees. Sal Bando—a player remaining with the A's—maintained that Finley had a right to downgrade the team because after all, he had built it in the first place.

Bill Veeck disagreed. He believed that Finley's actions breached the owner's "custodial" handling of the team for the fans.[43] And one prominent sports reporter challenged the commissioner to act in preserving baseball's integrity. "Make me a liar, Bowie Kuhn. Don't just stand there. Veto the sales. Show Marvin Miller who is commissioner. Show Charley Finley. Show the world."[44]

Kuhn made a landmark decision in voiding Finley's player sales because he considered that "public confidence in the game was at stake."[45] Finley countered with a $10-million lawsuit filed in U.S. District Court in Chicago that charged Kuhn with violating antitrust laws, conspiring to deprive Finley of his rightful money from the sale, and several civil rights violations. The suit also asked the court to declare that the commissioner "has no power or authority to void the sale or assignment of players."[46] Some sided with Finley, who found Kuhn to be a "village idiot." The columnist Red Smith considered Kuhn's decision to be wrong because the commissioner thus

sets himself up as a one-man counsel on wage and price stability and final judge of the wisdom of all player exchanges. He permits Calvin Griffith to collect $300,000 in a deal for Bert Blyleven but rules $1 million too high for Rollie Fingers. He lets Finley dispose of Reggie Jackson but not Joe Rudi.[47]

American League President Lee MacPhail urged Kuhn not to void Finley's sales, for two reasons: (1) No specific baseball rules had been broken; and (2) there were historical precedents in which large cash transactions had been made for players. In a rare display of labor and management officials sharing the same attitude, MacPhail's comments were fully supported by Marvin Miller. And MacPhail's second argument was further supported by history. Babe Ruth—for example—was sold to the Yankees for $150,000; also, Joe Cronin was sold to Boston in 1934 for $250,000 ($1.4 million in 1976 dollars).

Judge Frank McGarr ruled in Kuhn's favor, however, because: (1) the owners agreed the commissioner has the capability to determine what is detrimental to baseball and what are appropriate remedial actions; (2) there was no evidence of ill will or capriciousness on Kuhn's part when he violated the player sales; and (3) the owners intended that the commissioner should have broad discretion in these matters since there was no formally established appeal system and the owners had foreclosed their own access to the courts. Kuhn considered the decision to be a good one since "it's much clearer now that the commissioner was intended to be able to step into a situation and say, 'No, you can't do that because it would be bad for the game.' "[48]

Approximately three months after this decision, the commissioner allowed the Mets to trade Tom Seaver to the Reds for four relatively obscure players. Finley believed Kuhn's inaction in the Seaver trade to be a vindictive, irrational act that demeaned his office's traditional stature. Kuhn countered that Finley was to have received no other players for his sales, which would have decimated his 1975 Western Division Championship Club.

Ted Turner also had a confrontation with Kuhn when he was suspended for "tampering" with free agent Gary Matthews (as defined and prohibited by Rule 3G of the labor agreement). However—unlike Finley—Turner did not challenge Kuhn's decision. Indeed, he was glad that Kuhn had not ordered him executed for his infraction.

In January 1978 Kuhn again prohibited Finley from trading Vida Blue—this time to the Cincinnati Reds. Finley then turned his attention to removing Kuhn from office. At one time there were an estimated nine owners who wanted Kuhn out. George Steinbrenner was not a member of this group; he publicly cited the commissioner's attributes and urged other owners to endorse his position. Twenty owners then sent to Kuhn a resolution supporting him—an action that effectively ended any chance of dismissal. Some of the six owners (Kroc, Veeck, Corbett, Finley, Howsam, and Hoffberger) who did not sign the resolution would again find themselves tangling with the commissioner.

In 1979 Kuhn fined a number of owners for tampering with free agents. The highest fine by far was $100,000 assessed to Ray Kroc, who had been quoted nationwide as saying he wanted to spend $10 million on free agents such as Graig Nettles and Joe Morgan. Some thought that Kroc had not in fact violated Rule 3G because he neither "negotiated" nor had personal "dealings" with players under contract with another club.

Kuhn was up for reelection in 1982, and faced many problems. Since the

American League had expanded to 14 teams, the three-quarters rule meant that five negative votes in the American League or four negative votes in the National League could terminate his employment.

A compromise was proposed whereby Kuhn would retain his current powers while financial and other business matters would be handled by a chief operating officer who was technically to be under the commissioner. Most criticism of Kuhn had focused on his business acumen—like not obtaining sufficient television revenues—and on his low profile during the 1981 strike.

In November 1982 the final vote was 7–5 in the National League and 11–3 in the American League, both in favor of Kuhn. Yet the rule requiring a three-quarters vote in each league meant that he was defeated. Kuhn mused philosophically that the 70-percent affirmation after 14 years' experience was positively a landslide. Executives of the Angels, the White Sox, and the Orioles expressed their concerns respectively:

No self-respecting man would accept this job after the abuse Bowie Kuhn has taken.

For the last 50 years in baseball, our own worst enemies have been ourselves. Looks like it's not going to change. . . . We can't solve our problems with our present mode of voting.

We are victims of a system where four people can dictate to 22. . . . It's chaos.[49]

At least one columnist, Shirley Povich, found the situation incomprehensible, as he regarded Kuhn to be a "decent, intelligent man" who stood for the game's integrity and financial success.

Antagonism and distrust among the owners increased. Much of this anger was directed toward Cardinals owner Gussie Busch, who was considered the ringleader of the dump Kuhn movement. Cardinals manager Whitey Herzog told Busch that his attitude would cause the team to loose clout in the commissioner's office, and Dodgers' president Peter O'Malley—a strong supporter of Kuhn—removed Busch's beer product (worth $15 million in annual revenues) from his stadium. This situation of distrust placed management at a collective bargaining disadvantage, particularly when dealing with a very solid union.

Ueberroth and Giamatti

Kuhn remained in office until September 30, 1984. Peter Ueberroth—who received tremendous acclaim for his previous handling of the 1984 Olympics—believed he had a measure of business acumen, leadership ability, and a fairly strong sense of integrity. Yet he also felt that he was an "average guy," and certainly no miracle man. Once in office, the new com-

missioner quickly resolved the umpire's strike that was in progress, and—
as discussed in Chapter Three—played perhaps the most direct role ever
employed by a commissioner in resolving the 1985 owner-player labor dispute. Although he took over the office with some administrative aspects in
disarray, Ueberroth did eventually establish that the owners were working
for him—not vice versa.

Commissioner Ueberroth faced—but did not resolve—certain other very
tough challenges during his first term, such as removing drugs from the
game (see Chapter Six), defining and implementing affirmative action (Chapter Seven), monitoring owner "collusion" on free agency (Chapter 8), determining whether there should be expansion teams, and creating some
economic balance between baseball's haves and have-nots. This latter challenge may someday entail some type of revenue sharing, whereby teams
that market themselves through local television will pay reparations to the
teams whose TV markets they invade. In any case, these challenges were
not made any easier by the divided ownership. According to Ueberroth,
some of the executives were not completely content with how he was performing his job.

In June 1988, Ueberroth announced that he would not accept another
five-year term when his initial contract expired on December 31, 1989. The
commissioner gave no further elaboration, or even new job choice, although
he did say that he feels he is leaving the game in better financial condition
than he found it. Part of this improvement is due to two of Ueberroth's last
acts, involving television contracts negotiated in 1988 (discussed in the next
section).

A. Bartlett Giamatti, a former president of Yale University and also of the
National League, was elected commissioner by a unanimous vote of the club
owners in September 1989. Giamatti shared Ueberroth's top priorities (substance abuse and minority hiring), although he did not want to alter drast-
ically the game's "geometric beauty."

Giamatti had no sympathy for either the union or management during the
1981 strike, and labeled the situation an example of "deny side" economics.
He said that baseball's current labor-management relations has exhibited a
time-warp nature, with owners sometimes acting like nineteenth-century
capitalists and the players acting like union members from the 1930s. His
non-presence at the bargaining table during a bitter strike of technical/
clerical employees at his previous place of employment suggested a hands-
off bargaining approach in baseball. However, Giamatti insisted that any
involvement he does attempt will include more than the owners' perspective:
"People say, 'You work for the owners.' Nonsense. You work for everybody—
players, managers, fans, umpires, groundkeepers, concessionaires, everybody. I won't feel that, in a labor situation, which is adversarial, . . . I will
be the captive of one part of the institution or another."[50]

Giamatti exerted a more direct and frequent influence on one particular collective-bargaining issue: player discipline. His reputation as a disciplinarian is in part based on a 30-day suspension he gave to manager Pete Rose for touching an umpire, and a 2-day suspension given to Los Angeles pitcher Jay Howell for having pine tar on his glove during the National League Championship playoffs in 1988.

Within a year, Giamatti and Rose became embroiled in a disciplinary incident that involved various courts. Rose first met with Ueberroth and Giamatti on February 20, 1989, to discuss alleged gambling activities. Ueberroth indicated that Rose voluntarily agreed to attend, and that "There's nothing ominous and there won't be any follow through."[51] Some three months later Giamatti received a 225-page report on Rose's activities from his hired lawyer, John Dowd.

Giamatti scheduled a hearing with Rose on May 25 but granted Rose's postponement request to June 26 so that Rose's lawyers could review the report. This hearing was never held, since Rose's lawyers successfully persuaded a Hamilton County Common Pleas Judge to place a temporary restraining order on the hearing. Subsequent legal encounters occurred in the Ohio Supreme Court, the U.S. District Court, and the U.S. Court of Appeals, which affirmed that Rose's request for a temporary injunction would be heard by federal judges.

Giamatti and Rose precluded the preliminary injunction hearing with an "Agreement and Resolution," jointly signed on August 25, 1989, that declared Rose "permanently ineligible" in accordance with Major League Rule 21 but subject to reinstatement under Major League Rule 15. Under this agreement, Rose recognized the commissioner's authority to investigate the incident and to determine the appropriate disciplinary penalty. He also acknowledged that the commissioner had a factual basis to impose this penalty. Therefore Rose agreed to challenge neither the commissioner's penalty nor subsequent reinstatement decision(s) in court or otherwise.

Why would Rose, who had challenged gambling allegations for six months, accept this disciplinary action before a pending judicial review? A continued legal challenge in federal court would have likely reinforced previous judicial decisions upholding the commissioner's broad disciplinary authority, while adding to Rose's already expensive legal fees. Also, a continued battle probably would compound rather widespread public sentiment against Rose. Investigative reports released during Rose's attempt to remain out of federal courts reflected taped conversations with bookies, betting sheets featuring Rose's alleged handwriting and finger prints, and even his own admission that he made illegal, nonbaseball bets with bookies. It is likely that Rose realized that this trend would not be reversed if these and other incidents were revealed and discussed in subsequent judicial and quasi-judicial proceedings.

Rose was also influenced by the disciplinary agreement's exclusions. For example, his Hall of Fame eligibility in 1992 and his salary contract to manage the Reds for the 1989 and 1990 seasons were neither protected nor eliminated by the agreement. Also, the agreement did not charge Rose with betting on baseball. Rule 21's subparagraphs indicate that a player can be rendered "permanently ineligible" for gambling and/or betting on his team's games (21-d) or for engaging in conduct "not in the best interests of baseball" (21-f). The agreement levied the permanent ban under Rule 21 but no lettered paragraph was specified. This omission enabled Rose to continue his claim, "I've made some mistakes and I'm going to pay for those mistakes, but one of those mistakes was not betting on baseball . . . I'll continue to say that until the day I leave this world."[52]

Giamatti and much of the media and public doubted Rose's contention. Moreover, reports of this incident revealed little public sympathy for Rose. General sentiment believed that Rose's actions violated a reasonable rule and that his penalty was appropriate for the offense. Rose indicated that he was "dumbfounded" to hear Giamatti's public statement that he believed Rose bet on baseball: "Just 12 hours earlier, we signed the agreement in good faith, and there he was saying he thinks I bet on baseball. The only reason I signed that agreement was that it had no finding that I bet on baseball." Giamatti countered, "I was very clear about the fact that I was not going to be constrained from saying what I thought was the case."[53]

Giamatti died of a heart attack a few days after the Rose decision. He was eulogized by many as being "the fans' commissioner." Perhaps the most eloquent eulogy came from Ira Berkow of *The New York Times*: "He might have become the best baseball commissioner we've ever had. He had brains, sinew, and the best wishes of the game. And he was honest."[54]

Giamatti was replaced by Fay Vincent who was deputy commissioner of baseball. Vincent shared Giamatti's disapproval of the 1981 strike because it was not based on economic considerations. He hoped that negotiations over the 1990 collective bargaining agreement would be grounded in economic realities; however, he has also indicated that he will follow his predecessor's preference for an indirect, behind-the-scenes approach to these efforts.

MEDIA ROLES

The media represent both a revenue source and a conduit, for the owners and for the players. The revenue role has been discussed in Chapters One through Three (in terms of the World Series and All-Star Game revenues contributing to players' pensions and benefits) and is further explained in Chapter Nine.

On December 14, 1988, CBS outbid NBC and ABC for noncable rights to 12 regular-season games, the All-Star Game, and all post-season games for four years: 1990–93. Owners were pleased with the price—$1.1 billion over the four years—and the reduction of 20 regular-season games that occur on the weekends. Teams can, in turn, sell the fewer nationally televised games to local markets—thereby raising additional revenues. (Case in point: The Yankees recently received a 12-year cable TV agreement worth $500 million—enough to buy about 150 free agents.) CBS executives were most happy about the purchase because they had not heretofore covered the sport. Executives at NBC were "saddened" that they could not continue the network's 41-year relationship with baseball.

A second negotiated contract was signed with cable TV's ESPN network: four years for $400 million. These two television contracts pay each team $57 million, or $14 million each contract year. Commissioner Ueberroth effected neither equal employment opportunity nor a drug-free environment during his tenure, but these television negotiations directly met his revenue-sharing objective.

Television as revenue generator has introduced scheduling considerations that in turn have affected labor relations provisions. For example, in 1971, World Series games were first played at night—prompting one baseball observer to remark, "If television wanted a game played in six inches of snow it just might be aired."[55] Something of the kind did occur during the 1988 National League Championship Series. Mets owner Nelson Doubleday blamed TV for "screwing with the national pastime" when it rescheduled a rain-out to be played at noon the next day. Doubleday threatened a "strike"— not allowing his team to show up the next day—because the field's conditions would not contribute to the optimum playing performance required of the fall classic.

The media's second role—as conduit—can affect individual players as well as team unity or dissension. Although not proven, it is very likely that the media have played a major influence in increasing salaries, simply by reporting the alleged terms of players' contracts to the public. This can backfire, however, by creating negative public opinion when high-priced players go out on strike. Sometimes the media puff up certain players. Dave Winfield, for example, believes that New York–based media turned Bucky Dent—"an average player"—into an all-star. And Sparky Anderson felt that the press caused George Foster—"a simple kid, a country boy"—to start behaving like a superstar. Foster decided to live up to the image by getting a driver's license for the first time and buying a Mercedes-Benz.

Praise for a player can quickly turn the other way, as Denny McLain found out. Headlines like "More Glory Awaiting Denny" and "McLain Passes Test for Mound Greatness" become "Denny's Tragedy: He's Destroying His Career."[56]

Sometimes the media develop an adversary relationship with a player. Roger Maris became angry with the media people who were constantly asking him if he was going to break Ruth's season home-run record in 1961. "Don't ask me about that fucking record. . . . All I'm interested in is winning the pennant. The only time I'm by myself is when I'm taking a crap."[57] Another such player-media relationship allegedly occurred between reporter Dick Young and Tom Seaver. In 1977—for example—Young reported that Seaver "pouts and stomps, and that he 'lacks the guts' to play out his option and go on the open market."[58] Recent Hall of Famer Willie Stargell figures that reporters overly stress players' bad points because they themselves have not experienced the players' jobs, and often forget that players know better than anyone when they have played a poor game.

Sometimes media accounts distort an event and—as Dave Winfield contends—"create problems" for players and the team. One such occasion arose when a reporter wrote that New York Yankee pitcher Ryne Duren—being quite drunk—tried to shove a lit cigar down manager Ralph Houk's throat. Houk is supposed to have responded by punching Duren in the face. In Duren's version, however, both he and Houk had a few drinks, Duren bumped into Houk by accident, and then Houk gave a playful backhand swat that opened a cut over Duren's eye. Duren said, "It was no big deal, certainly not a brawl. But that's the way headlines in the *New York Post* reported it."[59]

Another time, Mike Marshall gave up a grand-slam home run, was taken out of the game, and informed the press that he should have finished the game. According to another player, what Marshall meant was that he should have been good enough not to give up the home run and good enough to hang in the game. Yet other players thought he was criticizing the decision to pull him and were furious over Marshall's remarks.

Media accounts can disrupt a team whether or not the remarks are accurate and in context. A fistfight between Dodger players Don Sutton and Steve Garvey occurred after Sutton questioned Garvey's value to the team, to the *Washington Post*. In 1977 the Yankees experienced a lengthy, widespread clubhouse conflict that started when Reggie Jackson apparently informed a *Sport* magazine reporter that "this team . . . all flows from me . . . I'm the straw that stirs the drink." Jackson also found fellow player Thurman Munson to be "insecure," as "I'll hear him telling some other writer that he wants it to be known that he's the captain of the team, that he knows what's best. Stuff like that. And when anybody knocks me, he'll laugh real loud so I can hear it."[60] Years earlier a similar situation occurred: The press apparently manufactured a feud between Jackie Robinson and Roy Campanella over the proper role of blacks in baseball and in society.[61]

Players and managers have tried to counter the media in several ways. Some managers are like Ted Williams of the Red Sox, who had a rule banning the media from the clubhouse for a certain time period (15 minutes, say) after the game. This delay enabled the players to become more relaxed and more capable of giving rational interviews.

Williams, who in his autobiography admitted to hating the media, also used intimidation effectively in his dealings with the press. One reporter noted, "Williams is great copy. He intimidates us, and if we knock him at all, he'll shut us out and refuse to talk with us. We have a good thing going and we can't afford to screw it up."[62] Sometime Yankees manager Billy Martin also attempted intimidation on occasion. Martin once informed anyone who would listen that reporter Henry Hecht was

the worst fuckin' scrounge ever to come around this clubhouse [because] he got me fired twice, and now he's trying to make it a third time. And if you talk to him, don't talk to me, cause I don't want to have anything to do with anyone who talks to this little prick.

When Hecht called Martin a "paranoid," Martin responded,

I'm not paranoid. I don't have to be paranoid, to see that you're a little prick. You're not welcome in my office. You can come into the clubhouse—I wouldn't ever take away a man's right to earn a living—but you're not welcome in my office because I don't trust a fuckin' thing you say. . . . [Walking to his office Martin stated,] If that little bastard comes in here, I'll put him in the fuckin' whirlpool.[63]

Both pitcher Ron Guidry (Yankees) and manager Whitey Herzog (Cardinals) have a policy of not lying or misleading reporters. However, they do not volunteer more information than is called for, and when they do not like the question they do not answer it. Herzog also has a policy of never talking to a reporter who has previously let something loose in public that he or she knew was not true.

PLAYER AGENTS

The MLBPA bargains for the annual salary minimum for all players. While other labor-contract provisions such as those involving free agency and salary arbitration can raise salaries above this minimum, the amount and length of the individual contracts is a matter outside the MLBPA's jurisdiction.

Oftentimes a player will employ an agent to negotiate and structure his financial agreement with the club. The agent's general role is to serve as a negotiation equalizer. Otherwise, a somewhat naive and fearful athlete would have to go up against an experienced club official. This broad role is subject to several variations depending on the particular agent's style and financial philosophy.

For one thing there is variation in the types of activities that the agent is paid to perform. Some agents limit themselves to negotiating the player's contract while other agents serve as financial advisors and/or managers of the negotiated monies. There are also differences over the extent to which the negotiated monies are deferred. Consider, for example, a 30-year-old player who receives a five-year contract at $1 million a year. If an agent negotiated for the provision that each year $200,000 would be deferred and the player avoided touching this sum for another five years, then the player would have enough principal to draw down $242,000 annually to age 64.[64] Agents also differ over the particular investments made with the negotiated funds. Some prefer real estate while others look for tax-deferred investments. Finally, agents differ over their fee derivations and amounts. Agents like Ruven Katz charge an hourly fee. Katz once negotiated a $3.5-million contract between the Philadelphia Phillies and Pete Rose. He received a fee of between $20,000 and $30,000 for his efforts, and stated, "I'm just a lawyer. . . . I get paid by the hour."[65] Other agents charge 5–10 percent of the negotiated contract value and an annual fee (5 percent of the negotiated value, for example) to manage the funds. Another charge can occur if agents also obtain product endorsement advertising fees for the players.

Sports agents assume tremendous responsibilities, as Nick Buoniconti suggests in the account he gives of representing player Bucky Dent in a potential trade from the Chicago White Sox to the New York Yankees.

I feel I have a fiduciary obligation as an attorney. . . . There's a lot of pressure. When I was dealing with the Yankees or with Chicago for Bucky, it was . . . very difficult because I had this man's career in my hands, and if I . . . made a mistake by making . . . a demand in excess of what they thought was reasonable [I] probably would have blown the trade for the kid.[66]

Yet many industrial relations participants believe that agents neglect their responsibilities. Marvin Miller has contended that many agents have a bent for "fee gouging, breach of fiduciary relations, conflict of interest, and outright fraud." Ted Turner considers agents to be parasites or worse. "When they smile, blood drips off their teeth."[67]

Some owners feel that agents can control the game. For example, an agent who has several players on one club could conceivably advise them all to play out their options and then deliver them all to another team, to assure a pennant there.[68] One such situation could have occurred—for instance—when one agent, Jerry Kapstein, represented five players on the Oaklands A's in 1976. Charley Finley's unsuccessful negotiations with Kapstein for Don Baylor's services is reflected in a last-minute discussion that Finley had with Baylor, over the telephone.

Don, I don't feel too good, Don. This Jerry Kapstein. I'm gonna tell you and the rest of the players. I think you fellows have one helluva lousy agent if he can't represent you face to face. He never came to look me in the eye. Is there a chance of signing you, Don? What? But I can't talk to your man. I've invited him to my office and he wants to do everything over the phone.

Oh, I don't even want to talk to the son of a bitch. He's taken me up to six hours before the deadline. Is there any chance of you and I getting together? . . . Right now. . . . I'll go three years. . . . You still want that no-cut deal. . . . No, I'm not threatening you. I don't want to press you into anything. I just hoped I could do something tonight.[69]

There have been several cases of agent abuse. Recently, two players—Jack Clark and Johnnie LeMaster—were awarded $1.94 million when they sued their agent for poor real-estate deals. Another agent's investments cost 14 athletes (including Bill Campbell, Dave Goltz, Rich Wise, Doug Rau, and Don Sutton) $6 million; they also stand to lose $15 million more in IRS suits claiming their tax shelters should be disallowed.[70] One of these 14 athletes, Ken Reitz, arrived in the majors with no financial knowledge or experience. "I was just 21, sitting in the locker room in St. Louis with Jose Cruz, and neither one of us knew how to bank, how to write a check. . . . We used to cash our paychecks, take what we needed and put the rest of the money in the closet."[71] Reitz has no idea what happened to the $1 million he grossed over four years. He ended up $90,000 in debt.

The athletes are not always wholly blameless in these transactions. After all, agents seldom have complete control over them. Athletes may not follow the agent's advice, as when they break up a deferred-payment plan to obtain needed cash. Then also some players benefit very well from their agents. Gary Maddox made $54,000 with the Phillies in 1975. Thanks to free agency and agent Jerry Kapstein, Maddox was making $675,000 five years later. In 1980 he signed his final contract: six years and and $4 million. Kapstein raised Maddox's income through investments as well as negotiations, and today Madox's net worth is more than $3 million.[72]

The major problem facing the player-agent relationship is that there are no professional educational requirements to be met before becoming an agent. The MLBPA has negotiated a labor agreement provision (Article IV) that requires agents to be certified by an organization of their own.[73] Also beginning in 1988 the baseball players' union will limit player-agent contracts to one year.

Five

Manager-Player Relationships

Paradoxically enough, baseball managers represent a vital aspect of player-management relationships and yet a rather insignificant aspect of union-management relationships. Managers are paid to win games by achieving optimum player performance. This direct and often intense player-management relationship is basically ignored by the collectively bargained labor agreement, which does not seriously curtail managerial decisions or leadership styles. Players often protest managers' "unfair" actions to the team's owners. Indeed, managers may have more confrontations with owners than with the union or players.

Yet manager-player relationships can affect and reflect the collective bargaining agreement. Hostile relationships on some of the teams will likely cause players to encourage their union to reject and/or strike over a proposed contract settlement. On the other hand, generally friendly relations are associated with the desire for a labor agreement settlement and an uninterrupted playing season. Player-manager relationships can also involve discipline, which in turn can be appealed through labor agreement provisions.

Sometimes, managers have occupied or will occupy higher levels in the organization. Dallas Green—for example—has been both field manager and president of the Cubs. Presumably, such individuals carry their field experience and attitudes with them when they become more directly involved in union-management negotiations.

Managers are not all cut from the same cloth. Each has a unique personality, expectation, and method for team leadership. Sparky Anderson has often been labeled "a real nice guy" by his players, while Herman Franks was described as so abrasive he would make caffeine nervous. Alvin Dark's actions reflected his deeply held religious convictions, while Danny Ozark attempted to inspire his players by shouting, "Come on you guys, I can hit this guy with my cock!" (Ozark's managerial philosophy was, "You can't play baseball with a tight asshole.")[1] Rogers Hornsby never went to the mound to pull a pitcher out of the game, but instead yelled from the top of the dugout steps. This way the pitcher would have to walk to the dugout alone and then sit next to the manager for the rest of the game in silence. Hornsby also allegedly urinated on players while they were taking a shower. Managerial styles in baseball really do cover the spectrum.

The first section takes a closer look at these varied managerial styles and measures for success. Then examined are the capabilities and activities employed by the more successful managers. Perhaps this may lead us to discover the factors that tend to limit a manager's success.

WHAT MAKES A SUCCESSFUL MANAGER?

Some feel that management styles have had to change over time because today's players are different. Eddie Mathews reflected a widely held belief when he said that contemporary players are different because they place their welfare above the game.

They don't run to first base and you ask them why, and they say they can't get their head together. You ask them to come out for extra batting practice and they can't because they have to take their wives grocery shopping. . . . I feel sorry for someone making as much money as they do and not being happy. The uniform doesn't fit right, their locker is too close to the shower. We never had those problems. When I played, the manager said do that and they did it. Today it's, why do you want me to do that?[2]

Joe Pepitone, the first player to have a hair dryer in the clubhouse, believes that today's fun-loving, individualistic, and "want to be friends" attitudes among the players are destroyed by managers who stress "gung-ho shit"—beat the rival team at all cost.[3]

This suggests that managers can no longer rely on players' blind loyalty as they once could—that instead they must recognize and satisfy players' concerns, to motivate them. Yet managers were saying the same thing some 60 years ago. In 1927 Miller Huggins complained that there were no more of the "tooth and nail" players who had typified earlier years. Huggins regarded players of his own day as being too comfortable because they would not play with injuries and only viewed the game as a means to an end.

John J. McGraw also believed that players in the 1920s were more pampered than their predecessors. And according to McGraw, there has always been a basic difference between players and managers. The player "is young and impatient, while the manager must be responsible for the team as a whole and for results. The player's concern is for his own advancement."[4] Perhaps player attitudes and corresponding managerial approaches have changed less over time than one might imagine.

Whatever changes may or may not have been wrought in manager-player relationships, certain individual managers have definitely changed over time. Phil Rizzuto once noted that Casey Stengel was a different man after winning the pennant in 1949. A shy, cautious individual when he first managed the Yankees, Stengel became a rather loud know-it-all in 1950—taking too much credit for the good things the team did, sarcastically criticizing his players when things went wrong, and ingratiating himself with the press. Other examples include managers Al Lopez and Birdie Tibbetts, who apparently became sterner over the years, and Frank Robinson, who learned not to speak when he was very angry. A manager's age may influence his particular attitude and style. A young manager often wants to be friends with his players, many of whom might even be former teammates. Pete Rose—for instance—wanted the Reds to "like" him, instead of considering him a "lousy SOB." Billy Herman had the same philosophy when he retired as a player to manage the Pirates. He tried to be one of the guys and maintain his friendships among the players. Yet he found that other players resented this, and his team "got out of hand."

As his experience with players increases, a manager may change his style. He has seen that extensive happiness among the players does not necessarily generate more victories. Also, he comes to realize how unchangeable players' characters are. With experience, a manager usually learns how inventive alibis can be and how seldom certain promises materialize. An older manager knows that it is never possible to explain everything to everyone. He is therefore likely to say "We'll do it *this* way," and then let it go at that.[5]

Finally, variation in style has been noted in the same individual manager within the same day and even the same hour. Many players regarded John J. McGraw—perhaps the most famous manager of all time (he managed the Giants from 1902 until 1932)—as a tyrant. "But when his guard was down and he thought no one was looking, he often revealed a surprising warmth and compassion and a generous tolerance for human weakness."[6]

Objectively measured accomplishments may not determine a manager's "success" or tenure with a team. In 1969 Billy Martin took the Minnesota Twins from seventh place to a division title, yet he was fired. He was then fired after turning Detroit into a first-place team—and again, after making sixth-place Texas a division contender. He was also fired when he led the Yankees to their first pennant in 11 years, and then to a world championship the next season.

Sparky Anderson was fired after managing the Cincinnati Reds for nine seasons. Anderson had averaged 96 victories a year and an overall .596 winning percentage that was topped in baseball's modern times only by the

Yankees' Joe McCarthy (.614). Today, therefore, a good win-loss percentage does not ensure a manager's tenure, as he has to "answer to an owner who is . . . more than likely eccentric; to the various vice-presidents hired by the eccentric owner; to the players, who are emboldened by huge salaries and greater bargaining power all around; to the press, which second-guesses his every wrong move; and probably to some guy in the marketing department."[7]

Ty Cobb attempted to refute charges that he was an "awful" manager by using objective statistics other than wins and losses. In 1921 when he took over the Tigers, it was a team with the second-lowest group batting average in the circuit—.265. In his first season, the Tigers' average rose to .316. Cobb suggested that this figure—not team standing—best reflected his managerial-instructional capabilities. Similarly in 1989 Pete Rose pointed to his Reds' strong finishes for September–October games (96 wins, 56 losses, .632 average) during his four full seasons as manager, as evidence of his leadership skills.

These statistical measures might illustrate—but do not completely satisfy—a commonly reported managerial success indicator: *getting the most out of the team by helping its different players pull together.*[8] Dallas Green, a manager with experience, believes that keeping all 24 players reasonably happy in the dugout is a far more difficult and significant skill than knowing when to bunt or hit and run.

Unfortunately, the ability to get the most out of a team cannot be quantified or set forth in a step-by-step procedure. There are several general factors, however, associated with team victories and/or managers' continued employment by one or more teams. These factors can be divided into two general categories: managerial capabilities, and managerial activities.

MANAGERIAL CAPABILITIES

The Friendship–Respect Debate

Some successful managers have been friends with their players, approachable both on and off the field. Rod Carew expressed appreciation for Billy Martin's significant "fatherly advice" when he needed it. Pete Rose must also have thought of his manager—Sparky Anderson—as a friend, since both Rose and his wife felt free to discuss a marital problem with him.

Media reports on the constant flow of Dodgers in and out of manager Tommy Lasorda's office, and on Lasorda's habit of passing out Italian food and exchanging small talk with his troops, indicate that he is another manager who is very friendly with most of his players. Yet Lasorda knows that all players will not like the manager—particularly when they are benched, moved down in the batting order, or taken out of a game they are pitching. Lasorda notes that players are "highly competitive, often egotistical, proud men" involved in a situation where nine are on the field and 16 are on the bench. "Casey Stengel once said that the key to managing was keeping the players on the team who hate you away from the players on the team who are undecided about you."[9]

One of Lasorda's former players—Candy Maldonado—when he was traded to the San Francisco Giants expressed a decidedly unfriendly attitude toward his ex-boss and commented about his new manager, Roger Craig, that "there's so much difference between him and Tommy. He's honest and reliable for one thing."[10] In the world of baseball—as in any other sphere— a manager who is universally loved is rare, indeed. Even those who strive for friendship with their players are bound to have some enemies.

Then too, the friendship dimension, which often extends to helping players resolve off-field problems, can be physically and mentally draining to the manager. Eddie Mathews—for one—would receive calls from players' wives wondering where the men were after curfew. And Mathews believes that player problems can easily become manager problems when the fatherly advice results in a player's breaking up his marriage, going to jail, or worse.

Managers who have few or no player friends (Rogers Hornsby, for example) may not have a successful season. Yet the unpopular manager can still be successful if players respect his playing/managerial skills. Billy Herman explained this situation, using Leo Durocher as an example:

A manager can never allow personal popularity to be a factor in running the club. Leo was great that way. He didn't give a damn whether you liked him or not as long as you put out for him on that field. And you'd be surprised how many guys there were who hated Leo's guts but who still went out there and broke their necks for him because they respected his baseball know-how. Those kids, Reese and Reiser, idolized Leo and played their hearts out for him.[11]

Similarly, Joe McCarthy—who managed the New York Yankees—is said to have had tremendous control of his players without being "buddy-buddy" with them. Boston's Ted Williams said that McCarthy obtained more performance from a team than any other manager. A lesser known player—Joe Page—agreed with Williams. Nicknamed the "Gay Reliever" because of his love for late-evening merriment and his role as relief pitcher, Page was used very little by McCarthy, who felt the player was not living up to his capabilities. After his career was over, Page commented, "I hated his guts . . . but there was never a better manager."[12]

Respect does seem to be necessary to the successful manager. This, however, does not have to exclude friendship. Joe Pepitone both liked and respected Yogi Berra, who was able to ignore Pepitone's chronic excuses— getting him to play in 160 games and have 100 runs batted in in one season. Still, respect can be earned without friendship—too—by using three other capabilities: (1) consideration of individual differences; (2) patience; and (3) knowledge of the players and the game. These capabilities can determine whether a manager's several activities (discussed later in the chapter) are effective and successful.

Consideration of Individual Differences

Most players and managers would agree with Hall of Fame pitcher/manager Burleigh Grimes's observation that a manager's success depends largely on the ability to identify and act on individual differences among players. Words and actions that help and/or motivate one player may produce the opposite effect or none at all in another. Thus a successful manager should be somewhat accessible and be a good listener to uncover the unique considerations and motivations of each player.

One of the more interesting—if not significant—applications of this capability concerned Casey Stengel, when he discovered that his star shortstop Phil Rizzuto had received a death threat. Someone wrote Rizzuto a letter indicating that he would be shot during batting practice. When Rizzuto expressed his concern, Stengel formulated what he thought was a fine solution: He ordered Rizzuto to switch his uniform (number 10) with Billy Martin's (number 1) to make sure that Rizzuto would be safe. After 20 minutes in the switched uniform, Rizzuto asked for his own number back. According to Martin, Rizzuto said, "I'll take my chances on the guy with the gun. . . . If I wear Martin's number, I'm liable to get hit in the head with a pitch or slugged by one of the players on the other team."[13]

Then too, this considering of individual differences among players—while important—should never be the top managerial priority. If he were to carry it to such an extreme, a manager would be "absorbed in judging morale instead of ability, psychology instead of strategy, personality instead of performance, the peripheral influences instead of the actual events."[14] Walter Alston, legendary manager of the Dodgers, agreed with this sentiment. On the one hand—Alston said—recognizing and acting on individual differences is necessary: The manager should know which players "to pat on the back, which ones to give a kick in the ass now and then."[15] Yet the good of the team always comes first, and this must at times push aside the interests of individuals.

Patience

Paul Richards, an experienced baseball manager, has cited "restraint under duress" (a good definition of "patience") as the most significant managerial capability. Danny Murtaugh—regarded as one of the most patient managers in the business—agreed: "Two angry men don't get anywhere. . . . I used to be fiery. The Irish blood. But I learned to control my emotions long ago."[16] Tim McCarver also expressed this sentiment. He believed that one of the best managers was Bobby Cox, who sat in the dugout during a long losing streak and "never blinked an eye." Players relate well to managers who are even tempered and do not panic.

One of the more unusual examples of managerial patience occurred when Bill Virdon was managing the Yankees. Sparky Lyle decided to "change his luck" one playing day by unzipping his fly and exposing his genitals during warm-up practice. Virdon heard secondhand about this exhibition. Lyle later described his manager's self-controlled response as follows:

The next day when I came to the ball park, Virdon called me into his office. He said, "I have favor to ask of you." I said, "What's that, Bill?" He said, "Please don't shag balls in the outfield with your nuts hanging out anymore."[17]

Patience is not easily maintained in the baseball arena. As will be discussed later, even Murtaugh has had his stormy encounters with players. One of the worst combinations is a rookie manager whose team is off to a bad start. In 1987 Larry Bowa faced this situation. And Bowa says that everyone was telling him that patience is the key, but nobody could tell him where to find it.

Sometimes a manager may think of himself as patient, while conveying just the opposite impression to some of his players. Ted Williams, for example, thought that he had developed patience through his devotion to fishing: "Show me an impatient fisherman, and I'll show you no fisherman at all. And don't you ever forget that ole Teddy Ballgame is the best fucking fisherman anywhere."[18] While many players did agree that Williams had this quality, the opinion was not universal. Denny McLain was certainly one dissenter. In his autobiography, McLain noted that Williams introduced himself by opinioning that the only thing "dumber than one fucking pitcher" is "two of you dumb fucking pitchers." McLain regarded Williams to be a "gibbering idiot" whose approach was based on intimidation and fear.

Knowledge of the Players and the Game

Tom Kelly, manager of the world champion Minnesota Twins in 1987, contends that "the players have to know a couple things about their manager during a game: that he's in the ballgame, and that he's confident."[19] Billy Martin believes that managers now have to demonstrate knowledge, because today's players—unlike their earlier counterparts—frequently challenge the manager's judgment.

Gene Mauch has the reputation of being a thinking man's manager: He is always prepared for every possibility and is therefore not surprised by game developments. Preparation means knowing players' strengths and weaknesses as well as what particular play might work, given certain circumstances. Leo Durocher, for example, had the reputation of making sharp and split-second decisions during the game—which earned him the players' respect in spite of his irascible personality.

One source of managerial knowledge is playing experience. Some think that infielders and catchers have particularly valuable playing knowledge, and therefore make good managers (John McGraw, Joe Cronin, Leo Durocher, Buckie Harris, Frankie Frisch, Hughie Jennings, Miller Huggins, Connie Mack, and Al Lopez are examples). Pitchers have seldom been offered manager jobs—a situation that Warren Spahn explained this way:

I didn't get to manage for two reasons; I was a pitcher, and a good one. . . . There's a prejudice in baseball against pitchers as managers in the big leagues, and against guys who had good playing records. It's spread by all those little bench warmers who get the managing jobs. They'll tell you that things came easy to the stars, so we're no good as teachers. That's bull. We got good because we studied the game and ourselves and did what it took to excel.

When a manager's job comes open, who gets it? . . . Some ex-catcher or utility infielder. They're supposed to know strategy. Hell, who knows more about the steal or the hit-and-run than a pitcher? He's in the middle on both those plays. He knows the most about pitchers because he was one, and about hitters because it was his job to get them out.[20]

Some managers (Tony LaRussa, Dick Howser, and Frank Robinson, for example) have relied on extensive mathematical player-situation probabilities generated through computers. The proper information can indicate that a player hit .220 by day and .304 at night and/or .321 on artificial turf and .239 on the grass.

It is the opinion in some quarters, however, that managers do not need much in the way of specialized knowledge. For example, noted sports analyst Bill James believes that most of the decisions managers make are obvious, and that the unique strategies are seldom employed and never necessary. Indeed, problems arise—some say—when managers overmanage or are always looking over their players' shoulders.

MANAGERIAL ACTIVITIES

Managerial activities can be grouped into three general categories: (1) determining team composition and playing roster; (2) teaching baseball skills and strategies; and (3) devising and enforcing player rules.

Determining Team Composition and Playing Roster

It is the manager's responsibility to identify and develop talent for the enhancement of team performance. He can only go so far in this endeavor, however. Reggie Jackson tells how his nonetheless good manager Dick Howser was not able to advance that team (the Yankees) beyond the division playoffs in 1980: "Howser couldn't be faulted for the way we played in the playoffs. He didn't throw that pitch to George Brett. He didn't make me go 0-for-4."[21]

Some of the most important personnel decisions made by a successful manager are not generally recognized by players and newspaper reporters. A manager's job may be, say, to look over three kid pitchers who were all 15–6 in the minors last year and figure out which one deserves the fifth spot in the starting rotation. Al Lopez—who had himself a fine managerial reputation—believed that Casey Stengel's greatest asset was in his taking a chance on the bunch of young kids (Mantle, Ford, Martin, and McDougald) with whom he won ten pennants in 12 years. A successful manager must also know whether an older player who has less than a .200 batting average in April is in a slump or is through. These decisions are the kinds of decisions that determine team victory or failure—more than any overall managerial strategy.

Assessing a team's strengths and weaknesses can be a painful experience. Consider—for example—Whitey Herzog's analysis of the Saint Louis Cardinals in 1980, when he found a bunch of "misfits": Players who were lazy, on drugs, or drinking vodka during the game. He informed the owner thus:

You've got a bunch of prima donnas, overpaid SOBs who ain't ever going to win a goddamned thing. You've got a bunch of mean people, some sorry human beings. It's the first time I've ever been scared to walk through my own clubhouse. We've got drug problems, we've got ego problems, and we ain't ever going anywhere.[22]

Billy Martin has indicated that his first task after joining any team is always to get rid of "clubhouse lawyers," "alibiers," and "complainers," which Red Sox Manager Joe Morgan intends to do for his team after the 1989 season.

But getting rid of undesirable players by trading them to other teams is not easily accomplished. Aging players who have become less productive may have inflated salaries and/or no-trade clauses in their contracts. Martin was unsuccessful in removing Reggie Jackson, even though he felt that "we have to get rid of him. He is a disruptive force."[23] Whitey Herzog was more successful in getting his team's "disruptive force"—Keith Hernandez—traded to the Mets. Herzog contended that he, other players, and coaches had observed Hernandez loafing, not being on time, having "atrocious" practice habits, and generally "poisoning the whole ball club."[24]

Many times, player acquisitions and removals are determined by the manager in conjunction with another team official, such as the general manager. Long-time manager Earl Weaver explains this situation:

That's the manager's job: to tell the general manager what he needs to win. What do we need to win? OK, we need some speed in the outfield, more power in the infield and a catcher who's going to drive in 40 to 60 runs—you tell those things to the general manager. You've got to know that you need a Lowenstein, who you pick up for $20,000; last year, John hit .320 for the Orioles with 24 home runs. You need a [Terry] Crowley, who'd been traded by Cincinnati and released by Atlanta; when the time comes to win a ball game in the seventh, eighth or ninth inning, or when the player you counted on is hitting .214 in June, now you've got a move you can make.[25]

The cooperation between team officials is not always smooth. For example, one general manager, Dallas Green—when asked why he had not informed manager Gene Michael that he was trading a starting pitcher—replied, "He doesn't tell me when he's going to bunt. Why should I tell him when I'm going to trade?"[26] Michael subsequently surprised Green by resigning. To which Green commented, "It's nice he told somebody. . . . He didn't tell me."[27]

Whitey Herzog both realized and resolved this sort of problem when he was hired to be both the general manager and manager for the Saint Louis Cardinals. This rare situation was due to Herzog's past success with the Kansas City Royals, his belief that the Cardinals needed a huge facelift to be competitive, and his attitude that most general managers have never played the game but hide their poor player decisions by firing the manager. Larry Bowa felt this way about Padres official Chub Feeney, who fired Bowa during the 1988 season. Bowa could not respect Feeney because he felt that Feeney was out of touch with the game and would not recognize his own players in the hotel lobby. Feeney did resign at the end of that season, and he contended that this action was not prompted by his giving an obscene hand gesture to two fans who paraded a "scrub Chub" sign at the ballpark.

In addition to designing the composition of the team, a manager also has to successfully cultivate his existing players by way of many interconnected decisions—such as planning and readjusting his pitching rotation and bull-pen, selecting his regulars, platooning his not-quite regulars, and ensuring that substitute players are ready for an emergency. The manager also "has to settle on a batting order, change it when necessary, and decide when to leave it alone."[28]

Teaching Baseball Skills and Strategies

The main object of a manager's communication is to let players know where they stand on the team, particularly when they are in trouble. Difficulties usually do arise in this process. Earl Weaver, for example, dreaded even going to the ballpark when he had to continue benching a player who wanted to be in the game.

Sooner or later, I'd have to tell him, "Look, you're playing horseshit baseball; you're lousy." You've got to come out with the words—not necessarily those—and you're going to hurt the guy's feelings. But if you don't do it, you're not doing your job right.[29]

The manager's personality can be another stumbling block in communication. Hall of Famer Bill Terry recalled that, despite manager John McGraw's tremendous accomplishments, he was so sarcastic in dealing out blame to the players (including Terry) that blowups were common. One such confrontation between McGraw and Terry resulted in neither individual speaking to the other for the next two years.

Actually, managers have often used sarcasm over the years to let certain players know where they stand. Connie Mack was managing when a rookie batted against 400-plus game winner Walter Johnson for the first time. After the rookie struck out twice, Mack asked him what he was waiting for and the rookie indicated that he would like to hit a curveball. Mack retorted, "Son . . . I have very valuable news for you. Walter Johnson doesn't have a curve ball. In fact, he doesn't need one. So please don't bother to wait for it."[30] When Mike Cuellar was knocked out by the other team in 13 straight starts in 1976, his manager—Earl Weaver—noted, "I've given Mike more chances than my first wife."[31]

Casey Stengel often used sarcasm constructively, as when his words stung Yogi Berra (about the way Berra had called pitches in the previous game) to the point where Berra finally yelled, "So if I'm doin' so bad . . . why don't you catch?" Berra then hit 3 for 5 in the next game. Stengel grinned at Berra in the clubhouse and said, "Got you mad, didn't I?"[32]

Billy Martin also recalled manager Stengel's effective communication style in an instance when Stengel benched Martin and then wanted him to play in the seventh inning. Martin was "pissed," sulked over the situation, and was ready to nail Stengel when the manager did finally ask him to go out on the field. But Stengel confronted Martin this way: "Whassa matter? Is widdo Biwwy mad at me? . . . Will you take you widdo gwove and go out and pway second base?" Martin recalled, "It was all I could do to keep from cracking up, but that cleared the air and pulled me out of my mood. I never said a word. I just grabbed my glove and headed out to second base."[33]

There are three communication avenues; private (manager–individual player only), quasi-public (such as team meetings), and public (which typically involve fans and/or the media). Private one-on-one discussions with players are frequent, but the effectiveness of these meetings depends on the personalities involved. Miller Huggins had several private communications with Babe Ruth. In one such encounter Huggins informed Ruth that he was being fined $5,000. Ruth allegedly responded—in a nasty manner—"Five thousand dollars? Fuck you, you little son of a bitch. Who the hell do you think you are? . . . If you were even half my size I'd punch the shit out of you."[34] It is probably safe to say that this is an example of very ineffective private communication with Ruth. A much more effective one followed, with owner Jake Ruppert—as discussed later.

Quasi-public communication in the form of clubhouse meetings with the manager and some or all of the players can be extremely varied with regard to frequency, subject matter, style, and effectiveness. Some managers—like Billy Gardner, Sparky Anderson, and Whitey Herzog—do not find such meetings useful. Herzog has not held a post-game clubhouse meeting in 14 years. On the other hand, Larry Bowa held 15 meetings with the Padres in his first month of regular season. One veteran player has noted that some meetings are funny, dry, and commonsensical while others are witless, ungrammatical, and totally nonsensical. A few team meetings have even managed to be inspirational. Jim Bouton believes that the best pep talk ever was given by Don Hoak, the manager of a minor league team. Hoak reportedly held his thumb and forefinger about an inch apart and told the players, "you're just this far away from big-league pussy."[35]

A far more serious team meeting—one with a large impact—occurred when newly hired Cardinals manager Johnny Keane believed that pitcher Mickey McDermott was being disruptive to team performance. Tim McCarver recalls the somber moment when John Keane spoke.

"We checked your room four nights in a row, and you weren't there. . . . We gave you cab fare and we gave you a job. You came to spring training and you were broke. I will not have guys like you tear down the tradition of this organization."

Nobody uttered a word. You could hear a pin drop. The clubhouse was as quiet as an ancient church. In a hoarse voice, McDermott finally spoke up. "John, if you feel that way, maybe I oughtta take my uniform off," he half whispered.

"That's exactly what you'll do. Here's your pink slip," answered Keane, and he pulled the paper out of his pocket. Most players, almost to a man, are released quietly, normally in the manager's office. But Keane wanted this made public. He was making a statement. Mickey never pitched another game in the majors.

Johnny Keane's decisive action had quite an impact. At least it did on me. The general reaction was that he'd been fair and just. Interestingly enough, the team finished out the year playing 47–33 ball under Keane. Could it be that Keane knew what he was doing?[36]

To be effective, a team meeting must have a topic that players perceive to be relevant to the game and consistent with past managerial actions. Charlie Dressen violated the first requirement in what has come to be known as his "brussel sprouts" meeting. During a rain-delayed game, Dressen brought the players together to discuss their eating habits. He indicated that the club was generously paying for player meals, but that some of the players were abusing this privilege—like charging brussel sprouts, which amounted to a $1 side-order. Duke Snider—tired of the topic—objected, "Fer crissake, Charlie, it stopped raining. Let's go out and hit; and forget about the goddam brussels sprouts. I don't know who ate it, but put it on my tab. And I didn't even eat in the hotel."[37]

Managers must also make their remarks consistent with past practice, if a meeting is to be effective. One manager yelled at his players for being too carefree or—as he put it, in more typical baseball language—having a "horse-shit" and "given up" attitude. Yet, according to one player on the team, these words were never backed up with disciplinary action because the manager wanted to be everyone's friend.

Clubhouse meetings can backfire unexpectedly, too—creating problems, rather than solving them. In 1975, pitcher Dock Ellis believed that he had some useful observations to make as to why Pittsburgh was playing so poorly, so he asked manager Danny Murtaugh to set up a team meeting. At this meeting—right off the bat—Ellis informed the players that he had lost respect for Murtaugh, and then started to go on with his criticism of the players. Murtaugh became enraged—first challenging Ellis to fight, and then ordering him out of the meeting. Ellis was initially suspended for 30 days, although after two weeks he was reinstated with back pay minus a $2,500 fine.

Communications made in public increase the chances for mistake, which can lead to embarrassment and anger. Therefore, some managers avoid discussing players with the press. Others, though, like to take this route. In 1897, manager Cap Anson attempted—without success—to motivate his team by having a sportswriter friend print the following in his article: "Captain A. C. Anson desires me to announce, in black type, at the head of this column, that the Chicago Baseball Club is composed of a bunch of drunkards and loafers who are throwing him down."[38] Herman Franks described some of his former players to the press as being "flaky," "nuts," and "selfish." He also called one Chicago Cub outfielder a "constant whiner," and added, "There isn't enough money in the world to pay me to manage if I have to look at that face everyday."[39]

Another Cubs manager, Leo Durocher, publicly lambasted "Mr. Cub"—Ernie Banks—during later days as a player, when some of his skills had inevitably declined. When reporters asked Durocher about Banks, Durocher replied, "Mr. Cub, my ass. . . . I'll give Mr. Banks $100 any time he even attempts to steal second."[40]

Actions can speak louder than words even in public communication. One day, against Nolan Ryan—the fastest pitcher in baseball at the time—Banks struck out three straight times. The Mets replaced Ryan with another pitcher when Banks went up for his fourth at-bat. Durocher then lifted Banks for a pinch hitter—the first time that had been done in 19 seasons.

One of the more celebrated "lifting" incidents occurred in 1977, when Billy Martin pulled Reggie Jackson from his right-field position after Martin felt that Jackson had not hustled enough for a flyball. Angry words were exchanged when Jackson returned to the dugout, and the television cameras showed players and coaches physically restraining Martin and Jackson from fighting. Martin defended his actions, in part by citing the precedents of Casey Stengel pulling Mickey Mantle out of a game and Gil Hodges once doing the same to Cleon Jones.

About a year later, Reggie Jackson found his opening, and he—too—used actions rather than words to communicate his displeasure toward Martin. Jackson was at bat in the tenth inning with a player on first base. Martin told Jackson through third-base coach Dick Howser to sacrifice bunt and advance the runner to second. Jackson followed directions, but his bunt went into foul territory. Martin then gave signals for Jackson not to bunt, but Jackson—claiming later that he was confused—bunted foul again. Dick Howser then called time-out and informed Jackson that the bunt signal was off, but Jackson told Howser that he wanted to bunt and proceeded to bunt the ball foul a third time—for an automatic out. Jackson received a five-day suspension ($9,273 salary loss) for his behavior; but in the end—as mentioned later in this chapter—Martin was forced to resign over his statements about this incident.

A dramatic on-field confrontation once occurred between Lenny Randle and Frank Lucchesi, manager of the Texas Rangers, in which Randle broke Lucchesi's jaw with several punches to the face—necessitating plastic surgery for the manager. Randle excused his actions on the grounds that he was angry because the manager did not give him much playing time and had also called him a "punk." Suspended 30 days ($13,407 salary loss), fined $10,000, and traded to the Mets, Randle filed a grievance. His was the first such grievance since the labor agreement was signed in 1966. However, Randle subsequently waived the arbitration hearing (and accepted the discipline), only to find himself sued by Lucchesi. Eventually, the two reached an "amicable" out-of-court settlement. Lucchesi admitted he did know that among blacks "punk" often means "sissy" or "queer."[41]

Managers rely on communication to teach and develop player skills. A manager's knowledge and experience are of great benefit in teaching players, but only if he is able to communicate them. Charlie Dressen's communicative ability made all the difference to Gil Hodges after the player was benched because of a batting slump. Dressen viewed several movies of Hodges at bat; he found Hodges to be off balance and have poor timing, with no weight or accuracy in his swing. So Dressen told Hodges,

"Keep your front foot where it is, but move the back foot farther from the plate. See what I mean. Now when ya pull back, the way ya do, you'll just be stepping into line. It won't hurt ya so much, stepping outa the way like ya do, cuz ya won't be really stepping out of the way, you'll really be stepping into it. I wancha to over-compensate, or some word like that."

That season, 1953, Hodges batted .302. In the World Series of 1953 he led all the Dodger hitters with .364. His weakness persisted, but his career was saved.[42]

Many have said that Ted Williams was the best hitting teacher of all the managers. John Roseboro claimed that Williams taught him more about hitting than he had learned in a lifetime. Rod Carew, one of the finer contemporary hitters, also benefited from Williams's advice.

Ted and I talked about what I did when the bat gets heavy as the season progresses. I said I choked up. He said he did too. He also said he used a shorter bat; it gave him more control. He gave me some interesting advice. He said, if you want to use a shorter bat, switch to one about a half inch shorter, but turn the trademark away from you so that the bat will seem longer because you're looking at all wood. I tried it and it worked.[43]

Physical skills are reinforced through constant practice. Lou Piniella recalled that Bill Virdon constantly worked the players at spring training—for example, hitting flyballs to the outfields for several hours every day. When Piniella made a fine catch during the season, his former manager, Earl Weaver—unaware of Piniella's extensive practice sessions—asked him, "When in hell did you become an outfielder?"[44] And Ted Williams always appreciated Joe Cronin's frequent batting practices where the pitcher was instructed, "Look this is batting practice, this ain't pitching practice. Get the ball over. Throw strikes."[45]

Some players just respond poorly to all training and teaching techniques. Williams remembered one outfielder who had impressive natural ability but no desire to take any additional batting practice during the regular season. The player was traded before the next season began. Casey Stengel had a similar problem with none other than Mickey Mantle—an athlete with seemingly unlimited potential. Stengel—a great teacher of baseball—was frustrated with Mantle, who preferred to do things his own way. Another Yankee player once observed that Stengel would "grab Mickey by the back of the neck and shake him hard when he did something the old man didn't like. He said, 'Don't let me see you do that again, you little bastard!' "[46]

There are also several mental mistakes that can be minimized—if not eliminated—through consistent drill. Dick Williams said that he could accept a player who makes "physical mistakes" such as a pitcher hanging a curveball or an infielder fumbling a groundball. He could not, however, excuse a player who makes "mental mistakes" such as missing a sign from a coach, manager, or player (an outfielder missing the cutoff man, for example).

Devising and Enforcing Player Rules

Collective bargaining agreements do not preclude a baseball club from establishing rules governing player conduct. Some managers, like Sparky Anderson, prefer very few rules. "The only way an athlete can perform is when you let him loose. If you're going to hold his reins and tie him up and tell him every time he moves that this is how you want it, well, he's not going to perform his best."[47] Pete Rose also followed this philosophy since he had only two rules: "Be on time and play hard."[48] Dave Johnson, the Mets' manager, has only one rule: "Do not embarrass me or the ballclub."[49] Billy Martin, on the other hand, preferred that players' conduct be governed by a wide range of rules during the 1985 season. Martin ordered his players as follows:

Wear coats and ties while traveling. [All players] have to be in three hours after a night game, or by midnight after a day game. No golf or public appearances on game days. I'll have additional rules on drug abuse. All radios must have headsets. When I call a practice on an off day, attendance will be mandatory. I'll have a system of fines: $500 for a first offense, $1,000 for a second, $1,000 and a suspension for a third.[50]

Some managers keep their rules reasonable—that is relating to the job and not subjecting the players to undue humiliation—and others do not. The reasonable rules are easier to enforce and produce the best results. Presumably some sort of curfew on nighttime player return to the hotel is reasonable, although some may think that John J. McGraw's 11.30 P.M. time limit was not. Miller Huggins went further by not only imposing the same curfew time but also forbidding players to smoke when in uniform. Some managers—notably, Ted Williams—have even attempted to prohibit players from having sex during the season.

Williams was most fanatic about sexual abstinence during the season. He enforced celibacy as best he could on the road. He claimed that women were an unnecessary distraction during the season and that the players should save up all that energy for baseball. He thought sex took too much out of the players, especially before a game. Pitchers especially should lay off sex for at least a couple of days before pitching.[51]

Rogers Hornsby was another manager who was considered to be unreasonable, when he would not let players eat or drink (soft drinks included) in the clubhouse even between games of a doubleheader.

However, there are players—like Joe Pepitone—who find almost any rule to be unreasonable.

After I got traded to Houston, I once walked out on the field during batting practice without a hat, and Harry Walker, the manager, yells at me, "Goddamn it, Pepitone. Put your hat on. You're a ball player." Pull my pecker. You know what I mean? I'm also me. When I was traded to Houston, Walker gave us a paper with twenty-five rules and regulations on it. He said to me, "If you don't like some things, just cross them off and hand the paper back to me."

So on the top of the paper it said, "Rules and Regulations." I crossed that out. I said, "I don't want to read the rest of it. Leave me alone and just let me play my game." He said, "Those rules are going to help us win ball games." I said, "Ain't nothing going to help you win ball games except us players. You're not going to win them."[52]

Pepitone may be at least partially right. Casey Stengel used to say, "Look at Bobby Richardson. He doesn't drink, he doesn't smoke, he doesn't chew, he doesn't stay out late, and he still can't hit .250."[53]

In addition to being reasonable, effective work rules should be clear. Sparky Lyle once sat next to the pitching coach during a game and began to enjoy two hot dogs. When the coach reminded Lyle of the rule prohibiting eating just before a game, Lyle replied that the game had already started. Another example of baseball players' inventiveness concerning any rules that are less than crystal clear was provided by Miller Huggins's players. In 1927 Huggins decided to place a gambling limit of 25 cents a round of poker. Babe Ruth and the other players got tired of playing poker all night for just a few dollars so they switched to bridge where Ruth set the limit at 50 cents (25 cents from each partner) a point. Under this arrangement, each player could win or lose $350 or more in a few minutes.

To ensure effective player performance, managers also have to consistently enforce rules. Some baseball managers interpret "consistent" to mean one rule for all, regardless of playing ability. Casey Stengel once violated this rule when he decided to excuse Mickey Mantle from taking a brutal (in time, distance, and location) three-day road trip during spring training that all the other players had to take. Yet Stengel reversed his decision when he learned that Mantle was bragging about his "vacation" to other players.

Consistent can also mean identical treatment under identical circumstances. Bill Veeck decided to fire his manager, Roger Hornsby, when Hornsby refused to let a player visit his extremely sick wife during a road game in Washington, D.C., even though the wife lived only half a mile farther from the ballpark than the hotel. When informed of the situation, Veeck had asked Hornsby to change his mind, and was told, "All players are alike to me. . . . I can't have two sets of rules." Hornsby's view on consistency here was quite a bit misguided, and Veeck fired him over it, exclaiming,

That's just ridiculous. If everybody lived in Baltimore and had a wife who was pregnant and in ill health, and you let some of them go and didn't let others go, than you'd have two sets of rules. You have only one player in that situation, so you let him go and you'll only have one set of rules.[54]

Some managers or owners go to the opposite extreme from Hornsby, and give special privileges to players with superior performance credentials. For example, Hughie Jennings instituted one set of team rules for Ty Cobb and another set of rules for the other players. Cobb did not have to attend team batting practice, for instance. The players told Jennings that they thought

Cobb was receiving special treatment and Jennings agreed, offering them the same consideration if they had Cobb's performance statistics.

More recently, Bo Jackson received permission from Kansas City Royals management to pursue his "hobby": playing professional football in the off-season. This angered many other Royals players, who are contractually prohibited from pursuing physically dangerous activities (water skiing and football, for example).

Rules are effective only to the extent that they are enforced. According to Sparky Lyle, Billy Martin failed in this regard because Martin did not back up his threats about fining players who did not wear jackets and ties on the road or who played cards before a game. Lyle thought that more respect would have been generated if Martin had simply deducted $50 from a player's paycheck for each dress infraction, and if he had just yelled, "Knockoff the goddamn card game."

Ever since Billy took over as manager in 1975, he's been setting down rules and not enforcing them. It was always "All right, Goddamn it, there's not going to be any more of this or I'm taking your money. I don't want to take it, but I'm going to take it." Then the player would do it again, and still nothing would happen. He still didn't fine him. Then Billy would hold another meeting and he'd say, "All right, I said I was going to take your money, and I didn't. I was lenient 'cause I thought maybe you'd learn. Now I'm going to do it. If you don't want to obey, I'm going to take your money for sure.' " Still, nothing would happen. After he cried wolf like that, you started not to believe him.[55]

Sometimes rule enforcement means that higher level baseball officials have to step in and back up the manager's decision. Jake Ruppert was an owner who was ready to enforce the rules that his manager, Miller Huggins, set for the players—including Babe Ruth. As noted earlier, Ruth once obscenely threatened the manager when informed of a $5,000 fine. However, Ruppert upheld the fine. In his autobiography, Ruth reports that he quickly learned a major lesson:

I was given to understand that Huggins was boss on the ball club and that I was just another player. What's more, I was told my suspension would last until such time as Huggins lifted it. . . .

I am not proud of this chapter of my baseball life . . . but . . . I believe I learned something from this one. I knew that although Huggins was a little man in stature, he was the boss, and I had acted like a spoiled child.[56]

Eddie Mathews found rule enforcement to be complicated at times. He posed the example of a player breaking curfew by only five minutes.

Do you fine him two hundred dollars, or do you accept his claim that he had a tough time getting a cab or some silly thing. Now suppose you let him off for only five minutes late. Next time somebody else is a half hour late. What the hell do you do with him?[57]

Mathews (and also Sparky Lyle) observed too, that today's player can well afford to violate the rule and pay the fine. Someone like Reggie Jackson can afford to pay any fine set for missed spring training practice, particularly since he probably makes more money on business deals the days he is absent from baseball.

Some managers have enforced their rules in innovative ways. Ty Cobb remembered that a team official once commissioned a private detective to follow the players past curfew and complete a detailed written report of what was said and done. Gil Hodges made this clubhouse speech when he learned that four of his players had violated curfew.

I know who you were. You're each fined one hundred dollars. But a lot of us are married and I don't want to embarrass anyone. There's a cigar box on my desk. At the end of the day, I'm going to look into that box and I want to see four hundred dollars in it. Then the matter will be closed.[58]

At the end of the day, Hodges found $700 in the cigar box. George Steinbrenner has—on at least one occasion—paid a hotel bellhop for every player autograph on a ball signed when they returned to the hotel after curfew.

FACTORS LIMITING MANAGERIAL SUCCESS

All in all, for the baseball manager, "success" is not easily defined—particularly because there are so many factors beyond his control. Despite the manager's influence on player selection and use, he is nonetheless limited to the team's talent and luck. Yogi Berrra notes in his autobiography that nobody has all the answers since even your best players will get on base only three out of ten times and a terrific season occurs when a team only loses a third of its games. Tommy Lasorda tempers the many accolades received for his Dodgers' World Series victory in 1988.

The players do it, not the manager . . . Say Whitey Herzog has his boys hit and run, and the batter lines into a double play. Say Sparky Anderson does it, and the batter swings and misses and the runner is thrown out at second. Then say I do it, and the batter gets a hit, and the runner on first goes to third. Which one of us is the genius? "You, Tommy."[59]

Managers often receive too much credit for team victories and too much blame for team losses. It is the players who make the difference. A manager can help a player develop his potential, but that manager cannot make the player better than his natural abilities decree. Injury is another factor that takes success out of the manager's control. A lot of player injuries (a situation faced by the league-leading Saint Louis Cardinals in 1987, for instance) can help defeat the sharpest managerial skills and strategies.

Furthermore, teams need a few players who can assume a leadership role, in addition to a good manager. Billy Herman said that the success of the Milwaukee Braves during the late 1950s was in large part due to three player leaders—Spahn, Burdette, and Matthews—who were effective role models. Joe Morgan explains the necessity of having players who are leaders.

[A] manager can only do so much. If a manager has to raise hell every five minutes about things that are going wrong, players stop listening to him. But if something goes wrong and two or three guys on the team turn around and say, Hey, that wasn't right, don't do that anymore, the manager's out of it and the team's better off. A manager can't be the only guy on top of everything, and that's a problem with a lot of teams, not just the Expos.[60]

Yet Don Zimmer believes that leadership does not necessarily equal "rah-rah." His leaders on the Chicago Cubs—Andre Dawson, Ryne Sandberg, and Vance Law—say nothing but "play hard, even when hurt."

Managers sometimes have to deal with players who feel they can ignore the manager because they have a good relationship with the owner. Dick Williams—for example—believes he was fired in Boston because he had an altercation with the owner's favorite, Carl Yastrzemski. Steve Garvey agrees that managers have a tough time disciplining or benching the superstars with a high-priced multiyear contract because top management wants that player on the field.

Players have been known to attempt to get rid of a manager they do not like by playing halfheartedly—thus spurring the owner to fire the manager for poor team performance (because it's easier to replace one manager than 25 players). Denny McLain and four other players once formed the "Underminers Club," dedicated to removing manager Ted Williams and his coaches from the payroll.

Thus, the owner-manager-player triangle can clearly influence managerial performance and tenure. Perhaps the most dramatic example of owner-manager relationships is reflected in the following summary of George Steinbrenner's operation of the New York Yankees.

MANAGER SHIFTS UNDER GEORGE STEINBRENNER'S YANKEES

1/73   *George Steinbrenner acquires the New York Yankees.*

Steinbrenner used his first press conference on the subject to announce that he would be an "absentee" Yankee owner because he would not pretend to know anything about baseball.

9/73   *Manager Ralph Houk (80–82)*[61] *resigns and is replaced by Bill Virdon* *(1/3/74).*

Virdon was not the Yankees' first choice: Steinbrenner wanted Dick Williams, who remained the property of the Oakland A's.

8/75   *Virdon (142–124) is fired and is replaced by Billy Martin.*

Many of the players thought that their own poor attitudes—not Virdon's managerial skills—had resulted in the team's poor performance. Virdon's replacement, Martin, may have continued to encounter this situation, in the person of Reggie Jackson.

On July 23, 1978, Jackson returned to the Yankees lineup after a five-day suspension for continuing to bunt despite Martin's orders. Martin informed reporters that "[Steinbrenner] can replace me right now if he doesn't like it. . . . I'm sick and tired of this crap. We've got a smooth running ship here, and I don't want him [Jackson] coming along and breaking it up. If you want to play ball, Reggie, fine—then shut your mouth and play." Thirty minutes later Martin told two newsman, "They [Jackson and Steinbrenner] deserve each other. One's a born liar [Jackson], the other's convicted [Steinbrenner]."[62]

7/78   *Martin (279–192) "resigns"—although Al Rosen indicates that Martin was about to be fired for his remarks—and is replaced for one game by Dick Howser (0–1) and then by Bob Lemon.*

Martin refused to comment further about this situation because "I am a Yankee and Yankees do not talk or throw rocks."[63] Steinbrenner indicated that he was shocked by the aforementioned remarks, expressed concern for Martin's well-being, and wished him luck.

Lemon managed the team for the rest of the season, rallying the players from a 13.5-game deficit to win the World Series.

6/79   *Lemon (82–50) is fired and is replaced by Martin.*

This decision surprised the media since there was little advance indication of a managerial change. Steinbrenner did, however, observe the team a couple of days before the announced decision and said, "This doesn't look like a baseball team . . . There's no spark. I've been around athletes long enough to know when there's spark. There isn't any."[64]

In October 1979 Martin was allegedly involved in a fight with a marshmallow salesman, who required 30 stitches to close a badly cut lip.

10/79   *Martin (55–41) is fired and is replaced by Dick Howser.*

Martin did not like this move and has some harsh comments to make about Steinbrenner: "George was born very rich and he thinks everyone can be bought and then he finds someone (like myself) who can't be bought

... I feel the man is sick, I'll be honest with you. ... I'll only go back if George is gone."[65] Howser's team won the American League East Division Championship.

11/80   *Howser (103–59) resigns and is replaced by Gene Michael.*

Near the end of the 1981 season, George Steinbrenner felt that the team needed a practice. Michael disagreed and said, "I can live with anything. ... My mother died in 1978, I went through a divorce, I had friends who died. He can take the job. It won't bother me. I don't resign."[66] Steinbrenner replied, "I'm the boss, I'm the leader, and he should have shown more loyalty. No one anywhere keeps a job acting that way."[67] Michael's team won the first half of the strike split season.

9/81   *Michael (46–33) is fired and is replaced by Lemon.*

Steinbrenner called this decision the most agonizing he had ever made, claiming that Michael was "like family." Steinbrenner seemed to guarantee Lemon the entire 1982 season when he stated, "I'm not going to make a change in 1982 unless it's dictated by something other than how the team is doing."[68]

4/82   *Lemon (19–23) is fired and is replaced by Michael.*

This action was taken only games into the 1982 season, with the following logic: "Like Lem, we are all disappointed in the slow start of the club. Our entire organization feels that we have the talent to win. This is the deepest and best-balanced team we have had in some years. It is the players who are not producing the wins and perhaps this change will get them going."[69]

8/82   *Michael (44–42) is fired and is replaced by Clyde King.*

Steinbrenner appointed King—a former pitching coach—to complete the season. He would rather have fired some of the players instead of Michael, and indicated, "Some of the players ... will be well advised to start playing as good as they think they are."[70]

1/83   *King (29–33) is replaced by Martin.*

Steinbrenner was likely correct when he praised Martin as "a winner" who increases fan attendance. Both Martin and Steinbrenner felt that they were sealing their relationship. Steinbrenner said that he and Martin would deal directly with each other, instead of through the media as they had in the past. Under Martin, team victories and attendance (an extra 200,000 paid units) increased. However, many players (Goose Gossage, Ken Griffey, and Steve Kemp, for example) stated they did not want to play for Martin the next season. Also Martin received two suspensions for altercations with umpires, allegedly invited a female researcher to perform an oral sex act, and destroyed a toilet with a baseball bat.

12/83   *Martin (91–71) is fired and is replaced by Yogi Berra.*

Berra made it through the 1984 season. During spring training in 1985, Steinbrenner said, "Yogi will be the manager this year, a bad start will not affect his status." Steinbrenner also said, "I just can't understand all these teams changing managers the way they do. The lack of stability is alarming."[71]

During Berra's stay, a very serious argument allegedly occurred when Berra thought Steinbrenner was wrong in wanting certain players on the team. Berra blamed Steinbrenner for the poor team performance and got so mad at Steinbrenner that he threw a pack of cigarettes at him.

4/85   *Berra (93–85) is fired and is replaced by Martin.*

This action occured just 16 games into the 1985 season. Berra was never given a reason for his discharge, although he thinks that Steinbrenner had not forgotten the cigarette-throwing incident. A Yankee official said Steinbrenner "would rather fire 25 players than to fire Yogi, but we all know that would be impossible."[72] Under Martin's leadership, the Yankees compiled a 91–54 record. During this season, Martin was also involved in two barroom brawls. He got a broken arm and two cracked ribs in the second fight, against pitcher Ed Whitson.

10/85   *Martin (91–54) is fired and is replaced by Lou Piniella.*

Martin's lawyer contended that this action was no surprise, as Steinbrenner had indicated that Martin's stint this time around would be for one year or two until Lou Piniella had enough experience to assume managerial duties. A big feud erupted between Piniella and Steinbrenner near the end of the 1987 season. On August 8, 1987, Steinbrenner—irritated that the manager had failed to accept his telephone call regarding a personnel decision—stated that he would have nothing to say to Piniella in the near future. Steinbrenner said, "I don't know of too many guys—even sportswriters—who if their boss told them to be available for a call at a certain time, wouldn't be there."[73] Piniella replied that everyone had worked very hard all season and that any disagreements should be in private. Piniella also said that the controversy "has taken a piece of my heart away," while Steinbrenner indicated that the manager would have been gone "If I weren't forgiving."[74] Piniella seems to have had strong player support. Pitcher Tommy John said, "The guys here like playing for Lou. There's a reason why this team is in first place. He's managed exceptionally well and we'll go to the wall for him."[75] Steinbrenner continued not to speak to Piniella for at least two weeks, but did state that the manager would complete the 1987 season. The Yankees did not go on to win the American League Championship that year.

10/87   *Piniella (179–145) is "promoted" to general manager and is replaced*
by Martin.

Piniella said, "I feel this is a step forward in my baseball career and gives
me the opportunity to learn a new facet of the game."
Martin indicated that Steinbrenner "has my heart, and I have his bank."[76]
Martin kept the Yankees in first place most of his tenure, but also managed
to receive 40 stitches from a fight in a topless bar. He also received a three-
day suspension for throwing dirt at an umpire, and the umpires pledged to
throw him out of a game the minute he should step on the field to protect
a call. Lou Piniella resigned as general manager at the end of May 1988,
indicating some interpersonal difficulties with Martin.

6/88   *Martin (40–28) is fired and is replaced by Piniella.*

Martin was most surprised about this decision, contending that he was
still the best manager in baseball.

10/88   *Piniella (45–48) is fired and is replaced by Dallas Green.*

Steinbrenner explained his latest managerial change this way: "I'm sick
of watching superior Yankee teams throw away pennants because they lack
discipline . . . Dallas is tough. He's outspoken. He won't back away from
anyone, including me. Last year, it was a mistake to put Lou Piniella on
the spot. He wasn't ready for the job, and the team got out of hand." Green
did not appreciate his team's efforts during spring training season, and
warned them of potential problems if their regular season performance was
not an improvement. And he was quite aware that he might be fired on any
given day. "Comes July Fourth, George might show up at the stadium to
throw out the first manager."[77]
Steinbrenner initially backed Green when players complained about his
criticism of them. He then favorably compared Green's demeanor to that of
Billy Martin who "couldn't discipline himself" let alone the players.
By July, Steinbrenner's support of Green eroded. He felt the club was
too skilled and too well paid to have more losses than wins. He also expressed
concern over Green's coaches. By August, Green expressed concern over
Steinbrenner's use of the newspapers instead of face to face discussions to
correct alleged managerial/coaches' mistakes. Green also expected to be fired
although Steinbrenner reiterated support of Green, indicating that he had
no plans to replace him.

8/89   *Green (56–65) is fired and is replaced by Bucky Dent.*

Steinbrenner fired Green some ten days after his nonremoval pledge
mainly because Green told Steinbrenner that he surrounded himself with
people (Bill Martin, Lou Piniella, Clyde King, Syd Thrift, and others) who
"steal" from him. Green offered a somewhat different explanation for his
removal:

Now George is back with his puppet machine. He doesn't want anybody around he can't command. He couldn't make me change the lineup. He couldn't make me change personnel. He couldn't make me fine people or do anything I didn't want to do. He had no way of knowing what was going on in the clubhouse. Now he's got the right people back. They'll say, "Yes, George," to anything George says.[78]

Green's replacement, Bucky Dent, acknowledged that his tenure under Steinbrenner was uncertain. Indeed, he did not know his salary or the anticipated duration of his contract at the time of his managerial appointment. Dent lost 11 of his first 13 games as the new Yankee manager, while Steinbrenner heard an unprecedented chant by fans—"George Must Go!"—at three Yankee games. Steinbrenner assessed the situation: "I may have rushed Bucky." However, a nine-game winning streak changed Steinbrenner's mind, and Dent was given a contract to manage the Yankees through the 1990 season.

Overall, from a statistical standpoint, Steinbrenner's record has shown some success. The Yankee managers compiled a 1,474–1,175 win-loss record through Green, or a .556 winning percentage. But his record and his comments—if they have been quoted correctly by the press—also reveal some inconsistencies. Steinbrenner once said (without smiling), "If all I did was read the newspapers I wouldn't even want to go home with myself."[79]

One consistency does emerge, however. The players' preference for one particular manager or another seems not to have influenced Steinbrenner's decisions. Managers were fired rather than players disciplined when the team was not performing well. Perhaps this reflects an attitude that managers are very replaceable. Charley Finley once said, "A monkey could stand out there and wave at pitchers. It doesn't take a genius to manage."[80]

Bill Veeck also believed that baseball players—not managers—are the ones in short supply: "You could find 100 fans in the stands on any given day who could call the right strategy at the right time with the exact degree of accuracy as the manager."[81] However, Veeck's statement does not mean that he thought anyone can manage any team. He wrote a letter to his co-owners of a minor league team when they hired Casey Stengel to manage the team, in which he declared that Stengel had never managed a winner and that he was a poor manager and a poor judge of players. "If these aren't reasons enough, I don't like him and want no part of him."[82]

Some owners (Marge Schott of the Reds, for example) attempt to remove themselves from the operational end of the game. They feel they know far less about baseball players and successful team strategies than do managers, and thus they are relatively content to let the manager perform his job. Charley Finley was probably at the other end of the scale. According to one of his Athletics players—Dave Duncan—"It doesn't matter who manages this ball club. There's only one man who manages this club, Charlie Finley.

And we'll never win as long as he manages."[83] Finley had great faith in his own ability to identify and resolve player problems, and would become frustrated when his hired managers did not agree with him. After just one game with Alvin Dark managing, Finley humiliated Dark in front of the players by yelling,

I don't know what the fuck you're in this game for . . . but I'm in it to win. And if you don't get your fucking ass in gear, you're gonna be gone! We won two straight without you and we can make it three without you, too. All you got to do is write the fucking names down on the piece of paper and let them play. We got the best goddamn team in baseball, goddammit, and if you can't win with the talent we got you can't win.[84]

Yankees owner George Steinbrenner's involvement in managerial decisions at least equals Finley's—a fact that has on occasion frustrated sometime Yankee's manager Billy Martin.

Steinbrenner's involvement drove Martin mad. Martin hated Steinbrenner's coming to him with stacks of statistics and telling him, based on the statistics, who should be in the lineup and who should be pitching. Martin wouldn't believe the numbers because he didn't believe Steinbrenner. He hated Steinbrenner's questioning every move he made that backfired, every pinchhitter who failed, every relief pitcher who struggled. He hated Steinbrenner's acting as if he knew something about baseball or any other sport. Billy had played ball in schoolyards and in the minor leagues, on bad fields and under bad lights, had felt ninety-mile-an-hour fastballs dig into his ribs and had ducked under pitches that were supposed to take off his head. What did Steinbrenner know about baseball, about strategy, about when to go with the percentages, and when to buck them?[85]

A team is likely to experience several different managers if the owners believe that managers are easily replaced, or that the current manager does not conform to their own management style and/or personal preferences. Whitey Herzog had several "successful" (winning) seasons managing the Kansas City Royals and yet he did not personally get along with the Royals' owner, Ewing Kauffman, and his wife. Herzog was eventually fired, and he heard from another owner—Gene Autry—who indicated that he was not surprised about the decision. When pressed for a further explanation, Autry replied that he had recently asked Ewing Kauffman's wife "how my old friend Whitey was" and that Ms. Kauffman replied, "Who gives a shit?"[86] Uncertain tenure appears to be a frequent feature of the baseball manager's job, and probably makes player-manager relationships more difficult. It constitutes still another factor limiting managerial success, since it is largely beyond the manager's control.

---------------- *Six* ----------------

Player Pressures and Problems

Which one of the following five incidents occurred after 1906?

1. A second baseman was arrested for running away with the wife of a fruit dealer and the fruit dealer's savings.
2. A 17-year-old girl had a catcher arrested for being the father of her unborn child, after yielding "to his unholy desires last May."
3. A pitcher went to the mound drunk—"his head the size of a brewery tub"—and blew the game.
4. An outfielder was fined by his team for being charged with indecent exposure.
5. Several players were arrested for throwing baseballs and luggage, fighting, and waving a gun on public transportation to another game.[1]

The fourth incident is the correct answer. The others preceded 1906, although it is likely that similar situations have occurred several times thereafter. Baseball players have endured the same types of pressures from early days to the present that might have been associated with these problems.

These historical similarities do not minimize the extremely varied relationships between players' pressures and problems. For one thing, players do not all recognize the same pressures. The legendary Walter Johnson, for example, was respected by everyone for never losing his temper. Johnson believed that no player can give his best when he is worried, angry, or resentful; and so basically, he avoided these reactions in himself. For another thing, players react to pressures in a variety of ways: Some want to participate in the winning game play (whether hitting or fielding), while others try to avoid it at all costs. Tim McCarver maintains that, in pressure situations, "one guy's heart pumps twice as fast as usual. Another guy is as calm as three in the morning."[2]

Sometimes, a player's reaction to pressures will elicit disciplinary actions, administered by the team or league officials and or the commissioner of baseball (who, traditionally, has had a great deal of latitude in this area). Perhaps the broadest based application of discipline was the 1947 season suspension of manager Leo Durocher. Commissioner Chandler was worried about Durocher's comments regarding other league personnel, as well as his association with at least one noted gambler. (Durocher seems to have received full pay for this suspension, and returned in 1948.) More recently, Denny McLain received three suspensions in 1970 for admitted involvement with bookmakers, dousing two sportswriters with water, and carrying a gun without a license.

Management's disciplinary action against a player can be subject to union challenge through the labor agreement's grievance procedure (Article X), and allows for the possibility of a third party neutral—the arbitrator—determining whether management's action was correct. Article XI indicates that any discipline must be for "just cause"—a vague term that usually means the grievant must have clearly committed the offense and that the penalty (fine, suspension, and so forth) must be appropriate for the infraction.

An arbitrator determined that both of these dimensions were missing in the case of Alex Johnson. In 1971, the manager of the California Angels accused Johnson of continually calling other players obscene names and not giving his best effort. Johnson was suspended for his behavior. However, the arbitrator decided that Johnson's suspension was inappropriate since two psychiatrists testified that he had been unable to perform because of an emotional condition. The arbitrator believed that Johnson should have been placed on the disabled list, rather than disciplined. Some 15 years later Dennis "Oil Can" Boyd of the Red Sox exhibited some emotional displays, and was admitted to a hospital for counseling. However, he also accepted a three-day suspension and $6,450 in lost wages.

Section A1(b) of the labor agreement enables the commissioner to exempt any of his disciplinary actions—"making the presentation of, or the maintenance of public confidence" in the game—from the grievance procedure. Thus, the commissioner could take disciplinary action against a player where he—not the arbitrator—makes a binding decision. Yet, included in the current labor agreement is a letter written by Commissioner Kuhn to Marvin Miller in which Kuhn indicates that he would never take such action.

ON-FIELD PRESSURES AND PROBLEMS

Surviving in the Majors

The biggest on-field pressure is in maintaining acceptable performance levels for a long, consistent time frame. Baseball players' careers average four years in length—very short. Writer Phil Hersh observes, "We treat athletes the same way Europeans used to treat royalty. The difference is the queen is royal for life. The athlete is only on the throne as long as he can play."[3] This situation is all the more urgent when a player realizes the less than satisfactory conditions in the minor leagues and the possibility that he may return there.

Marvin Miller believed that football players are not as solidly behind their union as baseball players because football players come to the deluxe atmosphere of their employer (the National Football League) directly from the first-cabin environment of big-time college football. Most baseball players—on the other hand—have spent time in the minor leagues, where they learn how "cheap" and "cruel" management can be when it holds all the cards. There are about 154 minor league teams and 3,400 players; only one out of 15 players who enter the minors ever enters major league baseball. Moreover, that experience in the majors may only occur during spring training when players are cut and returned to the minors before the major-league regular season starts. Consider, for example, the experiences of two players—Ray Searage and Hipolito Pena—who at the start of the 1989 season had been on 16 minor–major league teams in 14 years, and 12 minor–major league teams in 8 years, respectively.

Who goes and who stays is often based on very slight differences, like the way a pitcher holds a runner on base. Jim Bouton shaved his moustache and got a haircut before spring training, contending that his chances to stay in the majors were borderline and his hair length might make the difference. Bouton has seen a lot of players cut in spring training. "You walk into the clubhouse and you see a guy packing his bag and you both try not to look at each other."[4]

Replacements can also happen after spring training—sometimes even affecting superstars. Consider Sparky Lyle in 1978. He had won the Cy Young award the previous season for having a 13–5 win-loss record, 26 saves, and an earned run average of 2.17. George Steinbrenner rewarded Lyle's performance by adding $35,000 to his $140,000 yearly salary and extending his contract a year, through 1980.

Steinbrenner also signed two other relief pitchers: Goose Gossage (26 years old) and Rawly Eastwick (27 years old). Gossage received a $2.75-million contract ($460,000 a year), and Eastwick received a $1.1-million contract ($220,000 a year); and Lyle was traded to the Texas Rangers in

1979. Eastwick pitched in only eight games before being traded to the Philadelphia Phillies in 1978. Gossage managed to last with the Yankees for six more seasons before being traded to San Diego in 1984.

Job insecurities can be compounded by lack of playing time; by the several publicized riches-to-rags stories, involving both rookies and veterans; and by injuries and/or declining skills. Many versatile infielders and outfielders sit on the bench when seven others on the team play these positions on a regular basis. Starting pitchers experience this frustration even more often. Some feel that a pitcher with a .500 win-loss percentage is as marginal as a .250 hitter. Also, the chances for redemption are farther apart. Batters come to the plate some 500–600 times a season. A pitcher will likely get only 30 chances—about once every four or five days—to start. When the pitcher does start, many other pressures then arise:

Little is more inspiring than watching one man strike out batter after batter; little sadder than one man who cannot retire the side. Read the strain in a pitcher's eyes as he stares at his catcher: he knows that one bad pitch may lose the game. Talk to a pitcher when he is in a slump: he knows that his high salary is questioned with every bad performance. And watch the pain register on his face as he throws more than 100 pitches at 90 miles per hour in one evening. The final pressure is knowing that any one of these pitches could be the last violent act he will ever perform on his own body. It happens.[5]

Many baseball rookies have had sensational starts, only to fade quickly into obscurity. One young phenomenon, Bo Belinsky, ended his career with a total of 28 pitching victories and 51 losses. Mark Fidrych—"the Bird"— won 19 games during his rookie season and accounted for three straight sellouts at Tiger Stadium—something no other Detroit player (Cobb, Cochrane, Greenberg, Gehringer, and McLain included) had ever done. Yet Fidrych hurt his shoulder in 1977 and only appeared in 11 games. In 1979, Fidrych had an 0–3 record with a 10.20 earned run average before he was sent down to the minors. Another rookie, David Clyde, was fresh out of high school when he won his first game for the Rangers. He completed his career one season later with an overall record of 7 and 17. More recently, Gregg Jefferies, a rookie "phenom" at the end of the 1988 season, struggled at the plate through 1989. Jefferies contended that pitchers weren't even working the ball around him, an observation partially supported by Cubs' pitcher Mitch Williams: "All I know about Jefferies is that he's short and not swinging the bat too well right now."[6]

Veterans have also gone from riches to rags, even while their playing abilities were still good. Jimmie Foxx—probably the first player to hire a butler—consistently spent more than his salary and ended up dying broke. Mickey Cochrane and Connie Mack both lost money in the stock market crash in 1929. Many decades later Denny McLain recognized several financial difficulties during the 1970 season. "My wife, the FBI, the Internal Revenue Service, the commissioner of baseball, eighty-six creditors, and a few other vultures were on my back—all at the same time. On the outside, I was as happy as a whore in a lumber camp. Inside, I was dying."[7] McLain filed for bankruptcy in 1970, listing debts of $446,000 and assets of only $413. More recently, Ron Guidry—superstar Yankee pitcher—had to deal with a $4-million debt resulting from bad investments. And Graig Nettles and Harmon Killebrew have experienced severe economic difficulties.

Other veterans have to fight off career-ending injuries. Some positions—such as catcher—almost mandate a short career for this reason. Writer Jim Murphy believes that "catchers have the career security of U-boats" because they catch balls thrown at more than 90 miles an hour, and block players from home plate—which is like "stopping a run-away truck with a sheet."[8] Recent Hall-of-Famer Johnny Bench experienced this catcher's jeopardy when he went to the doctor with what he thought was a broken foot. X-rays revealed no current break, but did indicate five previous ones that Bench did not even know had happened. And not just catchers fall prey to this syndrome. Players in other positions are subject to injuries, as well.

At least such injuries make a veteran's retirement decision easier. Normally, the decision rests on a confusing combination of objective and subjective indicators that can be interpreted in varying ways. The wrong interpretation can lead to an embarrassing last season. Joe DiMaggio quickly retired after a .263 season. He claims that he kept telling his body what to do and his body replied, "Who me?" Willie Wilson mulled over retirement during the 1988 season when he wore tape on his knees, ankles, and feet, and said he felt like a broken-down racehorse.

Other players' retirement decisions require more time and effort. Reggie Jackson felt he could still benefit a team in his final playing years. However, he knew that the situation would require him to train harder to play less.

Greg Luzinski figured that his past—if not potential—productivity would be of value to another team when his employer—the Chicago White Sox—said "enough."

Luzinski has been wounded in the process. . . . You would have been, too, if you had hit 307 home runs in your big-league career and had to watch the loutish Cliff Johnson sign a fat contract with Texas and the lethargic Jeff Burroughs saved from unemployment rolls by Toronto. Add to that the forsaken feeling of having offered your services to everyone as a free agent and found no takers. Then you should understand why Luzinski has wrapped his emotions in barbed wire.[9]

Many players persist in playing as long as they can anywhere they can. When the Yankees released Roy White after one poor season, White could not yet quit and wound up playing three more years in Japan because— White said—"There's nothing else that gives you the same excitement and challenge as building your skills for years, then going into a pressure situation and hitting a home run, or getting the key hit in a pennant race."[10]

Phil Linz believes that the retirement problem occurs because players have no transferable job skills when they get out of the game. Ernie Banks agrees. "I think I had a fear of failure in doing something outside of sports, like a lot of athletes do. And people don't help, because they keep talking to you about your past. They are trying to be nice, but they don't understand the problems an athlete has in adjusting to a new career."[11]

Yankee legends Mantle and Ruth have both gone on record stating that retirement from baseball represented a large irrevocable loss. Both lived only to play ball—which made their post-baseball endeavors seem hollow by comparison.

In summary, baseball players are under much pressure to survive in the majors, and to extend their playing careers. Along the way, it is likely that their skills will decline; and thus their playing careers will end—far in advance of the age when most of us seek retirement. Their post-baseball options will probably not be so meaningful or lucrative, when compared to their playing days. Most players therefore have to cope with failure; the ultimate inability to adjust can be suicide. Loren Coleman, author of *Suicide Clusters*, has uncovered some 77 suicides of major league players, many apparently due to retirement adjustment problems. Donnie Moore, who shot his estranged wife and then killed himself in the summer of 1989, represents an extreme example of coping inability. Many attributed his suicide to a home run pitch he threw three years earlier. The pitch, to Dave Henderson, helped Henderson's Red Sox win the game and the pennant from Moore's California Angels. After the game Moore said, "I'm the goat. . . . I know this is supposed to be a team sport, but I'll take the blame."[12] Moore likely took the blame and related aftermath until he died. Less dramatic adjustments can result in three general player problems on the field: (1) altercations with fans; (2) taking performance shortcuts; and (3) altercations between teams.

Altercations with Fans

The baseball spectator, or fan, is—en masse—a major source of baseball revenues and player salaries. Thus, some fans believe in expressing their dissatisfaction when a player and/or team is not living up to their expectations.

Fans have always been expressive, but there is some reason to think that their recent behavior has taken an ugly turn. Joe DiMaggio, for example, says that he cannot believe the obscenities fans hurl at players today. "In my day . . . they just called you a bum."[13] In his autobiography, Willie Stargell talks about the physical violence that fans can inflict. "During the course of my career, I saturated many a towel with my blood after being struck by an object thrown from the stands." Some teams have taken action to correct these situations, such as not selling beer after the seventh inning. Commissioner Ueberroth even formed a Fan Behavior Committee to study the situation.

Some players admit to being noticeably affected by fan pressure. Mike Schmidt says that the fans in Philadelphia hurt his productivity. "I'll tell you something about playing in Philadelphia: Whatever I've got in my career now, I would have had . . . more if I'd played my whole career in Los Angeles or Chicago, you name a town—somewhere where they were just grateful to have me around."[14]

John Hiller retired because of fan abuse. He saw Detroit fans boo Al Kaline at the end of Kaline's career. And fans urged Hiller himself to have another heart attack when he was warming up. One of the more publicized series of altercations between fans and a player involved Ted Williams. In 1956 Tom Yawkey, owner of the Red Sox, fined Williams $5,000 for spitting at fans (although other fans organized a fund-raising drive to pay off the fine). Williams—who was in the lineup the night after the spitting incident—responded, "I'll do the same thing over again if I get mad enough. . . . If I could afford it, I'd pay a $5,000 fine every day to do the same thing."[15] Again in 1958 Williams was fined $250 by the league president for spitting at fans who booed when he did not run out a roller to first base.

More recently, Sparky Lyle recalled a real "asshole" fan with mustard all over his T-shirt who hollered, "You bum, Lyle. You suck." An upset Lyle gave the fan a "double bird" (two raised middle fingers), even though Lyle's mother saw the action.[16]

Taking Performance Shortcuts

Baseball players have long employed various ways to enhance their individual and/or team performance that do not exactly mesh with the game's rules or sportsmanship philosophy. When he was retired, Ty Cobb coached a high school all-star team. After a speech on fair play, Cobb pulled the catcher aside before starting the game and said, "Remember. . . . Just before a batter swings, flip a little dirt in his eye."[17] Today some baseball players are still taking performance shortcuts used by their predecessors when hitting or pitching.

Babe Ruth was rumored to use a "corked" bat on occasion. Earl Weaver once hit six home runs in a month in the minors and was distressed when his corked bat was seized and thrown out of the game. A corked bat is easily made: A hole is drilled in the top of a bat for about eight inches, and white glue is poured into the hole as a sealer. Cork or little rubber "super balls" are tightly packed into the hole—causing the bat to serve as a charged springboard for the hit baseball. The top of the bat is replugged to match the grain, and then sanded and varnished. These bats give the hitter a further advantage because the new bat has the density of a regulation bat, but actually weighs less.

Commissioner Ueberroth devised a new rule regarding corked bats in

1987, after hearing several allegations of their use. Each manager could impound one bat used by an opponent per game and have the bat x-rayed to see if it was corked or doctored. Many players have had their bats confiscated, only to have the x-rays prove them normal. Some managers consider the rule to be pretty silly. Tommy Lasorda maintains that he cannot detect a tampered bat while sitting on the bench, so how would he know to object? And Jim Leyland contends that a team could bring in a truckload of corked bats after a bat has been confiscated in the first inning. Another problem with the rule is that the umpire can overturn a manager's request for inspection. This happened when the Mets' manager asked that Andre Dawson's bat be inspected and the plate umpire rejected the move.

Billy Hatcher of the Houston Astros became the first and only player to be ejected during the 1987 season for using an illegal bat. The bat in question literally exploded when Hatcher hit the ball, and an opposing player observed the cork inside the broken bat. Hatcher claimed that the bat belonged to relief pitcher Dave Smith and that he did not know the bat was doctored. Yet he served ten days' suspension for using Smith's bat.

Pitchers have traditionally doctored a baseball by putting a substance on it that would make the ball hard to hit. In the early days of the game, a baseball remained in the game for five or six innings or until it was knocked out of the park. The pitcher was allowed to "rub the ball in the dirt, splatter it with licorice and tobacco and pound it against his cleats. . . . In the late innings, in the shadows, you had to hit a dark streak that almost defied detection."[18]

The "spitter" was legal in baseball's beginning years, and then restricted in 1920 to 17 pitchers who were judged to be capable of throwing the ball safely. One of these pitchers was Burleigh Grimes of the Giants, who finished his career in 1934 and represented the last of the legal spitballers.

Several subsequent pitchers have been known to apply various substances to the ball—despite its being illegal. Preacher Roe, a spitballing ace, preferred to chew Beech-Nut gum because it generated the slickest saliva. He used a fastball pitching motion, but squeezed the ball when he released it— "like letting a watermelon seed shoot out from between your fingers." To "load one," Roe "wiped his large left hand across his brow and surreptitiously spat on the meaty part of the thumb. The broad base of the hand was his shield. Then, pretending to hitch his belt, he transferred moisture to his index and middle fingers. Finally, he gripped the ball on a smooth spot— away from seams—and threw. The spitter consistently broke down."[19]

Jim "Mudcat" Grant, who pitched from 1958 through 1971, has admitted using detergent and sandpaper to alter baseballs. Grant said that his actions were meant to gain a psychological—not physical—advantage over the hitter. "It was to plant an idea in a hitter's mind. If you threw one pitch that the hitter knew that something was on the ball, then you had that hitter for the rest of the game."[20]

Jim Bouton thinks that Whitey Ford was the best at using a doctored ball. His catcher, Ellie Howard, would fake losing his balance in order to dip a ball in the mud. Ford could then make this ball "drop, sail, break in, break out, and sing 'When Irish Eyes Are Smiling.' "[21] Ford also used his wedding ring to scuff up the ball and make it dance to an even different tune. The most recent publicized scuffing controversy involved Roger Craig, manager of the San Francisco Giants, and pitchers Mike Scott of the Houston Astros and Orel Hershiser of the Dodgers. Craig—along with many others—has accused Scott of throwing a scuffed ball; however, he and Scott appear to have a mutual "admiration society" over this situation. Scott is not offended by Craig's claim. He maintains that Craig does not speak ill of him; moreover, Scott feels that if a manager's players make these claims then a manager has to challenge the pitcher to keep his players happy.

Orel Hershisher has also questioned Scott's pitching performance—in a more critical tone. "He's got sandpaper on the side of his glove, and he takes the ball and hits it into the glove to scuff it. It's not fair when the opposing teams, the National League office and even his teammates know it, and still nobody does anything about it."[22] Scott did not appreciate Hershiser's remarks. Neither did Roger Craig, who challenged Hershiser:

Well, I don't know why Orel's making with that kind of talk, . . . because I ain't so sure he's all that legal himself. He stands out on the mound and goes to his face or spits in his hand and then he pitches the ball without wiping it. Our hitters have had a lot of complaints about him doing tricks with the ball . . . not scuffing it; just using liquids.[23]

Other pitchers have scuffed baseballs with sandpaper or thumbtacks hidden in their gloves or with other tools at hand such as a sharpened belt buckle, a rivet in the catcher's shinguard, or a sharpened eyelet in the pitcher's glove.

In 1987 pitcher Kevin Gross was ejected and suspended for ten days when he was found with a "sandpaper substance" glued to his glove. Giamatti's suspension of Gross indicated that he felt player cheating was worse than player substance abuse.

Acts of physical excess, reprehensible as they are . . . often represent extensions of the very forms of physical exertion that are the basis for playing the game; regulation and discipline seek to contain, not expunge, violent effort in sport. Cheating, on the other hand, has no organic basis in the game and no origins in the act of playing. Cheating must be clearly condemned with an eye to expunging it.[24]

The incident invoked both the game's historical aspects and the just-cause disciplinary dimension discussed earlier in this chapter.

"Just cause" dictates that there be clear and convincing evidence that an offense has been committed. Gross admitted to having and using the sandpaper; but without such an admission, the offense is not easy to prove. Phil "the Vulture" Regan was once accused of applying Vaseline to a baseball, when a tube of this substance was found on the ground after Regan ran the base paths. Regan claimed he had never seen the Vaseline "before in my life," and escaped discipline. Baseballs can become "scuffed" many ways— in particular, by hit pitches. A team that collects scuffed balls thrown by an opposing pitcher will not get very far with the umpires, who typically view these items as "inadmissible evidence."

The second dimension of discipline for just cause is that the penalty should match the offense. Doctored baseballs and maybe doctored bats have been a part of baseball's heritage. Mudcat Grant believes that yesterday's players were hit with a wink in reprimand when they were caught. Today's players guilty of the same infraction are treated as if they had committed a serious crime. Other people feel that the rules must be enforced, and infractions penalized. In some cases, however, this attitude may be self-serving. Consider the infamous "pine tar" incident, where the amount of this substance on George Brett's bat exceeded baseball's rules—thereby eliminating a home run hit off a ball pitched by Goose Gossage, who recounted,

Shit, he hit it out of here. And I'll tell you, that sombitch is fucking Houdini, man. He can fucking hit. The man is amazing. They had that pitch at ninety-six on the speed gun, and it was up and in. . . . He's a great hitter. I think next time I'm gonna . . . give him a lob—or maybe roll it in.[25]

Yet Gossage—not so surprisingly—supported the rule that cancelled Brett's home run: "A rule's a rule, and is he gonna be heartbroken if they find me out there with an itty-bitty piece of sandpaper tucked in my glove? You wanna know what I think? I think 'Tough shit.' "[26]

Rick Sutcliffe believes that light or no penalties for infractions will encourage all pitchers to engage in these activities since any pitcher can learn to doctor a ball, and "if they suspend a pitcher for only two games [10 days] and they have a chance to win four or five more games [by cheating], anybody would."[27] Sutcliffe feels that a two-month suspension would be more appropriate since few pitchers would take a chance on losing that much money. Whitey Herzog takes the hard stance that you either play by the rule or you do not play—whether the player is a hitter or a pitcher. He feels that any player who violates the previously discussed rules should be banned for life.

Altercations between Teams

Players want good individual performance statistics, but they also realize that some of their pride and more of their financial status depends on their team's standing at the end of the season. In this sense, all of the players on other teams have to be viewed as the enemy (Joe Pepitone's comments in the preceding chapter notwithstanding). However, most baseball players are not fighters, and some "fights"—like one that occurred between Bill Madlock and Ted Simmons—are farcical in nature. Madlock had become disgusted waiting for a pitch from Al Hrabosky, who would walk off the mound and psyche himself up with monologue before returning to throw the next pitch. Madlock decided to do the same thing—walk away from the batter's box and talk to himself. When the umpire told him to get back to the plate, Madlock refused—whereupon the umpire told Hrabosky to pitch. Hrabosky then proceeded to throw two strikes at the unguarded plate. Madlock jumped in to avoid the third strike, and catcher Ted Simmons punched him in the face. When asked what Madlock did to provoke this fight, Simmons replied, "He didn't say anything. I didn't like the way he was looking at me."[28]

Other altercations look very serious in the buildup, but never do materialize. Babe Ruth recalled a day when shortstop Leo Durocher threw a hip at the base runner, Ty Cobb—knocking Cobb down and enabling the outfielder to throw Cobb out at third base by 20 feet. Cobb threatened that he would spike Durocher or "cut your legs off" if that happened again. Durocher replied, "Go home Grandpa. . . . You're through . . . , and if you try to cut me I'll ram a ball right down your throat."[29] Many fans and players were actually disappointed when actions never followed these words. As mentioned before, Leo Durocher had a knack for bringing out people's antagonisms. Babe Pinelli—"the most mild mannered umpire you'd ever see"— once watched a fight in which Carl Furillo was choking Durocher. Another observer, Duke Snider, recalls the incident. "Leo is turning white; I'm afraid the guy is going to die. And there's Babe Pinelli, Mr. Nice Guy—in all his umpire's neutrality—yelling, 'Kill him, Carl! Kill him!' "[30]

Some confrontations are more physical than others. Perhaps the most famous incident occurred between Juan Marichal, pitcher for the Giants, and John Roseboro, catcher for the Dodgers. Roseboro wanted his pitcher, Sandy Koufax, to "knock down" some Giants because Marichal had been knocking down Dodger batters. Koufax would not comply, so Roseboro told Koufax to throw a low inside pitch when Marichal was at bat. Then Roseboro deliberately dropped the pitch, picked it up again behind the plate, and threw it back to Koufax—missing Marichal's nose by two inches. Marichal responded by hitting Roseboro in the face with a bat. He received an eight-day suspension and a $1,750 fine for his action.

Most altercations start after a pitcher hits an opponent with the ball. Some pitchers do not throw at batters. Sandy Koufax, Vida Blue, Nolan Ryan, Mike Scott, and Dwight Gooden never have. Indeed, some pitchers—on rare occasions—have "fed" batters. In 1910, Nap Lajoie was just a few points away from Ty Cobb, poised to win the batting championship with seven or eight hits against the Saint Louis team. With the cooperation of the Saint Louis manager, pitchers, and third baseman (none of whom liked Cobb),

Lajoie received his "hits." The Saint Louis manager ordered his third base-man to play very deep; and Lajoie—normally a slow runner—had seven successful bunts in the final two games of the season.

One day Denny McLain wanted to see just how far Mickey Mantle could hit his pitch, so he simply tossed the first ball to the plate. The catcher ran out to the mound to find out what was happening, and McLain said, "Just tell Mantle to be ready. The next one will be right down the cock soft as I can get it up there."[31] Mantle caught on, signalled for a waist-high pitch over the plate, and hit the ball into an upper deck seat and broke a seat board. The next batter up—Joe Pepitone—wanted similar treatment and asked McLain where the ball would be thrown. McLain pointed to the side of his head and knocked Pepitone down.

Many pitchers, however, have intentionally thrown near or at the batter in retaliation and/or to establish their game. Sometimes a pitcher knocks a batter down when the batter has had prior success—a situation that may explain a curious comment about one of baseball's greatest unresolved ques-tions. Babe Ruth was alleged to have "called his shot" in the 1932 World Series—pointing to center field before hitting a home run off Cubs pitcher Charlie Root.

Billy Herman maintains that Ruth was pointing to the Cubs' dugout be-cause the bench was calling him everything, including "a big, fat baboon." Herman further notes, "If he'd have pointed and hit it there, he'd have been on his ass the rest of the Series."[32]

More recently, Mike Schmidt hit a first season homer against Bob Gibson, and ran the bases with "my head down"—in effect saying, "I'm sorry I hit the home run, Mr. Gibson." Nevertheless, as Schmidt noted, "He knocked me down the next time up."[33]

Then too, pitchers like Don Drysdale believe that their effectiveness depends on using the entire plate. Batters often crowd the middle portion of the plate; therefore, a pitcher throwing away from the batter gives up a large strike-zone area. Drysdale contends, "Show me a guy who can't pitch inside and I'll show you a loser." It was from Sal "the Barber" Maglie that Drysdale learned to watch the batter's feet while throwing him a pitch low and outside. If the batter moved his front foot in that direction, then Drysdale would "jam him" by throwing a high inside fastball. "Then you're in mental charge of his at-bat."[34] Drysdale has probably been the only pitcher to give an intentional walk by throwing four pitches at the batter's (Frank Robinson's) head—knocking him down each time. "Batter" Moose Skowron shares Drys-dale's opinion that a pitcher has the right to establish his game by throwing at the batter. Skowron maintains further that Early Wynn is a Hall of Fame pitcher because he would have knocked down his own mother.

According to one player, Dizzy Dean would "come into the visiting club-house and threaten us. 'So and So, you been hitting me pretty good. You're gonna go on your *ass* today,' and he'd go out and do it and he'd throw the ball *hard.*"[35] Dean once knocked down nine out of ten consecutive hitters, skipping only the pitcher. He also once became infuriated when a batter "dug in" with his back foot—the ultimate disrespect shown to a pitcher. Dean asked the hitter whether he was done with his digging, and then told him to get a shovel for his subsequent "burial" at the plate.

More recently, Dock Ellis decided to load the bases by hitting the first three Cincinnati Red batters. Ellis did not want to hit Pete Rose because he knew Rose would take it too well. Nonetheless, he changed his mind and hit Rose in the side.

Pete Rose's response was even more devastating than Dock had anticipated. He smiled. Then he picked the ball up, where it had fallen beside him and gently, underhand, tossed it back to Dock. Then he lit for first as if trying out for the Olympics.

As Dock says with huge approval, "You have to be good, to be a hot dog."[36]

Goose Gossage received a similar response from Thurman Munson when he hit Munson with a 100-mph fastball and Munson grinned. Gossage remembers, "Christ, [Munson's] tough . . . Later in the clubhouse, I got a note from him, 'I took your best fucking shot, you cockroach.' "[37]

Most players are not so self-controlled as Rose and Munson. In 1987 there were 14 bench-clearing brawls before the most publicized one of them all occurred on July 7, when Andre Dawson of the Cubs hit a home run against the Padres' Eric Show. Dawson was on a tear: This hit meant four home runs, two doubles, and nine runs batted in his previous ten at-bats. The next time at bat, Dawson was hit in the face with a Show pitch. Cubs pitcher Rick Sutcliffe and other Cubs players expressed their feelings about the situation by fighting with Show and other Padres. Dawson received 24 stitches and an apology from Show, who said that he had not intentionally thrown at the hitter. Dawson responded to the apology, "[Show] said in his statement that he would regret it the rest of his life. If I have anything to do with it, I'll make sure he does."[38] Show was not penalized for the incident.

OFF-FIELD PRESSURES AND PROBLEMS

Traveling

Road trips seem to be punctuated with three common pressures: (1) lack of privacy; (2) boredom and loneliness; and (3) proximity to bars and female companionship. The first pressure is probably the worst. Reggie Jackson laments, "Being a star's a fake world, man. Hell, I can't even conduct a decent relationship with a woman."[39]

Players wanting to maintain their privacy on the road confine themselves to rather dull places like the hotel room, the newspaper stand, or a shopping mall. Thus enters the second pressure: boredom and loneliness.[40] Some players are concerned that they are never home to help with child-raising functions.[41] Others are happy with this circumstance. "Some don't have families, some have families they don't care too much about, some care but also prize the 'freedom' being away from home represents.' "[42] Lonely players and those seeking to break out of a dull pattern are constantly confronted with the option of the third-named pressure: bars and women. Player drinking is discussed in detail later on. Yet, consider for a moment here the legendary player-drinker, Babe Ruth. Ruth would enter a bar on a sweaty summer day and ask for a Tom Collins with two fistfuls of ice chunks and so much gin in it that the other bar patrons would laugh.

In one shot, [Ruth] swallowed the drink, the orange slice and the rest of the garbage, and the ice chunks. He stopped for nothing. There is not a single man I have ever seen in a saloon who does not bring his teeth together a little bit and stop those ice chunks from going in. A man has to have a pipe the size of a trombone to take ice in one shot. But I saw Ruth do it, and whenever somebody tells me how the Babe used to drink and eat when he was playing ball, I believe every word of it.[43]

"Hitting the trail" is the way Jimmy Bouton would describe seeking women while on the road. According to Bouton's wife, he was a participant as well as recorder of this diversion. Rod Carew has indicated, "I won't tell you that I haven't gone out when I've been on the road. I would be lying. The fact that I have has been the source of more friction in our marriage than almost anything else."[44] Willie Davis left the game because of domestic difficulties. The Saint Louis Cardinals then placed Davis on the disqualified list for the remainder of the season—thereby avoiding salary obligations to him. Davis, however, liked this turn of events because his ex-wife's lawyers could not garnishee a nonexistent salary, and he figured that if she wanted the money she could play baseball in his place.

One of the more unusual domestic alterations involving players was the Kekich–Peterson "family exchange" incident of 1973. Fritz Peterson and Mike Kekich both pitched on the Yankees. Mrs. Kekich and her two children moved in with Peterson, while Mrs. Peterson and her two children joined Kekich. Mrs. Kekich explained the situation: "We were all attracted to each other and we fell in love. . . . We didn't do anything sneaky or lecherous. . . . There isn't anything smutty about this."[45] The other Yankee players appeared relatively unconcerned about their teammates' activities, particularly since Kekich and Peterson seemed to have no difficulties with the situation. Lindy McDaniel was maybe the only player who publicly expressed any concern. Yet even he added, "If I took the position that I'd play only with the players who agree with my moral standards, I wouldn't play."[46]

Commissioner Kuhn, however, was most concerned about the incident when he finally made a public announcement two weeks later. Kuhn described the event as "appalling, regrettable and deplorable." He never did take any action on it, but he felt that it hurt the game's image and that "it's the commissioner's role to try to protect the image and honesty of the game. This does not help the image of the game."[47]

Team Tensions Off the Playing Field

A warm attitude toward teammates is not a prerequisite for success in baseball. Johnny Evers and Joe Tinker formed baseball's most celebrated second-base combination, yet they did not get along at all.[48] Sam Crawford played the outfield next to Ty Cobb, and they rarely said more than "I got it" to each other. In fact, Cobb almost prided himself on not being able to get along with teammates. "Every man, from the minors on up, is not only fighting against the other side, he's trying to hold on to his own job against those on his own bench who'd love to take it away. Why deny this? Why minimize it? Why not boldly admit it?"[49] Some teams like the Chicago White Sox in 1919 and the Oakland A's of the 1970s played very well with a lot of dissension within the ranks.

Yet team dissension has also been known to result in game losses, disciplinary action against players, and team roster changes. There are many sources of such tension. For example, Reggie Jackson claimed that Billy North provoked a fight when he called Jackson a "fucking faggot" for allegedly moving in on his girlfriend. Ed Kranepool recalls in *After the Miracle* that he went "crazy" after hearing that Tom Seaver took a couple of his dollars without his permission for a team collection.

I thought about it for a long time, but I never apologized. Here's a guy, the best pitcher of his time, a guy who is going into the Hall of Fame, and I blew any chance of ever being close to him by something this small. We stayed away from each other after that. I look back at it now with a little more maturity. I can see the reason. I was jealous of him; that's all it was. I wanted to be the best in the game at my position; I wasn't. He just made it look so easy, was so good—and it just frustrated me so much. I wasn't blowing up because he went into my pants pocket. I was blowing up because I wasn't as good at my job as he was at his.

Although these and other tensions spring from unique circumstances, many team dissensions can be grouped into three categories: (1) application of player humor; (2) team arguments over player performance; and (3) sociodemographic differences.

Application of Player Humor

A player's humor can provoke the ire of teammates since it so often represents a persistent combination of qualities that can only be described as childish, earthy, blunt, and sarcastic. In Sparky Lyle's autobiography, he tells his favorite joke played on Gene Michael, who was afraid of anything that moved—even an ant. Mel Stottlemyre and Fritz Peterson replaced the steel cup in Michael's jock pouch with a large bullfrog, and then snapped the pouch shut. Gene started getting dressed.

He put his shirt on, and son of a bitch he puts the jockstrap on, and then he pulls his pants up and his belt, and as he puts his cap on and gets ready to grab his glove and go out onto the field, the frog starts to kick. I swear to you, Gene looked down at his fly, and he screamed, 'Something just kicked my dick!' I don't know how he did it, but in one movement he jumped right out of his uniform. As his pants and jock lay on the floor, Gene was just walking around the clubhouse, looking at the jock.

Some players will go to great lengths with their earthy humor. Joe Pepitone—for example—put a piece of popcorn under his foreskin, and claimed to the team doctor that he had a new venereal disease. " 'Jesus Christ, Joe, what the hell have you done?' the doctor said. Pepitone didn't start laughing until the doctor had carefully used a forceps to liberate the popcorn."[50] Sparky Lyle was usually able to draw a lot of clubhouse laughs when he would remove his clothes and sit on birthday cakes.

This type of humor can grate on teammates, though, when it is directed at their personal lives. Reggie Jackson contends that players often rib each other about their wives' sexual habits.

Guys kid other guys about their wives, but some guys get angry if they're worried about their wives. Or if they've been screwing around, themselves. A guy will get to the clubhouse late and another guy will ask him what took him so long. The first guy will explain, "I had to wait until you left, so I could get into your wife."

And the second guy will laugh and say, "Jeez, thanks, if somebody didn't service her, I'd have had her on my back the rest of the home stand."[51]

Jackson did also mention something about a physical altercation that resulted when John "Blue Moon" Odom told teammate Rollie Fingers, "Hey, man, you better beat it back to the hotel. Your wife might be in bed with somebody by the time you get there, if you wait too long."[52]

Team Arguments over Player Performance

Players' critiquing of other player's performances is sometimes necessary, although telling a player when he is out of line or is not performing well is primarily the manager's responsiblity. Still, teammates can often help. Sometimes players use humor to get their point across, particularly if the point has to do with a player in a slump. Lyman Bostock actually appreciated the jokes from his teammates about his batting slump because he felt that the joking was intended to keep him "loose." Goose Gossage recalls when he first got to the Yankees he lost three games in a row. Outfielder Mickey

Rivers would throw himself across the hood of the car used to bring Gossage in from the bullpen, yelling, "Don't let him in the game." Another time, Rivers got into a three-point track stance with his rear toward Gossage— ready to chase down the ball.

This type of humor can also produce unproductive team tension. For example, a serious fight between Vida Blue and Blue Moon Odom occurred when Blue held his hands up to his neck—indicating "choke"—because Odom had a particularly rough game. In other cases it is difficult to determine whether a statement was supposed to be humorous or not. Catfish Hunter once said of Reggie Jackson, "He could be better if he'd just stop talking about what he's going to do and do it."[53]

One of the more serious team hassles in 1987 occurred between Darryl Strawberry and a couple of his Mets teammates. During spring training, Strawberry missed two straight practices, for which he received a $1,500 fine from his manager and several criticisms from his teammates. Wally Backman said that Strawberry needed to straighten up; and Lee Mazzilli let it be known that he, too, could not condone Strawberry's actions. When three months later Strawberry missed a game because of a low-grade fever, Lee Mazzilli and Wally Backman indicated that nobody gets sick 25 days a year, and that Strawberry had again let everybody down by his actions.

Strawberry countered both remarks with some of his own. "They rip me and they can't even hold my jock." He also threatened Backman, "I'll bust him in the face, that little redneck."[54] A ten-minute meeting was held behind the clubhouse door, to clear the air. Whether it did or not is uncertain; and whether or not Strawberry's performance was affected by his teammates' reaction is uncertain, too. But Strawberry became the Mets' cleanup hitter shortly after the incident, and hit .307 with 17 home runs and 46 runs batted in during his first 60 games in this position.

Strawberry became a definite team leader through the 1988 season, particularly when he rejoined the Mets for a night game after attending his wife during childbirth. Appearing in the game without having slept, he still managed to produce a home run—and respect from teammates like Bob Ojeda.

What was impressive about Darryl returning to Pittsburgh was that he did it for his teammates. . . . He could have stayed away, and it would have been totally understandable. But he felt it was imperative for him to be there with us in an important series.

None other than Wally Backman agrees: "By wanting to be out there every day and by busting his tail, he has shown everybody he is a leader. He has earned my respect."[55]

Sociodemographic Differences

A baseball team is subject to many diverse sociodemographic characteristics that can cause team tensions, disunity, and fights. Tom House, author
of the *Jock's Itch*, recalls his orientation to one sociodemographic characteristic. Team manager Andy Pafko, during his initial meeting with the
players,

stands up in his inimitable way and says, "I want all the California ballplayers on
that side of the clubhouse. Everybody else come over here with me." And he proceeds
to tell everyone else to "stay the fuck away" from California ballplayers because
they're weird and a detriment to baseball. California is the fucking land of fruits and
nuts, he says.

Race is the most obvious such characteristic and it forms the basis of
Chapter Seven. Race may have been an influence in fights among the Kansas
City Royals players during the 1988 season. Royals' second baseman Frank
White commented on this situation, "Why haven't we seen two whites fight,
or two blacks fight? It's always black–white. . . . I'm not saying we have a
racial problem, but I'm not sure it's just a coincidence either."[56] Players
from other countries may face extra problems caused by language and cultural
barriers. For Roger Moret, these problems led to an emotional breakdown
that found him one day standing naked—fixed at attention, and holding a
shower shoe in one hand—as he faced his new team, the Texas Rangers.
He had just compiled two impressive seasons (13–2 and 14–3) with the Red
Sox.

Age differences among players can also create problems, from two stand-
points. First, the veteran's job security is threatened by younger players.
Second, the age difference can be so great (in some cases, veterans being
old enough to be the fathers of their young teammates) that serious differences of opinion can arise in terms of social and even financial objectives
and behavior.

Reggie Jackson once heard a younger player bragging that he was about
to enter arbitration and would stand to make a lot of money for the next
season. Jackson asked the player what his "numbers" (hits and runs) were,
and the player did not know. Jackson then proceeded to lecture his young
teammate on the ways agents can cheat the player and on the types of
financial skills (structuring a bank loan, for example) that can be used in
negotiations. The younger player wanted out of this discussion and Jackson
said, "Hey man, don't listen to me. I'm just an old shit. I don't know nothing."
Later, when asked if he thought the player would listen to his advice, Jackson
spit through his teeth and replied, "I don't give a shit if he listens or not,
to be honest."[57]

ALCOHOL AND DRUG ABUSE

Sometimes, players use alcohol or drugs in response to all the pressures that they face. Maury Wills spent four years locked in his $500,000 house with blankets covering the windows. He was addicted to drugs. Wills said that his drug problems began after he was fired as manager of the Seattle Mariners in 1981. "There was depressions and disappointment. . . . All the people I let down. The embarrassment. . . . Some people get old but never grow up. That's what happened to Maury Wills."[58] Other players have offered various reasons for their introduction to alcohol and/or drug abuse: insecurity about playing (Sam McDowell); social requirements, like proving masculinity (Johnny Blanchard); struggling and loneliness (Darrel Porter); a lot of money and an emotional roller coaster of a season, including a troubled marriage (Keith Hernandez); desiring to forget the many demands on one's time (Willie Wilson); idle time due to an elbow injury (Dale Berra); trying to match one's previous best season (Dwight Gooden); and fear of life's being "dull" (Dennis Eckersley).

Yet this is not to suggest that alcohol and drugs are an almost natural reaction to baseball's pressures. As pitcher and acknowledged alcoholic Bob Welch points out, the stresses and strains of baseball are no better excuses for alcoholism than deadlines are for writers, and housekeeping and child-drearing are for mothers. "Can 10 percent of the population stand around and blame their occupations, when alcoholics reach into every possible job and income level in this country? . . . Alcoholics are great people for a denial, excuses. Bullshitting, really."[59] While the following sections on alcohol and drug abuse are baseball specific, no real attempt has been made to differentiate baseball from other workplace situations.

Alcohol

There are several differences between alcohol abuse and drug abuse in baseball. Alcohol has a longer history in the game. Legends as well as ordinary mortal players have apparently enjoyed their share of liquor, including Grover Cleveland Alexander, Rollie Hemsley, Sam McDowell, Babe Ruth, Mickey Mantle, Whitey Ford, Bobo Newsom, Mickey Cochrane, Jimmy Foxx, Don Newcombe, Rabbit Maranville, Bugs Raymond, Joe Page, Hank Thompson, Dick Allen, Paul Waner, and Hack Wilson (who allegedly always drank a quart of milk before the game to offset a quart of whiskey the night before). In his autobiography, *Crash*, Dick Allen recalls one day when he was playing third base and collided with Mickey Mantle who was trying for a triple. The umpire close on the play informed Allen and Mantle, when they were sprawled on the ground and the dust had settled, "I've never smelled so much booze in my life. . . . Get off your asses before you set each other on fire."

Because of this longer history, alcohol is more associated with the tradition of the game than drugs are. Beer is a principal TV sponsor and a big concession item in the ballpark. Players have drunk alcohol in the clubhouse after the game, and elsewhere later. The owner of the Cardinals used to have a policy of giving his players a free case of his own beer each week; and according to pitcher-alcoholic Ryne Duren, many times the traveling secretary will indicate that the drinks are "on him" if there is a plane delay. As a matter of fact, some managers and coaches drink more than their players, and—sometimes—view drinking as therapy.

One of their tricks to shake a club out of a slump is to say the curfew is off for that night and to go out and relax by raising a little hell. When we boarded the bus the next morning after one of those nights, one of our best players looked like he'd been on skid row for two or three weeks. He was in no shape to perform for two or three days. The writers were told he was sick.[60]

Willie Mays recalls that Leo Durocher often lent money to Dusty Rhodes for his drinking bouts, and Dusty always told Leo the truth about what time he got back—sometimes, 6 A.M. Sam McDowell said that the police on at least six occasions arrested him for drunken driving—only to give him coffee and a ride home when they realized he was a baseball player. So society in general—as well as managers—tends to condone the drinking players.

At a very minimum, this supportive sort of environment may have precluded any likelihood of active players publicly announcing their alcohol problem. Bob Welch and Darrel Porter were probably the first players ever to do so, in 1980.

And at a maximum, this supportive environment keeps players from perceiving their drinking as being serious enough to warrant treatment. Many times, their drunken behavior has to be extreme before players consider the implications. Don Newcombe returned home drunk one night only to find his wife intoxicated. He then started to beat her and put a pistol to her head and said he was going to kill her. "Fortunately, something told me, 'Don, you'd be foolish to do that.' "[61] Ryne Duren once passed out with a lit cigarette; his house was gutted by fire. Another time, Duren had to be coaxed off a bridge by Gil Hodges.

One day, Bob Welch put on an exhibition of bizarre behavior during pregame activities on the field. Welch started slobbering tobacco juice all over his uniform and wept that he was drunk. He attempted to catch a long flyball, but fell on his face. He then wandered toward home plate, where the opposing team was taking batting practice; cursed out a player on that team whom he did not know, "in the worst language you can imagine" and challenged him to fight. Teammate Rick Sutcliffe had to slap Welch across the face five times and shove him into left field to get him away from the encounter. Welch ended up in the clubhouse, telling manager Tommy Lasorda that "you wouldn't care if I got drunk if I could pitch. You just throw me out there to win for the team."[62]

Two of the differences between alcohol and drugs are related. Alcohol is legal; and disciplinary action is seldom taken against players who are drinking, because the just-cause requirements would make it mandatory to determine whether the player had "too much to drink." Drugs, on the other hand, are often illegal; mere possession may result in a criminal conviction and team discipline. The union has filed more grievances over alleged drug activity than over alcohol abuse. Therefore, the arbitrator plays a much larger role in this situation, as discussed below.

Drugs

Historical Overview with Two Case Studies

Reno Bertioa was probably the first publicized player to have taken drugs—tranquilizers—to help ease his nervous tension. In 1957 his batting average at the time of this disclosure was slightly under .400—a big improvement over his sub-.200 average the year before. A *Wall Street Journal* editorial wondered if future record books would look something like this: "Jones, Brooklyn, 1959: Played 30 games on Miltown, 20 on Equinol, 7 on Suavitil, and 40 on Thorazine."[63]

Marijuana was reportedly in use on some teams in the 1950s, and by the 1960s, some players were using "greenies"—an amphetamine-barbiturate combination that might give added energy or strength, particularly after a long night with little rest. This practice was publicized by Jim Bouton's 1970 book, *Ball Four*. Stars such as Reggie Jackson and Pete Rose have taken some form of this pill on occasion.

Commissioners Bowie Kuhn and Peter Ueberroth devised and implemented various drug abuse programs, with little success. This can be seen in a brief history of two players' drug involvements that have concerned one or both of the commissioners.

Steve Howe

—In 1982, Steve Howe, an All-Star pitcher for the Los Angeles Dodgers, and Rookie of the Year in 1980, spent five and a half weeks in a rehabilitation clinic, for cocaine abuse.

—In May 1983, he reentered treatment and returned to the active roster near the end of June. He was fined $53,867. Don Newcombe considered the fine to be proper: "Who does Steve Howe . . . think he is, that he can use illegal drugs, and nothing is supposed to happen to him?"[64]

—During July to December 1983 Howe was suspended (July 16) for being late to a game, and was reinstated a day later when he took a drug test. He was again suspended for the rest of the season after being late to a game and refusing to take a drug test on September 22. (He was 4–7 for the season, with 18 saves and a 1.44 ERA.) The MLBPA filed a grievance over this action, but withdrew it when Commissioner Kuhn transferred Howe from the suspended list so that Howe would receive service time for the benefits plan. Howe again tested positive the day after Thanksgiving and was ordered by the commissioner to sit out the 1984 season to rehabilitate himself.

—During the 1985 season, Howe was once fined for being late to a game, and missed another game in June. In 20 games, he was 1–1 with three saves and a 4.84 ERA. He was released by the Dodgers on July 3 and was signed by the Twins for $480,000 with another $270,000 in incentives and no drug testing requirement. The Twins' president commented, "Minnesotans are very forgiving people. . . . They like to root for underdogs, for people who have made mistakes and are trying to overcome them. That's one reason I gave him an opportunity."[65] The Twins' fans gave Howe much initial support. However, he was 2–5 in 13 games, with no saves and a 6.16 ERA. In September, Howe experienced a two-day alcohol/cocaine binge after appearing on a "Nightline" show focusing on drugs in baseball. Howe then met with Twins' president Harold Fox, apologized, and indicated that this situation could occur again. He was then released from the Twins' organization.

—In the 1986 season Howe joined a minor league team (the San Jose Bees), where he was suspended twice for testing positive for cocaine. For the first time Howe challenged the drug test, claiming that it was incorrect and that it reflected Commissioner Ueberroth's eagerness to eliminate him from the game. He did, however, acknowledge the second test's results in his autobiography. "Since the spring, Ueberroth had searched for evidence that I was still a dirtball. This time, the Commissioner didn't have to manufacture his proof. I handed it to him."

—In July 1987, the Texas Rangers signed Howe to a minor league contract (July 12) after reviewing documentation that he had been free of cocaine for 18 months. He was called up to the Rangers on August 6. However, the team was fined $250,000 by Commissioner Ueberroth, who maintained that players returning from drug rehabilitation should stay 60–90 days in the minors to make sure they have their problems under control before joining the majors.

—In January 1988 Howe was given an unconditional release from the Rangers because he failed to comply with his drug recovery program. More specifically, he tested positive for alcohol. Howe claimed that his having a drink at a bar should not have voided his two-year $1.2-million contract. But management contended that more than one incident and more than alcohol were involved. He pitched in Mexico during the 1988 season. In his book, *Between the Lines*, Howe assessed his drug-related baseball career in uncertain but not hopeless terms:

I've been severely wounded by drugs, but my health is good. I still have my family, and I have no criminal record of drug-related offenses. I've fallen down often, but thanks to all the loving people who didn't give up on me, I've been able to let God guide me in the right direction.

LaMarr Hoyt

—In February 1986 LaMarr Hoyt's previous accomplishments included the Cy Young award when he was with the White Sox (24–10 record) in 1983. After a 13–18 record in 1984, he was traded to the Padres where he pitched 16–8 in 1985 and

8–11 in 1986. On February 10, 1986, he pleaded no contest to being caught with Valium, Quaaludes, and marijuana. He was fined $620 but not arrested.

On February 18, Hoyt pleaded guilty to a public nuisance charge for possessing two marijuana cigarettes and a switchblade knife. He was placed on probation for three years.

—In October 1986, he pleaded guilty to two misdemeanor charges for possessing 500 pills of valium and propoxphene. Penalties included a 60-day jail sentence, commuted to five years' probation, a fine of $5,000, submission to regular drug testing, and forfeiture of his 1986 Porsche 944 Sports Turbo (valued at $33,000).

—From January to June 1987, the San Diego Padres—adhering to their team policy of no second chance for players with drug problems—fired Hoyt. They also sought to void Hoyt's individual player's contract with the team, contending that his actions violated the "good citizenship clause." Commissioner Ueberroth suspended Hoyt for one year—the 1987 season.

The MLBPA filed a grievance, and arbitrator George Nicolau upheld it with the following reasoning:

There is not a sliver of evidence that Hoyt used cocaine at any time during his major league career. . . . Nor is there any evidence that he sold, distributed or faciliated the distribution of drugs at any time. Neither is there evidence of recreational use of drugs.[66]

The arbitrator was apparently influenced by a psychiatrist's report that Hoyt's problems were in part due to a sleep disorder known as "intractable insomnia." Nicolau felt that this condition prompted Hoyt to seek sedatives. The arbitrator's remedy also supported Hoyt. Ueberroth's suspension was reduced from one year to 60 days. The Padres were also obligated to pay Hoyt $2.8 million on his remaining three-year contract.

Dallas Green of the Cubs was one of the few baseball executives to comment on the arbitrator's decision.

I read the Hoyt decision, and I'm still in a state of shock. . . . The surprising thing is that nobody has really said anything about it. It just came out like it was expected, and you don't hear baseball guys getting upset about it. . . . I used to have enough faith in ballplayers that they had the right character. . . . I just don't know anymore. In tough situations, it always looks like the player comes out scot-free. What LaMarr Hoyt did was illegal. I don't care what any damn do-good doctor said.[67]

Padres owner Joan Kroc said, "We may be forced to pay him, but we will not be forced to play him."[68]

—In July 1987 the Chicago White Sox hired Hoyt for the 1988 season for an estimated $1.1 million. Owner Jerry Reinsdorf reasoned, "We are satisfied that LaMarr's character is as good as it was when he was here."[69]

—In December 1987, Hoyt was arrested and charged with intent to distribute cocaine—the first time he had been associated with this drug.

—In January 1988 Hoyt was sentenced to one year in federal prison for violating his probation in the October 1986 drug case. He had tested positive for cocaine use three times in October 1987.

—In July 1988—after serving about four and a half months at the Allenwood Federal Prison Camp—Hoyt was transferred to a halfway house.

Both of these cases indicate that drug involvement can occur over and over again in one player's career, entailing complicated discipline considerations. Also, there is no one policy agreed on by all teams. Indeed, for every team seeking to rid itself of a drug-involved player, there seems to be another team likely to pick that individual up. Another complicating factor is that the commissioner's authority can be severely checked by an arbitrator—a situation further illustrated below.

Drugs and the Kuhn Administration

In 1971, Bowie Kuhn started what was probably the first formal drug program (the Drug Education and Prevention Program) in professional sports. Regional seminars were held to educate management officials in the identification and dangers of drug abuse. Players were not directly involved in these efforts. The program's major focus was on grievances. In 1978 the subject of alcohol abuse was added to the educational program, with Don Newcombe coordinating related efforts.

Kuhn first experienced the arbitrator's impact on this issue in 1980 when Ferguson Jenkins was arrested in Canada for possession of two ounces of marijuana, four grams of cocaine, and two grains of hashish. Jenkins refused to explain his awkward situation to Kuhn; therefore, he was suspended from playing, although he received his salary. The MLBPA filed a grievance; and arbitrator Raymond Goetz overturned Kuhn's suspension decision, for the following reasons:

1. Jenkins might have jeopardized his subsequent court case if he had answered Kuhn's questions.
2. Canadian authorities did not view Jenkins's offense as being so serious (he was found guilty but given no sentence).[70]

Jenkins did agree to donate $10,000 to a drug education and prevention program in Texas, as well as time for public service announcements.

Employee Assistance Programs (EAPs) for drug and alcohol abuse were suggested by Kuhn in 1980.

I asked the clubs to give consideration to establishing EAPs. In the ensuing months some did, but many did not. It was a common problem in baseball. Unless direct orders were issued, there were always clubs that would behave irresponsibly. It was the simple reality of living with these complex personalities. Whenever possible I tried to use persuasion to bring about my goals at the club level. When it worked it was a better approach than issuing orders.[71]

Kuhn changed his approach in 1981. He and the league presidents established a policy that mandated severe discipline for involvement with dangerous drugs or trafficking in any kind of illegal drugs. This action would not be taken against players who came forward voluntarily for treatment. Over his remaining years as commissioner, Kuhn had more than one opportunity to consider—if not apply—these penalties.

San Diego Padres player Alan Wiggins was arrested in 1982 for possessing cocaine. Kuhn suspended Wiggins for 30 days without pay. Two years later, however, the commissioner learned that Wiggins had continued to receive his pay while on suspension. Kuhn then fined the team $50,000.

In 1983, four players of the Kansas City Royals—Willie Wilson, Willie Aikens, Jerry Martin, and Vida Blue—pleaded guilty to a charge of attempting to possess cocaine. The four players received a $5,000 fine each and three-month prison sentences—the first time any player had received a prison sentence for drug violations. Kuhn suspended them for the 1984 season, subject to review on May 15, 1984. Jerry Martin's lawyer thought that Kuhn's penalty was continuing to apply an uneven standard to the drug problem and that it failed to take into consideration the heavy price the players had paid with their prison sentences. The MLBPA filed a grievance; and arbitrator Raymond Block found that the players' use of cocaine and their criminal convictions—and the resulting negative publicity on baseball—justified discipline. However, he considered the penalty to be excessive and ordered the players reinstated on May 15. This decision directly pertained only to Wilson and Martin, but Kuhn applied it to Aikens, as well. Vida Blue also challenged his suspension for the 1984 season; however, arbitrator Block upheld Kuhn's decision.

He [Blue] was far more than a mere passive user or a possessor. He was vigorously involved in continuous, heavy use of cocaine. He served as an active connection between other ballplayers who were, or became, users and their supplier, Mark Liebl. He placed himself between the players and the distributor as a liaison, even to the extent of ordering cocaine from the clubhouse.[72]

Pascual Perez was the next player to be jailed (in the Dominican Republic) for cocaine involvement. He waited approximately three months in prison before being fined $400. Bowie Kuhn issued a one-month suspension and a year's probation to Perez for his drug involvement and his failure to cooperate with the commissioner's office in the related investigation. According to Kuhn, Perez had not conformed to the "high standard of personal conduct" required by the Uniform Player Contract. Arbitrator Block eliminated both penalties, citing lack of evidence that Perez was involved with cocaine. The arbitrator further held that the court proceeding had been so flawed that Perez's conviction should be given no weight in the suspension consideration. Kuhn called arbitrator's decision "inexplicable, indefensible and highly destructive of baseball's efforts to deal with its serious drug problem."[73]

Also during 1984, the MLBPA, owners, and players devised a joint plan regarding cocaine use. A player could ask for help with no fear of penalty, or a team could suggest that a player should seek help. Conflicts would be resolved through a three-member panel of experts to determine whether the player had a chemical dependency problem. Any player obtaining treatment would be paid full salary for 30 days, half salary for the next 30 days, and the player salary minimum if the team agreed to continue the treatment beyond 60 days.

A player who voluntarily seeks help would receive no discipline for the first offense, but would be subject to discipline for repeated offenses. The commissioner could also discipline a player convicted of a drug charge (one year suspension without pay, or permanent ineligibility) or a player who had used or possessed a controlled substance on the stadium's premises (one year suspension without pay).

The program did not cover alcohol or drugs other than cocaine. It also did not include what the owners wanted: mandatory and random drug testing.

Drugs and the Ueberroth Administration

Peter Ueberroth made removing drugs from baseball a major priority when he replaced Bowie Kuhn. The new commissioner figured that drugs were no more prevalent in baseball than in any other organization, but he felt that professional baseball had an added responsibility to remove the problem because of its high visibility. When asked how drugs could be eliminated, Ueberroth responded, "It's built on trust and players helping players. It's not grandstanding."

The commissioner then announced a mandatory drug-testing program for all baseball personnel (Ueberroth's office staff, the owners, the managers, the coaches, and union league personnel)—except the major league ball players. Just prior to this announcement, Alan Wiggins had been suspended by the Padres and then traded because of a cocaine addiction relapse. Don Fehr, president of the MLBPA, described Ueberroth's surprising move as "grandstanding," and added, "We already have a joint drug program and it's working. . . . We've always felt that mandatory testing was demeaning."[74] Fehr also noted that the "handful" of players who had appeared before the joint review council had almost all been relapse cases. In his opinion, the drug problem was not growing in baseball.

Publicity over players using illegal drugs intensified in September 1985, however, when a Pittsburgh grand jury investigated an accusation that one Curtis Strong was supplying baseball players with cocaine. Many players testified to their own or others' involvement. Keith Hernandez admitted that he had used the drug from 1980 to 1983 and had played a game under its influence. Other cocaine-use revelations included: Enos Cabell, "off and on" from 1978 to 1984; Dave Parker, from 1976 to 1982, purchasing the drug from Strong; Dale Berra, who also claimed he had obtained amphetamines from Willie Stargell and Bill Madlock (Berra recanted under cross examination); Jeff Leonard, buying cocaine from Cabell; Lonnie Smith, from Strong; and so forth.

The trial generated some controversy after Strong was found guilty on 11 of 14 counts. Some legal observers felt that granting immunity to the players for their testimony against Strong violated the traditional notion that you immunize Mr. Little to get at Mr. Big. Writer Pete Axthelm—for example—contended, "You immunize a John Dean to get a Richard Nixon, not the other way around."[75]

Billy Martin agreed that too much immunity was given to the players: "I hate stool pigeons, and these guys are copping on their own pals." Regarding the only Yankee player in the trial—Dale Berra, son of Yogi Berra—Martin commented,

I told Yogi two years ago about that kid of his. Although I wasn't managing then, I had friends in Pittsburgh who told me things.

I told Yogi I was telling him this about his boy because if I had a son I'd expect him as my friend, to be giving me any information a father needed to know. Yogi said he'd check it out.[76]

Ken Moffett, former president of the MLBPA, said that the decision would not alter professional baseball's basic approach toward drug-using players.

Greed stops the owners from really going after the drug problem in the game. They still want to win, and they will overlook a player's drug problems if they think it will help them win. . . . The use of [amphetamines] is so rampant [that] if you penalized people using pills, you would have to suspend entire teams in some cases.

People in the game know who the drug users are, but the owners do not really do anything about it because of greed and because the Players Association does not want to deal with the problem.

There are plenty of big-time players with drug problems whose names have not yet come to the surface. This thing is a lot more widespread than in Pittsburgh. . . . There is a lot more to the problem than the public knows. Baseball has covered it up. And nothing will change unless the owners and the players really work together to bring it to an end.[77]

Baseball fans were not moved either way by the trial, although fan magazines such as *Sports Illustrated* editorialized that something had to be done about drugs and baseball since "the integrity of the game is at stake." Ueberroth gave to seven players who were implicated in the trial (Keith Hernandez, Jeffrey Leonard, Dale Berra, Lonnie Smith, Joaquin Andujar, Enos Cabell, and Dave Parker) the choice of a year's suspension or a 10 percent donation of 1986 base salary to drug prevention programs, plus submission to random drug testing throughout their careers and 100 hours of community service. All the players chose the second option. Ueberroth also assigned lesser penalties (5 percent of their 1986 salary and 50 hours of community service) to four players (Al Holland, Lee Lacey, Larry Sorensen, and Claudell Washington). Dave Parker was sued by the Pittsburgh Pirates, to keep from paying $5.3 million in deferred payments on his five year contract negotiated in 1979. The Pirates contended that Parker's fraudulent refusal to disclose cocaine use during the playing season legally cancelled the team's financial obligation to him. Parker's lawyers countered that the team was aware of the player's problem and chose to ignore it. An out-of-court settlement was reached whereby the Pirates paid Parker nearly $2.65 million, or half the disputed amount.

Ueberroth used the Pittsburgh trial as a rationale for sending a personal letter directly to every major league player, urging each of them to submit voluntarily to drug tests in 1986. He said that the three tests would be "totally confidential" and free of any penalties. Any player testing positive would be offered medical treatment and counseling. Don Fehr urged the players to throw the letters in the trash because the commissioner had no legal right to bypass the union. Fehr wanted management to make a specific proposal which would in turn be considered by the union in a collective bargaining sense. In making his complaint, Fehr also recalled his first meeting with Ueberroth after Ueberroth had announced the plan.

They asked us if we'd agree to testing, even if it was just for the sake of public relations.
We asked a number of questions such as, "What kind of tests?" They didn't know. We asked, "Who would give it?" They said they didn't know. We asked what accuracy figures they could give and they couldn't know that because they didn't know what kind of tests they'd be giving.
They said they'd let us know, and the next thing was them cancelling the Joint Drug Agreement [the previous management-union plan, without mandatory testing] before the third game of the World Series so they could generate the most publicity.[78]

Most players had no objection to testing but thought the matter should be handled by the MLBPA. Don Baylor—the American League player representative—explained,

The barrier goes right back up. . . . If you're going to get the players to do something, you have to go to the union first. I don't think the commissioner realizes how far he got set back. A lot of players had been in his corner. Whether true or not, they thought he had something to do with settling the strike. He already had some votes for President of the United States.[79]

Ueberroth eventually agreed with Fehr and Baylor, and indicated that he had made a mistake in attempting to force a drug program on the MLBPA.[80]

In October 1985 the owners voted unanimously to end the one and a half year old agreement—started under Kuhn's regime—between management and the union over drug enforcement. The owners contended that mandatory drug testing would have been necessary to make the plan effective.

In 1986 the Baltimore Orioles instituted the first voluntary drug-testing program. Fehr did not object to this because the program was not a condition of employment and therefore not subject to collective bargaining. Fehr was more concerned about management's practice of inserting drug-testing clauses into several hundred standard player's contracts. However, arbitrator Tom Roberts determined that those provisions were unenforceable: management must negotiate the drug-testing issue with the MLBPA. Under the labor (Basic) agreement between players and owners, only benefits could be added to the standard players' contract; and the arbitrator disagreed with management that drug testing was a benefit.[81]

The current labor-management position on drug testing and related issues is indefinite. Commissioner Ueberroth described management's current policy thus:

We have a player who has a problem, our pattern is to do exactly as follows: First time, cooperative player, we take him out of the game and we let the medical people decide when he comes back. We don't decide, the union doesn't decide, we don't argue about it because we all have the same ambition. We don't let the coaches and the managers decide, either; that's another problem because they want to get the player back on the field. We hold the medical institution, wherever the person has gone, with responsibility to make the very best effort—because recovery rates are not very good in drugs—the very best chance that the individual has to lead a normal life, to be recovered. And then we test them the rest of their career, two times a week, sometimes three times a week. We don't abandon the player, and that's why today the record is incredible.[82]

Management has also reserved the right to enforce a range of disciplinary sanctions if a particular player commits additional drug-related offenses. However, there is no formal drug program testing agreement with the union, which reserves the right to grieve any aspects of this issue—depending on the particular circumstances involved.

The future of drug testing in baseball will likely be influenced by two considerations: (1) the extent to which the player's role model responsibilities are agreed to exceed their individual rights; and (2) whether any other method comes along that is effective in identifying a drug problem. As regards the first consideration, some observers see no conflict at all with the rights of individuals. Note the comments of Dallas Green and Whitey Herzog;

Green: All they have to do is go in a bottle. The union dictates they don't have to do it, but this goes beyond the union. . . . I feel very strongly about this. Don't they owe it to their families? No matter how you shape it, they owe it to the public, their families and the Man upstairs who gave them all this talent. What is there to being a role model?

Herzog: It's a sorry situation when the players say that it's humiliating to take a drug test. If I was a ball player, I'd be the first one to use the bottle. I don't want them thinking that, because I struck out four times, I'm messed up. If an owner gives a player a guaranteed contract for three years or four years or whatever, he sure ought to be able to get him to urinate into a bottle any time he wants him to. Who's guaranteeing that money? The owner is the only guy today taking the risks.[83]

On the other hand, there are some players who take exception to being treated differently from most other employees—assumed guilty until they prove themselves innocent. One of their arguments is that the higher standard is not justified since baseball players—unlike police, fire fighters, and pilots—are not responsible for public safety. Writer Peter Richmond notes that the media and fans inflate athletes like Dwight Gooden . . . "100 times the size of what they are—and then, when they prove human, we treat it as a sin of hundredfold proportions."[84] Willie Wilson probably spoke for many players when he said that he accepted being a public role model on the field but that his off-field role model responsibilities were limited to his own children.

The second consideration has to do with finding a substitute for drug testing. Many players and managers alike declare that they are unable to recognize drug problems because they are not familiar with the physical and behavioral indicators. For example, many Mets players—including Keith Hernandez—were shocked to learn that Dwight Gooden admitted using cocaine on the eve of the 1987 baseball season. The recognition problem is further accentuated by Gooden's denial after the 1986 season: "Beer is what I drink and not much of that. . . . Wine makes me sick. Drugs? No, I never use them and I never will."[85]

The different management attitudes toward handling drug-involved players include a reluctance on the part of some to confront the player about the situation. This may also be true for alcohol abuse.

People don't like to talk about alcoholism. They will laugh about the person who passes out at the party, and they will cry about the person who swerves into oncoming traffic or destroys a marriage, but between, too often, there is silence.[86]

Occasionally, an official will even prefer to trade his team's problem to another team, rather than expose and resolve it.

Part Three

Remaining Player-Management Issues

Seven

The Race and Ethnic Issue

Professional baseball has had two opposing traditions of discriminating against minorities and yet also furthering equal employment opportunity. Its biased background was never a collective bargaining issue, since serious collective bargaining efforts were not really taking place until recently.

Minority players' advancement occurred only slowly but did start before the Civil Rights Act was passed in 1964. Title VII of this act mandated equal employment opportunity, or representation of minorities at all organizational levels. By that time baseball was probably more integrated than any other major organization in the United States—having a larger proportion of minority professional employees (players) than related proportions found in other U.S. firms.

The presence of minority players can reflect social progress while at the same time creating a potential for uncontrollable factions within the MLBPA—a situation that could dissolve collective bargaining unity. The MLBPA must minimize this situation by stressing racial equality and/or convincing minority players that negotiated labor-agreement provisions prevent employment discrimination.

Ray Burris maintains that, although the MLBPA is "supportive" of affirmative action, it seldom—if ever—becomes directly involved with related efforts, on grounds that this area is management's responsibility. There are only two labor-agreement provision that pertain to racial equality. Article XIV-A states: "The provisions of this Agreement shall be applied to all players covered by this Agreement without regard to race, color, religion or national origin." Article XIV-C provides that labor agreements be printed in Spanish for Spanish-speaking players. Yet other labor agreement provisions such as minimum salary, free agency, and salary arbitration—when coupled with management's personnel decisions—may contribute to nondiscriminatory labor practice, as well.

Baseball's discriminatory tradition before and during Jackie Robinson's playing days is discussed here first, and then contemporary attitudes toward minority players and managers are examined. The final section pertains to a most controversial player-management issue: Are black and hispanic players discriminated against today?

BEFORE AND DURING JACKIE ROBINSON

The Situation before Robinson

Babe Ruth received racial abuse decades before Jackie Robinson became the first contemporary black player. People thought Ruth's features (lips and nose) resembled many blacks. He was called "nigger" so often that people thought that he was part black and had managed to cross the color line.[1] Ty Cobb once refused to share a hunting cabin with Ruth stating, "I've never bedded down with a nigger and I'm not going to start now."[2]

There were always other white players who carried the potential for discrimination and abuse along ethnic lines. For example, Tony Lazzeri, a 12-year infielder for the New York Yankees, was nicknamed "The Wop." Hall of Famer Hank Greenberg endured ethnic slurs from both players and media. One newspaper account stressed that this "Jewish boy . . . made good without going into the ready-to-wear line [because he had] little suggestion of the Jewish characteristics in his appearance, the nose being straight."[3]

Greenberg once got into a half-hour fight with teammate Rip Sewell because of ethnic insults. He thought Sewell had called him "bush," or minor league player. Sewell recounted Greenberg saying,

"Who you calling a bush, you Southern son of a bitch?" Well, you know that's fightin' words in my part of the country. Son of a bitch is bad enough, but Southern son of a bitch, that was the kicker. So I said, "You, you big Jew son of a bitch, if it fits you."

He said, "I'm gonna take your ass on when we get to Lakeland."[4]

As for his unsuccessful attempt to beat Babe Ruth's home run record, however, Greenberg did indicate, that it was not due to anti-Semitism on the part of opposing players. "So far as I could tell, the players were most rooting for me, aside from the pitchers. I remember one game Bill Dickey was catching for the Yankees, he was even telling me what was coming up. The reason I didn't hit 60 or 61 homers is because I ran out of gas; it had nothing to do with being Jewish."[5]

There were black baseball players in the 1880s.[6] However, by 1901, professional baseball was segregated. Blacks were pushed off white teams and forced to form their own leagues, such as the Negro National League. One black standout, James "Cool Papa" Bell, indicated that white management would not subsequently sign other black players even if they were good.

There were never any explicit discriminatory policies against black players. Commissioner Landis stated, "There is no rule, formal or informal, or any understanding—unwritten, subterranean, or sub-anything against the hiring of Negro players by the teams of organized ball."[7] However, the unwritten law was powerful enough. Columnist Westbrook Pegler wrote in 1931 that he was amazed at never having received even one letter commenting about racial segregation in baseball. This might explain baseball management's inaction. One former umpire noted that Landis "had convenient hiding places for his ideals. If the populace was not looking, he had little compunction about defending the underdog, but if the spotlight were turned on in full focus, he would defend anyone to the last camera."[8]

A poll taken in the late 1920s found that four-fifths of the National League players and managers had no objection to integration. Also southern and northern players regularly competed in interracial post-season games. Yet few—if any—owners pressed for black players, possibly using one or more of the following lame excuses:

(1) About a third of all major-league players were Southerners and they would not play with or against Negroes; (2) Negroes could not travel with a big-league club, because hotels would not accommodate them; (3) the clubs trained in the South, where Negroes and whites were forbidden by law to play together; (4) fans might riot in the stands if there was trouble on the field between a white and Negro player; (5) Negroes were not good enough to play in the big leagues anyway.[9]

Perhaps the most serious reason for not hiring blacks in baseball was the fear that white fans in northern states would not come to the ballpark. This rationale was rendered absurd and should have been overturned during World War II, with the tremendous migration of southern blacks to the north for employment.

For instance, in 1944 Bill Veeck—anticipating a large market of black fans—attempted to buy the Philadelphia Phillies and stock the team with black players. Yet when Veeck informed Landis of his intentions, the team was quickly sold to another buyer at a price far lower than Veeck had anticipated paying. Four years later, Veeck owned the Cleveland Indians; he hired the legendary black pitcher Satchel Paige, who drew 201,829 cash customers for his first three starts.

Branch Rickey of the Dodgers was more successful in placing a black player on his team. He thoroughly distrusted other club owners, believing that they would prevent his hiring efforts. He also believed that his baseball scouts were biased against blacks. Therefore, he informed his employees that they were to be low-keyed and find the best players possible for an "all-Negro" team. In reality, Rickey was looking for a carefully selected black player to be placed on the Brooklyn Dodgers.

Rickey's research turned up Jackie Robinson—a man who was evaluated as being both a superior athlete and an outspoken individual. Rickey was not discouraged by this latter quality. Indeed, he seemed to be impressed with reports of a court-martial trial that Robinson had experienced in the army. The prosecution unsuccessfully attempted to establish that Robinson was guilty of insubordination and conduct unbecoming an officer because he refused lawful orders of a superior officer who insisted that he move to the back of a bus.

Rickey held a three-hour interview with the ballplayer before hiring Robinson, to determine if he had the necessary interpersonal qualities to integrate baseball. Rickey indicated that few people were going to help Robinson and that there would be endless attempts to agitate him. A player might—say—purposefully collide with Robinson or slash him with his spikes, and then grin and say, "How do you like that, nigger boy?" Having to listen to these emotional scenarios made Robinson quite angry, and he asked Rickey, "Do you want a ballplayer who's afraid to fight back?" To which Rickey shouted in response, "I want a ballplayer with guts enough not to fight back."[10]

Robinson's Playing Days

The hiring announcement in 1947 was greeted with some skepticism and anger. A. B. "Happy" Chandler was baseball commissioner at the time. His behavior then and now illustrates discrimination's convoluted, multifaceted nature. Frank Robinson notes in his autobiography, *Extra Innings*, that Chandler was even more responsible than Rickey for bringing Jackie Robinson into the game. Commissioner Chandler ruled for Rickey and against the 15 other owners, who did not want baseball integrated with Robinson. This ruling cost Chandler his job as commissioner.

Yet, some 41 years later Chandler commented, "You know Zimbabwe's all nigger now. There aren't any whites." He defended his statements with past and present actions he took with blacks. He also noted that his remarks were due to his hometown upbringing. "There were 400 whites and 400 blacks. We called them niggers and they didn't mind. We loved each other."[11]

Satchel Paige was hurt by the decision to hire Robinson, since Paige thought of himself as the first black player to call for integration and draw white fans into the park. Other players in the Negro leagues felt that there were better players than Robinson—a feeling probably shared by Bob Feller, who said that Robinson lacked some physical qualities necessary for outstanding performance. Rogers Hornsby predicted that Rickey's racial integration attempt would not "work out. . . . A mixed baseball team differs from other sports because ball players on the road live much closer together. It's going to be more difficult for the Negro player to adjust himself to the life of a major league club, than for the white players to accept him."[12]

Dixie Walker—the National League's batting champion, and favorite of the Brooklyn fans—indicated, "As long as he's not with the Dodgers I'm not worried."[13] When it turned out that Robinson was in fact playing on the Dodger team, Walker was influential in circulating a petition indicating that the team would not play if Robinson were included. Many players did not wish to get involved with this, for a variety of reasons. Leo Durocher called a team meeting and obscenely told the team what they could do if they conducted the strike. He also reasoned that Robinson was a fine player who would put money in their pockets, and that many more black players would be hired, and would take their jobs from them if they did not produce.

Another much more personal rationale came from Hall of Famer Billy Herman. Recently, his young daughter had become suddenly and seriously ill. Herman, who was new to the town, called a doctor and then took his daughter to the doctor's office. The doctor—who was black—cured his daughter. Herman related this story to a player who wanted him to sign the petition against Robinson. The player said that he himself would have stayed away from the black doctor. "I told him I thought he was a goddamn fool, and then I told him what he could do with his petition. Here's a guy asking me not to play ball with a man because he's black—after I'd just told him that without any doubts or hesitations I'd entrusted my daughter's health to a black man!"[14]

Branch Rickey investigated the petition and found Bobby Bragan, Cookie LaVagetto, and Carl Furillo involved. Rickey convinced Bragan not to place any stumbling blocks in Robinson's way—at least—and was pleased that Pee Wee Reese was neutral and that Gil Hodges would not sign the petition. Rickey did not even talk with Furillo because "I regarded him as a man in whom talk could arouse no moral dilemma because he had no basic moral concept of his own. I would almost wager that today Furillo will argue as rabidly in Robinson's behalf as he was arguing against Robinson in those days."[15]

When this challenge was finally defused, the Dodgers with Jackie Robinson then faced another; the racist taunting of the Philadelphia Phillies and manager Ben Chapman—who cited every slur in the book, from thick lips to restricted brain growth and animalistic behavior. Chapman also speculated on the repulsive sores and diseases that Robinson's teammates were going to get if they touched the combs or towels that he used. Other insults focused on his baseball capabilities—with Chapman yelling at Robinson, "If you were a white boy, you'd have been shipped down to Newport News long ago!"[16]

Chapman received widespread and severe criticism for his remarks. He countered that this type of "bench jockeying" (verbally rattling the opposing player) is common. He noted that he and other players had received ethnic insults and that Jackie Robinson should not be patronized with different treatment. Many Dodger players came to Robinson's defense, however, because of the intensity of the remarks and the fact that Robinson was under strict orders not to respond.

Robinson particularly appreciated the response of his teammate Eddie Stanky, who—after three days of the insults—yelled back at the Phillies, "Listen you yellow-bellied cowards why don't you yell at somebody who can answer back?"[17] Yet Stanky also agreed with Chapman that some racial/ethnic insults are just part of the game. In 1954, Stanky was with the Saint Louis Cardinals' organization; he was asked by a reporter if the Cardinals were race-baiting Robinson. Stanky replied that he had only heard "nigger" and "black bastard"—phrases that "are not out of line."[18]

Shortly after the Philadelphia incident, a rumor developed that the Saint Louis Cardinals had agreed to strike if Robinson were going to play against them. The strike vote was later categorically denied by a Cardinals player, Stan Musial. However, the situation did galvanize the National League president, Ford Frick, to impose baseball's first written policy concerning black players. His message to the Cardinals stated:

If you do this you will be suspended from the league. You will find that the friends you think you have in the press box will not support you, that you will be outcasts. I do not care if half the league strikes. Those who do it will encounter quick retribution. They will be suspended, and I don't care if it wrecks the National League for five years. This is the United States of America, and one citizen has as much right to play as another. The National League will go down the line with Robinson whatever the consequence.[19]

The Cardinals did not strike. However, the racial heckling continued—a situation that seemed to unify the Dodger team with Robinson. Pee Wee Reese was perhaps the player most responsible for this eventual integration. At the end of the season, even Dixie Walker publicly announced his respect for Robinson's performance and Rookie of the Year award.

Players around the league were aware of Robinson's intensity. Leo Durocher reflected, "This guy didn't just come to play. He came to beat ya. He came to stuff the goddamn bat right up your ass."[20] In 1949 Rickey told Robinson he was now on his own as a Dodger—free to say whatever he wanted. And so, Robinson then directed at least part of his considerable verbal energies toward heckling umpires and players. Roger Kahn transcribed Robinson's loud conversation with his pitching teammate Ralph Branca when Branca walked a player:

[Ball one] "Oh, no. Ball shit. Don't worry. Bear down, Ralph. Where was it? Where was the pitch? Goddamnit, ump, do the best you can. Don't let him bother you

Ralph. Bear down. [Ball two] Good pitch. Goddamn good pitch. Where you looking, ump? Stay in the game. Bear down, Ralph. Don't mind him. [Foul ball] There's one he didn't blow. Bear down. [Ball three] Oh no; oh, shit. Where was it? Where the hell was it?" He trotted to the mound, said something to Ralph Branca and walked slowly back to second base. "Play ball," the plate umpire shouted. " What?" Robinson was moving to his normal fielding depth. "Wait'll I'm back. Don't mind him, Ralph. He can't hurt us. We already *know* where he stands. Attaboy. Good pitch. [Ball four] Hey, ump, what the fuck you trying to do?"[21]

Duke Snider recalls an incident where Robinson at bat shouted "terrible obscenities" at Sam Jones, the pitcher—getting Jones so mad that he hit Robinson with a pitch. Robinson continued his heckling at first base and Jones threw the ball wildly, trying to pick him off. He ran all the way to third and scored when his heckling prompted Jones to throw a really wild pitch.

According to his wife, Robinson also used baseball as a forum where he could present his ideas concerning racial protest and equality.[22] Eddie Mathews suggests that in his latter playing years, Robinson stressed "race crap" over performance. Robinson would claim a pitcher knocked him down because he was black when he was really thrown at because he was a "helluva hitter."

Larry Doby, the next black player hired in the major leagues, encountered experiences similar to Robinson's. He recalled the racial taunts and bench-jockeying he received everywhere in the league.

I'd get the usual—"nigger," "coon," "shoeshine boy." I could understand from some fan or some jerk sitting on the bench. But I'd get it from managers, too. Like Casey [Stengel]. He'd call me jig-a-boo.

All game he'd be yelling, "Hey, jig-a-boo." But you'd mention this to the writers and they'd say, "No, not Casey."[23]

Few of Doby's white co-players would shake hands with him, and none would room with him. Doby eventually roomed with Satchel Paige, but this arrangement did not last long. Paige kept a loaded gun on the night table and informed Doby that he would shoot anything that moved in the room at night. Doby went back to staying by himself.

By 1949, there were seven black players on three teams. Jackie Robinson, Don Newcombe, and Roy Campanella on the Dodgers; Henry Thompson and Monte Irvin on the Giants; and Larry Doby and Satchel Paige on the Indians. The other 13 baseball teams remained segregated. The millionaire owners Yawkey of the Red Sox, Briggs of the Tigers, Busch of the Cardinals, Carpenter of the Phillies, and Wrigley of the Cubs were the last to bring black players to their teams. This situation also applied to the New York Yankees where general manager George Weiss allegedly once said, "I will never allow a black man to wear a Yankee uniform. . . . Boxholders from

Table 7.1
Offensive Player Yearly Leaders, 1957–1986

	NATIONAL LEAGUE			AMERICAN LEAGUE		
	Blacks/ Hispanics	Total	Percentage of Hispanics and Blacks	Blacks/ Hispanics	Total	Percentage of Hispanics and Blacks
Doubles	22	34	65	16	37	43
Triples	22	39	56	18	39	46
Home Runs	17	33	52	16	39	41
Batting Average	22	30	73	13	30	43
Stolen Bases	30	30	100	29	30	97
Runs Batted In	18	32	56	14	30	47
At Bats	20	30	67	9	30	30
Hits	20	34	59	19	30	63
Runs	20	33	61	14	31	45
	191	295	65	148	296	50

Note: Totals are sometimes higher than 30 because some years had more than one individual with the same leadership statistic.

Source: David S. Neft and Richard M. Cohen, *The Sports Encyclopedia: Baseball,* 7th ed. (New York: Sports Products, 1987), pp. 566–73.

Westchester don't want that sort of crowd. They would be offended to have to sit with niggers."[24] The Yankees did eventually bring a black player (Elston Howard) to the team in 1955; and the Boston Red Sox were the last team to hire a black (Pumpsie Green), in 1959.

At first, the National League made more progress with black players than the American League. For example, blacks in the National League received eight out of the ten Most Valuable Player awards in the 1950s. Yet black and Hispanic players eventually benefited both leagues in various performance categories. Consider—for example—the leaders in various offensive categories for the years 1957–86, as indicated in Table 7.1.[25] When all nine offensive-measure categories (batting average, at-bats, runs, hits, doubles, triples, home runs, runs batted in, and stolen bases) are considered, 65 percent of the leaders in the National League were Hispanic or black, along with 50 percent in the American League. These proportions are higher than the proportion of black and Hispanic players currently playing in the majors.

In 1964, Jackie Robinson reflected on the more qualitative aspects of baseball's integration:

Integration in baseball has already proved that all Americans can live together in peaceful competition. Negroes and whites co-exist today on diamonds south, north, east, and west without friction, fist fights, or feuds. They wear the same uniforms, sit side by side on the same benches, use the same water fountains, toilets, showers; the same bats, balls, and gloves. They travel from city to city on the same buses, trains, or planes. They live in the same hotels, eat in the same dining rooms, kid each other in the same baseball jargon. Negro and white ballplayers play cards and golf together, go to movies together, swap inside information about opponents, defend each other in rhubarbs, pound each other's backs after a winning game. They attend postseason banquets together, go on club picnics, visit each other's homes. Fans no longer notice the color of a ballplayer's skin. Willie Mays is San Francisco's hero. . . . Ernie Banks is the most respected Cub.

Now, let's broaden the focus.[26]

Yet baseball is not free of racial discrimination and abuse, as the rest of this chapter will demonstrate.

BLACK PLAYERS IN CONTEMPORARY TIMES

Attitudes of Other Baseball Participants

The racial-attitude dimension within baseball is both significant and confusing. Racist, discriminatory attitudes toward black players will likely affect them negatively (causing less pay or playing opportunities, for example). Yet attitudes are subjectively expressed and received, affect people differently, can change over time, and can be very unclear. For example, Reggie Jackson told a reporter the story of when, as a teenager, he and his Pennsylvania all-star youth team played against a Fort Lauderdale team. According to Jackson, the coach of the team—fearing racial unrest—only let him up at bat once. And Jackson was so upset that, when he did get up, he was afraid to swing and struck out on three called strikes. The coach's daughter read Jackson's remarks in *Sports Illustrated*. She wrote to the magazine and countered by saying that Jackson had played every inning in the series and received honorable mention as MVP. The opposing pitcher in one of the games also wrote in and said that he nearly had his head taken off with Jackson's line drive.

Altercations do occur between white and black players in which racism is not a factor. Larry Doby—for example—hit Art Ditmar, a white pitcher, after Ditmar told Doby to commit a sex act on himself.

Yet some comments carry serious discriminatory potential. Calvin Griffith, owner of the Minneapolis Twins, once indicated that he relocated his team from Washington, D.C., because Minnesota had few blacks and many "good, hardworking" whites. Griffith also called his black star, Rod Carew, a "damn fool" for signing a contract far below his worth. Carew responded, "I will not come back and play for a bigot. I'm not going to be another nigger on his plantation. . . . I will never sign another contract with this organization."[27]

According to Willie Mays, manager Alvin Dark was quoted as saying that

Spanish-speaking and Negro players cause problems because they do not have mental alertness, pride in themselves, and ability to be a team player. More recently, George Bell's manager said that Bell's baseball skills kept him from cutting sugarcane in his native country, the Dominican Republic. Other comments—while racially explicit—may reflect nothing more than heavy-handed clubhouse humor. Roy Campanella of the Dodgers told the Giants' Willie Mays that his team's star, black pitcher Don Newcombe, would knock Mays down because Newcombe hated "colored rookies." And Reggie Jackson recalled that the following conversation started when Rollie Fingers yelled at Sal Bando, " 'Hey, you damn dago, you're so fucking fat you make the fat-ass manager look thin!' Sal told him he'd been hanging around with the Jew Holtzman so long, he was beginning to think he was smart, too. When he said it, it seemed pretty funny."

Comments and actions are not always taken the same way. For example Jackie Robinson harbored some bad feelings toward Casey Stengel because Stengel called black players "jig-a-boos" or "jungle bunnies." Stengel also commented on Elston Howard, the first black Yankee—who was also a slow runner—"Well, when they finally get me a nigger, I get the only one who can't run." Yet, apparently, Howard never indicated in public that these remarks seriously bothered him.[28]

There are black players who express outright resentment against perceived racist actions on or off the playing field. Reggie Smith told the media that the city of Boston was very racist. And Bob Gibson has indicated, "I am prejudiced against all those who have contempt for me because my face is black and all those who accept me only because of my ability to throw a baseball."[29]

Dock Ellis informed the media before the 1971 All-Star Game that the National League would never let him be the starting pitcher, even though his record was 14 wins and three losses. His rationale for saying this was that the American League was starting another black pitcher, Vida Blue, and he figured that two black pitchers would be more than baseball could handle. Ellis did start the All-Star Game; he contended that he had made those remarks to goad management into taking action. More recently, George Foster successfully sought release from the final year of his five-year contract with the New York Mets when he was benched in favor of white players.

Other black players do not outwardly react to racial abuse. Jim Rice was asked about the Red Sox's dismissal of Tommy Harper, a black coach who protested the policy of distributing invitations to an Elks Club party only to white players and coaches.

What's the big thing? Tommy never wanted to go to the Elks Club, he just wanted to make an issue out of it. It was an issue for him, not for me. Why do you guys always bring up those things? . . . I have a house down here, my wife can cook, why would I want to go to the Elks Club? Why should I care if they don't want me if I don't want to go?

[*Reporter*:] But it must have made you angry?

[*Rice*:] Why should it make me angry when I never had any desire to go there in the first place? And why get angry about things you can't change?[30]

Ken Griffey and John Mayberry have expressed similar attitudes in print; and a 1977 "CBS Reports" show, "The Baseball Business," noted that black Yankee players were still holding their card games in the back of the bus, but because of selection—not segregation. Mike Schmidt has observed, "You walk into any major league clubhouse today and you'll see the black guys at one end listening to black music and the white guys at the other end listening to country music."[31]

Attitudes and behaviors can also vary within the individual player over time. Hank Aaron once preferred not to speak out on racial issues.[32] More recently he has commented that baseball's management officials "want to look at us [blacks] as monkeys."[33] Roy Campanella remembers an incident with Lew Burdette, a white pitcher. Burdette threw at Campanella twice when he was at bat. Burdette then yelled, "Nigger, get up and hit." Campanella "then got so mad I missed the next pitch," and struck out. Some time later Burdette visited the retired and paralyzed Campanella at his store and asked how he was feeling. "The onliest thing I want to remember about Lew Burdette is that whatever he called me, and he shouldn't have, later on he come all the way to Harlem to say hello."[34]

Expressions of discriminatory attitudes and actions are not always clear. Dick Allen maintains in his book, *Crash*, that discrimination/prejudice occurs when he and other black players are called "naturals" while Stan Musial and Ted Williams are regarded as being "great students of the game." Allen notes this attitude attributes blacks' baseball success to luck and physical blessings instead of to the tremendous amount of mental and physical effort that is necessary to learn the craft. Some whites are friendly, "pat-on-the-back" types with black players, but then—as soon as they think there are no blacks around—start throwing "n's" (their code word for "nigger") around. Some say that a discriminatory attitude can be communicated in many non-verbal ways, too—like when a white catcher keeps looking at the dugout while a black pitcher is arguing with him.[35] But people may also disagree over the discriminatory nature of a particular act. Bowie Kuhn did not attend the game in which Hank Aaron hit the historic 715th home run that broke Babe Ruth's record. Instead, he sent Monte Irwin—a black Hall of Famer—to represent the commissioner's office. Years later, Kuhn attended a ceremony to present Aaron with an award for producing the 1970s most memorable moment. Aaron, however, sent a representative to accept the award.

Promotional Barriers, and the Campanis Incident

While some black players have at least a few good memories of the minor leagues and spring training, many autobiographies talk only of brutally discouraging conditions. Segregated eating and resting facilities and even barbershops were still the rule, rather than the exception. Fan abuse was also extreme at times. One black player recalls that although he gathered his strength from some minor league fans who loved the game irrespective of player's color, he experienced other fans who "got off on racial intimidation":

Between innings, coming in from the outfield to the dugout, I would hear the voices— "Hey, Chocolate Drop" or "Watch your back, nigger." I would look up, but I could never find the guy who made the remarks. Racist fans have a way of hissing and mumbling under their breath that makes them hard to locate. Black players know this and after a while learn not to look up. I would have loved to go a round with any one of them. I think a one-on-one slugfest with one of those racist cowards would have given me all the release I needed.[36]

Willie Stargell once had a shotgun put to his temple; the gunman informed him that he would be killed if he played the game that night (which he did). Discrimination was also facilitated through such team practices as listing "race" on player scouting reports—a practice that, according to Frank Robinson, still occurs on some teams today.

Once in the major leagues, black players have seen very little movement into coaching, management, and front-office positions. Jackie Robinson realized this situation, as noted in his last public comments (at the 1972 World Series): "I won't be satisfied . . . until I look over at the coach's box at third base and see a black manager there."[37] Frank Robinson became the first black to manage a professional baseball team—the Cleveland Indians—in 1975.[38] He was fired during the 1977 season. At the time, Robinson maintained that his dismissal was not due to race, although he did feel that some player unrest would have been eliminated if top management had supported him more. Some seven years later, Robinson reflected that he had probably been trying too hard at Cleveland and should have been more patient.

Robinson's second managerial assignment was with the San Francisco Giants in 1981—a team that had a great deal in the way of player tensions. One report described its previous season this way: "The club had its share of carousers and an equal number of born-agains. Between were a couple of quitters and several whiners. The number of dedicated players, those who came out to play every day as hard as they could, could be counted on the fingers of one hand."[39] Robinson won the National League Manager of the Year award in 1982. Nevertheless, he was fired in August 1984. This time Robinson was concerned, believing that "the next black manager will have to be a very low-keyed person who has not accomplished a lot on the field." When asked to give advice to black players who hope to manage, Robinson replied, "Don't even think about it. . . . Take as much as you can on the field as a player. Don't get into it off the field. There's nowhere to go. I know I'm right."[40] Robinson proved himself wrong by becoming the next black manager (of the Orioles) in 1988—a situation perhaps inadvertently prompted by Al Campanis (see below).

Both Commissioners Kuhn and Ueberroth instituted affirmative action programs (in 1970 and 1987, respectively), with unsuccessful results. Frank Robinson cited the following statistics for 1987: 21 out of 180 coaching jobs filled by blacks; nine blacks or Hispanics out of 180 managers for major and minor league teams; and 30 minorities (17 blacks and 13 Hispanics and Asians) out of 879 administrative positions in baseball.

Al Campanis, vice-president of the Dodgers, may have motivated some serious affirmative action changes through his comments in an April 1987 television interview with Ted Koppel of *ABC News*. This program signified the 40-year anniversary of Jackie Robinson's debut in baseball, and the following excerpts illustrate its unexpected significance:

Koppel: Why is it there are not black managers, no black general managers, no black owners?

Campanis: Well, there have been some black managers, but I really can't answer that question directly. . . .

Koppel: Is there still that much prejudice in baseball today?

Campanis: No, I don't believe it's prejudice. I truly believe that they may not have some of the necessities to be, let's say, a field manager, or perhaps a general manager.

Koppel: Do you really believe that?

Campanis: Well, I don't say all of them, but they certainly are short. How many quarterbacks do you have? How many pitchers do you have that are black? . . . Why are black men, or black people, not good swimmers? Because they don't have the buoyancy.

Koppel: It may just be that they don't have access to all the country clubs and pools.

Campanis: How many [black] executives do you have on a higher echelon in your business? How many black anchormen do you have?

Koppel: Yeah, fortunately, there are a few black anchormen, but if you want me to tell you why there aren't any black executives, I'm not going to tell you it's "cause the blacks aren't intelligent enough." I'm going to tell you it's because it is that whites have been running the establishment of broadcasting just as they've been running the establishment of baseball for too long and seem to be reluctant to give up power. . . .

Campanis: Well, we have scouts in our organization who are black, and they're very capable people. I have never said that blacks are not intelligent. I think many of them are highly intelligent, but they may not have the desire to be in the front office.[41]

Campanis's bottom line—that blacks may lack certain necessities for moving into baseball management—produced an immediate and intense controversy. Columnist Carl Rowan observed that "he was dumb enough to suggest on nationwide TV that blacks are too dumb to be field managers."[42] Ira Berkow interpreted Campanis's word, "short," to mean that blacks lack capabilities in thinking positions.

These interpretations may be incorrect. Ted Koppel was the first person in the interview to equate lack of necessities with lack of intelligence. Campanis directly denied that he ever made this connection.[43] Also, Campanis was previously on record as citing physical—not mental—differences between blacks and whites. In 1981 he stated, "I think black athletes are the best in everything but swimming, pitching and long distance running. They have many physiological advantages—quick movements and less fat on them per pound, for example."[44]

Campanis also said that black stars do not want to pay the dues, such as taking lower paid management jobs in the minor leagues and obtaining necessary experience before moving into the major leagues. This statement— while sometimes correct—is irrelevant. Some black stars (like Bob Gibson) would consider being a manager, but not a coach—believing coaches to be underpaid for all the traveling they do. Pete Rose was of a similar opinion. And he became a major league manager without having minor-league managing experience. Moreover, Rose is the exception, rather than the rule. In 1987 only three out of the 26 teams were managed by someone who did not have minor league coaching or managing experience.

Yet some black players—like Bobby Tolan, Ray Burris, and others—have paid or are willing to pay minor league dues for a major-league managerial position. Black playing star Joe Morgan has this to say about the situation:

Why can't baseball give a chance to black players who were not big stars, and did not make huge salaries? Players like Curt Motton or Gene Clines—I can name a lot more who would do a great job. Sparky Anderson was the best manager I played for, and he was not a star as a player; but he was given the opportunity to manage, and he took advantage of it. . . . However, they will only consider a black player for a managing job if he was a big star.[45]

Morgan's comments do make a great deal of sense, since many of the best managers today (Tommy Lasorda and Dick Williams, along with Anderson, for example) are high on the list in qualities other than player performance record.

Additional controversy focused on the extent to which the remarks made by Campanis reflected a personal racism that extends to other management officials, as well. Campanis issued an immediate apology, particularly to black Americans, for his inability to express his beliefs accurately.

Some of the Dodgers as well as manager Tommy Lasorda believed that the remarks made by Campanis did not reflect his personal beliefs and actions. Sportswriter George Vecsey commented, "I have never heard him say anything faintly resembling the foolish phrases he used on television."[46] Roy Campanella had once commended Campanis for his devotion to the advancement of minority ballplayers' careers: "Dear Al . . . I want to thank you again for your friendship. You're one good Greek. . . . "[47] Campanis probably was not malicious in his thoughts and words. Nonetheless, "his unwitting prejudice offers evidence of a color bar that may be every bit as hard to overcome as the blatant one Jackie Robinson conquered."[48]

AFTER CAMPANIS

The Campanis interview produced two tangible results: his dismissal from the Dodgers, and the institution of an affirmative action program. Dodger President Peter O'Malley asked for and received his vice-president's resignation, maintaining that "comments given by Al Campanis are so far removed from what the organization believes that it is impossible for Al to continue his responsibilities."[49]

Edward Williams, owner of the Baltimore Orioles, could see right away that the remarks made by Campanis would prompt change. The Orioles had one black front-office employee (a secretary) out of 45. Williams stated, "Those comments were so embarrassing they'll be productive. . . . What we have to do is correct this, and we're going to. We're going to have an affirmative action policy. I'll match my record on racial justice in the last 40 years with anyone in this country."[50]

Commissioner Ueberroth indicated that Campanis had been speaking for himself, not for baseball—although Ueberroth still had not filled the long-time vacancy left in his office when black executive Monte Irvin retired. Civil rights leader and presidential hopeful Jesse Jackson met with Ueberroth about two weeks after the Campanis remarks, to discuss affirmative action in baseball. Jackson mentioned the likelihood of a picket line—including ex-players—on July 4 if an affirmative action plan were not enacted by then. Marvin Miller labeled Jackson's plan "a worthy purpose."

Ueberroth accepted Jackson's demand that each baseball team should devise its own affirmative action plan, but he also indicated that the agenda and timetable would be established by baseball management—not someone else.[51] Some greeted this turn of events with cynicism. Bernie Linicome of the *Chicago Tribune* said, "One can only step back in honest admiration of what good can be accomplished when two self-promoting schemers see votes at the other end of injustice."[52]

In any case, Ueberroth did quickly initiate affirmative action by appointing Dr. Harry Edwards, an outspoken black sports sociologist and associate professor at the University of California, as a special assistant. Edwards decided that his first objective was to create a pool of women and minorities who would be candidate material for front-office and field-management jobs in baseball. These names would then be matched with each team's published job openings and related job specifications.

Some baseball executives and players did not think that Edwards's program would be an unqualified success. Don Baylor, for example, was both optimistic and reserved. "I know Harry Edwards is a doer and has gotten things done outside of baseball. . . . But this is a different group of people he will have to deal with. They make their own rules and hire who they want. They've done that for a long time."[53]

Indeed, there is a network in baseball whereby coaches and other management officials are selected on a political patronage/companionship basis. And indeed, Edwards was only the second black ever to hold an executive position in the commissioner's office. (Monte Irvin was hired as special assistant by Commissioner Eckert in 1968.) Edwards apparently realized and met this situation by employing none other than Al Campanis to help him. He gave the following explanation for this decision.

We really can't go around demanding open and candid discussions of the problems and solutions to racism in baseball and then lynch people when they openly and candidly display their feelings. Al Campanis has been in baseball for 40 years and has a tremendous store of knowledge. . . . He will be very valuable in preparing me for dealing with those people in baseball. We're going to have to deal with Campanises in baseball, and it's good that I have a person in-house who knows how they think.[54]

Still, all this affirmative action business has produced very little in the way of immediate results. Jesse Jackson called off his threatened demonstrations after the promotion of two former black players (Gary Maddox in Philadelphia and John Roseboro in Los Angeles). Yet—as Jim Bouton observed—eight months after the Campanis incident there had been more blacks hired to figure out how to promote black employment: (one: Edwards) than were actually hired to occupy management positions (none, for 12 manager or general manager openings, which were filled by white "no-names or retreads").

No managers were fired in 1987 until June 18, when the Philadelphia Phillies fired John Selske and replaced him with Lee Elia—a white third-base coach. Not since 1976 had baseball gone so long into a season without a manager being fired. Perhaps this was due to a relatively tight pennant race at this time of the season. Yet some think that the delay was due to baseball owners' fears that the replacement manager would have to be black.

Phillies owner Bill Giles had to spend quite a bit of time defending his managerial selection of Elia. Yet the media was quiet in the fall of 1987 when George Steinbrenner promoted manager Lou Piniella to general manager and hired Billy Martin as manager. After the Campanis incident, Steinbrenner had commented, "I'll stand on my record anytime. . . . It doesn't make any difference to me where a person goes to church or the color of their skin. The only thing that matters is whether they can get the job done. It always has."[55] Steinbrenner's record at the time of this statement showed two blacks out of 46 front-office employees. He had previously labeled Piniella as "the worst judge of talent" (a major aspect of the general manager's job) in the organization, and had already fired Martin as manager four times before. Why he did not hire at least one new employee—white or black— for the management positions is unclear.

Some have criticized that baseball's affirmative action efforts are a sham. Six months after Campanis, baseball had not yet identified a list of qualified minorities for nonplaying positions. Edwards appeared more concerned about what players' parents do for a living than about what makes an individual qualified for a job.[56] No blacks were hired to fill the 14 top decision-making vacancies for managers and general managers, for example, in 1987. Hank Aaron judged Edwards to be both unproductive and noncommunicative. Edwards countered that he was in touch with top management but that results take time—and also that "egos are involved here." Frank Robinson is one such "ego" who wondered why Edwards had not sought his counsel and 35 years of related experience. Robinson also criticized the long-run approach that Edwards was taking, instead of emphasizing short-run results.

Edward's lack of urgency is not shared by the qualified blacks who have been denied the opportunity to work in baseball. When a strong-voiced black man like Harry Edwards is given the baseball commissioner's ear, that man should help make things happen for minorities as soon as possible, not produce a five-year plan. Edwards was given a budget of $250,000 and an annual salary of $250,000, so he can afford to take his time. In addition, Edwards is paid $80,000 a year by the University of California at Berkeley, and he says he makes up to 100 speeches, at $5000 per appearance, each year. I know black ex-players who are willing to work in baseball for the equivalent of three of Edwards's speech fees, yet they can't find a job.[57]

Some people think that black superstars will have to play a major role in finding and publicizing qualified black candidates for vacancies. In November 1987 a group of 60 blacks tied to organized baseball formed the "Baseball Network" to facilitate the hiring, recruiting, and promoting of minorities in baseball and sports administration. Ben Moore was appointed as the executive director. Willie Stargell, Ray Burris, Frank Robinson, Curt Flood, and Jim Grant were named board members. The Baseball Network is not a direct rival of Harry Edwards and baseball's internal affirmative action efforts, although board-member Robinson hopes that Edwards will eventually match his words concerning minorities in baseball with actions and results.

Commissioner Ueberroth—in his final state-of-the-game address in December 1988—stressed a fivefold increase in minority employment (from 2 percent to 10 percent) in two years, but also acknowledged that he was disappointed in the lack of minorities in two very visible positions: general manager/manager, and positions that deal with the press. Ueberroth's successor, Bart Giamatti, indicated that it will take a long time to achieve equal opportunity—perhaps even longer than his tenure as commissioner.

In late 1988, Bob Watson became an assistant general manager of the Houston Astros—a hiring praised by Harry Edwards and others. In early 1989, an even more visible position became available when Bart Giamatti left the National League's presidency to become commissioner of baseball. There were two immediately obvious and seemingly qualified candidates, who would also have satisfied the purposes of an affirmative action program.

Giamatti himself at least indirectly suggested his own replacement by praising the National League vice-president, Phyliss Collins. Another possible choice was Santiago Fernandez, a general counsel for the Dodgers who was a magna cum laude from UCLA with a law degree and valuable baseball operations' experience. As it turned out, Bill White—a black former major-league player and sportscaster—was chosen. Dodger owner Peter O'Malley said that race had played no part in White's selection. This assertion was echoed by noted sports-reporter Dave Anderson, who said, "Of all Bill White's credentials, the most comforting is that he has been in baseball all his adult life. He understands baseball and he understands its people."[58]

Thus far in our account, racial discrimination in baseball has been approached somewhat randomly and anecdotally. The subject will be more systematically analyzed in the next section.

ARE BLACK AND HISPANIC PLAYERS DISCRIMINATED AGAINST?

For the purpose of analysis here, black and Hispanic players have been combined into one category and compared with other players to determine if there are any current indicators of employment discrimination. There are two major reasons for the combined category. First, "blacks" and "Hispanics" are both employee categories that come under the mandate and jurisdiction of the 1973 Equal Employment Opportunity Act and the Equal Employment Opportunity Commission (EEOC). An employer can be found guilty of illegal discrimination if its hiring practices adversely affect either category. Second, contemporary black and Hispanic players were first admitted to the game in 1947 and 1948, respectively; and both have suffered the effects of its tradition of discrimination.

Many autobiographies of black players (Willie Stargell, Jackie Robinson, Roy Campanella, John Roseboro, Dock Ellis, Hank Aaron, Bob Gibson, and so forth) depict the adverse employment conditions in the minors, spring training, and the majors and connect them more to their color than to their race. There is little reason to think that dark and black Hispanics have not faced similar employment constraints.[59] For example, in 1987 the media engaged in some curious debate over the Texas Rangers' assertion that they were employing the first black coach in the team's history by hiring Davey Lopes—who considers himself to be equal thirds of white, black, and Portuguese. Lopes said that the press and the management could consider him anything they want.

Positional Restrictions of Black and Hispanic Players

Black and Hispanic players may be discriminated against by not being considered for all playing positions. This restriction would likely reduce the number of minority players entering the majors. It would also reduce their flexibility to move to other positions, and therefore possibly reduce their playing years. An additional adverse impact can occur if the positions not containing black and Hispanic players typically carry more salary and/or are regarded as necessary stepping-stones for career advancement (to manager, general manager, and so forth) after the players' field days are over.

The positional restriction of black and Hispanic players would probably reflect certain underlying stereotypes assigned by baseball management. For example, one study found a lack of black and Hispanic players at the pitcher and catcher positions. This study's author contended that these positions are central to every play of the game. A similar lack of black and Hispanic players was found at other "thinking" positions: second, shortstop, and third base.[60]

Table 7.2 displays the evidence for positional restriction of black and Hispanic players on the 1987 playing roster. This table and Tables 7.3 and 7.4 represent all 626 major league players who were under contract as of August 31, 1987, and who had at least 51 at-bats or, in the case of pitchers, 30 or more innings pitched in 1987. Blacks and Hispanics represented 30.7 percent of all major league players in 1987. Statistical (difference of proportion) tests were run for the various positions to see if the minority players had either a significantly higher or a significantly lower proportion than the total proportion. The results indicate that blacks and Hispanics are restricted from the central positions of pitcher and catcher (American League only), and are overrepresented in the outfielder positions. However, these individuals are also overrepresented in two other thinking positions; second base (American League only), and third base.

Caution must be exercised in formulating the implications of Table 7.2. For example, the underrepresentation of black and Hispanic players in the pitching and catching positions could indeed prevent minor league players in these categories from entering the majors. Yet its effect on their careers once in the majors is less clear.

Blacks and Hispanics may contend that their exclusion from the pitching and catching positions prevents them from obtaining necessary experience to become a baseball manager after their playing days are over. Yet, as noted by Warren Spahn in Chapter Five, pitchers are seldom picked to become

Table 7.2
Positional Distribution of Black and Hispanic Players on the Major League Teams, 1987

Position	AMERICAN LEAGUE (proportions)		NATIONAL LEAGUE (proportions)		BOTH LEAGUES (proportions)	
	Whites	Blacks/Hispanics	Whites	Blacks/Hispanics	Whites	Blacks/Hispanics
Pitcher	87.5	12.5*	88.7	11.3*	88.0	12.0
Catcher	93.3	6.7*	79.2	20.8	87.0	13.0*
First Base	68.4	31.6	56.3	43.7	62.9	37.1
Second Base	39.1	60.9*	73.7	26.3	54.8	45.2*
Shortstop	47.4	52.6*	34.8	65.2*	40.5	59.5*
Third Base	85.0	15.0	76.2	23.8	80.5	19.5
Outfield	40.9	59.1*	28.1	71.9*	35.2	64.8*
Total Players	70.4	29.6	58.1	31.9	69.3	30.7

N = 626 major league players in 1987
*Statistically significant at the .05 level

managers. A review of managers on the 26 teams as of June 15, 1987, found only two former pitchers.

Some people would figure that Table 7.2 reflects a situation of pay discrimination as well, since pitchers and catchers probably receive more money than players at other positions. This possibility will be examined later.

Differential Performance Considerations

Former Commissioner Ford Frick believes that performance measures should determine who is on or off the team. "Whether you have one or twenty-one black players on a major league roster is irrelevant. The one question that baseball and all sports must face up to is simply this: 'Is the selected player the best available for the position?' If he is, no apologies are necessary."[61] Unfortunately, the simplicity of Frick's delivery obscures a fairly complicated perspective. Performance is subject to diverse interpretations and measurements.

In other organizations, equal employment opportunity takes into consideration the "relevant labor market"—the proportion of qualified individuals in some geographical proximity that could be employed. This concept is far from precise for most organizations, and becomes very muddled indeed in professional baseball where potential players are scarce—but available—throughout North and South America. They come from the minor leagues, college campuses, and various semi-pro teams in the United States and elsewhere. Further, the prevalence of whites among the players taken from the minor leagues and/or colleges may reflect the discriminatory selection practices of these organizations, rather than of the major leagues.

In any case, given a narrowly defined focus, it should be quite revealing to examine the relative playing abilities of players in the major leagues. More directly put: Do Hispanics and blacks need better performance statistics than their white counterparts to be in the major leagues? One prominent black player—Gary Templeton—believes this to be the case. "The white establishment keeps blacks to a minimum. If you look around the league, only a certain amount of players are let in. If a black player is 10 or 20 percent better than a white player, the white guy gets the nod. Face it, this is just a white man's game."[62] The issue can be approached in different ways. Several studies have focused on just one performance indicator: batting averages for black and white players. One such study examined batting averages for a 13-year period (1953 through 1965). As a group, black players consistently hit better than their white counterparts (the difference ranged between .012 to .025), although no statistical tests were conducted for these differences.[63]

Another study (with rather small samples) indicated that blacks have a higher batting average than whites when the particular position is controlled for. Black shortstops hit better than white shortstops, for example.[64] A third study of career batting averages of black and white players on the 1986 roster found that twice as many black baseball players as whites had career averages greater than .281 (32 percent versus 15 percent); and 47 percent had better than .270, versus only 30 percent of whites. On the other hand, almost three times as many whites as blacks had career averages below .241 (28 percent versus 10 percent).[65] However, no insights were presented into how the batting average distinctions were selected or how the statistical measures (standard deviations for number of playing years, for example) were controlled and tested.

Differential performance expectations/considerations can be also statistically examined and tested by comparing the proportion of black and Hispanic players to their proportionate share of leaders in various offensive performance categories. This suggestion was offered by Jim Bouton, who reasons,

There are a lot of Negro stars in the game. There aren't too many average Negro players. The obvious conclusion is that there is some kind of quota system. It stands to reason that if 19 of the top 30 hitters in the major leagues are black, as they were in 1968, then almost two thirds of hitters should be black. Obviously, it's not that way at all.[66]

There are many offensive performance categories that can and will be used in this analysis. However, one remaining problem is to determine an ap-

Table 7.3
Proportion of Black and Hispanic Players Found in the Top 25 Percent of Selected Performance Categories, 1987

Offensive Categories	American League (proportions)	National League (proportions)	Both Leagues (proportions)
Batting Average	34.7	53.5	46.9
At Bats	42.9	53.5	45.7
Runs	42.9	58.1	48.4
Hits	44.0	55.6	48.9
Doubles	45.3	51.2	47.9
Triples	43.5	57.6*	50.0
Home Runs	36.0	51.1	42.1
Runs Batted In	34.7	55.8	43.6
Stolen Bases	57.1*	61.4*	61.0*
Proportion of Hispanic and Black Players in Hitting	42.9	52.5	48.3
Category Total	42.1	45.9	43.8

*Shows items that are statistically significant at the .05 level. The null hypothesis is that the individuals in the top 25 percent represent a random sample drawn from a population with a proportion of 42.1 percent black and Hispanics for the American League, 45.9 percent for the National League, and 43.8 percent for the combined leagues.

propriate proportion of players for our investigation. One extreme sometimes used by sportswriters over the years is to look only at the top individuals in each category. This approach, along with related statistics (see Table 7.1), was discussed earlier in the chapter; and it supports Bouton's hypothesis. To reiterate, the proportion of black/Hispanic performance leaders is far greater than their employment representation has been over the years. However, focusing on accomplishments of the top individuals ignores the contribution of the other black and Hispanic players. A more appropriate reference point would be the upper quartile of players in both leagues.

Table 7.3 indicates the proportion of black and Hispanic players found in the top 25 percent of players in various offensive categories in 1987. Pitching was not eligible to be considered because the small number of Hispanics and blacks in this position does not permit statistical testing for differences.

The table indicates that Hispanics and blacks represented 43.8 percent of the eligible offensive players in both leagues. If the proportion of the top 25 percent for the ten offensive categories turns out to be significantly higher than 43.8 percent, then Jim Bouton's argument is correct: Black and Hispanic players have to perform better than their white counterparts in the majors.

Table 7.3 shows that the proportion of Hispanics and blacks in the top 25 percent is indeed higher than the total proportion of eligible blacks and Hispanics, for eight out of ten performance categories. However, these both-league overrepresentations are statistically significant for only one performance category: stolen bases. Black and Hispanic players were also significantly overrepresented in the triples category for the National League, although it should be noted that three triples would enable a player to enter the top 25-percent performers in this offensive category. Furthermore, no significant differences were found when so-called power infielders (first base, third base, and catcher) and fielding infielders (second base and shortstops) were separated from and compared with the totals.

Potential Salary Discrimination

Previous research has not found that black players have been discriminated against regarding salary treatment. Rather, these studies have come to the following conclusions:

—Black veteran nonpitchers are not being discriminated against with regard to pay. Also, the results of statistical correlations showed that management tends to use the same factors (runs, hits, runs batted in, and home runs, with at-bats and years also exercising close variational influence) for both white and black employees.[67]

—Black players earn more than white players in every position in major league baseball. A nonrandom sample of 148 black and white players found higher salary averages among the former ($66,000 versus $56,900 for outfielder; $53,100 versus $40,800 for infielders; $59,900 versus $38,400 for pitchers).[68]

Many of the surveys generating these conclusions have methodological problems, however. Incomplete salary data for all players are compounded by rather subjective and inconsistent data sources, such as newspaper accounts. These problems have been enhanced by the recent trends in multiyear contracts and deferred incomes with varying—sometimes unknown—interest rates paid over, say, a 20-year period. And because of the often small sample sizes, no study has differentiated between the American and National Leagues to see if the initial reluctance of the American League to hire black and Hispanic employees has lingered in other employment practices affecting these individuals in the 1970s and 1980s.

Table 7.4 is designed to show whether blacks and Hispanics were overrepresented or underrepresented among the highest paid (upper quartile) players, with future guaranteed payments discounted to present value. Since 30.7 percent of all players are black or Hispanic, it would be expected that this upper quartile group would contain a like percentage of blacks and Hispanics. Actually, as shown in Table 7.4, the minority group constitutes 36.7 percent of the upper quartile range. While this difference is not sta-

Table 7.4
Percent of Blacks and Hispanics in Selected Populations and Those in the Upper
Quartile Salary Range

	Percent of Blacks and Hispanics	
	In Population	In Upper Quartile
All Positions		
American League	29.6	35.3
National League	31.9	39.4
Both Leagues	30.7	36.7
All Nonpitching Positions		
American League	42.1	54.0
National League	45.9	51.2
Both Leagues	43.8	56.7*
Selected Positions - Both Leagues		
1B, 3B and C	21.6	18.2
2B and SS	52.4	57.1
OF and DH	58.2	76.3*

*Statistically significant at the .05 level

tistically significant (.05 level), it certainly offers no indication of salary discrimination against black/Hispanic players, neither in professional baseball
as a whole nor in its constituent American and National League components.

Since blacks and Hispanics make up so small a percentage of pitchers, it is
necessary to analyze the salary data for nonpitching positions only. These
data are also presented in Table 7.4. In each case—except for the first-base/
third-base/catcher (power infield) category—blacks and Hispanics are overrepresented in the upper salary quartile; and in two of the cases, the difference in proportions is statistically significant. Certainly, none of the data
in Table 7.4 indicates salary discrimination against black/Hispanic players.

Therefore, black/Hispanic players do not currently experience statistically
measurable discrimination in either positional-performance restrictions or
salary treatment. This finding does not, however, minimize the discriminatory behaviors and attitudes that are directed toward black/Hispanic players. Further, those desiring to remain in baseball after their playing days
are over do experience tremendous discrimination from a statistical standpoint.

Eight

Player Mobility and Salary Arbitration

Thomas Boswell maintains that the first reserve clause occurred over the price of a uniform. A player was angry that his team was too cheap to pay for his uniform, and so he signed with another team. In the intervening century, baseball players "have been sold for as little as 25 cents and traded for a bulldog, a bird dog, a turkey and an airplane."[1]

As discussed in Chapter One, most of baseball history—particularly the nonunion years—has witnessed the exercise of managerial discretion over players' careers and wages. This chapter discusses how this discretion was gradually reduced over time through collective bargaining provisions concerning player mobility and salary arbitration.

THE RESERVE RULE

Baseball has long been involved with the reserve rule (see Chapters One through Three).[2] In 1879, owners established the first reserve rule to stop players from jumping clubs and receiving higher salaries. Each team was allowed to reserve five players who could not be acquired by any other owner. This rule became part of the Uniform Contract signed by each player and gave the employing club the sole right to assign or renew the contract. The player either accepted the employer's salary offer and almost unlimited control over his career, or retired from baseball. Over the years, players have not been consistently against the reserve clause. Mickey Mantle, Ted Williams, Pee Wee Reese, Lou Boudreau, Pete Rose, and Stan Musial—

for example —have either claimed to be unconcerned about its rule, or were actually in favor of it.

There have been several rationales given for the reserve rule over the years—each surrounded by its own debate.

1. *The reserve clause is needed for balanced competition and economic stability among teams.*

Commissioner Kuhn placed the "balanced competition" argument in perspective before a congressional committee. Kuhn believed that the clubs with the most revenues would attract the better players and dominate other teams. Unbalanced races, lower fan interest and attendance, and lower team revenues would result.

Kuhn also believed that many players—if free to choose their own team— would select a club that is a winner and/or is located in a good geographic area that is also conducive to endorsements and other types of outside income. One study has supported Kuhn's concerns: Free agents signed before January 1, 1980, who also made more than $150,000 tended to gravitate toward teams having larger markets.[3]

Yet there are those who believe that Kuhn's arguments and predictions regarding competitive balance are wrong. Some players recognize that they may be worth more to a lesser team. Dale Murphy, for example, receives $2 million a year to play for the Atlanta Braves. This figure was not approached or countered by the New York Yankees when he recently became a free agent.

Also, at least one management representative—Earl Weaver—believes that relaxation of the reserve rule (via "free agency" for players, discussed later in this chapter) can help each team to become more competitive.

The attitudes in spring training are 1000 percent better than they used to be [under the reserve rule,] especially on pennant-winning teams. When players had to sign for what the general manager and the owner wanted to pay them, they'd come into spring training and say things like, "Screw this; I worked my butt off last year and got nothing for it, so they'll accept what I give'em this year." Players have more of an incentive to play.[4]

Further, teams may soon be discouraged from buying up all the talent: A team that buys a lot of superstars will always have some of these players sitting on the bench. And when the stars are not playing regularly, they do not play so well. Then they start complaining and attempt to get traded to another team.

Even the statistics do not always support Kuhn's argument. In the 1976 draft—under reserve rule changes—the first ten "million-dollar" players to sign all went to teams with worse records than their previous teams. Also, the last ten World Series have been won by ten different teams—an unprecedented situation.

2. Public confidence in the integrity of the game would be preserved through retention of the reserve clause.

There are people who say that baseball's early days before the reserve clause was enacted was a time of criminal chaos. Alfred Spink wrote about this situation in 1875.

Bribery, contract breaking, dishonest playing, poolroom manipulation, and desertion of players became so commonplace that the respectable element of patrons began to drop out of attendance, until the crowds which attended the game were composed almost exclusively of gamblers, criminal element, and men who went to the grounds to bet money on the results.[5]

The reserve rule prevented players who committed these offenses from freely joining an opponent team. It also prevented local fan favorites from jumping teams—thereby enhancing public confidence in the sport's consistency, and maybe even integrity.

There is no evidence to suggest that the reserve rule's relaxation through labor-management negotiations in 1976 has resulted in any corrupt player behavior. However, Red Sox pitcher Bill Lee believes the reserve rule's counterpart—free agency—adversely affected the performances of free agents Freddy Lynn, Carlton Fisk, and Rick Burleson in 1976. Lee noted that these players performed as well as they could but were not at optimum levels because of unsigned contracts and related front-office and media pressures.

There is also little reason to expect that management would not trade star players and local favorites if the reserve rule did remain in force. According to Hank Aaron, the Milwaukee Braves traded fan favorites like Bill Bruton and Juan Pizzaro, and moved other players around, like "livestock." And then (jeopardizing this reserve rule argument even further), the Braves' management moved the entire team from Milwaukee to Atlanta. One study conducted by *Sports Illustrated* in 1982 found that 109, or 88 percent, of the players inducted into the Hall of Fame had been traded once or more during their careers.

3. Professional baseball's unique legal status reflects and perpetuates the necessary importance of the reserve rule.

This argument was used after the Supreme Court decision *Federal Baseball Club v. National League* was issued in 1922. The Federal League of Professional Baseball Players had sued the National League for buying up constituent clubs and inducing those clubs to leave the Federal League. Damages were sought under the Sherman Antitrust Act.

Judge Oliver Wendell Holmes agreed that the teams were in different states and needed to travel across state lines to play each other. He also contended that this transportation was incidental and was not enough to change the character of the business and bring it under antitrust regulation. "As it is put by the defendant, personal effort, not related to production, is not a subject of commerce."[6]

Some 30 years later, baseball's unique legal status was reaffirmed by the Court in *Toolson v. New York Yankees*. George Toolson, a minor league player in the Yankees' farm system, refused to report to a particular minor league club because he felt that it would be more difficult to make it onto the Yankees team than onto other major league teams. The Yankees invoked the reserve rule, which then banned him from playing professional baseball at all. The Supreme Court noted the previous *Federal Baseball* case and subsequent congressional investigations (without resolution) of baseball's antitrust exemption, and concluded that any potential correction of this exemption should be determined and legislated by Congress.[7]

Two years later the Court reaffirmed baseball's unique status when it placed professional football under the scope of the Sherman Act. This decision agreed with William Radovich, a football guard, who—like Toolson before him—claimed that the professional sport had entered into a conspiracy to monopolize by curtailing his choice of employer teams. Justice T. C. Clark admitted that the ruling was inconsistent with the court's 1922 baseball decision, but commented that his court would have also placed baseball under the Sherman Act if the *Federal Baseball* and *Toolson* cases had not been written earlier.[8] Baseball was the only professional sport to remain outside antitrust protection—a situation that would again be tested in the *Curt Flood* case (as discussed below).

The reserve rule has seldom—if ever—given management total discretion in compensating, retaining, and dispensing players; there were several historical safeguards that have been incorporated into current labor-agreement provisions. For example, the player's minimum salary discussed through this book has at least set a floor for player compensation. Article V of the labor agreement stipulates this figure and also the maximum salary reduction that a player can receive (no more than 20 percent of his previous year's salary or 30 percent of his salary two years previous). Article V also establishes the salary arbitration procedure (discussed later in this chapter).

The waiver rule will not allow a team to send a player to the minor leagues until the other major league teams have had a chance to hire him. There are also current labor-agreement provisions that regulate trading within and between the National and American Leagues. In addition, a player who has ten major-league seasons with at least five years on his current club has the right to veto any trade. These limitations notwithstanding, management's ability to control player mobility through the reserve rule remained judicially untested for 17 years after the *Toolson* case.

CHALLENGES TO THE RESERVE RULE IN THE 1970s

The *Curt Flood* Supreme Court Decision

In 1969, the Saint Louis Cardinals traded Curt Flood, an outfielder who had compiled an overall .293 batting average in 12 seasons with the Cards. He was traded to the Philadelphia Phillies. Flood refused to be moved, in part because he had received no advance notification. In his book *The Way It Was*, Flood bitterly recalls getting a phone call from an assistant to the Cardinals' general manager, after the fact.

If I had been a foot-shuffling porter, they might have at least given me a pocket watch. But all I got was a call from a middle-echelon coffee drinker in the front office. Was I not entitled to a gesture from the general manager himself?

Flood said that management's behavior in his case was a reflection of the player's total helplessness or dependence on his club to make a living.

A salesman reluctant to transfer from one office to another may choose to seek employment on the sales force of a different firm. A plumber can reject the dictates of his boss without relinquishing his right to plumb elsewhere. At the expiration of one contract, an actor shops among producers for the best arrangement he can find. But the baseball monopoly offers no such option to the athlete. If he elects not to work for the corporation that "owns" his services, baseball forbids him to ply his trade at all. In the hierarchy of living things, he ranks with poultry.

Flood petitioned Commissioner Bowie Kuhn to make him a free agent so that he could negotiate with any club. When Kuhn did not comply, Flood took his request to federal court on May 19, 1970. Some players agreed with Hall of Famer Edd Roush that since management was spending money to develop players, it needed the reserve clause (or something like it) to have control over its investment. Others—like Hank Greenberg and Jackie Robinson—felt that the reserve clause was one sided and that players should be given some control over their own destinies.

The three defendants in the suit—Charles Feeney, president of the National League; Joe Cronin, president of the American League; and Commissioner Bowie Kuhn—were unpleasantly surprised when the MLBPA supported the *Flood* case, since the jointly agreed-on labor agreement neither challenged nor weakened the reserve clause. However, Marvin Miller cited a labor agreement provision calling for a "joint study" of the reserve clause, and contended that management had not seriously acted on the issue. For his part, Kuhn believed that Miller was blundering in pursuing this case because it had little chance of judicial support and would sour future labor-management negotiations on the subject.

The judge ruled against Flood but did not rule on the reasonableness or the legality of the reserve clause. "Instead he ruled that Organized Baseball was exempt from the requirements of all federal and state antitrust laws and that the reserve system did not subject Flood to involuntary servitude."[9] Flood fared no better with the court of appeals, which in 1971 upheld the lower court's decision. Flood sat out the 1970 season without receiving any pay, and was then traded to the Washington Senators in 1971. He quit some 20 days after the appeals court decision was issued.

The case was then appealed to the Supreme Court, which issued its decision on June 6, 1972. No majority opinion was written in regard to the 5–3 vote, although the written decision incorporated the following reasoning: "We continue to be loath, 50 years after *Federal Baseball* and almost two decades after *Toolson*, to overturn those cases judicially when Congress, by its positive inaction, has allowed those decisions to stand for so long and, far beyond mere inference and implication, has clearly evinced a desire not to disapprove them legislatively."[10]

This decision indicated that Congress should become actively involved in the reserve rule and related issues. However, as the *Washington Post* pointed out, baseball's continuing exemption from antitrust laws meant that tradition and history had won out over logic and consistency. Six of the justices said that baseball was "interstate commerce"—contrary to the 1922 Supreme Court decision. However, three of those six justices, along with two others, simply voted to stick to the precedents. Baseball was therefore regarded as an anomaly and an exception to the court's holding that other sports and entertainments are subject to antitrust laws.

In any case, the Court's decision suggested that the reserve rule could be altered only through Congress or through collective bargaining. Flood realized collective bargaining's potential when he heard the Supreme Court's decision. "If I had 600 players behind me there would be no reserve clause."[11] Yet Congress did not act, and the players did not immediately receive reserve-clause alterations to their labor agreement. Consider the provision negotiated in 1973:

Article XV—Reserve System

Except as adjusted or modified hereby, this Agreement does not deal with the reserve system. The Parties have differing view as to the legality and as to the merits of such system as presently constituted. This Agreement shall in no way prejudice the position or legal rights of the Parties or of any Player regarding the reserve system. During the term of this Agreement neither of the Parties will resort to any form of concerted action with respect to the issue of the reserve system, and there shall be no obligation to negotiate with respect to the reserve system.[12]

The Hunter and the Messersmith–McNally Grievances

Changes were made in the reserve system in 1974. These changes were not made by Congress or negotiation efforts. Instead, arbitrator Peter Seitz modified the reserve issue in the process of rendering two grievance decisions. The first decision involved Jim "Catfish" Hunter, who was to be paid $100,000 in 1974—with half the sum to be applied in any manner he should designate. Hunter told the Athletics owner, Charles Finley, to apply half his salary to an insurance annuity. Finley refused to make this purchase because it would not be a deductible tax expense for the team.

Hunter filed a grievance claiming that he should not be bound to the Athletics because Finley's action violated provisions of Paragraph 7(a) of the American League Uniform Player's Contract, which read:

The Player may terminate this contract, upon written notice to the Club, if the Club shall default in the payments to the Player provided for in paragraph 2 hereof or shall fail to perform any other obligation agreed to be performed by the Club hereunder and if the club shall fail to remedy such default within ten (10) days after the receipt by the Club of written notice of such default.

Arbitrator Seitz agreed with Hunter and declared that he was a free agent.

Much of baseball management thought that the arbitrator was exceeding his authority by awarding anything more than a financial payment and renegotiation of Hunter's contract. They felt that Seitz had failed to consider the *Curt Flood* decision and the fact that the reserve system was not a part of the labor agreement.

Finley was not upset that Hunter used arbitration, even though Charley Finley had often become angered with "disloyal" players in the past. Indeed, Finley made a rare public admission of having made a mistake, and acknowledged Hunter as a "class act."

Let me tell you what kind of a person Jim Hunter is: After he won the arbitration case, he offered his services back to me. That's right, I could have re-signed him. And all he wanted was $200,000 so he could buy a farm in North Carolina. But I had been so positive I was gonna win that case, I was hurt—so hurt that I said "no." It was stupid.[13]

Finley was—however—outraged with the arbitrator's decision, which he believed to be unfair. In a rare situation, Commissioner Kuhn agreed with Finley and contended that it almost looked as if arbitrador Seitz were punishing Finley on general principles. And Seitz seemed to agree with Kuhn. The arbitrator once stated, "If Mr. Finley had neglected to supply Mr. Hunter with the white sox ball players use, I would have found that way [to make Hunter a free agent]."[14]

Seitz's decision was upheld by two courts,[15] and Hunter did become a free agent. Many teams sought his services.[16] However, in the end, George Steinbrenner signed the player to a five-year contract with the Yankees at an estimated salary of $3.7 million. Kuhn called this act "fiscal insanity." Hunter's salary was more than a third of the purchase price for the entire

Yankee franchise two years earlier. "Baseball did not know it yet, but the Hunter deal heralded an era of fiscal irresponsibility by ownership that has not abated to this day."[17]

Pitchers Andy Messersmith of the Los Angeles Dodgers and Dave McNally of the Baltimore Orioles played the 1975 season without signing their contracts. At the end of the season they filed a grievance and claimed to be free agents. They did not follow Flood's unsuccessful strategy of contesting the reserve clause's legality. Instead, they contended that they were free agents because management had violated Paragraph 10(a) (Contract Renewal Clause) in the Uniform Player's Contract, which was also included in the collective bargaining agreement and in part read:

10(a) On or before December 20 ∗ ∗ ∗ in the year of the last playing season covered by this contract, the Club may tender to the Player a contract for the term of that year. ∗ ∗ ∗ If prior to the March 1 next succeeding said December 20, the Player and the Club have not agreed upon the terms of such contract, then on or before 10 days after said March 1, *the Club shall have the right by written notice to the Player* ∗ ∗ ∗ *to renew this contract for the period of one year on the same terms,* except that the amount payable to the Player shall be such as the Club shall fix in said notice.(emphasis added)

The Orioles management believed that this issue was beyond arbitration's scope. Therefore, they asked Federal Judge John W. Oliver to exclude the grievance from arbitration. Judge Oliver stated that management should first pursue arbitration and then contest any possible jurisdiction problem in the courts.

Management had two basic contentions in the grievance:

1. Contract renewal and possible free agency are parts of the reserve system, which are specifically excluded from the labor agreement (at Article XV, given above).
2. Paragraph 10(a) becomes a part of the renewed contract and can be invoked by the owners as long as they wish.

Arbitrator Seitz found no specific definition of the reserve system in the labor agreement. He indicated that, although Paragraph 10(a) and the grievance might be related to a general consideration of the reserve system, yet he found no evidence that Paragraph 10(a) was to be specifically exempt from the grievance procedure. He also ruled against management's second contention. Seitz agreed with the union's interpretation of Paragraph 10(a): that owners have a right to renew an unsigned player's contract for one year, and one year only.[18]

This decision did not materially affect McNally, who had retired from baseball. However, Messersmith made use of his newly acquired free-agent status, and negotiated with several teams. The Cincinnati Reds were interested, but dropped out of contention due to club president Bob Howsam's reasoning that

Andy is a good athlete and would make a desirable addition to our pitching staff, but we have to operate our team on a sound basis. To sign him under these terms is poor business. No club in our industry can truly afford this and survive.

In addition . . . we cannot allow the acquisition of one player to undermine the relationship we have with our other players and the soundness of our approach to them.[19]

Messersmith eventually signed a multiyear, estimated $1.75-million contract with the Atlanta Braves.

Seitz's decision affected but did not resolve the reserve issue. He had not determined whether the reserve system was good or bad. He had just interpreted the agreements and understandings of the union and management officials. Standing alone, the decision meant that all players could become free agents by refusing to re-sign with their present clubs and then playing one season without contracts. Interestingly enough, before his arbitration decision was finalized, Seitz had informed management officials of his leanings, and urged them to resolve the issue through collective bargaining.

I begged them to negotiate. . . . I had no deadline. I could have withheld my decision indefinitely had the owners shown the slightest inclination to adjust their differences. But they rebuffed me completely and said they wanted my decision now. Right now.

What I did was inevitable. . . . The owners were too stubborn and stupid. They were like the French barons in the 12th Century. They accumulated so much power they wouldn't share it with anybody.[20]

According to a Louis Harris survey, this decision was favored by the public, who considered it wrong (57 to 31 percent) that "the players could not sell their services or pick their employers once they had signed up."[21] This attitude was not shared by the baseball owners, who exercised their option to discharge Seitz after he issued the decision. Management's labor relations representative, John Gaherin, made this announcement: "Professional baseball has instructed me to terminate Peter Seitz as chairman, because it no longer has confidence in the arbitrator's ability to understand the basic structure of organized baseball."[22]

American and National League presidents MacPhail and Feeney issued a joint rationale for their judicial appeal of Seitz's decision, contending that it had neither jurisdictional nor substantive merits.

For the arbitrator to assume the power to restructure the essential framework of the game when the United States Supreme Court, the United States Congress and other authorities have clearly placed the reserve system above narrow, individual disputes is clearly an over-reaching of authority.[23]

Judge Oliver heard the initial appeals and upheld Seitz's jurisdiction over the grievance.

This court . . . cannot review the merits of substantive disputes that were submitted to the arbitration panel. In this case, the rights of the parties are controlled by the 1973 Basic Agreement. That agreement is governed by the same federal law applicable to any other collective-bargaining agreement between employers engaged in an industry affecting commerce and a recognized labor organization representing the employees in that industry.[24]

Oliver's decision was subsequently upheld by a federal appeals court that reasoned: "We hold that the arbitration panel had jurisdiction to resolve the dispute, that its award drew its essence from the collective bargaining agreement."[25]

This reasoning is very consistent with three 1960 Supreme Court decisions (nicknamed "the Trilogy") indicating that third party neutrals—arbitrators hired jointly by union and management officials under negotiated labor agreement provisions—are better qualified than judges to interpret the terms of those agreements and fashion an appropriate remedy for grievances.

As discussed in Chapter Two, hard bargaining then occurred over the reserve issue. The details of subsequent negotiations over free agency are discussed in Chapters Two and Three. The sections below discuss free agency's economic impact, as well as management involvement in the procedure.

FREE AGENT EXPERIENCES AND CONTROVERSY

1976–1984

Seitz's arbitration decision immediately applied to approximately 50 players who had not signed their 1976 contracts. The situation was so pressing that it prompted union-management negotiations over free agency: The four-year labor agreement ultimately signed that year provided free agent status for players who had been at least six seasons in the major leagues. Several studies have examined the salaries and performance of the 1976 class of free agents, and have rendered these related findings:

1. Free agent status was worth $40,000 to affected players in 1977.[26]

2. Multiyear player contracts—very rarely given before 1976—were included more frequently as owners sought to protect their investments.[27]

3. Free agents in 1977 received higher pay than did non–free agents with comparable playing ability.[28]

4. The salary gain for free agents does not mean they were overpaid: One statistical interpretation is that they were paid closer to their marginal revenue product than were non–free agents.[29]

Bill Campbell—the first player to sign under the new arrangement—increased his previous year's salary $22,000, to a five-year contract worth $1,075,000. Campbell summarized his experience thus: "Look, this business seems insane to me. . . . No player is really worth what they're paying me, but if they want to, then fine."

Approximately $25 million was spent on 24 free agents in 1977. This price is even more impressive when applied to various player performance measures. Buzzy Bavasi, owner of the Padres, commented on the situation this way: "Let's face it. . . . It was a big ego trip for all of us." A 1986 book written about off-season player mobility and negotiations, *A Baseball Winter*, chronicles the frustrations experienced by Atlanta Braves owner Ted Turner during this free-agent buying frenzy. Turner actively sought many star players like Pete Rose, Reggie Jackson, and Dave Winfield and then settled instead for Mike Lum, Al Hrabosky, Terry Forster, and Pete Falcone. Turner finally did sign a free agent whom many teams wanted—Bruce Sutter—to a contract estimated at a healthy eight-figure salary. At which point, Turner exclaimed, "I finally got me one."

Commissioner Kuhn believed that this first year's experience with free agency was giving valuable publicity to baseball, and was enabling some of the weaker teams to become more competitive. He also expressed concern, however, about the increase in player's salaries—a concern that intensified over the next two years ($21.3 million was paid for ten free agents in 1978; and $15.6 million, for ten free agents in 1979). Nolan Ryan signed a record $3-million pact for the 1980–82 seasons; and at least one owner—Edward Bennett Williams—wanted Kuhn to take action against the higher salaries resulting from free agency.

Nevertheless, the salary gains from free agency (and salary arbitration, discussed later in this chapter) continued. In 1976 the average salary for major league baseball players was $51,501; in 1984 the average salary was $329,408. Some of these gains probably reflected the signs of a new baseball prosperity: increased attendance and television revenues. And much of this prosperity was due to the greater competition and wider distribution of talent caused by free agency.

As noted earlier in the words of Buzzy Bavasi, owners' egos continued to remain involved with the free agent process. Free agency caused a new kind of instant player-owner relationship in which the owner shared the spotlight at the moment of signing—and felt freer than ever to attack the star afterward. "If the star failed, it was not the owner's fault, for he could show how much he had paid; he remained a good owner who had hired a bad player."[30]

Owners' egos gave way to a more results-oriented, bottom-line approach in 1985, however.

1985 to the Present: The Collusion Grievances

The current free-agent procedure has three key annual dates:

1. December 7. By this date, a club must offer salary arbitration. If it does not, the club cannot sign the player until the next May 1.
2. December 19. If the club does offer salary arbitration, the player must accept or reject the offer by this date. If the player accepts, he is considered signed. If he rejects the offer, the third key date comes into play.
3. January 8. A club extending an arbitration offer that is rejected has until this date to sign the player. If it does not sign him by then, the club cannot sign him until the next May 1.[31]

On the face of it, the January 8 date places pressure on both the player and the club to agree on a contract before the playing season opens. A club might suddenly get serious in the last-minute negotiations, fearing the nearly four uninterrupted months in which the player could be negotiating with other teams. Yet January 8 can put real pressure on a player, particularly if he has neither received nor anticipated a realistic offer from another team: The earliest next opportunity to sign a contract—May 1—is five weeks into the regular playing season.

Since 1985, the January 8 deadline does seem to have put more pressure on the players than on the teams. The 1985 labor negotiations forced management to open its books—which created the impression that fiscal restraint was needed to correct alleged widespread financial malaise. In any case, restraint was clearly shown in salary discussions with the 1985 free agents, most notably in the instance of Kirk Gibson. Some thought that Gibson would sign a five-year contract worth at least $8 million. When his team—the Detroit Tigers—offered Gibson a three-year $3.6-million contract, Gibson responded that he would "vomit" if he had to sign this agreement and then shake hands with Tiger management. After receiving no offers from any other teams, Gibson did eventually accept a Tiger contract (three years at $4.1 million)—one minute before the January 8 deadline. George Steinbrenner maintained that Gibson's and other free agents' situations represented

a re-awakening of owners, and if anyone deserves credit here, it's the commissioner, Peter Ueberroth, who got us together on numerous occasions—always with four lawyers in the room to guard against anything that might be construed as collusion—and made us tell each other how stupid we'd been in the past.[32]

Despite the four lawyers and management's guard being up, Don Fehr—

president of the MLBPA—charged it with collusion because each player would no longer be dealing with one club, but would now have to deal with all 26 clubs working together. As Fehr also realized, only five of the 62 free agents in 1985 had signed with new teams—each for less than the original team offered. Fehr grieved the 1985 free agent situation and cited the following collusion evidence:

the simultaneous decision by all teams to carry one less player this year to save money; the unanimous decision to limit contracts to three-year terms shortly after the owner's Player Relations Committee circulated a negative analysis of player performance after signing long-term contracts; the refusal to include incentive clauses in player contracts and the attempt to insert drug-testing clauses.[33]

Arbitrator Thomas T. Roberts was selected by union and management officials to decide this grievance (nicknamed "Collusion I") concerning the 1985 free agent players. The grievance was still unresolved when the 1986 free agents class sought consideration. One of these players, Jack Morris—baseball's most successful pitcher from 1980 to 1986—was looking for a new situation and with an arbitrator determining his salary. Yet the Yankees, the Phillies, and the Twins all rejected Morris's offer; he finally elected salary arbitration with his original team—the Tigers. Morris's agent, Dick Moss, believed that the situation represented collusion since certain baseball owners—like George Steinbrenner—would have signed Morris, had they been acting independently. Barry Rona, executive director of the Player Relations Committee (PRC), argued that the owners' action represented only prudent business sense—not conspiracy—particularly since any written oral agreement between the clubs would have become public knowledge within a couple of days.

Dal Maxvill, once general manager of the Saint Louis Cardinals, suggested that management would continue to be conservative in bargaining with these individuals. "Over the past few years, 85% of the free agents have had worse years than they did prior to signing these contracts. . . . I don't think I'm smart enough to find the 15%."[34] After the hard line was established, many clubs followed suit by not giving their players a contract. The PRC even came out with a form letter by which management could turn its players into free agents for the following season. The letter read:

(Dear Player:) Please be advised that after careful consideration, we have made a determination not to tender you a contract for the 1987 Championship season. By not tendering you a contract . . . we understand that . . . you will become a free agent and be able to negotiate with any Club. By taking this action we are not foreclosing the possibility of your signing a 1987 contract with the Club should our plans change or should events dictate that it is mutually advantageous to do so. The Club appreciates your efforts during the past season and we wish you every success for the future.[35]

Yet some players continued to test the free agent waters, even going past the January 8 deadline and thereby allowing themselves the extra time to negotiate with other teams until May 1, 1987. However, the situation did not work to their advantage. Bob Horner, for example, saw Atlanta's wage offer of $4.5 million for three years dwindle to $3.9 million during free agent negotiations, before deciding to play in Japan. Horner reflects, "People keep saying I made a terrible mistake, that I misread the market. . . . But I'd have to be Merlin the Magician looking into a crystal ball to foresee being worth $1.3 million to a team one week and then worth nothing at all to the rest of the league."[36]

The MLBPA filed a second collusion grievance—this one in regard to the 1986 free agents. This grievance was heard by arbitrator George Nicolau (who was also assigned the third collusion grievance filed in 1987). Once again, many key free agents chose to re-sign with their own teams. Cal Ripken and Jack Morris each signed two-year contracts with the Orioles ($1.7 million) and the Tigers ($3.98 million) respectively. Dale Murphy also signed with his original team—the Braves—for three years ($6 million), because he felt that there was no longer a free agent market. The fate of free agency after 1985 and 1986 is further discussed below.

The Collusion I Decision

Tom Roberts issued his arbitration decision in September 1987. His task was to determine if management had violated Article XVIII-H of the labor agreement—and to prescribe an appropriate remedy, if need be.

Article XVIII-H

The utilization or non-utilization of rights under this Article XVIII is an individual matter to be determined solely by each Player and each Club for his or its own benefit. Players shall not act in concert with other Players and Clubs shall not act in concert with other Clubs.

To begin with, Roberts observed that management had suggested Paragraph H of Article XVIII, in the first place—to prevent joint player holdouts like the Koufax–Drysdale action in 1956. He also noted the heritage of owners' active and aggressive bidding for free agents from 1976 through 1984.

Roberts realized that some major league teams (the Kansas City Royals, Minnesota Twins, Oakland Athletics, and Seattle Mariners, for example) had never signed free agents. He also understood management's contention that "what occurred during the 1985–86 winter was nothing more than the culmination of a predictable evolution to a more sober and rational free agent market from that present during the 1970s."

However, Roberts was strongly influenced by the sharp change that had taken place in the owners' behavior in just one year's time. During the winter of 1984–85, 26 of the 46 re-entry free agents changed clubs; in 1985–

86, only one (Carlton Fisk) of 32 free agents received an offer from a new club. Further, four owners' meetings had been held between September and December 1985, in which the commissioner and others stressed problems with free agents and long-term player contracts. These meetings and the results that showed up in the 1985–86 season could only mean that "the right of the clubs to participate in the free agency provisions of the Basic Agreement no longer remained an individual matter to be determined solely for the benefit for each club. The contemplated benefit of a common goal was substituted (thereby violating the labor agreement)."[37]

Barry Rona of the PRC indicated—predictably enough—that this was a bad decision and would offer no more public discussion on the topic. Don Fehr of the MLBPA was equally predictable, contending that arbitrator Roberts had correctly understood the owners' violations and would subsequently formulate an appropriate remedy. Roberts did determine in January 1988 that all of the affected 62 players in the free agent classification could file for individual damages. Seven of these individuals had until March 1988 to test the free agent waters and still hold onto their former contracts. This three-month "free bite of the apple" would then expire; the players could continue to be free agents, but the contracts with their former clubs would no longer exist.[38]

The 1986 free agent Jack Morris (Potentially, a free agent again in 1987) commented on the arbitrator's decision:

Hey, it's foolish for a guy making $1.85 million to look for sympathy and I'm not doing that. . . . My salary is not the issue here. The issue is that the owners were found guilty of collusion.

I know that George Steinbrenner wanted to hire me. I could see it in his face. I could hear it in his voice. He finally had to say, "Sorry, buddy, I can't do it." Steinbrenner said no one told him what to do. In fact, he swore on his mother's name about it. All I can say now is, "poor mom."[39]

Kirk Gibson, the only 1985 free agent who actually changed teams as a result of Robert's decision, was even more direct.

It would be nice if I got a money settlement, and, yeah, my pocket's open. All I know is that the owners signed an agreement to permit free agency and then changed the rules in the middle of the game—just when it was my turn to go to bat. That isn't the way you do business. You make an agreement, you stick to it. Instead, they got together and decided to break the law and they're going to pay for it.[40]

Roberts released his initial remedy for Collusion I in September 1989. The $10.5 million figure pertains to 139 players, although additional arbitration remedy hearings might be necessary since the MLBPA submitted specific claims for these players totaling $16,622,000. Other hearings might be necessary to resolve what the remedy does not include, such as the possible money lost because of a decrease in the number of multi-year contracts.

The Collusion II Decision

Arbitiation George Nicolau's decision concerning the 1986 free agents beat Robert's decision by 8,346 to 5,674 testimony pages—but Nicolau clearly respected his predecessor's contribution to industrial relations' common law of the shop.

In theory, one arbitrator is not bound by another's determination on such matters. Yet, there is great value, particularly in labor relations, in the consistency of interpretation. Such consistency provides, to both parties in a collective bargaining relationship, a stable and continuing means of administering their agreement. For this reason, most arbitrators will not disagree with a prior contractual interpretation between the same parties unless they are persuaded it is irrational and clearly wrong. Chairman Roberts' interpretation of XVIII(H), insofar as it goes, does not fail that test and I adopt it. Thus, as he found, the exchange of information does not constitute a *per se* violation of XVIII(H). However, as he also found, what is done with that information, how it is thereafter used and to what end, is another matter. It is also apparent, under his analysis, that a plan or understanding, or the pursuit of a common scheme for a common benefit, or an agreement to that end does not require a seal or other formality. Moreover, it need not, as I understand him, be in writing and, if its presence can otherwise be discerned with sufficient clarity and force, may even be unspoken.[41]

Further, Nicolau found that a common scheme, plan, or understanding need not rest on absolute uniformity of action (that is, no deviations) and/ or formal penalties for noncompliance. He then focused on the 1986 free agency experience and the "exceptions" that—according to management— proved the absence of concerted action.

There were 79 reentry free agents (Andre Dawson, Lance Parrish, and Tim Raines, for example) after the 1986 season. "Nontender" free agents (such as Darrell Evans and Steve Balboni) were available, as well. This latter category occurs when clubs do not tender a contract for the following season to a reserved player. The practice results in the player's becoming a free agent, regardless of years of service. The club may risk losing this player to another team, but also eliminates the nontender free agent's arbitration possibility and is itself able to avoid the 20-percent maximum salary cut provision in the labor agreement.

Nicolau found that no club had sought to sign a nontender free agent in whom the player's former club held a continuing interest. The same situation occurred for reentry free agents at both the December 7 and the January 8 deadlines.

This striking absence of bidders before the contractual deadline cannot be adequately explained by the notion that "other" clubs don't "start thinking" about free agents until January or beyond; that the months of November and December are too early to do so. The evidence is otherwise. Historically, the bulk of free-agent signings by new clubs has occurred before January 8, not after.

Nicolau realized that Article XVIII-H "does not guarantee any particular level of market activity." However—he also noted—"the period at issue was not one of 'declining activity,' [and indeed] the record demonstrates that there was literally no market; no bid, save one: that of the former club."

Management contended, however, that the experiences of some of the free agents who bypassed the January 8 deadline indicated the prevalence of competition rather than concerted action. The owners acknowledged that four of these free agents—Ron Guidry, Bob Boone, Doyle Alexander (all of whom returned to their former clubs), and Bob Horner (who left for Japan)—had not received offers from other clubs and management claimed that this was because of their age, attitude, and/or versatility limitations.

But management insisted that two of the 1986 free agents—Andre Dawson and Lance Parrish—did sign with clubs other than their former employees, and that two others—Tim Raines and Rich Gedman—received offers from other teams even though they eventually returned to their former team. Yet the arbitrator found that all four of these examples supported the MLBPA's position more than management's.

—Dawson wanted to play on the grass in Chicago, and he was the one who made the overtures. Indeed, he told the Cubs to write in a figure that he would accept. This amount ($500,000 guaranteed plus another $150,000 if his knees were still holding up at the All-Star break) was far less than his previous year's contract with the Expos.

—Bill Giles, owner of the Phillies, did sign Parrish. Yet he had received several calls from fellow owners and major league officials urging his careful consideration and fiscal responsibility, prior to this event.

—The offers made to Raines and Gedman were found to be either "evanescent" or "not on the table at the same time" and therefore not "competing" with each other.

Also, all of this was occurring in the jointly concerned—if not concerted—atmosphere urged by Commissioner Ueberroth, who had spoke at a May 1986 meeting spoken of the millions of dollars still being paid to nonperforming players. "At the September 1986 meeting, the Commissioner expressed his continuing interest with individual club finances and distributed an analysis of the performance of the 1985 free agents." Two months later Ueberroth again spoke of players not being paid to play and indicated that owners had better get expenses down to avoid financial disaster.

Arbitrator Nicolau concluded that management did violate the labor agreement with its inaction toward the 1986 free agents.

In any one year, there may be a great deal of bidding between former clubs and other clubs; in another year, substantially less. But the abrupt cessation of activity in 1985 and the repetition of that pattern, with only minor post–January 8 deviations in 1986, cannot be attributed to the free play of market forces. Clubs have different personalities, different fiscal realities, different budgets, and different needs. Rather than reactions on the basis of those realities and those needs, there was a patent pattern of uniform behavior, a uniformity simply unexplainable by the rubric of financial responsibility or by other factors on which the Clubs have relied in this proceeding. In my opinion, their conduct with respect to the 1986 free agents was in deliberate contravention of Club obligations as embodied in Article XVIII(H), for which an appropriate remedy is fully justified.[42]

Beyond Collusion II

Nicolau furnished an "interim remedy"—a "second chance"—for 12 players, who were given about two months to seek another team even though they had a contract in force.[43] As of November 1, 1989, he had not finalized other aspects of the remedy. However, both union and management representatives have agreed in hearings that Collusion II's damages are more than Collusion I's. Management contends Collusion II's remedy should be no more than $17 million, while the union contends $60 million is more appropriate.

Also uncertain is management's reaction to the current class of free agents. Put simply, will the two adverse arbitration decisions, along with the substantial increase in funds newly received from television, prompt owners to resume their previous free-spending ways? Steve Sax—second baseman for the 1988 world champion Dodgers—claims to have received a three-year $3.5-million contract from his team, but he joined the Yankees for an additional $500,000. Sax mentioned that the two clubs exhibited very different attitudes during this process.

The Yankees treated me as someone they greatly respected. I felt it wasn't the same with the Dodgers. I felt [Dodger Executive Manager] Claire was really aloof. The tone of voice he spoke to me in and the way he looked at me really turned me off.[44]

Cincinnati Reds general manager Murray Cook maintains that the current free-agent spending—if it continues—will return the game to the dangerous economic levels of a few years ago. California Angels owner Gene Autry lost free agent Bob Boone to the Kansas City Royals for $1 more than he offered in 1988. An angry Autry then commented, "We will not be outbid for another free agent . . . It's absurd, but if others are going to do it, then so am I."[45] One reporter notes that "the owners are running amok, the way they did B.C. (Before Collusion)."[46] Another writer illustrates this situation with a rundown on the early free agent signings that took place in the latter months of 1988.

Andy Hawkins, a .500 pitcher, jumped from the Padres to the New York Yankees when they offered a raise from $435,000 last season to $3.6 million for three years. Nolan Ryan, 42 next month, got a 50 percent increase from his $1 million salary to join Texas.

Tom Niedenfuer and Jeffrey Leonard, unwanted by almost everyone, each got $1.75 million for two years from usually tight-fisted Seattle. Ineffective Jesse Orosco, let go by the Dodgers, found a home in Cleveland at $1.67 million for each of two years. Mediocre Dave LaPoint got $2.575 million for three years from the free-spending Yankees, who earlier gave $4 million to Steve Sax.[47]

Barry Rona of the PRC believes this recent activity supports management's contention that business trends and peer pressure—instead of collusion—occurred with the previous free agents. Don Fehr of the MLBPA says it only goes to show that the owners were consistently lying when they said they were not making any money.

SALARY ARBITRATION: PROCEDURES AND TRENDS

As indicated in Chapter Two, salary arbitration has been a player's collective bargaining objective for more than 40 years. In 1952, Commissioner Chandler maintained that this procedure would result in players' receiving more equitable salaries. However, owners did not agree with Chandler; and salary arbitration remained dormant for 22 years, until the 1974 season.[48] Salary arbitration procedures and trends will be discussed here, as well as its potential problem areas.

Current labor agreement provisions indicate that any club or a player with three[49] but less than six years' major league service may submit the player's salary to binding arbitration without the consent of the other party. Players who have six or more years of major league service, and who were not eligible to declare free agency at the end of the preceding championship season may also select salary arbitration; however, if the club refuses to cooperate with this procedure, then the player can become a free agent within ten days of such refusal.

Players submit their arbitration requests and salary figures to the MLBPA, and the clubs submit their arbitration requests and salary figures to the PRC, between January 12 and 22. Salary figures are then exchanged between MLBPA and the PRC. Salary negotiations between the player and the club may continue at that point, and the matter is considered withdrawn from arbitration if an agreement can be reached before the arbitrator's decision. The parties are also free to negotiate after the arbitrator's decision, although this practice is very rare. In 1988 Andre Dawson "lost" when an arbitrator indicated that management's last offer of $1.85 million a year was more appropriate than Dawson's last offer of $2 million a year. Yet Dawson and the Cubs subsequently renegotiated a three-year contract after this arbitration decision for one playing season had been rendered.

Arbitrators are jointly selected by the MLBPA and the PRC, and conduct hearings during the first three weeks of February at Los Angeles, Chicago, New York, and other major league cities—as the parties agree. These hearings are held at whatever site is closest to the home city of the club involved, and the arbitrator's expenses (including a $475 per diem) are shared by the player and the club. The hearings are conducted on a confidential basis, with each party limited to one hour of initial presentation and half an hour of rebuttal and summation.

The arbitrator's decision is binding and is limited to either the player's salary offer or management's offer (no compromise between the two). There is no opinion or explanation given for the particular offer selection, and the arbitrator is encouraged to give the decision within 24 hours of the hearing.

Table 8.1 displays arbitration statistics over the years and suggests three related conclusions. First, arbitration's popularity with the players has remained over the years even though arbitrator decisions have not been awarded predominately to the players. The number of arbitration cases (124) heard the first six years (1974–82; see table footnote) is similar to the number (132) for the second six years (1983–88) even though the percentage of decisions awarded to the players decreased 6 percent, when the two time periods are compared. Further, the total number of players filing for arbitration increased 62 percent in the second time period.

Second, players have sharply increased their salaries through the salary arbitration procedure. Of course, this situation applies to the players who receive a salary arbitration award in their favor. Dick Woodson, pitcher for the Minnesota Twins, had the first arbitration "victory" in 1974 when an arbitrator decided that his salary proposal of $30,000 was more appropriate than the club's offer of $23,000. Woodson won a $11,500 raise, which prompted him to say later, "I felt as if I'd struck it rich."[50] In 1987, Don Mattingly struck even more riches when an arbitrator selected his salary offer of $1.975 million. This salary amount was a record arbitration award and a 1,519-percentage increase over Mattingly's 1984 salary. Yet one study found that players who basically ignored arbitration had also significantly increased their salaries, when salary levels two years prior to arbitration were compared to salaries after two years of arbitration.[51] This may be because the owners fear the results of the arbitration alternative, and for good reason. In 1988, for example, 12 players who were eligible for arbitration for the first time used the procedure. Their new salary figures represented a substantial 259-percent increase.[52]

Table 8.2 indicates that players also increase their salaries when they file for arbitration but do not use the procedure, or even when they lose (that is, when the arbitrator agrees with management's salary figure). Only three out of 257 players receiving arbitration decisions had a cut in pay from their previous year's salary.[53]

Then too, a salary arbitration loser can still use the process to his advan-

Table 8.1
Selected Salary Arbitration Statistics, 1974–1988

Year	# Filing for Arbitration	# in Arbitration (%)	# Arbitration Awards to Players (%)	# of Arbitration Awards to Management %	Ave Player/ Management Offer Ratio	Ave Player Offer/ Previous Yr. Salary Ratio
1974	54	29 (54%)	13 (45%)	16 (55%)	1.19	1.44
1975	38	14 (37%)	5 (36%)	9 (64%)	1.21	n.a.
1979	29	12 (41%)	8 (67%)	4 (33%)	1.49	n.a.
1980	65	26 (40%)	15 (58%)	11 (42%)	1.44	n.a.
1981	108	21 (19%)	11 (52%)	10 (48%)	1.49	n.a.
1982	103	22 (21%)	8 (36%)	14 (64%)	1.53	n.a.
1983	88	30 (34%)	13 (43%)	17 (57%)	1.46	3.02
1984	80	10 (12%)	4 (40%)	6 (60%)	1.51	2.34
1985	97	13 (13%)	6 (46%)	7 (54%)	1.43	2.21
1986	159	35 (22%)	15 (43%)	20 (57%)	1.45	2.35
1987	108	26 (24%)	10 (39%)	16 (61%)	1.28	1.69
1988	111	18 (16%)	7 (39%)	11 (61%)	1.27	2.39
1989	131	12 (9%)	7 (58%)	5 (42%)	1.35**	1.41
Totals*	1171	269 (23%)	122 (45%)	147 (55%)	1.47	

*Salary Arbitration was not used in 1976 or 1977; totals include one case decided in 1978. The arbitrator accepted management's offer of $84,000 to Roy Smalley, Jr., instead of the players' offer of $110,000.
**Weighted average
Note: n.a., not available.

tage. Wade Boggs, for example, lost in 1986 when the arbitrator rejected his $1.85 million salary offer in favor of management's $1.35-million offer. Yet his loss needs to be put in perspective. Boggs increased his first-year contract of $32,000 in 1982 to $130,000 in 1983 and $525,000 in 1984. In 1985 the arbitrator agreed with his $1-million salary offer (management's offer was $650,000). However, in 1986 the arbitrator favored management as noted above. In 1987 Boggs again filed and considered the salary arbitration procedure. His offer was $1.85 million, compared to management's $1.6-million counterresponse. Salary negotiations continued, with Boggs eschewing the procedure. "Nobody wins in arbitration. It's a player's right, but it's hard on all involved . . . I don't like the things they say about you. The two arbitration hearings the last couple of years left me feeling pretty down."[54] Boggs averted arbitration at the last minute, signing instead a three-

Table 8.2
Year-by-Year Salary Gains for Players Who Have Filed for and/or Used Salary
Arbitration, 1983–1988

(Category of player in arbitration)	(Year and percentage increase over previous year's salary)					
	1983	1984	1985	1986	1987	1988
Winning Players	159	174	91	145	72	44
Losing Players	54	46	30	40	14	65
Winners & Losers	96	67	63	79	39	57
Settlements before Arbitration	69	75	72	54	33	65
All Players Involved with Arbitration	78	74	70	60	35	63

Sources: Murray Chass, "87: Vintage Year in Arbitration," *Sporting News*, March 2, 1987, p. 37; and Murray Chass, "Don't Jump to Wrong Conclusion," *Sporting News*, February 29, 1988, p. 35.

year contract that was conservatively estimated at $5 million. Should this amount be equally distributed over the three years, then Boggs's 1988 salary represented a nearly 5,200-percent increase over his first salary six years before.

Third, arbitrators have encouraged bargaining in the case of those filing for arbitration, but do not seem to have influenced bargaining efforts among those experiencing arbitration. As previously noted, an arbitrator can only select either the player's or management's salary offer. Since there is no possibility for compromise, each party will likely present a reasonable final offer out of fear that the arbitrator may select the other party's offer. This situation should narrow their proposal differences and prompt the parties to resolve these differences without resorting to the third party outsider.[55] In fact, this has increasingly been the case among players filing for arbitration. Far more players filed for arbitration and settled before using the procedure in the years 1983 through 1988 than in the years 1974 through 1982. Also, only one in five players who had filed for arbitration actually used this process in 1983 through 1988. A far higher proportion (nearly one out of three players) used arbitration in the first six years. And in the most recent year—1989— only 9 percent of the 131 eligible players continued with arbitration. All of these findings do support the previously cited advantage of final offer arbitration, which is intended to promote intensive, sincere bargaining between the participants.

Table 8.3
Salary Arbitration Decisions by Player-Management Salary Offer Ratio, 1974–1989

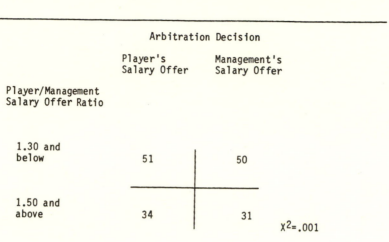

	Arbitration Decision	
	Player's Salary Offer	Management's Salary Offer
Player/Management Salary Offer Ratio		
1.30 and below	51	50
1.50 and above	34	31

$$\chi^2 = .001$$

Yet arbitrator's decisions have not noticeably encouraged the parties who actually enter upon the procedure to resolve or narrow their differences.[56] In 1974 the players' offers averaged 17 percent higher than management's offers. If players and managers were trying to resolve their differences, this ratio should be seen to decline over the subsequent years of salary arbitration. This is not what happened, as the annual average player-management salary offer ratio remained higher than the overall average (1.40) for the next eight out of nine years.

Harder bargaining may have occurred during 1987 and 1988, although many of the players and management officials must be aware that the size of the discrepancy between the player and management offers does not seem to influence the final arbitration decision. For example, in 1987 an arbitrator agreed with pitcher Jack Morris's offer of $1,350,000. This decision represented the largest absolute difference ($475,000) from management's salary offer.

Table 8.3 examines the extent to which the arbitrator's decisions have been associated with the player-management offer ratios for the years 1974 through 1989. Some people feel that arbitrators are conservative by nature and therefore will not be likely to agree with players' salary offers that are far apart from management's last salary offer. Continuing this line of reasoning, we may expect that arbitrators would be more inclined to agree with the players when the player-management offer ratio is low (1.30 or below) and with management when the player-management offer ratio is high (1.50 or higher). Yet Table 8.3 does not support this reasoning or show any as-

Table 8.4
Salary Arbitration Decisions by Player's Current Offer to Player's Last Year
Salary, 1983–1989

Arbitration Decision

Ratio of Player's Offer to Last Year's Salary	Player's Salary Offer	Management's Salary Offer
2.00 and below	50	51
3.00 and above	35	31

$$X^2 = .005$$

---

sociation of statistical significance between the arbitration decision and the player-management salary offer ratio.

Further, arbitrators do not appear to be particularly concerned over the size of the discrepancy between the player's salary offer and his previous year's salary. Dave LaPoint's 1987 salary arbitration experience represents a dramatic example. An arbitrator agreed with his salary offer of $425,000 even though this figure represented a 640-percent increase over his previous year's salary of $65,000. Table 8.4 summarizes results for the years 1983–89 and indicates that there is no statistically significant relationship between the arbitration decision and the ratio of the player's current offer to the player's previous year's salary.

The vast majority of players who filed for salary arbitration in 1989 did not have the arbitrator decide their salaries. The total settlement for individuals who filed for salary arbitration, exchanged "last" salary-offer information with the clubs on January 19, and then negotiated their salary settlement, was 9 percent less than the players' combined last offers and 15 percent more than the clubs' combined last offers. This player victory is even clearer as the negotiated settlement represented a 70-percent increase over the players' combined salaries in 1988.[57]

The players who did have the arbitrator decide their 1989 salaries had a total settlement that was 9 percent less than their combined last offers and 22 percent more than the clubs' combined offers. The arbitrators' decisions represented a 74-percent increase over the players' salaries in 1988. Again we find that players very seldom lose in the arbitration process. None of the 12 players in arbitration had their salary reduced from the previous season, and ten of these individuals received salary increases from the arbitrator.

The 1989 arbitration experiences and results also confirms management's fear of using the process. Arbitrators decided only 12 out of 131 eligible players' salaries; and among these 12, the average 1989 season pay ($764,583) was substantially higher than corresponding figures ($601,215) for eligible players who negotiated their settlements instead of relying on the arbitrator's decision. These results have been causing anger on the part of the owners toward the arbitrators and toward themselves—which will likely affect the 1990 labor-management negotiations.

This anger is symbolized in Steve Balboni's arbitration case. Balboni, who had a career batting average of .230 and 336 RBIs through 1987, was released by the Kansas City Royals and signed for $350,000 by the Seattle Mariners in 1988. The Mariners considered Balboni's 1988 performance (.251 batting average, 21 home runs, and 61 RBIs), and offered him $500,000 for the 1989 season. However, the arbitrator decided that Balboni's last salary offer of $800,000 was appropriate. Management arbitration consultant Tal Smith (a winner of 51 out of the 89 arbitration cases in which he has represented management) commented that this action was the most "unsupportable" decision in his entire experience.

Many owners are also angry at their peers for "giving in to players" instead of letting arbitrators make the decision. Orel Hershiser provides the most prominent example of this situation. He and management officials literally kept the arbitrator waiting while they finalized a three-year $7.9-million settlement. The Dodgers were afraid that Hershiser would become a free agent after receiving a one-year contract from the arbitrator. They were also influenced by other large settlements that have recently been given to Roger Clemens, Dwight Gooden, Eric Davis, and Jose Canseco before these players could enlist the arbitrator.

These "voluntary" settlements very likely affected arbitration hearings in 1989 and will do so in the years ahead, as both players and management invoke precedence and make their arguments on a comparative basis. Cleveland Indians president Hank Peters felt that the arbitrator's acceptance of his player Joe Carter's $1.63 million salary offer was influenced by a prior $2-million salary settlement that the Twins had reached with Kirby Puckett. And while Peters realized that all team owners are free to negotiate contracts with individual players as they see fit, he urged them to consider their salary negotiations' broader impact on the other teams instead of being guided solely by self-interest.

Tensions among the owners over these recent arbitration experiences as well as free agent bidding will probably translate into 1990 bargaining issues. It might be 1981 all over again, with the MLBPA countering that only 12 of its members were completely involved in arbitration and that the union cannot and will not be responsible for protecting the owners from themselves.

POTENTIAL PROBLEM AREAS WITH SALARY ARBITRATION

There are many possible problems that salary arbitration can pose for the player and/or club. These problems can be grouped into two general categories: (1) the arbitrator's decision; and (2) the negative impact on team finances and player performance.

The Arbitrator's Decision

Exhibit 8.1 indicates some of the criteria that arbitrators can and cannot consider in determining whether it should be the player's or the club's salary offer that is selected.[58] These criteria could offer player and club some potential guidelines for determining if their offers are reasonable and therefore likely to be accepted by an arbitrator. However, the potential is never completely realized since the arbitrator does not include a explanation in the decision. Neither the club nor the player knows whether the arbitrator considered certain criteria—and if so, the relevant weights and rationale. This omission hinders or precludes any serious wage decisions between players and management—even those who are sincerely interested in resolving their differences through good-faith bargaining.

Faced with such uncertainty, the parties tend to overprepare: They run as many statistics and computer printouts by the arbitrator as possible, on the assumption that the arbitrator will be influenced by at least one of the presented "facts." One experienced salary arbitrator contended, "I had more figures before me than exist in the files of the Census Bureau and the Bureau of Labor Statistics."[59]

Statistics are ever available but seldom conclusive, as problems remain in their interpretation. This situation is discussed in Chapter Nine, in terms of determining player performance. However, two examples will be used here for illustrative purposes. A certain club might argue that a certain player should receive its lower salary offer because he batted in fewer runs last year than the year before. Yet the player could counter this statistic with the argument that he was moved down the lineup (batted eighth instead of fourth, for example) and then present statistics to show that fewer players were on base when he was at bat.

A similar situation might occur when a pitcher claims that his win-loss average was worsened because his team failed to get him runs. In 1986—for example—the Boston Red Sox furnished pitcher Roger Clemens with the most run support in the majors (6.09 runs per start) while Danny Jackson

Exhibit 8.1
Criteria That Arbitrators Can and Cannot Use in Salary Arbitration (provisions
are from pages 12 and 13 of the 1980 Basic Agreement)

---

    (12) <u>Criteria</u>. The criteria will be the quality of the Player's
contribution to his Club during the past season (including but not limited to
his overall performance, special qualities of leadership and public appeal),
the length and consistency of his career contribution, the record of the
Player's past compensation, comparative baseball salaries (see subparagraph
(13) below for confidential salary data), the existence of any physical or
mental defects on the part of the Player, and the recent performance record of
the Club including but not limited to its League standing and attendance as an
indication of public acceptance (subject to the exclusion stated in (a) below).
Any evidence may be submitted which is relevant to the above criteria, and the
arbitrator shall assign such weight to the evidence as shall to him appear
appropriate under the circumstances. The following items, however, shall be
excluded:

    (a)   The financial position of the Player and the Club.

    (b)   Press comments, testimonials or similar material bearing on the
           performance of either the Player or Club, except that recognized
           annual Player awards for playing excellence shall not be
           excluded.

    (c)   Offers made by either Player or Club prior to arbitration.

    (d)   The cost to the parties of their representatives, attorneys,
           etc.

    (e)   Salaries in other sports or occupations.

    (13) <u>Confidential Major League Salary Data</u>. For his own confidential use,
as background information, the arbitrator will be given a tabulation showing
the minimum salary in the Major Leagues and salaries for the preceding season
of all Players on Major League rosters as of August 31, broken down by years of
Major League service. The names and Clubs of the Players concerned will appear
on the tabulation. In utilizing the salary tabulation, the arbitrator shall
consider the salaries of all comparable Players and not merely the salary of a
single Player or group of Players.

---

of Kansas City received the least support (2.93 runs per start). The offsetting
nature of statistics like this may be resolved by the arbitrator, but the reasoning behind this resolution is never made known to the parties.

Exhibit 8.1 also permits a wide variety of evidence to support salary
arguments. Some players have won their salary arbitrations by using video-
tape highlights of their defensive skills and taped interviews of club officials
complimenting the players' performance. Some say that Rick Cerone won
his salary arbitration in 1981 because a group of shrieking women showed
up at his hearing and requested his autograph.[60]

Arbitrators also have a difficult time in comparing player salaries. Sometimes one-year contracts are compared with multi-year contracts that can
include signing bonuses, tax shelters, and deferred payments at varying
interest rates. These figures can be averaged differently over the life of the

contract, and comparable annual salaries for any particular year do not represent absolute figures. Confusion can also occur when some players take limited partnerships instead of cash. Finally, some players like Doc Gooden and Gary Gaetti have "loaded up" the front ends if their multiyear contracts because of union-management uncertainties in the 1990 negotiations. Gaetti will make $2.4 million in 1989 and $500,000 in 1990 to minimize any salary losses due to a strike or lockout should there be a collective bargaining impasse.[61]

In short, arbitration is not bound by precise and commonly accepted principles, evidence, and weights. Instead, it can resemble a high-stakes crapshoot—a situation all the more dramatic if the arbitrator is not totally familiar with baseball. Rod Carew once described an early salary arbitration hearing where the arbitrator wanted to know what a "sacrifice hit" meant.

The Negative Impact on Team Finances and Player Performance

Many baseball management officials believe that any arbitrator's decision—no matter how accurately arrived at—has a very negative impact on team finances. Owners may bid up player contracts in salary negotiations or may even pay an extremely high salary figure to free agents. However, in salary arbitration, a third party neutral makes the decision, and management is incapable of controlling or even predicting its team's payroll costs.[62] Yet Marvin Miller has offered a counterargument to this contention.

The whining of the club owners and officials [concerning salary arbitration is] understandable. They liked it when they could dictate the dollar amount of their most significant cost—player salaries. They hate it when free market forces and impartial adjudication are substituted for owner fiat, all of which is so understandable that it is obvious.[63]

The arbitration hearing will often have a negative impact on player-management relationships, also. "Arbitration is not designed to create goodwill and fellowship. It is a dart throwing session [and] it tends to pad the players' bank accounts more than it nourishes their egos."[64] In justifying its salary offer, management may have to say critical things about the player, even though the player is also present at the hearing. The White Sox—for example—contended that its shortstop, Bill Almon, "lacked leadership qualities, tended to choke in the field, was inexperienced, hadn't made the All-Star team and . . . had batted .158 during a particular 13-game stretch."[65] Joe Rudi experienced a similar situation when Charles Finley, owner of the Oakland A's, bad-mouthed him in arbitration.

At my session, he said that I was the worst left fielder in baseball, that I was one of the slowest men in the game, that sure I caught everything but there were so many balls that fell in for hits that would be caught by normal ballplayers. He said that I had a very weak arm, that Campaneris [the A's shortstop] had to go halfway to the outfield to take relay throws. He said that you always put your most mediocre outfielder in left field. I expected him to say those kind of things but it ticked me off that the arbitrator bought his line of bullshit. After it was over Finley said, "I still love you like a son."[66]

Needless to say, players are not pleased when they hear such remarks. Sal Bando brought his wife Sandy to his arbitration hearings with Finley who nevertheless called Bando "the worst-field third baseman in the American League." Finley figured that Bando brought his wife to minimize this sort of criticism. "I hate to be critical of a player in front of his wife... It makes me uncomfortable." Actually, Bando had a different motive. "The only reason I brought Sandy with me... was to keep my temper under control. I felt like beating the shit out of Charlie for the things he said about me. But not with Sandy there."[67]

Arbitration hearings have sometimes included nonperformance factors, as well. Management noted in Orel Hershiser's 1985 hearings that the player had been diagnosed as having spina bifida when he was a child. Hershiser retorted, "I'm nearsighted too... but I can still throw strikes."[68]

Negative attitudes directed toward management for its remarks made in arbitration could very well affect player morale and performance. It is also possible that salary arbitration may contribute to jealousy among the players, because the salary decisions are now public knowledge—and so publicized.

Nine

Salary Trends and Controversy

Many baseball observers have long been concerned about players' high salaries. An article written before 1900, for example, indicated that players were paid "altogether too handsomely" for a workday that consisted only of "a little exercise for a couple of hours."[1] Salaries have increased at an even greater rate during the past 20 years—a situation largely due to collective bargaining and certain labor-agreement provisions (free agency and salary arbitration, discussed in Chapter Eight).

In this chapter, salary trends over the past 20 years are first discussed and contrasted with the negotiation experiences of earlier players. Then, the controversial dimensions of recent players' salaries are grouped into two general and related questions: Are players overpaid? and Is there a relationship between pay and performance?

SALARY TRENDS

Compensation can take many forms (travel and moving expenses and spring training allowances, for example), and it has increased over time through collective bargaining. World Series participants' shares for selected years[2] are presented below to illustrate this situation:

Year	Winning Share	Losing Share	Total Purse
1950	$5,738	$4,081	$486,371

Year	Winning Share	Losing Share	Total Purse
1960	8,418	5,125	682,145
1970	18,216	13,688	1,714,305
1979	28,237	22,114	2,854,824
1988	109,741	87,942	11,969,880

Salary represents the most significant and pervasive compensation element. Players' minimum and average salary statistics for 22 years are presented in Table 9.1.

The increase in minimum salaries grew at a sharper percentage than did the increase in average player salaries for the years 1967 through 1976. One reason is that the minimum salary had a smaller dollar base in 1967: Increases in average player salaries during this time period were higher in absolute dollars but lower in proportional increase, as the 1967 average salary was more than three times greater than the minimum salary counterpart. This proportional difference might also have reflected the union's strategy of appealing to the most members by increasing the salary minimums. The star players, who never showed much interest in unions to begin with, had to bargain for their own salary increases—a hard job, since the reserve rule was still in effect during this time period.

By 1979 the situation had reversed. The yearly proportional increase in average player salaries had far exceeded that for minimum player salaries. Indeed, the average salaries for these years were 5–8 times the minimum salary figures. This reversal can be largely explained by the development and expansion of free agency and salary arbitration. Other possible explanations are examined in the following section.

Negotiation Experiences of Earlier Players

Table 9.1 indicates the superior bargaining leverage and results that contemporary baseball players have had when compared to their earlier counterparts. "Monopsony" characterized the baseball players' wage determination process before the reserve rule was modified by free agency. Under monopsony, one buyer—a team—would confront many potential sellers— the players, who were not paid according to their contribution to team revenues.[3]

In his autobiography, Hall of Fame pitcher Sandy Koufax placed monopsony theory into the context of baseball practice:

Once you sign your first baseball contract, you are owned by the club, a condition that is never completely absent from the bargaining table. Management will talk to

Table 9.1
Minimum and Average Player Salaries in Major League Baseball, 1967–1987

Year	Minimum Salary	(Percentage Increase Over 1967)		Average Salary	(Percentage Increase Over 1967)
1967	$ 6,000			$19,000	
1968 (1)	10,000	66%	(2)	------	(2) -----
1969	10,000	66		24,909	31%
1970	12,000	100		29,303	54
1971	12,750	113		31,543	66
1972	13,500	125		34,092	79
1973	15,000	150		36,566	92
1974	15,000	150		40,839	115
1975	16,000	167		44,676	135
1976	19,000	217		51,501	171
1977	19,000	217		76,066	300
1978	21,000	250		99,876	309
1979	21,000	250	(3)	113,558	498
1980	30,000	400	(3)	143,756	657
1981	32,500	442	(3)	185,651	877
1982	33,500	458	(3)	241,497	1171
1983	35,000	483	(3)	289,194	1422
1984	40,000	567	(3)	329,408	1633
1985	60,000	900	(3)	371,157	1853
1986(5)	60,000	900	(3)	412,520	2071
1987(5)	62,500	942	(4)	412,454	2071
1988	62,500	942	(6)	449,862	2268
1989(7)	68,500	1033	(8)	512,804	2599

(1) First Basic Agreement between Clubs and Major League Players Association.

(2) Not Available.

(3) Salary figures have been discounted for salary deferrals without interest, at a rate of 9 percent per year for the period of delayed payments.

(4) Salary figures include 9 percent per year for contracts that have signing bonuses, which are prorated over the life of the contract but are usually given at the start of the player's contract.

(5) Murray Chass, "Salaries Down, But by How Much?" *Sporting News*, December 21, 1987, p. 49.

(6) Murray Chass, "$449,862? It's Just an Average Wage," *Sporting News*, April 18, 1988, p. 14.

(7) Reflects an inflationary adjustment pegged every two years to the consumer price index.

(8) "Major League Salaries Soar to $512,804 per Player," Jacksonville, *Florida Times-Union*, April 5, 1989, p. C–4.

Source: (for other than those listed) Major League Baseball Players' Association.

you and they'll let you make your points and, if you are patient enough, they'll come up to their maximum figure. But the threatening undertone is always there, the hidden clamp. The owner can always say, "All right, we've talked enough. You will now accept what we are offering or you are no longer in the business of playing baseball."[4]

Bob Grim explains salary bargaining in the pre–salary arbitration, free agency era in even more succinct terms: "[Then] the owners had the players by the short hair, now it's the other way around."[5]

Ty Cobb was one of the few early stars who requested and received a high pay raise (from $10,000 to $12,000 in 1913). Management considered the request to be wrong and threatening. But Cobb backed it up: He had annual batting averages of .385, .420, and .410; there was a U.S. senator who was wondering whether Cobb's contract dispute might be showing some signs of violation of the antitrust laws; and there was always the possibility Cobb himself might decide to join the rival baseball league (the Federal League; see Chapter One). In the end, Cobb may have liked his hefty salary but he was never pleased with certain other working conditions that he had to endure. The shower rooms had only one shower, no hot water, and no therapeutic devices such as whirlpools. At the end of a game, the players all dumped their uniforms into a common container where they lay in their "natural sweat-soaked state" and were worn many times before ever seeing a laundry.

Most players faced Leo Durocher's situation when they attempted to negotiate for a higher raise during this earlier time period. In 1925 Durocher asked for a $1,000 raise to $7,000, but his request was refused. He cussed the general manager, who did the same and then traded Durocher to the last-place National League team the next day.

Even "the" star—Babe Ruth—had to back off on his salary demands in 1927. The Yankees offered Ruth $52,000 for the season; Ruth wanted $100,000. Eventually he accepted a three-year contract at $70,000 a season— a figure that, adjusted for tax and inflationary considerations, would have equalled $900,000 in 1981. Ruth's adjusted salary would not make him the top-paid player in 1989, though: Twenty-one players—such as Gary Carter, Ozzie Smith, and Eddie Murray—earned more than $2 million for this season.

The economic depressions finally had an impact on baseball revenues in 1932, and great pressures were placed on players to reduce their salaries. Ruth, who was making an estimated $80,000 in 1931, signed a contract for $62,500 to play the 1933 season. Salary austerity continued and affected even Joe DiMaggio—the first player to earn $100,000 a season. DiMaggio made $8,000 in his first season in New York and $15,000 in his second season. He requested $40,000 for the 1938 season—an action he later regarded as "one of the biggest mistakes I ever made."[6] Yankees' owner Jake Ruppert wasted no time in drumming up public support for his salary offer of $25,000 which would make DiMaggio the highest paid third-year player in history. Further, DiMaggio's own salary request of $40,000—if granted—would make him the highest paid player in baseball history at age 23.

The press loudly noted that Lou Gehrig, a 13-season superstar, was only making $36,000 a season. DiMaggio considered this irrelevant: "My negotiations with the Yankees will be carried on entirely apart from what they pay Lou."[7] These remarks were reaching a public with more basic concerns—

like trying to purchase a car on an annual family income of less than $2,000. DiMaggio eventually accepted $25,000 for the 1938 season.

DiMaggio's salary negotiations in 1942 were also unsuccessful. He hit in 56 consecutive games—a nearly impossible feat—and won the American League's Most Valuable Player award in the 1941 season. Yet management informed him, "There's a war on [and] the country's in bad shape. We're going to have to cut you $2,500." And then the press was told, "Soldiers are making $21 a month but DiMaggio wants a big raise."[8]

Regular players probably met with even more bargaining resistance than did these early superstars. Dick Allen, in his autobiography, *Crash*, suggested that players even experience this situation when they start in the minors. In 1962 he hit .329 for Williamsport in the (minor) Eastern League. He asked Phillies management for a $50 raise for the next season. He was told that if he held out for a raise, he would spend another season in the minors. He held out and Little Rock, another minor league team, was the result.

Management's salary philosophy for players who reached major league teams often included the following dimensions:

1. A wage increase given to a young player remains each season of his career. It is less expensive to give very small wage increases at the beginning and larger increases toward the end of a player's career, particularly if the player is a star— that is, capable of drawing fans into the park.

2. The player's performance is second to team performance. Even a great player should not be given a large increase if the overall team performance was unsuccessful.

Ralph Kiner experienced this second dimension quite acutely. He was told that he would have to take a $25,000 pay cut the year after he led the league in home runs. His team—the Pirates—had finished last; and the team's general manager, Branch Rickey, informed Kiner that the team could always repeat that status without him.

Whitey Ford was handed a variation of this same reasoning. He had earned $5,000 as a rookie in 1950 and then served in the army during the 1951 and 1952 seasons. When he returned to the Yankees, Ford wanted $10,000 for the 1953 season. The Yankees said that they had won the world championship without him and were not sure he could pitch after two years of inactivity. The club did raise its initial offer of $6,000 to $8,000. Ford accepted the offer because of domestic expenses, a lack of funds, and no skills to do anything else. But recently, Ford compared his most lucrative contract to Orel Hershiser's three-year $7.9-million agreement negotiated in 1989. Ford noted that his own top salary was worth less than $30 a pitch; Hershiser's pitches are now each worth around $600.[9]

Management backed its hard-line bargaining philosophies with equally hard-line tactics such as:

—Restricting a player's production. According to Allie Reynolds, management once prevented him from winning 20 games that would have strengthened his next season's bargaining position. In more recent times, George Bell of the Toronto Blue Jays contended that management hurt his bargaining position by restricting him to a designated hitter's role.

—Having many people (lawyers, business manager, general manager, and team president, for example) in the bargaining session with the player, who was alone.

—Possibly revealing private information if the player would not agree to salary terms. The Yankees threatened to show Mickey Mantle's wife their private detectives' reports on Mantle's late-night activities. Another incident involved informing a holdout pitcher's wife that he had caught a venereal disease during the previous season.

—Deceiving players—for example, understating the salaries of other players on the team so that the negotiating player would sign for less.[10]

And for many players before 1966, wage austerity extended to another economic condition: pensions. Chapter One traced the nonexistent-to-meager pension plan results during this period. The MLBPA changed that situation.

Player Pension Gains

Table 9.2 illustrates pension benefit gains over the past 20 years. This increase has been impressive, particularly when Table 9.2 is subjected to certain additional considerations. For example, in 1967 a player needed five years service in major league baseball to qualify for a pension. Now there is an almost instant vesting, as a player with as little as 44 days' major-league playing experience can qualify for a pension payment. Also, the current top pension payout—$90,000 a year to eligible players—is the maximum allowed by federal law.

Yet the $90,000 maximum—like other baseball statistics—needs to be put into perspective. A player earning this amount must have had active service during or after the 1970 championship season, must have ten years of playing experience, and draw his pension at age 62. Also, the salary in his highest three consecutive years of active service must average $90,000 a year.

These qualifications are far more restrictive than many media accounts would lead one to believe when they infer that a baseball veteran automatically earns $90,000 a year upon retirement. The $90,000 cap—while attainable—is seldom received. For example, 988 retired players received $14,418,209 in fixed and variable retirement benefits in 1987.[11] The average pension payment of $13,593 in 1987 is only 16 percent of the $90,000 max-

Table 9.2

Comparison of Selected Statistics from the Baseball Players' Pension Fund, 1967 and 1987

	1967	1987	(%increase)
Monthly benefits to players with 5 years in majors retiring at age 50	$250	$1447*	579%
Monthly benefits to players with 5 years in majors retiring at age 60	$644	$3145*	488%
Monthly benefits to players with 10 years in majors retiring at age 50	$500	$2894*	579%
Monthly benefits to players with 10 years in majors retiring at age 60	$1288	$6290*	488%
Annual management contribution to pension plan	$4,100,000	$30,000,000	732%
Assets of pension plan	$16,300,000	$388,974,100	2386%

*Monthly variable and fixed payments for players having active service during or after the 1970 championship season ($90,000 benefit level).

Sources: Major League Baseball Players Benefit Plan, Annual Report, 1987, p. 13; *Major League Baseball Players Benefit Plan,* pp. 12 and 17; Thomas E. Ricks, "Plump Pensions in Baseball Are Sources of Envy," *Wall Street Journal,* September 22, 1986, p. 27; and Ken Walker, "The History of Collective Bargaining by Athletes Engaged in Professional Team Sports," Unpublished M.A. Thesis, University of Illinois, p. 41.

imum. Many players receiving pension payments had less than ten years of playing service, withdrew their pension before age 62, and/or left the majors before 1970. This last condition—especially—causes some controversy among both past and present players. Seemingly dramatic pension-benefit comparisons can be made between players leaving before and remaining after 1970. For example:

—Ted Williams, outfielder, Red Sox, 22 seasons, last year 1960—maximum pension (at 65): $30,348 per year.

—Walter "No Neck" Williams, outfielder, Chicago White Sox and others, 10 seasons, last year 1975—Maximum pension (at 62): $68,212 per year.

Hall of Fame pitcher Early Wynn sees this situation as "the shaft" that the players' union (the MLBPA) is giving to the old-timers. Post–1970 MLBPA members would counter that the earlier players paid little or no union dues and did not have to endure the emotional and economic hardships of the player strikes (discussed in Chapters Two and Three) that resulted in the pension plan improvements. The sharp increase in player pensions and wages has resulted in other controversies as well, though.

ARE PLAYERS OVERPAID?

Players' Reactions toward Their Salaries

The players know that their salaries are often far higher than those of their predecessors and most of the fans who follow the game today. Players regarded their large salaries in a variety of ways. Some may agree with Freddie Patek, a former Kansas City shortstop, who felt that his salary could not be justified.

To tell the truth, I don't think anybody thought the escalation of salaries would ever go this high. I feel we're all overpaid. . . . I got a phenomenal contract—much more money than I ever thought I'd make. I wouldn't say I'm embarrassed by it, but deep down I know I'm not worth it. To my shame, though, I have to admit I asked for it.[12]

Pete Rose, too, felt that some of the younger players were either overpaid or trying to become overpaid with their salary proposals. "I worked 14 years to get where I am, and they want it in two or three years."[13] Rose's displeasure notwithstanding, current players do expect to be on a fast track so long as they perform well. Kirby Puckett, for example, has had a fine four year's (plus 147 days) career capped by a .356 batting average in 1988 (the highest for a right-hander since Joe DiMaggio hit .357 in 1941). Puckett's salary has also done well during this time period: $50,000 as a rookie in 1984; $130,000 in 1985; $265,000 in 1986; $435,000 in 1987; $1.2 million in 1988; and $2 million in 1989. Roger Clemens equalled Puckett's starting year and salary ($50,000 in 1984); his three-year contract signed in 1988 is estimated at $7.5 million.

Rose also found that he had to justify his salary with the fans. Although at one time he used to worry about fan reaction when he negotiated his salary, Rose later said that he did not "give a shit about what people think."

I say the hell with them. I'm not going to worry about anybody. . . .
    . . . Some guy is sitting behind me when I'm getting in my car one night. He's getting in his truck and he's got his load of people with him and he's gotta yell at me. He's gotta tell me, "Got all your money in your suitcase?" I say, "I can't get it all in there, asshole." And he just shut up. I mean, why don't he just get in his car and move on?[14]

Rose's attitude regarding salary is shared by those players who see their profession as being very selective and unique. These individuals may also believe that their worth is basically established by those who are paying their salary.

The baseball occupation is certainly selective in that only the best make it to the big leagues. One estimate says that one out of every 4,000 high-school baseball players will ever play in the major leagues. Those who challenge a player's pay because it far exceeds that of the common man fail to comprehend this selectivity. Yet, as sportswriter Leonard Koppett puts it: "If the players weren't exceptional, what common man would pay to watch them?"

In many cases, a player's personality has a cash value distinct from his playing skills. He has a certain quality that attracts fans but cannot be precisely measured or estimated. Dizzy Dean, for example, continued to bring fans to the ballpark when his team—the Saint Louis Cardinals—was not particularly successful, and even after his pitching arm went dead.

Their distinctive job skills and personality characteristics prompt players to compare their salaries to those of entertainers and/or each other. Entertainers such as Johnny Carson, Sylvester Stallone, and Frank Sinatra receive multimillion-dollar contracts for their services in television, the movies and recordings. Perhaps players make the most realistic salary comparisons when they consider the salaries earned by other players. This comparison can involve symbolic as well as economic considerations. The salary amount is a way of keeping score—of determining one's relative status among players. Hank Aaron, for example, believed that his signing for $100,000 a year was one of the biggest off-field movements in his baseball career.

I'll just plain have to admit that getting into the $100,000 class gave me a feeling I'd never had before. Ted Williams, . . . Joe DiMaggio, . . . Stan Musial, . . . Willie Mays, . . . Mickey Mantle, . . . and Sandy Koufax had made it—and now I had made it.

I could have hit 62 home runs, batted .400 and driven in 150 runs and I wouldn't have felt any more like I "belonged" than I did when I signed that contract for $100,000.[15]

Most players would probably agree with Babe Ruth that they are neither greedy nor overpaid in their wage determination efforts. Ruth contended,

It isn't right to call me or any ballplayer an ingrate because we ask for more money. Sure I want more, all I'm entitled to. Listen, a man who works for another man is not going to be paid any more than he's worth. A man ought to get all he can earn. A man who knows he's making money for other people ought to get some of the profit he brings in. Don't make any difference if it's baseball or a bank or a vaudeville show. It's business, I tell you. There ain't no sentiment to it.[16]

Player "worth" should never be approached in a sarcastically philosophical sense. For example, a light-hitting, poor-fielding shortstop's salary should not be compared to that of a brain surgeon. Nor should alternative uses for the players' salaries be a matter for speculation. The money saved by lowering the Yankees' salaries—say—would probably not be funneled into cleaning up the South Bronx. And while it is true that Don Mattingly's salary would feed and shelter many poor people, the income of George Steinbrenner would feed a great many more. Babe Ruth's comments suggest that the players' worth be measured in more pragmatic terms: an owner's payment for player services, which are probably less than the revenues that the player brings in.

Players' Salaries and Team Revenues

The relationship between player salaries and team revenues is not clear, as team revenues are neither consistently calculated nor consistently reported for the same team or for all teams. For example, one major league team—the Red Sox—reported very different revenue figures to the press and to Congress for the same operating years. Differences occur between teams because owners apply different accounting options. Some of these practices were revealed when the owners opened their books during the 1985 strike. Consider the examples of George Steinbrenner writing off his hotel in Tampa on the Yankees, and the Anheuser-Busch corporation not counting parking and concession income from the Cardinals' games as baseball revenue.

An individual team owner can also use different accounting situations to arrive at different revenue figures. Whitey Herzog found it difficult to believe that Ewing Kauffman, the Royals' owner and Herzog's former boss, lost $1.8 million while drawing 2 million fans a year. Herzog estimated Kauffman's costs at $13.5 million (player salaries, $10 million; front-office costs, $1 million; player development costs, $2 million; and travel expenses, $500,000) and his revenues from fan attendance and national television at $21.1 million plus any local broadcast-rights fees. Herzog concludes, "There's no way—if you draw two million people—that you can lose money. Unless you're trying."[17]

Herzog's financial analysis relies on traditional revenue sources such as paid home attendance, parking and concessions, shared road attendance, local and national television packages, and various licensing and marketing rights incomes. Two other financial aspects not included in Herzog's or in other cost-revenue analyses underestimate the players' contributions to team revenues. Unlike any other industry, professional sports team owners can depreciate player employment contracts for federal income tax purposes. In 1983 Tom Monaghan, the founder of Domino's Pizza, reportedly paid $55 million to own the Detroit Tigers. One estimate indicated that his player employment contract depreciation reduced the Tigers' purchase price by $14 million.

Capital gains that result from the sale of a team to another owner are also neglected. The Baltimore Orioles, for example, who were sold for $12 million in 1977, were again sold in 1988 for $70 million—an American League record. In 1989, the Seattle Mariners were valued at $76 million—much more than the team's $13 million purchase price in 1981. Also in 1989, a 58 percent share of the Texas Rangers, who heretofore have not won a division title, went for an estimated $25 million. Players do not receive a defined share of these figures.

Although team revenues are not consistently calculated, some estimates have attempted to link an individual player's contributions to increased fan attendance and related club revenues. Mickey Mantle's retirement was predicted to cost the Yankees 250,000 fewer admissions at home and on the road. Eight days after the California Angels signed Reggie Jackson ($4 million for four years), season ticket sales went from 4,800 to 12,000. It occurred to Buzzy Bavasi, president of the Angels, that the additional $3-million drawing interest in the bank meant that Jackson would pay for his contract in one week. Other players such as Dwight Gooden, Roger Clemens, and Fernando Valenzuela have significantly increased fan attendance and all its related revenues even when they were pitching on the road.

Another more aggregate measure is the percentage of a team's revenues that goes to salaries. Marvin Miller has rather consistently maintained that the percentage of revenues that goes to players' (workers') salaries in baseball is one of the smallest of any industry in the country. Miller indicated that the players' salaries and pension plan amounted to less than 28 percent of baseball's revenues in 1978, compared to a 35-percent share in 1952. He also mentioned that baseball TV revenues alone—not parking, tickets, or concession sales—exceeded the combined cost of players' salaries and the player pension plan. Comparable salary-revenue ratios for the years since 1978 seem to be unavailable. However, in 1985 the *Wall Street Journal* confirmed Miller's earlier statement that television revenues alone more than covered player salaries.

In 1988, the Minnesota Twins share of home ticket sales was $5 million more than the team's payroll.[18] Even more illustrative is the Los Angeles Dodgers' player payroll (likely the major league's highest) in 1989. This figure, around $22 million, is more than offset by an estimated $70 million from stadium revenues and local national television contracts, not to mention other organizational income sources.[19]

In summary, players' wage gains since the MLBPA's formation have been most impressive over the years. Whether or not players are overpaid as a result, however, is very uncertain—largely because of their unique job characteristics (very selective skills, along with personality aspects).

Debates over player worth are seldom useful or revealing if "worth" is defined in some philosophical sense. Uncertainty remains even if worth is defined in more pragmatic terms (payment for services that contribute to revenues), since team owners do not calculate revenues in any consistent fashion. Yet there is a very real possibility that owners have long been able to cover player salaries with television revenues alone. Moreover, owners do not have to share with the players any fan attendance–related income, tax depreciation advantages, or capital gains when the team is sold.

There is a potentially justifiable relationship between an increase in player salaries and an increase in team revenues. One study over a 14-year time period (1969–83) found that every team win increases fan attendance 1.9 percent, or an extra 25,301 paying customers. This relationship assumes that higher paid players contribute directly to increased team victories and revenues more than lower paid players. This assumption is tested in the following section.

IS THERE A RELATIONSHIP BETWEEN PAY AND PERFORMANCE?

The question of a possible correction between pay and performance is related to whether players are overpaid: A player might be paid too much if his large salary does not seem closely related to his past and/or current performance measures. One of the more publicized examples of this situation occurred in 1980 when Dave Winfield signed a ten-year contract with the New York Yankees that was estimated to exceed $22 million.

In 1978 and 1979 Winfield batted .308, and in 1979 he hit 34 home runs and drove in a league-leading 118 runs. Yet his seven-year career average prior to the Yankee signing was 19 homers, 78 runs batted in, and a .284 batting average. Some feel that Winfield was paid too much. Jim Bunning—a former All-Star pitcher for the Detroit Tigers—protested thus: "The insanity of it all is just unbelievable to me. . . . To think that Dave Winfield is worth more than the entire Detroit franchise."[20] Winfield contends that part of his large salary settlement was due to George Steinbrenner's not realizing that a certain cost-of-living escalator in his contract compounded.

Sportswriters and fans alike sometimes take pleasure in applying singular performance statistics to players' salaries. Consider the figures for the first class of free agents (those who signed in 1977), as indicated in Table 9.3. Subsequent and even more dramatic data are presented below:

—Rennie Stennet made approximately $20,000 for every hit he made for the Pirates in 1981, while George Foster earned $16,327 for every hit ($25,232 for every RBI) he made for the Mets in 1985.
—Julio Cruz was paid $1,242,333 for batting .197 for the White Sox in 1985.
—Bud Black earned $120,000 for each of his five pitching victories for the Kansas City Royals in 1987.

The newspaper *USA Today* has started to systematize (and publicize) major pay and performance differences by announcing annually an "overpaid" and "underpaid" players' team for both the American and the National Leagues.

Even more dramatic are the salaries paid to players who are not performing at all for the compensating team. This can occur when a player becomes disabled, or when he no longer plays for a team that must nevertheless

Table 9.3
Pay-for-Performance Measures for the 24 Free Agents in 1977

The Hitters

	Ave.	HR	RBI	$ per hit
Jackson, Yankees	.286	32	110	3,867
Rudi, Cal.	.264	13	53	6,531
Matthews, Atl.	.283	17	64	2,389
Cash, Mont.	.289	0	43	1,660
Grich, Cal.	.243	7	23	7,045
Bando, Milw.	.250	17	82	1,939
Baylor, Cal.	.251	25	75	1,891
Tenace, S.D.	.233	15	61	2,598
Campaneris, Tex.	.254	5	46	1,443
Hebner, Phil.	.285	18	62	1,475
Fuentes, Det.	.309	5	51	474
McCovey, S.F.	.280	28	86	672
Allen, Oak.	.240	5	31	1,463
Soderholm, W. Sox	.280	25	67	465
Smith, Balt.	.215	5	29	633
Dade, Clev.	.291	3	45	347
Nordbrook, W. Sox–Toronto	.193	0	2	1,875
Stillman, W. Sox	.210	3	13	1,200

The Starters

	W	L	ERA	$ per win
Gullett, Yankees	14	4	3.58	22,619
Garland, Clev.	13	19	3.60	16,808
Alexander, Tex.	17	11	3.65	9,363
Stone, W. Sox	15	12	4.51	4,000

The Relievers

	G	W	L	$ per save
Fingers, S.D.	78	8	9	9,486
Campbell, Bos.	69	13	9	6,774

Source: Larry Keith, "Is It Daft or Deft to Draft?" *Sports Illustrated*, November 11, 1977, p. 32.

continue to pay some or all of his guaranteed salary. Between the years 1983 and 2014, owners will have paid $56.7 million to players who are not earning that money on the playing field. One pitcher—Rick Burleson of the California Angels—earned $815,801 while unable to play for 214 days during the 1985 season.

Yet the relationship between pay and performance is not really encompassed by citing the flashy but isolated examples. There are at least four problems that must be considered in interpreting performance statistics, and they apply to all players during the particular season.

Interpreting Performance Statistics

The first baseball averages—players' average runs per game—were calculated in 1859. Batting averages were officially recognized after 1876, and pitching win-loss statistics and earned run averages were also in general use at this time. Runs batted in were not officially compiled until 1920.[21]

Roger Angell, a noted baseball observer, has placed these performance statistics in perspective:

The statistics of baseball form the critical dimensions of the game. Invisible but ineluctable, they swarm and hover above the head of every pitcher, every fielder, every batter, every team, recording every play with an accompanying silent shift of digits. The true, grinding difficulty of this sport is to be found in its unwinking figures, and ballplayers on the field are in competition not just with the pitchers and sluggers of the opposing team but with every pitcher or batter who ever played the game, including their past selves.[22]

Nevertheless, performance statistics—while inevitable enough and almost objective—do come with their own set of problems.[23] For one thing, some performance statistics are based on subjective—not absolute—judgments. Many hits and all errors are determined by an official scorer. Umpires subjectively determine balls (leading to possible walks), call strikes (leading to strikeouts), and judge the difference between fair and foul balls. The "balk" is probably the most subjective performance statistic of them all, and large-scale controversy ensued when it was stringently applied in 1988. There are many possible moves that can result in a balk, with many of these moves having subjective nuances. A balk occurs when the pitcher

—fakes making a pitch;

—while on the rubber, fakes throwing to first;

—while on the rubber, fails to step toward the base he is throwing to;

—while on the rubber, throws or fakes a throw to an unoccupied base except for the purposes of making a play;

—makes an illegal pitch;

—pitches when he is not facing the batter;

—makes any pitching motion while not on the rubber or makes any pitching motion on the rubber without making the pitch;

—unnecessarily delays the game;

—stands on or astride the rubber without the ball;

—when in a pitching position, takes one hand off the ball without throwing;

—drops the ball while on the rubber;

—pitches when the catcher is not in the catcher's box; or

—fails to come to a complete and discernible stop in the set position.[24]

A second problem is that standard baseball statistics (runs batted in, pitching victories, and so forth) are very narrow as they ignore the effect of other equally countable items that should be related. For example, relief pitchers are eligible for performance awards given by Rolaids and the *Sporting News*. These awards are largely influenced by pitching victories. Yet relief pitchers often rack up pitching victories after poor performances. A relief pitcher might enter the game with a two-run lead in the top of the ninth inning— say—and give up two runs, only to have his team win the game by one run in the bottom of the ninth inning—which gives him the victory. Another common pitching-performance indicator—earned run average—may not even apply to a relief pitcher, as this statistic tells nothing about the reliever's ability to keep the previous pitcher's runners from scoring.

On the other hand, neglected statistics can affect the traditional pitchers who are paid to start and win games. Dave Stieb, who pitched for the Toronto Blue Jays, illustrated this situation by explaining why he should have won the Cy Young (best pitcher) award in 1982 and the Golden Glove (best fielding) award for a pitcher in 1984.

The case, your honor, is predicated on the fact that the [Cy Young] award is supposed to go to "the best pitcher" in the league. Therefore, let us examine the facts. I won 17 and lost 14 that season, with an earned run average of 3.25. In 38 starts, I led the American League in complete games (19), innings pitched (288 1/3) and shutouts (5). I gave up 271 hits, struck out 141 and walked 75.

Pete Vuckovich [Milwaukee] won 18 and lost 6, with an ERA of 3.34. He finished nine of 30 starts, with one shutout, gave up 234 hits in 223 2/3 innings, struck out 105 and walked 102. . . .

The '84 season has to be a different story. I made two errors, both on pickoff attempts at second base, and Ron Guidry of the Yankees made none. That alone might appear decisive except that at 195 2/3 innings, he pitched 71 1/3 fewer than my league-leading 267 and, therefore, had fewer chances. Given the fact that he is a lefthander, the pickoff play at first is a far simpler matter for him in that he does not have to pirouette.

I realize it might be a pain in the pencil sharpener, but it would be fairer if the judges had stats on the number of chances taken—a wild throw is counted an error, an accurate throw counts for nothing—as well as the number of assists and putouts a pitcher contributes.[25]

Kansas City Royals' second baseman, Frank White, probably had a cleaner claim to a voted performance award in 1988. White committed only four errors, while leading the American League in fielding with a .994 percentage. Yet managers and coaches awarded the "Gold Glove" that year to Harold

Reynolds, who made 18 errors and had finished ninth with a .977 fielding percentage.

Some measures have been developed to take into account such diverse yet relevant baseball statistics. In 1981 the Elias Sports Bureau began the most complete formula to date for comparing players statistically at each position and in ranking groups. These figures determine the draft compensation that a team signing a free agent must give to that player's team. For example, a team signing a type-A free agent (one whose rankings are in the top 30 percent of all players in that position) must give three extra selections to the player's former team in the June draft.

The Elias Sports Bureau Scale gives the average ranking of a player per position in the following seven performance categories over the previous two seasons: plate appearances; batting averages; on-base average; home runs; runs batted in; fielding percentage; and total chances accepted. In 1987 Don Mattingly of the Yankees was the first player ever to receive a perfect 1 on the Elias Scale.

Another comparative statistic—the "total average" (TA)—has also been suggested. The TA is a straightforward statistic based on two fundamental baseball units: the base, and the out. Each base is one step closer to a run, and each out is closer to the end of the inning. Total average is the ratio between the bases that a player gets for his team and the outs that he costs the team. Doubles count as two bases, whereas a double play counts as two outs. Walks and hit-by-pitcher count for one base. A successful stolen base counts as an extra base; an unsuccessful stolen base counts as an out. Sacrifices are not counted in the calculation.[26]

This measure can compare players with different styles and strengths. The bunt hit, home run, walk, and steal are all considered. It also removes the advantage that one player may have by being on a better team, since runs scored and runs batted in are not included in the calculation.

A third performance-statistic problem is that each statistic does not have an absolute meaning. Therefore, people can interpret the same figure differently. Some baseball statistics are difficult to interpret in positive or negative terms. For example, does a high number of double plays reflect positively or negatively on a team's pitching staff? This figure could mean that a pitcher(s) has good control in getting the batter to hit a ground ball to an infielder. It could also mean that a pitcher(s) has given up too many hits and walks to let runners get to base—which is necessary for a double play.

Also, a seemingly negative statistic—fielding errors—might be viewed in positive terms: A very fast and capable fielder might get a glove on more balls (that is, have more fielding chances, and therefore errors) than less skilled players. By the same token, "positive" statistics can be viewed in negative terms. Mickey Mantle—a baseball legend because of his offensive statistics, including base hits—realized that he had 1,700 walks and 1,800 strikeouts. Mantle observed, "That's a total of 3,500, and if you get up 500 times a year, you figure I spent seven years where I never hit the ball!"[27]

Player performance statistics have a fourth problem as they are not so individual as they may appear. The figures are influenced by other players and other factors. Some player offensive statistics such as runs scored and runs batted in are influenced by the player's particular place in the batting order, and the ability of other players to get on base and/or move the player to home. Other team players also affect a pitcher's ability to win games—a situation that Jim Bouton described in regard to Yankee pitcher Diego Segui. According to Bouton, Segui pitched "lousy" for two games (giving up four runs in six innings), but received two victories. The press thought Segui was pitching better than he was, because of the results. Bouton feels that legendary pitching coach Johnny Sain summarized this situation best, when Sain said, "The world doesn't want to hear about labor pains. . . . It only wants to see the baby."[28]

There are also many varied playing conditions that can affect players' performance statistics. Consider the ballpark, for example: A player's batting average can be affected by each park's unique characteristics such as visibility, foul territory, the weather, the altitude, and the playing surface.

Grounds crews have been known to alter playing conditions to benefit their teams. In 1962 the Giants were able to beat the rival Dodgers in a key series largely because the topsoil was replaced by a "squishy swamp of sand, peat moss, and water." This conversion kept Murray Willis from adding to his 104 stolen bases that season. Other grounds adjustments have included the following instances:

—Comiskey Park: slanting the White Sox baselines toward fair territory so that bunts by Nellie Fox and Luis Apancio would have more chance of staying in fair territory.
—Municipal Stadium: moving back the outfield fences when the Yankees visited Cleveland, then moving the fences in when the Saint Louis Browns came to town.
—Crosley Field: digging out the pitcher's mound to create a concave effect, "increasing the chances of visiting pitchers' floating high, fat fastballs to the Frank Robinsons, Wally Posts, and Gus Bells on the Reds' roster."[29]

Even stadium construction can affect player performance. Noise levels at the Minneapolis Metrodome have been measured at 92 decibels. While the hometown Twins have adjusted to the loud confusion of sounds, other teams have not been so fortunate. In 1988 the Twins visiting teams had made from 13 to 71 errors in the 13 other American League ballparks. In the Metrodome they made 85.[30]

Thus, making comparisons of players' performance statistics—particularly over time—becomes difficult, if not impossible.

If one tries to compare figures for different eras, one is immediately immersed in different conditions, many of which the statistic user doesn't even know. In 1930, the ball was different from the one used in 1920, or 1960. Parks were different, styles were different, even rules were different. Until 1950, even the height of the mound differed in various parks. (It was then standardized at 15 inches).[31]

Such varied playing conditions and the circumstances of different teammates and opponents may explain why Joe Tinker, John "Crab" Evers, and Frank Chance were elected into the Hall of Fame in 1946 even though the trio had very mediocre performance statistics.

Performance and Salaries

Preceding performance measurement problems notwithstanding, management needs to know if the salaries that they are paying to the players relate at least somewhat to subsequent performance. Table 9.4 represents the top 25 percent and lowest 25 percent paid players who were under contract as of August 31, 1987, and had at least 51 at-bats or, in the case of pitchers, 30 or more innings pitched in 1987.

Management does not expect a $1-million-a-year player to have ten times the hits or batting average or pitching victories of a player who receives $100,000 a year. Yet management does feel that a highly paid player should perform better than a player who receives far less pay. The frequency distributions and chi-square statistics found in Table 9.4 assume that

—the top 25 percent paid hitters' and pitchers' performance statistics will be in the upper half at the end of the 1987 season; and

—the bottom 25 percent paid hitters' and pitchers' performance statistics will be in the bottom half at the end of the 1987 season.

These assumptions do not suggest a very direct relationship between pay and performance as they only state that management should increase the odds of its top-paid (25 percent) players being in the upper half of the performance statistics at the end of the season. Yet the statistics only support even this loose relationship on three out of eight occasions (number of hits for the American and the National Leagues, and earned run average for the National League). There is no statistically significant relationship between pay and season batting averages or pitchers' win-loss percentages.

Another and perhaps more representative way to examine the relationship between pay and performance is to look at average team salary and team win-loss percentage at the end of the season (see Table 9.5). Spearman rank order correlations (r) were conducted for each team's rank order salary with rank order win-loss percentage for each league. In 1977 there was a very high significant correlation between salary and performance for both the American ($r = .74$, $p \leq .02$) and the National ($r = .71$, $p \leq .02$) Leagues. However in 1987 and 1988 there were no statistically significant relationships

Table 9.4

Relationship between the Top and Bottom 25 Percent of Salaried Players and the Top and Bottom 50 Percent of Performance Statistics, 1987

Player's Salary	Performance Indicator	Performance Statistic (American League)		Chi Square	Performance Statistic (National League)		Chi Square
		Top 50%	Bottom 50%		Top 50%	Bottom 50%	
	Batting Average						
Top 25%		30	20		24	18	
Bottom 25%		31	19	.04	18	29	3.16
	Number of Hits						
Top 25%		35	15		34	8	
Bottom 25%		20	30	9.09**	11	36	29.39**
	Earned Run Av.						
Top 25%		23	15		17	12	
Bottom 25%		15	23	3.86*	13	17	1.38
	Won-Loss Pitching Percentage						
Top 25%		24	13		14	15	
Bottom 25%		18	19	1.98	15	15	.02

*Significant at .05 level

**Significant at .01 level

Note: Based on the top 25 percent and bottom 25 percent paid players who were under contract as of August 31, 1987, and had at least 51 at-bats or, in the case of pitchers, 30 or more innings pitched in 1987. The figures for earned run average are reversed: The top 50 percent of performance statistics for earned run average represent the lowest numerical totals for this measure, and vice versa.

between average team-salary ranking and win-loss percentage ranking for the American League ($r = .28$, $p \leq .33$; and $r = .34$, $p \leq .24$, respectively) or the National League ($r = -.31$, $p \leq .33$; and $r = .03$, $p \leq .91$, respectively).

Several factors account for this changed situation. As previously noted in Chapter Eight, the relationship between salary arbitration and performance results cannot be clearly established. By 1977 this relationship only affected 92 players who filed for arbitration, with 43 players actually using the procedure. The potential for salary arbitration's distorting effects on the pay-performance relationship increased during the next 11 years: 1,079 players filed for arbitration during this time period, with 226 players using the procedure. In fact, salary arbitration's impact is even larger, as arbitrators'

Table 9.5
Average Player Salaries and Team Win-Loss Rankings, 1977, 1987, and 1988

Team	Average Player Salary			League Salary Ranking			League Performance Ranking (Win-Loss Percentage)		
	1977	1987	1988	1977	1987	1988	1977	1987	1988
National League									
Philadelphia	139,916	488,613	543,520	1	5	3	1	6.5	11
Cincinnati	110,392	332,285	357,190	2	9	11	4	5	3
Pittsburgh	99,419	221,380	237,540	3	11	12	3	6.5	4
Los Angeles	97,778	579,785	641,487	4	1	1	2	10	2
San Francisco	88,180	309,846	474,712	5	10	5	8.5	4	6
San Diego	73,860	412,000	370,537	6	8	10	10	12	5
Saint Louis	71,315	429,019	447,845	7	6	8	5	1	10
Chicago	69,018	576,273	541,936	8	2	4	6.5	6.5	9
Atlanta	68,567	527,756	464,045	9	3	7	12	11	12
Montreal	65,823	204,740	371,783	10	12	9	8.5	3	8
New York	58,782	519,429	634,674	11	4	2	11	2	1
Houston	55,973	421,796	474,000	12	7	6	6.5	9	7
American League									
New York	138,973	562,758	672,005	1	1	1	2	4	7
California	96,602	408,632	463,890	2	9	7	8.5	11.5	10
Kansas City	95,692	531,552	608,583	3	2	2	1	6	8
Texas	83,993	226,755	215,826	4	13	14	5	11.5	12
Boston	76,294	520,758	555,514	5	4	3	3.5	8.5	3
Baltimore	70,960	523,658	521,785	6	3	4	3.5	13	14
Cleveland	68,784	361,917	324,130	7	11	11	10	13	9
Chicago	65,220	372,386	266,188	8	10	13	6	14	11
Milwaukee	54,435	281,781	333,535	9	12	10	11	3	5.5
Detroit	46,665	486,272	526,980	10	5	5	8.5	1	4
Oakland	45,700	426,582	396,987	11	7	9	13	7	1
Seattle	38,161	181,580	288,798	12	14	12	12	8.5	13
Minnesota	38,074	431,926	523,028	13	6	6	7	5	2
Toronto	34,320	411,687	455,059	14	8	8	14	2	5.5

Sources: New York Times, October 3, 1977; Tracy Ringolsby, "Top Paid Club? Pirates at $140,000 Average," *Sporting News*, January 28, 1978, p. 53; *New York Times*, April 12, 1987, p. 66–A; *New York Times*, October 6, 1987, p. 30; Hal Bodley, "Average Salary Increases 9.6 Percent," *USA Today*, April 7, 1988, p. 5C; Murray Chass, "$449,862? Its Just an Average Wage," *Sporting News*, April 18, 1988, p. 14; and *New York Times*, October 3, 1988, p. 42.

decisions have influenced the contract negotiations of other players not directly involved with the process.

Owners' egos can also distort pay-performance relationships. Previous chapters have suggested that successful and rational business executives undergo severe managerial reversals when they operate a baseball team. Hall of Famer Robin Roberts believes that owners are more driven by the desire to be a winner than by the profit motive. According to Roberts, their player salary decisions are based on dreams, rather than sound business decisions.

Such lapses in the owners' rationality can result in at least two possibly counterproductive player wage-agreement features: long-term contracts, and performance incentive clauses. Whitey Herzog, current manager of the Saint Louis Cardinals, believes that many a player has gotten lazy right after signing a long-term contact and has only performed at full speed again when in the final year of his contract. Fellow managers Billy Martin and Frank Robinson agree that long-term contracts ruin a player's performance incentive, because he will receive the same salary next year whether he hits .250 or .350 this year. As baseball legend Willie Mays put it:

It makes no sense to me to give a twenty-two-year-old who has a big year a contract that sets him up for life. I don't say that we played only for the money. But we certainly understood that if we did well, and the team did well, we'd get paid more. We couldn't live off last year's stolen base or great catch. That is what incentive is all about. You have to have a reason to want to be better. You want to be rewarded for an outstanding season. Now, though, you hear so many stories of clubs that are saddled with a long-term contract for a player they no longer want. What does the club do? It trades the player and still pays part of his salary to the new team.[32]

Yet others counter that the long-term contract factor is irrelevant because players are motivated by pride, which means not letting yourself down and/or embarrassing yourself in front of fans who—for the most part—are waiting for the high-priced player to goof up. Regardless of the length of their contracts, players are in the game to win. Former Cincinnati Reds player Joe Morgan says that he would be willing to play the World Series for free just for the chance of being champion. "The pride of being the champions—that's what matters. In time, the money for the Series will be gone, but I will be a world champion forever."[33]

There is some hard evidence, however, to supports Herzog's, Martin's, and Mays's side of the long-term contract controversy. One study found that baseball players become "disabled" at an unusually high rate after signing multiyear contracts.[34] Another found decreased performance among players signing for the long term. This study calculated the following average performance comparisons for players signing contracts of longer than three years:

104 (Unnamed) Hitters

Year before signing a multiyear contract: 133 games; 13 homers; 63 RBI; .280 avg.

Year after signing multiyear contract: 124 games; 11 homers; 56 RBI; .273 avg.

Second year after signing: 117 games; 12 homers; 54 RBI; .267 avg.

Third year after signing: 118 games; 10 homers; 53 RBI; .263 avg.

57 (Unnamed) Pitchers (Starters and Relievers)

Year prior to signing multiyear contract: 39 games; won 12, lost 9; 3.33 ERA

Third year after signing multiyear contract: 35 games; won 9, lost 8; 3.91 ERA[35]

As noted in Chapter Eight, the owners are currently shying away from long-term player contracts. In fact, Dave Righetti's three year $4.3 million contract through 1990 was the first multiyear contract signed by a pitcher since Fernando Valenzuela signed with the Dodgers for $5.5 million in 1986. Some of management's reluctance may be due to the aforementioned performance drops. However, the owners are also likely concerned about the possible legal obligation to pay a multiyear player contract if a strike occurs during the 1990 season.

The second possibly counterproductive player wage-agreement feature— "performance incentives"—is actually a misnomer: Rule 3(A), which governs player baseball contracts, outlaws incentives for achieving certain skill measures such as victories, earned run averages, batting averages, or home runs. The thinking behind this rule is that a player needing a home run to meet an incentive bonus might ignore a bunt sign and hurt his team in the process. Yet performance incentives can legally include rather subjective media awards (Most Valuable Player, Rookie of the Year, and the Cy Young pitching award, for example) that are based on these measures. Players can also get paid more for various work-quantity milestones. Consider, for example, Dwight Gooden's 1985 contract after he was paid the minimum salary in his rookie season in 1984. His contract reportedly included a $10,000 bonus for making 33 starts and $25,000 for 36 starts; $50,000 for winning the Cy Young award; $25,000 for finishing second; and $15,000 for third, fourth, or fifth; $15,000 for making the All-Star team; and $15,000 for winning a Gold Glove. Dave Kingman's 1985 contract gave him an extra $1,000 for plate appearances 501 through 600, and $2,000 per plate appearance for 601 through 650. In the same year Ron Cey pocketed the most incentive income ($500,000) for fan attendance bonuses. His contract called for bonuses of $100,000 each when the Cubs' attendance reached 1.5 million, 1.6 million, 1.7 million, 1.8 million, and 1.9 million.

Some players have done very well with incentives. In 1987 Bryn Smith earned the $62,500 salary minimum while pitching for the Expos. However, he also earned an additional $404,919 because of a provision that based his bonuses on the average number of innings he lasted in his starts.

On the surface, this practice may seem to strengthen the relationship between pay and performance. George Brett said that he was very motivated by incentive clauses he received during the 1987 season. He earned a $50,000 bonus for appearing in his thirteenth consecutive All-Star Game and another $250,000 for making 625 plate appearances. Brett received these incentives—he said—because the Royals thought that he could not perform accordingly and he wanted to show them otherwise. In 1987, players earned 56 percent ($7,226,444) of the $12,859,318 incentive bonuses in their contracts; this proportion dropped to 51 percent ($6,545,083 out of $12,711,500) in 1988.[36]

However, a deeper consideration of performance rewards suggests an insignificant—even contradictory—relationship. There may not be a direct relationship between quantity and quality indicators (number of pitching starts and pitching win-loss percentage, for example). In some cases, the relationship is removed because the incentive is almost automatically attainable or unattainable. Examples of the first category are the recent incentives that would give $50,000 to Frank Viola for finishing in the top ten in the Cy Young award voting, and a $50,000 weight incentive clause to Tony Pena (who was never overweight a day in his life). An example in the second category occurred when the White Sox offered a pitcher $25,000 if he won the Silver Slugger award, given annually in November to the league's best hitter at each position. The American League almost always uses designated hitters to bat for the pitcher.

Some management officials wonder why performance incentives are needed to motivate players at all. One general manager believes, "You're paying a guy a fantastic salary. What is it for, showing up at the ballpark? . . . We feel that you pay a guy for a 162-game schedule so why pay him extra for playing 150 games?"[37] Further, incentives that motivate players can backfire against the player and the team. For example, Giants catcher Bob Brenly believes that performance incentives encouraged him to play on bad knees in 1984.

I probably could've saved some of my cartilage damage by not playing. . . . You not only risk permanent injury, but you may not be playing 100 percent, and that lets the team down. For most guys, I think incentives do more damage than good.[38]

Frank Robinson maintains that performance incentives really cause unfair arguments for the manager because incentives make a player even more angry when he does not play. And then the player's anger may be directed also at the front office when he believes that the owner is conspiring with the field manager to keep his playing time and related wage incentives down. Al Campanis tells how this situation could have developed when he was vice-president of the Dodgers: "Let's say Tommy [Lasorda] is managing the All-Star team and he leaves off one of our players who has a $25,000 bonus clause for making the team. The guy immediately thinks Tommy and I are in collusion at his expense."[39] In 1988 the Dodgers were the only team that did not offer any incentives in players' contracts, and they won the World Series in spite of—or was it because of?—this practice.[40]

Notes

CHAPTER ONE

1. Peter S. Craig, "Organized Baseball," Bachelor of Arts Thesis, Oberlin College, 1950, p. 26. For examples of club rules and sanctions, see Robert C. Berry, William B. Gould IV, and Paul D. Staudohar, *Labor Relations in Professional Sports* (Dover, Mass.: Auburn House, 1986), p. 48.

2. John Ward, "Is the Ballplayer a Chattel?" *Lippincott's Monthly Magazine*, August 1887, p. 311. The reserve rule initially applied to only five players a team for the 1880 season. It was extended eventually to cover all players on the team.

3. David Q. Voight, *America through Baseball* (Chicago: Nelson-Hall, 1976), p. 207.

4. Paul M. Gregory, *The Baseball Player: An Economic Study* (Washington, D.C.: Public Affairs Press, 1956), pp. 185, 186.

5. Anthony J. Connor, *Voices from Cooperstown* (New York: Collier Books, 1984), p. 161.

6. Lee Lowenfish and Tony Lupien, *The Imperfect Diamond* (New York: Stein and Day, 1980), p. 51.

7. Red Smith, "Tale of Yank Robinson's Dirty Pants," *New York Times*, April 3, 1972, p. 51.

8. James B. Dworkin, *Owners versus Players* (Boston: Auburn House, 1981), pp. 13–15.

9. See, for example, "Baseball Values Rise in the Major Leagues," *New York Times*, December 30, 1906, p. 12; "What Baseball Costs Each Season," *New York Times*, August 23, 1908, sec. 5, p. 4; and "The National Game in Dollars and Outs," *New York Times*, May 2, 1909, sec. 5, p. 10.

10. John D. McCallum, *Ty Cobb* (New York: Praeger Publishers, 1975), p. 83.

11. "Detroit Baseball Club on Strike," *New York Times*, May 18, 1912, p. 1.

Actually the Cleveland club was the first team to "strike in professional baseball." In 1911, the team voted to attend a funeral after Ban Johnson refused to cancel the game. The game was eventually cancelled. *New York Times,* May 19, 1912, p. 2.

12. John J. McGraw, *My Thirty Years in Baseball* (New York: Boni and Liveright, 1928), p. 249.

13. Lowenfish and Lupien, *Imperfect Diamond,* p. 95.

14. McGraw, *Thirty Years,* pp. 251, 253.

15. "Owen's Immediate Reinstatement Is Opposed by Many Big Leaguers," *New York Times,* August 8, 1946, p. 25.

16. Paul Gould, "Unionism's Bid in Baseball," *New Republic* 115 (August 5, 1946), p. 134.

17. "Seeks to Organize Baseball Players," *New York Times,* April 18, 1946, p. 32.

18. "Sees It Doomed to Fail," *New York Times,* April 18, 1946, p. 32.

19. This incident reflects varied interpretations of labor-management activities. One account had Sewell being soundly booed by the fans as he led the Pirates on to the playing field. Sewell recounts the same incident differently: "I led the way out on the field and brought them all with me, and the people in that grandstand stood up and applauded. They applauded for 35 minutes." Roy McHugh, "A Strike Was Called; Rip Sewell Balked," *Los Angeles Times,* July 23, 1981, sec. 3, p. 8.

20. "Pittsburgh Pirates Reject Guild as Bargaining Agent by 15 to 3," *New York Times,* August 21, 1946, p. 30; and Craig, *Organized Baseball,* p. 105.

21. Gregory, *Baseball Player,* p. 194.

22. U.S. Congress, House, Subcommittee on Study of Monopoly Power of the Committee on the Judiciary, "Organized Baseball," Report pursuant to H. Res. 95 (82nd Cong., 2nd sess.) May 27, 1952, p. 133. See also Louis Effrat, "Players Approve Minimum Salary," *New York Times,* July 30, 1946, p. V–3; "Major Leaguers Meet Tomorrow to Map New Contract Conditions," *New York Times,* July 30, 1946, p. V–3; and Lee Allen, *100 Years of Baseball* (New York: Bartholomew House, 1950), pp. 297–98.

23. "Pension Program for Players Voted by Major Leagues," *New York Times,* February 2, 1947, p. V–1.

24. Ibid. "Dues from players will operate on a sliding scale. A player must pay $45.45 the first year he subscribes to the plan, and $90.90 the second year. Thereafter the payments increase each year until the tenth year when the fee will be $454.75. However, when a player's total payments aggregate $2,500, his yearly payments shall be reduced to $250 annually."

25. Gregory, *Baseball Player,* pp. 196, 197. For more details on this representation system, see U.S. Congress, Senate, Subcommittee on Antitrust and Monopoly of the Committee on the Judiciary, "Professional Sports Antitrust Bill, 1964," Hearings (88th Cong.), January 30, 31, February 17, 18, 1964, pp. 39–41.

26. Gregory, *Baseball Player,* p. 200.

27. "Council Approves Five Proposals Submitted by Baseball Players," *New York Times,* September 29, 1953, p. 32.

28. "Frick Outlines Pension Operation in Action on Heels of 'Sniping," *New York Times,* January 22, 1954, p. 33.

29. "Lewis Criticizes Report by Frick," *New York Times,* January 26, 1954, p. 22.

30. "Players' Representatives and Baseball Officials Agree on Pension Plan," *New York Times,* February 17, 1954, p. 36.

31. "Players Endorse Frick on TV Pact," *New York Times,* December 6, 1959,

p. 38. In 1962 the owners agreed to devote 95 percent—instead of 60 percent—of All-Star gate and television reserves to the fund, and the players agreed to drop the second All-Star Game played during the season.

32. John Drebinger, "Plan Ties Majors' Pay to Receipts," *New York Times*, December 3, 1958, p. 48.

33. "Player Rep Friend Raps Proposal that Athletes Form Labor Unions," *Sporting News*, August 3, 1963, p. 4. Cited in Ken Walker's unpublished monograph, "The History of Collective Bargaining by Athletes Engaged in Professional Team Sports."

34. U.S. Congress, Senate, Subcommittee on Antitrust and Monopoly of the Committee on the Judiciary, "Organized Professional Team Sports," Hearings (85th Cong., 2nd sess.), July 1958, p. 40.

35. See, for example, S. E. Boderlund and Cal Brumley, "Diamond Duel: Baseball Clubs Serving at Cost Curves, Fret over Attendance Slide," *Wall Street Journal*, April 8, 1957, pp. 1, 10; and "National League Sets Gate Mark," *New York Times*, October 1, 1963, p. 44.

36. Erwin G. Krasnow and Herman M. Levy, "Unionization and Professional Sports," *Georgetown Law Journal* 51 (1962–63), p. 771.

37. Personal telephone conversation with Marvin Miller, November 8, 1978.

CHAPTER TWO

1. Lee Lowenfish and Tony Lupien, *The Imperfect Diamond* (New York: Stein and Day, 1980) p. 199.

2. U.S. Congress, Senate, Subcommittee on Antitrust and Monopoly of the Committee on the Judiciary, "Professional Sports Antitrust Bill, 1964," Hearings (88th Cong.), January 30, 31; February 17, 18, 1964, pp. 39–41.

3. Jim Bouton, *Ball Four*, (New York: World Publishing, 1970), p. 220.

4. David R. Jones, "Creative Labor Man to Go to Bat for Ballplayers," *New York Times*, March 7, 1966, p. 32.

5. Harold Parrott, *The Lords of Baseball* (New York: Praeger Publishers, 1976), p. 17. Jim Bouton reflects that the Saint Louis Cardinals were told by the front office that Miller was the worst choice. They voted for him unanimously. Bouton, *Ball Four*, p. 222.

6. Ibid.

7. *New York Times*, April 3, 1966, p. 2.

8. The NLRB's philosophy did change in 1969 when major league umpires sought union recognition. 1969 Commerce Clearing House NLRB Decisions, No. 21,448. It is therefore likely that representation election for baseball players could have been held in 1969 since the NLRB placed the umpires under federal labor-relations law. Joseph Durso, "N.L.R.B. Orders Union Election for American League Umpires," *New York Times*, December 17, 1969, p. 1.

9. Bowie Kuhn, *Hardball* (New York: New York Times Book, 1987), pp. 75–76.

10. Leonard Koppett, "Baseball Pension Fund Is Increased," *New York Times*, December 2, 1966, p. 47; and Leonard Koppett, "Baseball Labor Dispute Still a Battle of Words," *New York Times*, June 7, 1966, p. 58.

11. Frederick G. Klein, "Militant Athletes," *Wall Street Journal*, August 23, 1967, p. 1.

12. Joseph Durso, "Major League Players Seeking Annual Minimum of $10,000," *New York Times*, December 1, 1966, sec. 1, p. 64.

13. Leonard Koppett, "Baseball Players Seek Increase in Base Pay, Voice on TV Pacts," *New York Times*, August 1, 1967, p. 37.

14. David R. Jones, "New Era Looms in Baseball Players-Club Relations," *New York Times*, February 12, 1968, p. V-1.

15. *Wall Street Journal*, January 16, 1968, p. 1.

16. "Baseball Club Owners' $5.1 Million Pension Offer Is Assailed as Inadequate," *New York Times*, December 18, 1968, p. 58.

17. "Turning Back the Clock," *Wall Street Journal*, February 5, 1969, p. 12. See also Leonard Koppett, "The Club Owners View; No Justification for a Baseball Players' Strike," *New York Times*, February 20, 1969, p. 57.

18. "Strike One," *Time* 93 (February 28, 1969), p. 79.

19. Joseph Durso, "Mets' Ryan, Grote, and Frisella to Report despite Strike," *New York Times*, February 20, 1969, p. 58. According to this article, the Mets led the league in player contract signings, with 30; other teams having a lot of their players sign contracts were Houston, Detroit, and Kansas City. The Saint Louis team apparently signed the fewest number of player contracts.

20. Leonard Koppett, "Baseball Pension Dispute Is Settled with $5.45 Million 3 Year Agreement," *New York Times*, February 26, 1969, p. 50.

21. Barbara Dennis and Gerald Somers, *Arbitration of Interest Disputes*, Proceedings of the 26th Annual Meeting, National Academy of Arbitrators (Washington, D.C.: Bureau of National Affairs, 1974), p. 110. Cited in James B. Dworkin, *Owners versus Players* (Boston: Auburn House, 1981), pp. 125–26.

22. "Who Says Baseball Is like Ballet?" *Forbes* 107 (April 1, 1971), pp. 24–26; and Todd E. Fandell, "Baseball's Blues, The 'National Pastime' Fights Lagging Interest with Array of Changes," *Wall Street Journal*, April 7, 1969, pp. 1, 10.

23. Leonard Koppett, "A Strange Business, Baseball," *New York Times Magazine*, September 2, 1973, p. 11.

24. Leonard Koppett, "Ball Clubs Bar Rise in Pensions," *New York Times*, March 23, 1972, p. 57.

25. "Players Remain Idle," *Washington Post*, April 6, 1972, p. D-1.

26. Murray Chass, "Player's Offer Is Rejected; Long Strike Seems Likely," *New York Times*, April 4, 1972, pp. 49–50.

27. "Short: Some Owners Want to Break Union," *New York Times*, April 2, 1972, p. V-3.

28. "Officials React Firmly to Strike News," *New York Times*, April 1, 1972, p. 16.

29. "Players Reject Upgraded Offer," *Washington Post*, April 11, 1972, p. D-1.

30. "13-Day Baseball Strike Ends," *Washington Post*, April 14, 1972, p. C-1.

31. "Kuhn Explains 'Matter of Judgment,' on Part in Strike," *Washington Post*, April 16, 1972, p. C-3.

32. Joseph Durso, "Owners Wait as Players Study Peace Pitch," *New York Times*, February 10, 1973, p. 25.

33. Red Smith, "Historic, Slanted, and Incomplete," *New York Times*, December 8, 1972, p. 55.

34. Durso, "Owners Wait," p. 25.

35. Basic Agreement between the American League of Professional Baseball Clubs

and the National League of Professional Baseball Clubs and Major League Baseball Players Association, January 1, 1973, p. 26.

36. Douglas Looney, "O.K., What's the Pitch?" *Sports Illustrated*, March 8, 1976, p. 46.

37. "Spring Is Coming but Baseball Isn't," Jacksonville, *Florida Times-Union*, February 24, 1986, p. A–7.

38. Bob Addle, "Miller Says Owners Talk, 'Delay." *Washington Post*, February 5, 1976, p. F–3.

39. Looney, "O.K.," p. 46.

40. "Will Kuhn Make a Move in Impasse?" Jacksonville, *Florida Times-Union*, March 11, 1976, p. B–10.

41. "Baseball Club Owners Give In—Sort Of," *Los Angeles Times*, March 16, 1976, sec. 3, p. 1.

42. "The Final Offer: Miller Will Seek Rejection," *Los Angeles Times*, March 17, 1976, sec. 3, p. 1.

43. "Kuhn Orders Camps Opened," *Washington Post*, March 18, 1976, p. C–1.

44. Bobbie Bouton and Nancy Marshall, *Home Games* (New York: St. Martin's/ Marek, 1983).

45. "Majors Settle with Players," *Washington Post*, July 13, 1976, p. D–2.

CHAPTER THREE

1. These figures were given by the Player Relations Committee with an estimated player-salary average of $149,700, in 1980. Ralph Ray, "Grebey: Pay Averaging $149,000, Why Strike?" *Sporting News*, May 17, 1980, p. 38.

2. Harry Bernstein, "Big League Bargainers Warming Up," *Los Angeles Times*, August 4. sec. 1, 1979, p. 22.

3. Phil Pepe, "Baseball's New Labor Man Is a Fan," *New York Daily News*, March 30, 1980.

4. Ron Firmrite, "Yankee Stadium, Opening Day, 1980?" *Sports Illustrated*, March 30, 1980, pp. 60, 62.

5. "Strike Two," *60 Minutes, as Broadcast Over CBS Television Network*, Transcript, vol. 12, no. 29, March 30, 1980, p. 12.

6. "Players Cancel Remainder of Spring Games," Jacksonville, *Florida Times-Union*, April 2, 1980, p. D–1; and "Strike Insurance Could Turn Profit for Owners: Miller," *Chicago Tribune*, April 1, 1980, sec. 5, p. 3.

7. "War Chests Back Labor Talks," *Sporting News*, December 8, 1979, p. 47.

8. Some of these proposals are from Ralph Ray, "Baseball Negotiators Far Apart," *Sporting News*, February 2, 1980, p. 33.

9. Michael Janofsky, "Baseball Pact: Owners Balk at Fair Play," *Miami Herald*, February 10, 1980, p. 7–C.

10. Ralph Ray, "Plenty of Room for Profits, Miller Replies," *Sporting News*, June 23, 1979, p. 9.

11. Dave Nightingale, "Compensation: Why Owners Want It, Players Fight It," *Chicago Tribune*, April 4, 1980, sec. 6, p. 2.

12. Thomas Boswell, "Baseball Players Board Authorizes a Strike," *Washington Post*, March 5, 1980, p. D–1.

13. Ralph Ray, "Players Cool to 'Generous' Offer," *Sporting News*, March 8, 1980, p. 15.

14. "Baseball Rep Unimpressed with Owner Concession," *Jacksonville Journal*, March 19, 1980, p. 21.

15. Ross Newhan, "I'd Close Down for the Season, Says Angry Autry," *Los Angeles Times*, April 3, 1980, sec. 3, p. 1.

16. Richard Hoffer and Scott Ostler, "Fans Choose Up Sides in a Strike," *Los Angeles Times*, April 4, 1980, sec. 3, p. 1.

17. Richard Dozer, "Owners Insist on Compensation Plan," *Chicago Tribune*, March 29, 1980, p. 2.

18. Patrick Reusse, "Marshall Pours Gasoline on Labor Talks," *Sporting News*, April 5, 1980, p. 41.

19. Skip Hutter, "Baseball Strike? Likely in May," *Harrisburg* (Pennsylvania) *Partiot*, March 30, 1980.

20. Ralph Ray, "Labor Talks Halted—3 Week Issue," *Sporting News*, May 3, 1980, p. 11.

21. Ray, "Grebey: Why Strike?" p. 38.

22. David Lamm, "Baseball Owners Want a Strike—And It's a Bad Call," Jacksonville, *Florida Times-Union*, May 10, 1980, p D–1.

23. Milton Richman, "A Plea for Some Restraint Is Made in Baseball Strike," *Los Angeles Times*, April 6, 1980, sec. 3, p. 3.

24. Jane Leavy, "Baseball Talks Continue," *Washington Post*, May 23, 1980, p A–4; Jim Kaplan, "No Strike Is a Real Ball," *Sports Illustrated*, June 2, 1980, pp. 48, 51; Murray Chass, "A Breather for Baseball," *Sporting News*, June 7, 1980, pp. 9, 44; and Mike Kiley, "2 Owners Played Important Role in Baseball Settlement," *Chicago Tribune*, May 25, 1980, sec. 4, p. 8.

25. Kaplan, "No Strike," p. 48.

26. Mike Kiley, "How Baseball Agreement May Only Delay a Strike," *Chicago Tribune*, May 24, 1980, sec. 2, p. 1. After an investigation in October 1980, the NLRB did issue a complaint that management refused "to bargain collectively and in good faith." Management had not supplied data concerning its administration of negotiated minimum-wage adjustments. *New York Times*, October 30, 1980, p. D–4.

27. Murray Chass, "Plan for Compensation Study Is Basis of Pact," *Sporting News*, June 7, 1980, p. 9.

28. Kaplan, "No Strike," p. 51.

29. Jerome Holtzman, "Owners Flash Hard-line Signal to Players," *Sporting News*, June 21, 1980, p. 36.

30. Dave Nightingale, "Baseball's Fate Is in Miller's Hands; Strike Set," *Chicago Tribune*, May 18, 1980, sec. 4, p. 4.

31. "Strike One," Jacksonville, *Florida Times-Union*, February 20, 1981, p. C–1.

32. Frederick C. Klein, "Baseball Owners Want Something for Nothing," *Wall Street Journal*, June 17, 1981, p. 28; and Jane Gross, "Players Strike Creates Widespread Economic Impact," *New York Times*, June 13, 1981, p. 14. For specific details on how this policy worked, see Ross Newhan, "Buzzie Bavasi Says Those Numbers Are Wrong," *Los Angeles Times*, July 3, 1981, sec. 3, p. 6.

33. Thomas Boswell, "The Player's Position: Time to Draw the Line," *Washington Post*, May 24, 1981, p. E–1.

34. "Double Standard," *Sports Illustrated*, March 9, 1981, p. 12. See also Bob Rubin, "Owners Opposed to Free Enterprise," *Miami Herald*, June 14, 1981, p. 2–C; and Dave Kindred, "Shed No Tears for the Poor Owners," *Los Angeles Times*, June 11, 1981, sec. 3, pp. 1, 14.

35. Edwin Pope, "Owners Finally Match Players for Gluttony," *Miami Herald*, June 14, 1981, p. 1–C.

36. Murray Chass, "Adversaries in Baseball's Labor Dispute Are in Holding Pattern," *New York Times*, May 31, 1981, p. 22; and "Needy—or Greedy?" *Sports Illustrated*, June 8, 1981, p. 15.

37. Murray Chass, "Baseball Strike Off as Players, Owners Extend Deadline," *New York Times*, May 29, 1981, p. 17.

38. For related details, see Jane Leavy, "Baseball Strike Set Friday after Defeat in Court," *Washington Post*, June 11, 1981, p. A–2; and Murray Chass, "Impasse Continues in Baseball," *New York Times*, June 9, 1981, p. 19.

39. Jane Gross, "Strike Finds Mets' Staub Keeping Busy on Three Jobs," *New York Times*, June 20, 1981, p. 14.

40. Jim Kaplan, "No Games Today," *Sports Illustrated*, June 22, 1981, p. 20.

41. Ross Newhan, "Now It's Hawks vs. Doves," *Los Angeles Times*, June 20, 1981, sec. 3, p. 11.

42. Jane Leavy, "Back from the Brink: How the Season Was Saved," *Washington Post*, August 2, 1981, p. F–1.

43. The six owners on the PRC were Fitzgerald of Milwaukee, Burke of Kansas City, Griffith of Minnesota, Galbreath of Pittsburgh, Howsam of Cincinnati, and McHale of Montreal.

44. "Mr. Donovan's Batting Average," *Washington Post*, July 25, 1981, p. A–22.

45. "Presence of PRC Board Could Help Baseball Talks," Jacksonville, Florida, *Times-Union and Journal*, July 19, 1981, p. D–5.

46. Jane Leavy, "Hope Fades for Season; No Talks Scheduled," *Washington Post*, July 13, 1987, p. D–1.

47. "Lopes Takes Some Shots at DeCinces," *Los Angeles Times*, July 23, 1981, sec. 3, pp 1, 4.

48. Jane Leavy, "Owners Stand Firm on Bargaining Position," *Washington Post*, July 30, 1981, p. D–1.

49. Bart Barnes, "Players' Pool Compromise at Heart of Deal," *Washington Post*, August 1, 1981, p. D–1.

50. "Kuhn Says Clubs, Players Learned Bitter Lesson," *Los Angeles Times*, August 1, 1981, sec. 3, p. 1.

51. The 1981 strike cost figures are from two sources: Jim Kaplan, "Let the Games Begin," *Sports Illustrated*, August 10, 1981, p. 17; and *Los Angeles Times*, August 2, 1981, sec. 3, p. 2.

52. Thomas Boswell, "Split Season a Likelihood," *Washington Post*, August 2, 1981, p. D–1.

53. "Playoff Plan Is Revealed for Baseball's Second Season," Jacksonville, *Florida Times-Union*, August 11, 1981, p. C–2.

54. Whitey Herzog and Kevin Horrigan, *White Rat* (New York: Harper and Row, 1987), p. 35.

55. "Impact of the Baseball Strike," *U.S News and World Report* (June 29, 1981),

p. 64; and "Poll Finds Baseball Image Tarnished," Jacksonville, Florida, *Times-Union and Journal*, July 18, 1981, p. D–3.

56. Thomas Boswell, "A Good Strike, Not a Great One," *Inside Sports*, September 30, 1980, p. 21.

57. Murray Chass, "Moffett Links Ouster to Miller," *New York Times*, November 24, 1983, p. D–16.

58. Thomas Boswell, "Moffett Links His Firing with Drugs in Baseball," *Washington Post*, February 22, 1984, p. D–1.

59. Figures for these years are from Thomas Boswell, "Baseball Strikes' Reverse Effect: Player Salaries Continue to Rise," *Washington Post*, February 14, 1982, p. D–1; and "Owners Say 18 Teams Lost Money in 1983," Jacksonville, *Florida Times-Union*, March 13, 1985, p. D–5. See also Thomas Moore, "Baseball's New Game Plan," *Fortune* (April 15, 1985), pp. 17–21.

60. Murray Chass, "Just When You Thought It Was Safe to Go Back to the Ball Park," *Sport* (April 1984), p. 62.

61. "Baseball Owners List Losses," *Washington Post*, May 17, 1985, p. D–1.

62. U.S Congress, House, Subcommittee on Monopolies and Commercial Law, Committee on the Judiciary, "Antitrust Policy and Professional Sports," Oversight hearings (97th Cong., 2nd sess.), July 14, 15, 16, 1982, p. 474.

63. "Baseball Owners Want NBA Type Salary Cap," *Washington Post*, May 21, 1985, p. D–1; and Tim Cowlishaw, "Sides Differ Strikingly on Financial State of Baseball," *Dallas Morning News*, June 16, 1985, p. 8–B.

64. Curt Holbreich, "Ueberroth Won't Enter Strike Talks," *Pittsburgh Press*, June 22, 1985.

65. Dave Sell, "Ueberroth 'Can't Allow There to Be A Strike' in Baseball," *Washington Post*, July 27, 1985, p. D–2.

66. Dave Sell, "Owners Make Pension Proposal," *Washington Post*, July 31, 1985, p. C–1. See also "Fehr: Owners' Plan Is 'Crazy,' " *Dallas Morning News*, July 31, 1985, p. C–5.

67. Kenneth E. John, "Strike Is Strongly Opposed," *Washington Post*, August 1, 1985, p. C–5.

68. C. L. Smith Muniz, "Ubie at the Bat," *New York Daily News*, August 2, 1985.

69. Gene Guidi, "Some Tigers Urge Compromise," *Detroit Free Press*, August 7, 1985. See also Rich Hummel, "Failure to Settle Upsets Cards," *Saint Louis Post Dispatch*, August 7, 1985.

70. Players were docked half a day's pay if the games were made up through doubleheaders, but received full pay if the games were played on an off day.

71. Terms of this settlement were obtained from Dave Sell, "Baseball Strike Settled," *Washington Post*, August 8, 1985, pp. A–1, and A–8; "Memorandum of Settlement" (between the Major League Clubs' Player Relations Committee and the Major League Baseball Players' Association), 1985, p. 12 and exhibit H; Murray Chass, "Peace Be with Baseball," *Sporting News*, August 19, 1985, p. 3; and Jack Craig, "Sharing the Wealth: Baseball Settlement May Help the Poor Get Richer," *Sporting News*, August 19, 1985, p. 13.

72. Dave Sell, "About-face by the Owners Got the Ball Rolling," *Washington Post*, August 9, 1985, p. F–1.

73. *Sporting News*, June 20, 1987, p. 11.

74. Hal Bodley, "Baseball Owners OK Start of Strike Fund," *USA Today*, June 10, 1988, p. 3C.

75. Stan Isle, "Players Building Sizable 1990 Strike Fund," *Sporting News*, December 19, 1988, p. 7.

76. Murray Chass, "Once Again Labor Problems Threaten to Overshadow Game," *New York Times*, December 18, 1988 p. 27.

77. Jerome Holtzman, "Forget the Deals, Fans Worry about 1990," *Chicago Tribune*, December 13, 1987, sec. 3, p. 3.

78. Hal Bodley, "Two-Thirds of 1990 Contracts Include Lockout Clause," *USA Today*, November 2, 1988, p. 3C. See also Alvin E. Roth, "Further Thoughts from the Power of Alternatives: An Example from Labor-Management Negotiations in Major League Baseball," *Negotiation Journal* (October 1985), p. 361.

79. "Adversaries to Meet at the Bargaining Table," *USA Today*, December 22, 1988, p. 2C.

CHAPTER FOUR

1. Pete Axthelm, "The Perils of Ownership," *Newsweek*, December 12, 1980, p. 61.

2. Art Turgeon, "Memo Ignited Red Sox Warfare," *Providence Journal*, July 14, 1983; Robert Friedman, "They Get Little Ink, But 15 Other People Also Own Yankees," *Wall Street Journal*, April 16, 1985, pp. 1, 22; and Jolie Solomon, "Cincinnati Red's Marge Schott Faces Problems Other than Baseball Scores," *Wall Street Journal*, June 6, 1986, p. 45.

3. "Debartolo Rejection by Owners Leaves Veeck 'Ashamed,' " Jacksonville, *Florida Times-Union*, December 12, 1980, p. F–8. For another example of this situation, see Shirley Povich, "National League Doesn't Come Up Short," *Washington Post*, July 7, 1966, p. D–1.

4. "Ban on Beards Intact for Reds," *Miami Herald*, December 26, 1984, p. 3–C; "Scorecard," *Sports Illustrated*, June 21, 1976, p. 13.

5. Gary Smith, "A Lingering Vestige of Yesterday," *Sports Illustrated*, April 4, 1983, p. 110.

6. Steve Bisheff, "Baseball Too Protective of Weaker Sisters, Says Big Brother Kroc," *Sporting News*, May 12, 1979, pp. 9–10.

7. Leonard Koppett, "The Sport's Big Boys: The Club Owners," *New York Times*, November 15, 1968, sec. V–1; and, "The (Mostly) Invisible 26," Jacksonville, *Florida Times-Union*, July 9, 1981, p. D–1.

8. John Tullius, *I'd Rather Be a Yankee* (New York: Macmillan, 1986), p. 16.

9. "Scorecard," *Sports Illustrated*, January 2, 1978, p. 11.

10. Don Kowet, *The Rich Who Own Sports* (New York: Random House, 1977), p. 129.

11. Marguerite Michaels, "To George Steinbrenner, The Object Is to Win," *Parade*, March 30, 1980, p .4.

12. Kowet, *The Rich* p. 129.

13. William Nack, "A Team in Trouble," *Sports Illustrated*, August 11, 1980, p. 50. For a successful counterpart—Walter A. Hass, Jr., owner of the Oakland A's—see Andrew Pollack, "Oakland's Stars in the Front Office," *New York Times*, October 20, 1988, pp. 25, 31.

14. Murray Chass, "Message from Steinbrenner Comes Across Loud and Clear," *New York Times*, August 9, 1987, p. 18.

15. Richard M. Cohen and Leonard Shapiro, "Too Little Time Forcing Hoffberg Out of Baseball," *Washington Post*, February 16, 1975, pp. C–1, C–12.

16. Rick Talley, "New Boss Prefers Old Ways for Cubs," *Chicago Tribune*, May 22, 1977, sec. 3, p. 2.

17. Mike Downey, "Is Schott Steinbrenner's Long Lost Sister?" *Sporting News*, April 18, 1988, p. 6.

18. Dick Schapp, *Steinbrenner* (New York: G. P. Putnam's Sons, 1982), p. 200.

19. Ken Picking, "Horner, Turner Collide Head On," *Sporting News*, May 10, 1980, p. 21; and Tim Tucker, "Reinstated Horner Plans to Report," *Atlanta Journal*, April 30, 1980, pp. 1D, 4D.

20. "Horner Signs with Cards," Jacksonville, *Florida Times-Union*, January 15, 1988, p. C–3.

21. Richard Esposito, "Steinbrenner Documents How Winfield Used Funds," *Miami Herald*, January 20, 1989, p. 13–E. For details into Winfield's financial complexities and his current disputes with Steinbrenner, see Mel Antonen, "Winfield Fund in the Middle," *USA Today*, January 11, 1989, pp. 1C, 8C.

22. Red Smith, *To Absent Friends* (New York: New American Library, 1982), p. 230.

23. "Angels' Bostock Vows No Hits, No Pay," *Atlanta Journal*, April 20, 1978, p. 2–D.

24. Herb Michelson, *Charlie O* (Indianapolis: Bobbs-Merrill, 1975), p. 94.

25. Schaap, *Steinbrenner*, pp. 217, 273.

26. Ian MacDonald, "Expos' Chief Wants to Head Off Strike," *Sporting News*, March 23, 1987, p. 29.

27. Greg Larson, "Twins' Griffith Defends Frugal Dealings," Jacksonville, *Florida Times-Union*, April 4, 1979, p. C–3.

28. "Madlock Gets No from Cubs' Boss," Jacksonville, *Florida Times-Union*, January 15, 1977, p. F–9.

29. Gordon Verrell, "A Major Overhaul for the Dodgers," *Sporting News*, March 7, 1988, p. 13; and Pollack, "Oakland's Front Office," p. 25.

30. Roger Angell, *Five Seasons* (New York: Simon and Schuster, 1977), p. 265.

31. Michelson, *Charlie O*, p. 229.

32. Donald Gropman, *Say It Ain't So, Joe!* (Boston: Little, Brown, 1979), p. 198.

33. U.S. Congress, Senate, Subcommittee on Antitrust and Monopoly of the Committee on the Judiciary, "Organized Professional Team Sports," Hearings (85th Cong., 2nd sess.), July 1958, p. 23.

34. Ford C. Frick, *Games, Asterisks, and People* (New York: Crown Publishers, 1973), p. 109.

35. Red Smith, *Strawberries in the Winter Time*, (New York: Quadrangle, 1974), p. 74.

36. Lee Lowenfish and Tony Lupien, *The Imperfect Diamond* (New York: Stein and Day, 1980), p. 123.

37. Harold Rosenthal, *The 10 Best Years of Baseball* (Chicago: Critegacy Books, 1979), p. 20.

38. Frick, *Games*, p. 209.

39. "Frick Tells Owners They Must Arm His Successor with Authority of Landis," *New York Times*, November 6, 1984, p. 43.

40. "Majors' Official Vote Restores Commissioner's Broad Powers," *New York Times*, December 5, 1964, p. 36.

41. Steinbrenner was eventually pardoned by President Reagan the last days of his administration.

42. "Kuhn Stays as 2 Owners Change," *Washington Post*, July 18, 1975, p. D–1.

43. Steve Nidetz, "Veeck: Fans Betrayed," *Chicago Tribune*, June 17, 1976, pp. 4, 5.

44. Dick Young, "Frazier, A's Baseball Battered," *Fort Myers News Press*, June 17, 1976, p. 5–C.

45. "3.5 Million Oakland Deal Voided in the Best Interest of Baseball," *Miami Herald*, June 19, 1976, p. A–1, A–2.

46. "Finley Files $10 Million Court Suit," *Miami Herald*, June 26, 1976, p. D–1. See also Bill Densmore, "Finley Suit Strikes at Kuhn Intrusion, Baseball Hierarchy," *Miami Herald*, January 2, 1977, p. C–1.

47. Red Smith, "Bowie on a Long Limb," *New York Times*, June 20, 1976, p. S–3.

48. Nancy Scannell, "Judge Rules Kuhn Had Right to Nullify Sales by Finley," *Washington Post*, March 18, 1977, p. D–1.

49. Thomas Boswell, "Owners Vote Not to Renew Kuhn's Contract," *Washington Post*, November 2, 1982, p. C–1. The NL clubs voting against Kuhn were New York, Saint Louis, Houston, Atlanta, and Cincinnati. The AL clubs voting against Kuhn were New York, Texas, and Seattle.

50. Stan Isle, "Giamatti Expecting to 'Work for Everybody,'" *Sporting News*, November 14, 1988, p. 7; and Roger Argell, "Celebration," *New Yorker* (August 22, 1988), p. 56.

51. "Rose, Ueberroth Meeting Stirs Speculation," Jacksonville, *Florida Times-Union*, February 22, 1989, p. C–5.

52. Martin Merzer, "Rose Banned from Baseball for Life," *Miami Herald*, August 25, 1989, p. 4A.

53. "Giamatti's Remarks Irk Rose," *Miami Herald*, August 29, 1989, p. 2D.

54. Ira Berkow, "The Green Fields of Bart's Mind," *New York Times*, September 2, 1989, p. 29.

55. Richard O'Connor, "Will Free Agents Kill Baseball?" *Sport* (April 1978), p. 42. See also Glenn Dickey, "The T.V Tail Wags the Dog," *San Francisco Chronicle*, June 24, 1977.

56. Denny McLain with Dave Diles, *Nobody's Perfect* (New York: Dial Press, 1975), pp. 192, 198.

57. Tullius, *I'd Rather*, p. 264. See also Rick Telander, "The Record Almost Broke Him," *Sports Illustrated*, June 20, 1977, pp. 60–70.

58. Pete Axthelm, "There Goes the Franchise," *Newsweek* (June 27, 1977), p. 63.

59. Ryne Duren with Robert Drury, *The Comeback* (Dayton, Ohio: Lorenz Press, 1978), pp. 11 and 12.

60. Robert Ward, "Reggie Jackson in No-Man's Land," *Sport* (June 1977), p. 94.

61. Jackie Robinson with Alfred Duckett, *I Never Had It Made* (New York: G. P. Putnam's Sons, 1972), pp. 108–13.

62. McLain and Diles, *Nobody's Perfect*, p. 201.

63. Geoffrey Stokes, *Pinstripe Pandemonium* (New York: Harper and Row, 1984), p. 35. Vulgarity and anger are not uncommon when a manager confronts the press. Jay Johnstone once recorded a confrontation between Lee Elia and the press where there were 44 expletives. "There were 36 fuckins, two shits, four mother fuckers, and two cocksuckers in his speech and he didn't even need a deep breath." Jay Johnstone and Rick Talley, *Over the Edge* (Chicago Contemporary Books, 1987), p. 16.

64. William M. Bulkeley, "Sports Agents Help Athletes Win—and Keep—Those Super Salaries," *Wall Street Journal*, March 25, 1985, p. 31.

65. "Katz Got the Kitty," *Sports Illustrated*, December 18, 1978, p. 11.

66. "The Baseball Business," *CBS Reports, as Broadcast over the CBS Television Network*, Transcript, April 26, 1977, p. 7.

67. Carry Kirkpatrick, "Going Real Strawwng," *Sports Illustrated*, August 21, 1978, p. 77.

68. Jerome Holtzman, "Too Powerful?" *Los Angeles Times*, March 13, 1976, sec. 3, pp. 1, 7.

69. Don Pierson, "Charlie Blames Agent," *Chicago Tribune*, June 17, 1976, p. sec. 4, p. 5.

70. Craig Neff, "Den of Vipers," *Sports Illustrated*, October 19, 1987, p. 77.

71. Armen Keteyian, "At Times You Flat Cry," *Sports Illustrated*, October 19, 1987, p. 91.

72. Craig Neff, "A Clean Sweep: How to Deal with the Agents," *Sports Illustrated*, October 19, 1987, p. 104.

73. Details of this process are found in MLBPA Regulations Concerning Player Agents, including exhibits A–E.

CHAPTER FIVE

1. Tim McCarver with Ray Robinson, *Oh Baby, I Love It!* (New York: Villard Books, 1987), p. 121; and Jay Johnstone and Rick Talley, *Temporary Insanity* (Chicago: Contemporary Books, 1985), p. 92.

2. Murray Chass, "Mathews Is Elected into Hall," *New York Times*, January 20, 1978, pp. A–17, A–19.

3. Peter Golenbock, *Dynasty: The New York Yankees 1949–1964* (Englewood Cliffs, N.J.: Prentice-Hall, 1975), p. 362.

4. John J. McGraw, *My Thirty Years in Baseball* (New York: Boni and Liveright, 1928), p. 55.

5. Leonard Koppett, *A Thinking Man's Guide to Baseball* (New York: E. P. Dutton, 1967), p. 104.

6. Lawrence Ritter and Donald Honig, *The Image of Their Greatness*, 2nd ed. (New York: Crown Publishers, 1984), p. 1.

7. Steve Wulf, "Another One Bites the Dust," *Sports Illustrated*, June 6, 1988, p. 48.

8. McCarver with Robinson, *Oh Baby*, p. 121.

9. Tommy Lasorda and David Fisher, *The Artful D-O-D-G-E-R* (New York: Arkin House, 1985), pp. 206–7.

10. "A Shot at Lasorda," *Washington Post*, February 15, 1987, p. D–4.

11. Donald Honig, *The Man in the Dugout* (Chicago: Follet Publishing, 1977), p. 249.

12. Harvey Frommer, *Baseball's Greatest Managers* (New York: Franklin Watts, 1985), p. 160.

13. Billy Martin with Phil Pepe, *Billy Ball* (Garden City, N.Y.: Doubleday, 1987).

14. Koppett, *Thinking Man's Guide*, p. 86.

15. Honig, *Man in Dugout*, p. 105.

16. Ibid.

17. Sparky Lyle and Peter Golenbock, *The Bronx Zoo* (New York: Crown Publishers, 1979), p. 151.

18. Shelby Whitfield, *Kiss It Goodbye* (New York: Abelard-Schuman, 1973), p. 35.

19. Patrick Reusse, "The Calmest Man in the Dugout," *Sporting News*, October 12, 1987, p. 14.

20. "Baseball: Straight Talk from Spahnie," *Wall Street Journal*, August 2, 1985, p. 11.

21. "Reggie Says Howser Is Best for Yanks," New Orleans *Times Picayune*, November 20, 1980, sec. 4, p. 3.

22. Whitney Herzog and Kevin Horrigan, *White Rat* (New York: Harper and Row, 1987), p. 117.

23. Jacksonville, *Florida Times-Union*, September 19, 1979, p. D–3.

24. Herzog and Horrigan, *White Rat*, p. 149.

25. "Playboy Interview: Earl Weaver," *Playboy* (July 9, 1983), p. 70.

26. Jerome Holtzman, "Michael Out as Cub Manager," *Chicago Tribune*, September 8, 1987, sec. 4, p. 4.

27. Ibid.

28. Koppett, *Thinking Man's Guide*, p. 91.

29. "Interview: Earl Weaver," pp. 68, 70, 74. See also Dave VanDyck, "LaRussa Workaholic," *Chicago Sun Times*, August 12, 1984, p. 114.

30. Frommer, *Greatest Managers*, p. 188.

31. Ibid., p. 239.

32. John Tullius, *I'd Rather Be a Yankee* (New York: Macmillan, 1986), p. 187.

33. Martin and Pepe, *Billy Ball*, p. 45.

34. Robert W. Creamer, *Babe* (New York: Simon and Schuster, 1976), pp. 291–92.

35. Jim Bouton, *Ball Four* (New York: World Publishing, 1970), p. 205.

36. McCarver with Robinson, *Oh Baby*, p. 123. For a similar application to Casey Stengel, see Joe McGuff, "Hank Bauer Recalls the Yankees Glory Years," in John Kuenster, *From Cobb to "Catfish"* (Chicago: Rand McNally, 1975), p. 76.

37. Dick Young, "The Duke," *Inside Sports*, October 31, 1980, pp. 150–51.

38. Frommer, *Greatest Managers*, p. 26.

39. "Scorecard," *Sports Illustrated*, October 8, 1979, p. 11.

40. Tom Fitzpatrick, "Sometimes It Was Tough to Keep Smiling," *Los Angeles Times*, August 10, 1977, sec. 3, p. 1.

41. John Husar, "Randle Fights to Keep the Faith with Baseball," *Chicago Tribune*, June 13, 1980, sec. 6, p. 2.

42. Roger Kahn, *The Boys of Summer* (New York: Harper and Row, 1971), p. 346.

43. Rod Carew with Ira Berkow, *Carew* (New York: Simon and Schuster, 1979), p. 202.

44. Lou Piniella and Maury Allen, *Sweet Lou* (New York: G. P. Putnam's Sons, 1986), p. 130.

45. Ted Williams with John Underwood, *My Turn at Bat; The Story of My Life* (New York: Simon and Schuster, 1969), p. 162.

46. Robert Craemer, *Stengel: His Life and Times* (New York: Simon and Schuster, 1984), pp. 274–75.

47. "Baseball Ambassador Anderson Develops a Knack for Phrases," *Miami Herald*, March 18, 1979, pp. 12–C.

48. Paul Attner, "Pete Rose, Manager," *Sporting News*, May 18, 1987, p. 11.

49. John Eisenberg, "Bucky Beaver? No, But Mets' Manager Is . . . Different," Jacksonville, Florida, *Times-Union and Journal*, August 17, 1986, p. C–3.

50. Steve Wulf, "Oh No, Not Again," *Sports Illustrated*, May 6, 1985, p. 17.

51. Whitfield, *Kiss Goodbye*, p. 47.

52. Golenbock, *Dynasty*, pp. 363–64.

53. Tullius, *I'd Rather*, p. 189.

54. Bill Veeck and Ed Linn, *Veeck—as in Wreck* (New York: Bantam House, 1963), pp. 240–41.

55. Lyle and Golenbock, *Bronx Zoo*, p. 153.

56. Babe Ruth with Bob Considine, *The Babe Ruth Story* (New York: E. P. Dutton, 1948), pp. 142–43. For a more contemporary example of manager-player confrontation, see Bill Lee and Dick Lally, *The Wrong Stuff* (New York: Viking Press, 1984), pp. 230–31. Denny McLain recalled in his autobiography (with Dave Diles), *Nobody's Perfect* (New York: Dial Press, 1975), pp. 69–70, one of the louder confrontations that occured when manager Charlie Dressen found that Hank Aguire was out past curfew. Hank was urging Dressen to trade him, and Dressen said, "Hell, I've tried to get rid of you ever since I got here, but no one will have you. . . . You asshole; you won't be here twenty-four hours from now."

57. Anthony J. Connor, *Voices from Cooperstown* (New York: Collier Books, 1984), pp. 99–100.

58. Kahn, *Boys of Summer*, p. 346.

59. Frederick C. Klein, "It's a Game of Inches," *Wall Street Journal*, October 21, 1988, p. A–13.

60. "Sport Interview: Joe Morgan," *Sport* (June 1984), p. 20.

61. The managers' win-loss statistics are supplied by Phil Pepe in his article, "Piniella Replaces Martin," *Chicago Tribune*, June 24, 1988, sec. 3, p. 1.

62. "Martin's Final Day: A Bright Sun, Then the Storm," Jacksonville, *Florida Times-Union*, July 26, 1978, p. D–4. See also Martin and Pepe, *Billy Ball*, p. 203.

63. Murray Chass, "Martin Resigns; Bob Lemon to Manage Yankees," *New York Times*, July 25, 1978, p. A–1, B–11. See also Murray Chass, "Reggie Jackson Penalized: 5 Days, $9,000," *New York Times*, July 19, 1978, p. A–2, A–15.

64. Murray Chass, "Martin Is Called Back as Yankees' Manager," *New York Times*, June 18, 1979, p. 14.

65. "Martin Sizes Up Steinbrenner: 'Man Is Sick,' " Jacksonville, *Florida Times-Union*, December 12, 1979, p. D–2.

66. " 'Fire Me,' Yanks Michael Tells Steinbrenner," Jacksonville, Florida, *Times-Union and Journal*, August 29, 1981, p. C–3.

67. Ira Berkow, "King George," Jacksonville, Florida, *Times-Union and Journal*, September 27, 1981, p. D–7.

68. Murray Chass, "Yanks Dismiss Lemon and Name Michael Manager," *New York Times*, April 26, 1982, p. C–1.

69. Ibid.

70. Murray Chass, "Yanks Dismiss Michael after Losing Doubleheader," *New York Times*, August 4, 1982, p. A–15.

71. "Steinbrenner Fires Berra, Hires Martin," Jacksonville, *Florida Times-Union*, April 29, 1985, p. F–1.

72. Ibid.

73. Michael Martinez, "Piniella Receives Lashing," *New York Times*, August 9, 1987, p. 19.

74. Hal Bodley, "N.Y. Circus: On Tightrope in Pinstripes," *USA Today*, August 12, 1987, p. 3–C.

75. "A Favorite Son No Longer," *Sporting News*, August 17, 1987, p. 22.

76. "Martin's Back as Yankee Manager," Jacksonville, *Florida Times-Union*, October 20, 1987, p. C–3.

77. Eliot Asinof, "New Yankee Manager Dallas Green, On the Spot," *New York Times Magazine*, March 26, 1989, p. 19.

78. Frank Dolson, "Green: Steinbrenner Wants Control," *Miami Herald*, August 22, 1989, p. 2D.

79. Michael Goodwin, "Steinbrenner and 'Star' Quality," *New York Times*, August 23, 1987, p. Y–121.

80. Jim Brosnan, "The I's, We's, and They's of Baseball," *New York Times Magazine*, July 3, 1966, p. 14.

81. Veeck and Linn, *Veeck*, p. 237.

82. Craemer, *Stengel*, p. 201.

83. Herbert Michelson, *Charlie O* (Indianapolis: Bobbs-Merrill, 1975), p. 211.

84. Reggie Jackson with Billy Libby, *Reggie: A Season with a Superstar* (New York: Playboy Press, 1975), p. 68.

85. Dick Schapp, *Steinbrenner* (New York: G. P. Putnam's Sons, 1982), pp. 200–201.

86. Herzog and Horrigan, *White Rat*, p. 111.

CHAPTER SIX

1. Incidents are from the following sources: Harold R. Seymour, *Baseball: The Early Years* (New York: Oxford University Press, 1960), pp. 124–25; "Met's G. M. Needs More Time," Jacksonville, Florida, *Times-Union and Journal*, July 20, 1975, p. H–3; and "Riot on Central Train," *New York Times*, February 9, 1906, p. 1.

2. Tim McCarver and Ray Robinson, *Oh Baby, I Love It* (New York: Villard Books, 1987), p. 86.

3. Phil Hersh, "Seeing 'Superman' Go Bad," *Chicago Tribune*, December 28, 1986, sec. 3, p. 3.

4. Jim Bouton, *Ball Four* (New York: World Publishing, 1970), p. 17. See also Rod Carew with Ira Berkow, *Carew* (New York: Simon and Schuster, 1979), p. 73.

5. Tony Scherman, "The Pitcher's Game," *New York Times Magazine*, June 15, 1980, p. 14. See also Geoffrey Stokes, *Pinstripe Pandemonium* (New York: Harper and Row, 1984), p. 63.

6. "Jefferies Struggles to Regain Glory of '88," *Miami Herald*, May 21, 1989, p. 6D.

7. Denny McLain with Dave Diles, *Nobody's Perfect* (New York: Dial Press, 1975), p. 18.

8. Jim Murray, "A Perfect Name, And Quite a Catch," Jacksonville, *Florida Times-Union*, June 6, 1980, p. D–1.

9. John Schulian, "Cut the Bull: Is It All Over for Luzinski?" *Miami Herald*, January 25, 1985, p. 5–F.

10. Thomas Boswell, "Older Players Find Goodbye Is the Hardest Word," *Washington Post*, September 28, 1987, p. B–1.

11. Ira Berkow, *Pitchers Do Get Lonely* (New York: Atheneum, 1988), p. 193.

12. Bob Rubin, "One Fateful Pitch Is Not Worth a Man's Life," *Miami Herald*, July 20, 1989, p. 5–D.

13. Laurie Hays, "And It's One, Two, Three Beers I'm Out at the Old (Expletive Deleted) Ballgame," *Wall Street Journal*, June 16, 1986, p. 35. See also George Vecsey, "The Sober Section," *New York Times*, July 30, 1987, p. 45.

14. Bill Carlin, "Schmidt Strikes Out at Philadelphia's Fans," *Miami Herald*, July 2, 1985, p. 1–C.

15. "30,338 Cheer Ted's 4-Bagger as Boston Crushes Orioles, 7–2," *New York Times*, August 9, 1956, p. 18.

16. Sparky Lyle and Peter Golenbock, *The Bronx Zoo* (New York: Crown Publishers, 1979), p. 101.

17. Ira Berkow, "The Abundance of Skullduggery in Baseball," *New York Times*, August 23, 1987, p. 20.

18. Ty Cobb, *My Life in Baseball* (New York: Doubleday, 1961), p. 84.

19. Roger Kahn, *The Boys of Summer* (New York: Harper and Row, 1971), p. 306.

20. "Loading-up Lowdown from Mudcat Grant," *Miami Herald*, November 15, 1987, p. 3–D.

21. Bouton, *Ball Four*, p. 213.

22. Dave Nightengale, "Scott Speaks Off the Scruff," *Sporting News*, August 28, 1989, p. 12.

23. Ibid.

24. Murray Chass, "An Active and Eloquent Commisioner," *New York Times*, September 2, 1989, p. 29.

25. Stokes, *Pinstripe*, p. 89.

26. Ibid.

27. "Consensus: Sock It to Cheaters in Baseball," *Sporting News*, August 24, 1987, p. 15.

28. Roger Angell, *Five Seasons: A Baseball Companion* (New York: Simon and Schuster, 1977), pp. 176–77. See also Danny Thompson with Bob Fowler, *E–6* (Minneapolis: Dillon Press, 1975), p. 135; and Bill Lyon, "Fighting, Winning Mix Well," *Miami Herald*, August 6, 1978, p. 2–C.

29. Babe Ruth with Bob Considine, *The Babe Ruth Story* (New York: E. P. Dutton, 1948), pp. 166–67.

30. Duke Snider with Bill Gilbert, *The Duke of Flatbush* (New York: Kensington, 1988), p. 58.

31. McLain and Diles, *Nobody's Perfect*, pp. 156–59.

32. Jerome Holtzman, "Cub Legend Bill Herman Takes Stroll down Memory Lane in Cooperstown," *Chicago Tribune*, August 2, 1988, sec. 4, p. 3.

33. Dave Albee, "Gibson Kept Plate Clean in His Time," *USA Today*, July 30, 1987, p. 2 C.

34. Mike Ryan, "Drysdale Did His Best Work Inside," *USA Today*, July 30, 1987, p. 2 C.

35. Anthony J. Connor, *Voices from Cooperstown*, (New York: Collier Books, 1984), p. 141. Emphasis in original.

36. Donald Hall with Dock Ellis, *Dock Ellis in the Country of Baseball* (New York: Coward McCann and Geoghegan, 1975), p. 30.

37. Harry Stein, "Sparky and the Goose," *Sport* (April 1978), p. 28.

38. Dave Van Dyck, "Apology Fails to Mollify Dawson," *Sporting News*, July 20, 1987, p. 27.

39. Harry Stein, "Meet Reggie (Dr. Jekyll) Jackson (Mr. Hyde)," *Esquire* (July 1977), p. 118.

40. Paul Hendrickson, "The Birds on the Wing," *Washington Post*, June 26, 1983, pp. K–1, K–3, K–8, K–9.

41. Randy Ready, currently of the San Diego Padres, represents an archetype as his wife's sudden and severe physical disabilities have shifted childrearing burdens during the baseball season. Bill Plaschhe, "Padre Ready Copes with Wife's Tragedy," *Miami Herald*, October 21, 1988, p. 12–D.

42. Leonard Koppett, *A Thinking Man's Guide to Baseball* (New York: E. P. Dutton, 1967), p. 190. One recent study enhances this situation, indicating that 72 percent of all ballplayers' wives do not live in their husband's hometowns—"a statistic that doesn't bode well for a baseball marriage." "Playing by Her Own Rules," *Sports Illustrated*, July 6, 1987, p. 38.

43. John Tullius, *I'd Rather Be a Yankee* (New York: Macmillan, 1986), p. 46.

44. Rod Carew with Ira Berkow, *Carew* (New York: Simon and Schuster, 1979), pp. 177–87.

45. Murray Chass, "Mrs. Kekich Discusses Exchange of Families," *New York Times*, March 7, 1973, p. 29.

46. "Yankees as Team Hoping 'Situation' Will Not Hurt Them," *New York Times*, March 7, 1973, p. 29.

47. "Kuhn Boosts Morals," *Washington Post*, July 20, 1973, p. D–2.

48. "The Baseball Business," *CBS Reports, as Broadcast over the CBS Television Network*, Transcript, April 26, 1977, p. 20.

49. Ted Green, "Cobb Never Set Out to Be Voted Mr. Congeniality," *Los Angeles Times*, August 27, 1977, sec. 3, p. 1.

50. Bouton, *Ball Four*, pp. 337–38. Tom House, in his book *The Jock's Itch*, recalled a variation of this humor "[A player] was, shall we say, endowed like an uncircumcised horse, and one of his favorite tricks was to put a lit cigarette in the head of his dick and conduct an interview while it was smoking."

51. Reggie Jackson with Bill Libby, *Reggie: A Season with a Superstar* (Chicago: Playboy Press, 1975), p. 79.

52. Ibid.

53. "Scorecard," *Sports Illustrated*, February 6, 1978, p. 14.

54. Steve Wulf, "Taking the Rap," *Sports Illustrated*, July 13, 1987, p. 22.

55. Dan Castellano, "Stirring the Met's Drink," *Sporting News*, August 8, 1988, p. 6.

56. "Friction and Frustration in Losing Make Royals a Team Divided," *Sporting News*, August 15, 1988, p. 16.

57. David Remnick, "Reggie at Sunset," *Esquire* (June 1987), p. 138.

58. *Washington Post*, February 10, 1987, p. E–2.

59. Bob Welch and George Vescey, *Five O'Clock Comes Early* (New York: William Morrow, 1982), p. 33.

60. John Roseboro with Bill Libby, *Glory Days with the Dodgers, and Other Days with Others* (New York: Atheneum, 1978), p. 157.

61. Fred Mitchell, "Baseball Alcoholics Fight Their Battle in Public," *Chicago Tribune*, April 11, 1980, sec. 4, p. 1.

62. Welch and Vecsey, *Five O'Clock*, pp. 125–26.

63. "Drugstore and Dugout," *Wall Street Journal*, May 20, 1957, p. 10.

64. Gary Ledman, "Athlete 'Confessions' Concern Newcombe," Jacksonville, Florida, *Times-Union and Journal*, October 8, 1983, p. B–6.

65. Bruce Lowitt, "For Howe Now, The Sounds of Silence," *Miami Herald*, October 10, 1985, p. 2–C.

66. Bob Verdi, "Hoyt Has Three Strikes, But He Isn't Out Yet," *Sporting News*, July 20, 1987, p. 7.

67. Fred Mitchell, "Green Denounces Signing of Hoyt," *Chicago Tribune*, July 3, 1987, sec. 4, p. 3.

68. "Padres Release Hoyt, Will Pay Him $3 Million," *Chicago Tribune*, July 3, 1987, sec. 4, p. 3.

69. "White Sox Take a Chance on Hoyt," *Sporting News*, July 13, 1987, p. 30.

70. Robert C. Berry and Glenn M. Wong, *Law and Business of the Sports Industries*, vol. 1 (Dover, Mass.: Auburn House, 1986), p. 438.

71. Bowie Kuhn, *Hardball* (New York: New York Times Books, 1987), p. 307.

72. Ibid., p. 316.

73. "Perez Is Told He Can Play; Kuhn Fumes," *Washington Post*, April 29, 1984, p. D–2.

74. Thomas Boswell, "Ueberroth Sets Broad Baseball Drug Testing," *Washington Post*, May 8, 1985, p. D–1. See also Jim Kaplan and Ivan Maisel, "The Commissioner Gets Tough," *Sports Illustrated*, May 20, 1985, pp. 32–34, 39–40. Under Ueberroth's plan, 275 individuals were tested in 1985, with 28 drug users reported. In 1986, 600 were tested, with 30 drug users; and in 1987, 1,000 were tested, with 20 drug users. Dave Nightengale, "Ueberroth a 1-Term Commissioner," *Sporting News*, December 21, 1987, p. 44.

75. Pete Axthelm, "Baseball's Bad Trip," *Newsweek* (September 16, 1985), p. 64.

76. Shirley Povich, "Martin's Wrath Spills Over on Drugs and 'Squealers' at Pittsburgh Trial," *Washington Post*, September 15, 1985, p. F–3.

77. "Baseball and Sleaze (cont.)," *Sports Illustrated*, September 23, 1985, p. 17.

78. Richard Justice, "Drug Test Settlement Is Expected," *Washington Post*, March 6, 1986, p. C–1.

79. Murray Chass, "Players on Tests: Deal with Union," *Sporting News*, October 7, 1985, p. 35.

80. "The Ueberroth Years," *USA Today*, March 29, 1989, p. 1C.

81. Thomas T. Roberts, "Sports Arbitration," *Industrial Relations Law Journal* 10: 1 (1988), pp. 8–11.

82. "The Agents Were Outrageous in the Media," *Atlanta Journal and Constitution*, December 6, 1988, p. 1E.

83. Fred Mitchell, "Drug Tests Are a Must, Green Says," *Chicago Tribune*, April 6, 1987, p. 92.

84. Peter Richmond, "We Can't Have a Hero and Beat Him, Too," *Washington Post*, May 9, 1985, pp. D–1, D–3.

85. "Gooden Welcomes Drug Tests," Jacksonville, *Florida Times-Union*, November 12, 1986, pp. C–1, C–5.

86. George Vecsey, "Sports and Alcohol: Coming Out of the Drink," Jacksonville, *Florida Times-Union*, April 23, 1980, p. C–1.

CHAPTER SEVEN

1. Robert Creamer, *Babe* (New York: Simon and Schuster, 1976), p. 181.

2. Jerome Holtzman, *No Cheering in the Press Box* (New York: Holt, Rinehart, and Winston, 1974), p. 54.

3. Richard C. Crepeau, *Baseball: America's Diamond Mind, 1919–1941* (Gainesville: University Presses of Florida, 1980).

4. Donald Honig, *Baseball When the Grass Was Real* (New York: Coward McCann and Geoghegan, 1975), p. 251.

5. Lawrence S. Ritter, *The Glory of Their Times* (New York: William Morrow 1984), p. 317.

6. For some insights into this situation, see David Q. Voight, *America through Baseball* (Chicago: Nelson-Hall, 1976), pp. 110–14.

7. Jules Tygiel, "Beyond the Point of No Return," *Sports Illustrated*, June 21, 1983, p. 66.

8. Jules Tygiel, *Baseball's Great Experiment* (New York: Oxford University Press, 1983), p. 31.

9. Robert Peterson, *Only the Ball Was White* (New York: McGraw-Hill, 1984), p. 174.

10. Arthur Mann, *Branch Rickey* (Cambridge, Mass.: Riverside Press, 1957) pp. 222–23.

11. "Ex-Commissioner Chandler Apologizes for Racial Remark," *Chicago Tribune*, April 7, 1988, sec. 4, p. 7.

12. Tygiel, *Great Experiment*, p. 128.

13. Carl T. Rowan with Jackie Robinson, *Wait till Next Year* (New York: Random House, 1960), p. 122.

14. Honig, *The Grass Was Real*, p. 312.

15. Rowan with Robinson, *Next Year*, p. 176. For Bragan's version of his attitudes of Robinson and discussion with Rickey, see Donald Honig, *The Man in the Dugout* (Chicago: Follett Publishing, 1977), pp. 7–8.

16. Harold Parrott, *The Lords of Baseball* (New York: Praeger Publishers, 1976) pp. 194–95.

17. Jackie Robinson with Alfred Duckett, *I Never Had It Made* (New York: G. P. Putnam's Son's 1972), p. 73.

18. Roger Kahn, *The Boys of Summer* (New York: Harper and Row, 1971) p. 135.

19. Peterson, *Only the Ball*, p. 199.

20. Tygiel, *Great Experiment*, p. 190.

21. Kahn, *Boys of Summer*, pp. 120–21.

22. Juan Williams, "After the Cheering Stopped, Jackie Robinson Played Harder than Ever," *Washington Post Magazine*, April 12, 1987, p. 37.

23. Sam Smith, "Doby's Abandoned Dream," *Chicago Tribune*, July 5, 1987, sec. 3, p. 6.

24. Peter Golenbock, *Dynasty: The New York Yankees 1949–1964* (Englewood Cliffs, N.J.: Prentice-Hall, 1975) p. 139.

25. It should also be noted that the proportion of black players grew rather steadily during this time period: 7.5 percent in 1954, 12.5 percent in 1958, 17.0 percent in 1962, 24.0 percent in 1966, and 24.5 percent in 1970. Gerald W. Scully, "Economic Discrimination in Professional Sports," *Law and Contemporary Problems*, (Winter–Spring 1973) p. 68.

26. Anthony J. Connor, *Voices from Cooperstown* (New York: Collier Books, 1984).

27. "Scorecard," *Sports Illustrated*, October 9, 1978, p. 28. Carew's response might also pertain to John Roseboro, who was holding out for $45,000. Griffith's offer to Roseboro had a note that began: "Boy, where else can you work and make $40,000 a year? Take this or you'll never work again." Bryan Burwell, "Roseboro Victim of Baseball Color Barrier," *Chicago Tribune*, May 10, 1987, sec. 3, p. 2. Another example of racism in management may have occurred when a reporter presented a general manager with the Pittsburgh Pirates' official program, which had a solid black cover with the team's emblem in gold. The general manager—perhaps realizing that the Pirates were the first, if not only, team to start blacks at all nine positions—wanted to know if the program was a team photo. Alison Gordon, *Foul Ball* (New York: Dodd Mead, 1985), p. 43.

28. For fine tributes to Howard's qualities, see Red Smith, *To Absent Friends* (New York: New American Library, 1982) pp. 309–10: and Jim Murray, "A Born Yankee," *Los Angeles Times*, June 23, 1977, sec. 3, p. 1.

29. Bob Gibson, *From Ghetto to Glory* (Englewood Cliffs, N.J.: Prentice-Hall, 1968), p. 3.

30. Ross Wetzsteon, "What's Eating Jim Rice?" *Sport* (June 1987) p. 48. See also "Dodgers' Gilliam Keeps Feelings Guarded Closely as a Base Line," *Miami Herald*, May 29, 1977, p. 11–C.

31. Dick Allen and Tim Whitaker, *Crash* (New York: Ticknor and Fields, 1989), p. 186.

32. Tom E. Fandell, "Unsung Slugger: Baseball's Greatest, Aaron, Speaks Softly but Carries a Big Stick," *Wall Street Journal*, April 5, 1971, pp. 1, 14.

33. "Scorecard," *Sports Illustrated*, October 8, 1979, p. 21.

34. Kahn, *Boys of Summer*, p. 365.

35. Jim Bouton, *Ball Four* (New York: World Publishing 1970) p. 302; and Lynn Rosellini, "Strike One And You're Out," *U.S. News and World Report*, July 27, 1987), p. 52.

36. Allen and Whitaker, *Crash*, p. 20.

37. Wendell Smith, "The Jackie Robinson I Knew," in John Kuenster, ed., *From Cobb to "Catfish"* (Chicago: Rand McNally, 1975), p. 243.

38. As of September 1987, the only other blacks to manage in the majors were

Maury Wills (Seattle Mariners in 1980, 20 wins and 38 losses; and in 1981, six wins and 18 losses), Larry Doby (White Sox in 1978, 37 wins and 50 losses), and Cito Gaston (Toronto Blue Jays in 1989, record for the season not available at the time of this printing). Robinson's win-loss record reads like this: Cleveland, 79–80 in 1975, 81–78 in 1976, and 26–31 in 1977; San Francisco, 56–55 in 1981, 87–75 in 1982, 79–85 in 1983, and 42–64 in 1984. Richard Justice, "Speaking of Necessities," *Washington Post*, April 12, 1987, p. C–12. John "Buck" O'Neil, hired by the Chicago Cubs in 1962, was the first black coach in the majors. *New York Times*, May 30, 1962, p. 12. The late Bill Lucas was the only black general manager hired up until 1988.

39. "Giants' Manager Robinson Glad for Second Chance," *Miami Herald*, April 5, 1981, p. 5–C.

40. "Robinson Says Firing Bad News," *Chicago Sun Times*, August 7, 1984, p. 99.

41. "Dodgers' Companis: Blacks May Lack 'Necessities' to Be Managers," *Chicago Tribune*, April 8, 1987, sec. 4, p. 2.

42. Carl Rowan, "Not Just Baseball's Shame," *Washington Post*, April 11, 1987, p. D–7. See also Thomas Boswell, "Baseball's Scandal Isn't Secret Now," *Washington Post*, April 10, 1987, p. D–7.

43. Jerome Holtzman, "Campanis Guilty Only of Not Being Slick Enough to Escape Koppel's Trap," *Chicago Tribune*, April 9, 1987, sec. 4, p. 3.

44. For an interesting discussion of racial physiological differences, see Dave Hyde and Shaun Powell, "Sports: Open Door or Dead End for Blacks?" *Miami Herald*, August 28, 1988, pp. 1–A, 21–A.

45. Joe Morgan, "Piercing the Excuses in Baseball Hirings," *New York Times*, April 19, 1987, Sec 5, p. 8.

46. George Vecsey, "Thinking about the Chief," *New York Times*, April 24, 1987, p. A–26. See also Hal Bodley, "Campanis: 'My Intentions Were Good,' " *USA Today*, April 14, 1987, p. 3C; the article indicates that Campanis, a last-minute substitute, for Don Newcombe was on the playing field after a tough Dodger loss and could not hear the questions.

47. Roy Campanella, *It's Good to Be Alive* (Boston: Little, Brown, 1959), p. 133.

48. *New York Times* Editorial, April 10, 1987, p. 34.

49. Mark Asher, "Dodgers Fire Campanis," *Washington Post*, April 9, 1987, p. C–1.

50. Richard Justice, "Speaking of Necessities," *Washington Post*, April 12, 1987, p. C–1. For an account of owner Edward Williams's actions and attitudes toward affirmative action see Don Baylor with Claire Smith, *Don Baylor* (New York: St. Martin's Press, 1989), p. 273.

51. "Baseball Agrees to Affirmative-Action Plan," *Chicago Tribune*, June 11, 1987, pp. 1, 6.

52. Bernie Linicome, "Jesse and Pete Grab the Moment," *Chicago Tribune*, June 12, 1987, p. 6.

53. Frank Litsky, "Taking the Struggle beyond the Field," *New York Times*, June 21, 1987, sec. 5, p. 1.

54. *Jet* (September 14, 1987), p. 48.

55. Roy S. Johnson, "Few Blacks Reach Local Front Offices," *New York Times*, April 16, 1987, p. B–12.

56. Tracy Ringolsby, "Majors Have Done Little to Solve Minority Hiring Problem," *Florida Times-Union Jacksonville Journal*, October 25, 1987, p. C–13.

57. Frank Robinson and Berry Stainbach, *Extra Innings* (New York: McGraw-Hill, 1988), p. 12.

58. Dave Anderson, "Bill White Keeps Fighting," *New York Times*, February 5, 1989, pp. 27, 29.

59. For related insights, see "Diamond Sparklers," *Wall Street Journal*, April 3, 1984, p. 1.

60. Richard E. Lapchick, *Broken Promises: Racism in American Sports* (New York: St Martin's/Marek, 1984), pp. 229–30. For an earlier study with similar results, see Anthony H. Pascal and Leonard A. Rapping, "The Economics of Racial Discrimination in Organized Baseball," in A. Pascal, ed., *Racial Discrimination in Economic Life* (Lexington, Mass: Lexington Books, 1972), p. 147.

61. Ford C. Frick, *Games, Asterisks, and People* (New York: Crown Publishers, 1973), p. 101.

62. Andy Cohen, "Baseball? Or Is It Beanball?" Jacksonville, Florida, *Times-Union and Journal*, April 12, 1981, p. D–3.

63. Aaron Rosenblatt, "Negroes in Baseball: The Failure of Success," *Transaction* 4 (September 1967), p. 51.

64. Pascal and Rapping, "Economics of Discrimination," p. 138.

65. Richard E. Lapchick, "Racism in American Sports: A Series for United Press International," p. 3.

66. Bouton, *Ball Four*, p. 302.

67. Robert G. Mogull, "Salary Discrimination in Major League Baseball," *Review of Black Political Economy* (Spring 1975), pp. 269–79. See also Pascal and Rapping, "Economics of Discrimination;" James Richard Hill and William Spellman, "Pay Discrimination in Baseball: Data from the Seventies," *Industrial Relations* 23 (Winter 1984); and Marshall H. Medoff, "A Reappraisal of Racial Discrimination against Blacks in Professional Baseball," *Review of Black Political Economy* (Spring 1975), p. 267.

68. Scully, "Economic Discrimination in Professional Sports," p. 76.

CHAPTER EIGHT

1. Thomas M. Boswell and Richard B. McKeown, "From Trial by Law to Trial by Auction," *Journal of Contemporary Law* 4 (1978), p. 176–89.

2. For detailed accounts of the early history of the reserve rule, see Harold R. Seymour, *Baseball: The Early Years* (New York: Oxford University Press, 1960), pp. 106–15; James B. Dworkin, *Owners versus Players* (Boston: Auburn House, 1981), pp. 41–62; and Lionel S. Sobel, *Professional Sports and the Law* (New York: Law-Arts Publishers, 1977), pp. 81–89.

3. George Daly and William J. Moore, "Externalities, Property Rights, and the Allocation of Resources in Major League Baseball," *Economic Inquiry* 19 (January 1981), p. 93.

4. "Playboy Interview: Earl Weaver," *Playboy* (July 1983), p. 68.

5. U.S. Congress, Senate, Subcommittee on Antitrust and Monopoly of the Committee on the Judiciary, "Organized Professional Team Sports," Hearings (85th Cong., 2nd sess.), July 1958, p. 214.

6. *Federal Baseball Club v. National League*, 259 U.S. at 207 (1922). See also Jesse W. Markham and Paul V. Teplitz, *Baseball Economics and Public Policy* (Lexington, Mass: Lexington Press, 1981), pp. 7–8.

7. *Toolson v. New York Yankees, Inc.*, 346 U.S. 356 (1953). The Court appears to have been correct in assessing Congress's lack of interest in containing professional baseball or even other professional sports under federal antitrust laws. A survey taken some four years after *Toolson* found 42 percent of the congressional respondents undecided over this possibility. "62 of 147 Members of Congress Undecided on Laws for Sports," *New York Times*, April 20, 1957, p. 13.

8. Luther A. Huston, "Pro Football Placed under Antitrust Laws," *New York Times*, pp. 1, 36.

9. Sobel, *Sports and Law*, p. 63.

10. *Curtis C. Flood v. Bowie K. Kuhn, et al.* (June 19, 1972), *U.S. Supreme Court Reporter*, 407 U.S. 2112.

11. "Flood Works in Bar, Calls Players 'Slaves,' " *New York Times*, April 2, 1973, p. D–4.

12. Basic Agreement between the American League of Professional Baseball Clubs and the National League of Professional Baseball Clubs and Major League Baseball Players Association, January 1, 1973, p. 27.

13. Bill Madden, "Glory Days with Finley, Yankees," *Sporting News*, February 2, 1987, p. 37.

14. Roger Kahn, "Baseball: State of the Game," *Esquire* (July 1976), p. 22.

15. Timothy P. Beavers, "Case Comments: Labor Law—Professional Baseball Not Exempt from Federal Labor Laws—*Kansas City Royal Corp. v. Major League Baseball Players Association*, 532 F.2d 615 (8th Cir. 1976)," *Florida State University Law Review* 15 (Winter 1977), pp. 137–44.

16. For details of these negotiations, see Tom Clark, *Champagne and Baloney* (New York: Harper and Row, 1976), pp. 257–67.

17. Bowie Kuhn, *Hardball* (New York: New York Times Books, 1987), p. 143.

18. *Professional Baseball Clubs*, 66LA114 C(P. Seitz, 1975).

19. "Messersmith's Price Scares Away Reds," *Washington Post*, March 24, 1976, p. F–9.

20. Harold Parrott, *The Lords of Baseball* (New York: Praeger Publishers, 1976), p. 264; and Will Grimsley, "Baseball Strike's Roots Go Back to Arbitrator Seitz," *Los Angeles Times*, July 14, 1987, sec. 3, p. 1–4.

21. Louis Harris, "Qualms on Baseball's Free Agents," *Chicago Tribune*, December 27, 1976, sec. 3, p. 4.

22. "Arbitrator Rules 2 Pitchers' Free," *Washington Post*, December 24, 1975, p. C–7. Seitz was the third "permanent" arbitrator to be released. Marvin Miller pressured the first arbitrator, Lew Gill, into resigning; and Gabriel Alexander was terminated by mutual consent. Dick Young, "Did Seitz Have Extra Reason for Ruling for Messersmith?" *Fort Myers Press*, December 26, 1975, p. 8–C.

23. *Los Angeles Times*, December 4, 1976, Sec. 3, p. 1.

24. Ross Newhan, "Messersmith Wins Still Another Round," *Los Angeles Times*, February 5, 1976, sec. 3, p. 1.

25. "Messersmith Ruling Upheld on Appeal," *Washington Post*, March 10, 1976, p. 4–D.

26. James R. Chelius and James B. Dworkin, "Free Agency and Salary Determination in Baseball," *Labor Law Journal* 33 (August 1982), p. 539.

27. James Richard Hill and William Spellman, "Professional Baseball: The Reserve

Clause and Salary Structure," *Industrial Relations* 22 (Winter 1983), p. 4. Bowie
Kuhn estimated that 42 percent of the players had long-term contracts by 1980.
Kuhn, *Hardball*, p. 171.

28. Ibid. See also Paul M. Sommers and Noel Quinton, "Pay and Performance
in Major League Baseball: The Case of the First Family of Free Agents," *Journal
of Human Resources* (Summer 1982), pp. 426–36; Paul D. Staudohar and Edwin M.
Smith, "The Impact of Free Agency on Baseball Salaries," *Compensation Review* (3
Quarter 1981), pp. 46–55; and Henry J. Raimundo, "Free Agents' Impact on the
Labor Market for Baseball Players," *Journal of Labor Research* (Spring 1983), p. 192.

29. "The Threat of Free Agency and Exploitation in Professional Baseball, 1976–
1977," *Quarterly Review of Economics and Business* 25 (Winter 1985), pp. 68–82.

30. David Halberstam, "The Education of Reggie Smith," *Playboy* (October 1984),
p. 196.

31. Murray Chass, "More Barren Ground for '86 Free Agent?" *Sporting News*,
November 17, 1986, p. 53.

32. "Conspiring Not to Conspire," *Sports Illustrated*, January 20, 1986, p. 12.

33. Hal Lancaster, "Baseball Players, Owners, Gear Up for New Fight over Free
Agency," *Wall Street Journal*, October 10, 1986, p. 31.

34. Ibid.

35. Murray Chass, "It's the Great Salary Slowdown," *Sporting News*, February
9, 1987, p. 32.

36. "Horner Didn't Expect Lack of Interest," Jacksonville, *Florida Times-Union*,
March 25, 1987, p. D–6.

37. T. Roberts, Before the Major League Baseball Arbitration Panel, Grievance
No. 86–2, September 21, 1987, p. 15.

38. "Arbitrator Frees Fisk and 6 Others," *Chicago Tribune*, January 23, 1988,
sec. 2, pp. 1, 5. The seven players were Carlton Fisk, Kirk Gibson, Tom Brookens,
Donnie Moore, Butch Wynegar, Juan Beniquez, and Joe Niekro.

39. "Tigers' Gibson: My Pocket's Open," *Sporting News*, October 5, 1987, p. 16.

40. Ibid.

41. G. Nicolau, Before the Major League Baseball Arbitration Panel, Grievance
No. 87–3, August 31, 1985, pp. 22–23. This decision reflected 39 hearings over a
seven-month period.

42. Ibid., pp. 79–80.

43. The 12 players and their respective teams were: Doyle Alexander (Detroit);
Alan Ashby (Houston); Bob Boone and Brian Downing (California); Jim Clancy and
Ernie Witt (Toronto); Ken Daley (Saint Louis); Ron Guidry, Willie Randolph, and
Claudell Washington (New York); Rich Gedman (Boston); and Roy Smith (Minnesota).
Tim Raines (Montreal) waived his second-chance rights when he signed a three-year
$6.3-million contract; and Dave Concepcion was made a free agent, although he had
also obtained this status when he was released by Cincinnati. Andre Dawson and
Lance Parrish waived their rights when they signed 1989 contracts.

44. Murray Chass, "Randolph without Job after Yanks Sign Sax," *New York Times*,
November 25, 1988, p. 33. See also Ross Newhan, "Sax Blames Dodger V. P.,"
Miami Herald, November 25, 1988, pp. 1–E, 3–E.

45. Chris Mortensen, "Winter Meetings Marked the Return of Free Agent Bidding," *Atlanta Journal and Constitution*, December 11, 1988.

46. Glen Waggoner, "Collusion Is Over, But Excess Is Back," *New York Times*, December 18, 1988, p. 27.

47. Ben Walker, "Free Agents Were Big Winners," *Miami Herald*, December 18, 1988, p. 10-C.

48. James B. Dworkin, "Salary Arbitration in Baseball: An Impartial Assessment after Ten Years," *Arbitration Journal* 41 (March 1986), pp. 63–70.

49. Prior to the 1987 season, players having two years' service were eligible.

50. Stan Isle, "New Turf Is Braves' Protection for Bad Hops," *Sporting News*, February 9, 1987.

51. James B. Dworkin, *Owners versus Players* (Boston: Auburn House, 1987), p. 162.

52. Compiled from information in Murray Chass, "Don't Jump to Wrong Conclusion," *Sporting News*, February 29, 1988, p. 35.

53. The three players were Aurelio Lopez in 1983, Dwight Gooden in 1988, and Mike Moore in 1988. Murray Chass, "No New $2 Million Players in'87," *Sporting News*, February 2, 1987, p. 39.

54. "Red Sox Signs Boggs to Three-Year Contract," Jacksonville, *Florida Times-Union*, January 30, 1987, p. E–1.

55. Dworkin, "Salary Arbitration in Baseball," p. 63.

56. This finding differs from an earlier two-year study of salary arbitration cases conducted by James B. Dworkin, "How Final-Offer Arbitration Affects Baseball Bargaining," *Monthly Labor Review* 100 (March 1977), pp. 52–53.

57. Derived from statistics presented in Hal Bodley, "Arbitration Adds $35 M to 89 Payroll," *USA Today*, February 20, 1989, pp. 1C, 7C.

58. Section 12 of this exhibit was modified in the 1985 Memorandum of Agreement to include the following:

Effective with the 1987 Championship Season, the arbitrator shall, except for a player with five or more years of Major League Service, give particular attention, for comparative salary purposes, to contracts of players with Major League Service not exceeding one annual service group above the Player's annual service group. Nothing herein shall limit the ability of a player, because of special accomplishment, to argue the equal relevance of salaries of players without regard to service, and the arbitrator shall give whatever weight to such argument as he (or she) deems appropriate.

59. Peter Seitz, "Footnotes to Baseball Salary Arbitration," *Arbitration Journal* (June 1974), p. 100.

60. "Arbitration Arms Race," *Sport* (January 1984), p. 9. See also Franz Lidz, "Making a Most Important Pitch," *Sports Illustrated*, February 1, 1982, pp. 46–47.

61. Murray Chass, "Who's the Highest-paid Player? It Depends on Your Figures," *New York Times*, February 12, 1989, p. 32.

62. C. Raymond Grebey, Jr., "Another Look at Baseball's Salary Arbitration," *Arbitration Journal* 38 (December 1983), p. 25.

63. Marvin J. Miller, "Arbitration of Baseball Salaries: Impartial Adjudication in Place of Management Fiat," *Arbitration Journal* 38 (December 1983), p. 34.

64. Bob Verdi, "Dawson Learns Baseball Is a 'Cold Business,'" *Sporting News*, March 21, 1988, p. 5.

65. "He's Our Shortstop, Lord Love Him," *Sports Illustrated*, February 22, 1982, p. 12.

66. Herb Michelson, *Charlie O* (Indianapolis: Bobbs-Merrill, 1975), p. 276.

67. Ibid., p. 279.

68. Joseph Nocera, "The Man with the Golden Arm," *Newsweek* (April 10, 1989), p. 44.

CHAPTER NINE

1. "Scorecard," *Sports Illustrated*, April 11, 1977, p. 19.

2. "Series Riches," *Inside Sports*, October 31, 1980, p. 10; and Hal Bodley, "World Series Is Worth More to Dodgers," *USA Today*, October 28, 1988, p. 3C. Shares and purses after 1969 reflect playoff and World Series revenue.

3. For economic insights into this bargaining situation, see Gerald W. Scully, "Pay and Performance in Major League Baseball," *American Economic Review* 64 (December 1974), pp. 915–31; Timothy Tregarthen, "Players Head for the Courts," *Margin* (November 1987), p. 9; and James B. Dworkin, *Owners versus Players* (Boston: Auburn House, 1981), pp. 136–37.

4. Sandy Koufax with Ed Linn, *Koufax* (New York: Viking Press, 1966), p. 174.

5. John Tullius, *I'd Rather Be a Yankee* (New York: Macmillan, 1986), p. 174.

6. Joe DiMaggio, *Lucky to Be a Yankee* (New York: Rudolph Field, 1947), p. 169.

7. John Drebinger, "DiMaggio Wants Big Increase but Withholds Demand till Yanks Make Offer," *New York Times*, January 18, 1938, p. 9.

8. Tullius, *I'd Rather*, p. 158. In February 1943 DiMaggio volunteered for the wartime draft and earned $40 a month as a private.

9. "New York Yankee Manager Dallas Green on the Spot," *New York Times Magazine*, March 26, 1989, p. 52.

10. Duke Snider notes in his autobiography (with Bill Gilbert), *The Duke of Flatbush* (New York: Kensington, 1988), a rare instance where deliberate managerial deception benefited a player in wage negotiations. One year, Gil Hodges sought a $2,000 salary raise to $25,000. Dodger management official Buzzie Bavasi thought Hodges was worth $27,000 "but he couldn't offer a player more than the guy was asking or the word would get around and Buzzie would never have any leverage in his contract negotiations." Bavasi told Hodges that he would place salary figures ranging from $23,000 to $27,000 on five slips of paper and then have Hodges draw one slip out of a hat that would represent his new salary. Hodges was pleased when he drew $27,000, but Bavasi was not surprised since that figure was on every slip.

11. *Major League Baseball Players Benefit Plan Annual Report*, 1987, pp. 6, 7, and 19.

12. Roger Angell, *Late Innings* (New York: Simon and Schuster, 1982), p. 31.

13. "Rose on Teammates: Too Rich Too Fast," Jacksonville, *Florida Times-Union*, November 12, 1977, p. D-4.

14. "Playboy Interview: Pete Rose," *Playboy* (September 1979), pp. 82, 84.

15. Henry Aaron and Furman Bisher, *Aaron*, (New York: Thomas Y. Crowell, 1974), p. 5.

16. *Sports Illustrated*, March 25, 1974, p. 59.

17. Whitey Herzog and Kevin Horrigan, *White Rat* (New York: Harper and Row, 1987), p. 212.

18. Murray Chass, "Lesson to Be Learned from Twins' Success At the Gate," *Sporting News*, April 24, 1989, p. 53.

19. Ross Newhan, "Dodger Owner O'Malley Wants Economic Reform," *Miami Herald*, May 7, 1989, p. 40.

20. Frank Dolson, "Winfield's Stats Don't Add Up to $13 Million," *Miami Herald*, December 23, 1980, p. 7–D.

21. Paul M. Gregory, *The Baseball Player: An Economic Study* (Washington, D.C.: Public Affairs Press, 1956), p. 41.

22. Roger Angell, *Five Seasons: A Baseball Companion* (New York: Simon and Schuster, 1977), pp. 149–150.

23. My account of some of these problems is derived from Leonard Koppett, *A Thinking Man's Guide to Baseball* (New York: E. P. Dutton, 1967), pp. 272–79.

24. Jerome Holtzman, "Balk Rule's Enforcement Almost Certain to Get Some Backs Up," *Chicago Tribune*, April 7, sec. 4, p. 3.

25. Dave Stieb with Kevin Boland, *Tomorrow I'll Be Perfect* (New York: Doubleday, 1986), pp. 113, 117.

26. Thomas Boswell, "Dwight Evans Should Have Been MVP," *Inside Sports*, February 1982, p. 20.

27. Peter Golenbock, *Dynasty: The New York Yankees 1949–1964* (Englewood Cliffs, N.J.: Prentice Hall, 1975), p. 183.

28. Jim Bouton, *Ball Four* (New York: World Publishing 1970), p. 169.

29. Noel Hynd, "Giant-sized Confession: A Groundskeeper's Deeds," *Sports Illustrated* (August 29, 1988).

30. "Dome-inating the Game," *Psychology Today* (October 1988), p. 20.

31. Koppett, *Thinking Man's Guide*, p. 274. Some contend that recent changes in baseball construction have resulted in more home runs during the season. However, this contention appears to be wrong, since there have been no changes in baseball construction. Jeffrey Kluger, "What's behind the Home Run Boom?" *Discover* 9 (April 1988), pp. 78–79.

32. Willie Mays and Lou Sahadi, *Say Hey: The Autobiography of Willie Mays* (New York: Simon and Schuster, 1988), p. 271.

33. Angell, *Five Seasons*, p. 332.

34. *Wall Street Journal*, March, 2, 1982, p. 1.

35. Hal Bodley, "Long Term Payoff?" *USA Today*, November 15, 1985, p. 2C.

36. "No Dodger Deals Include Incentives," *Miami Herald*, November 6, 1988, p. 6–D.

37. Rick Ostrow, "No Lack of Incentive in Baseball," *USA Today*, November 14, 1985, p. 2C.

38. Ibid.

39. Rich Ostrow, "Incentives: Contract Clauses Catch Managers in the Middle," *USA Today*, November 14, 1985, p. 8C.

40. This practice changed in 1989, when pitcher Mike Morgan, acquired from the Orioles, could earn an extra $150,000 in award and appearance bonuses.

Selected Bibliography

Extensive and rather systematic use was made of the following publications, individual citations of which appear in the notes but not in the bibliography: Bureau of National Affairs, *Daily Labor Report*; *Chicago Tribune*; Jacksonville, *Florida Times-Union*; *Los Angeles Times*; Major League Baseball Basic Labor Agreements; *Miami Herald*; *New York Times*; *Sporting News*; *Sports Illustrated*; *USA Today*; *Wall Street Journal*; and *Washington Post*.

Aaron, Henry, and Furman Bisher. *Aaron*. New York: Thomas Y. Crowell, 1974.

Allen, Dick, and Tim Whitaker. *Crash*. New York: Ticknor and Fields, 1989.

Allen, Lee. *100 Years of Baseball*. New York: Bartholomew House, 1950.

Allen, Maury. *After the Miracle*. New York: Franklin Watts, 1989.

Anderson, Sparky, and Si Burick. *The Main Spark*. Garden City, N.Y.: Doubleday, 1978.

Angell, Roger. "Celebration." *New Yorker* (August 22, 1982): 50–60.

———. *Late Innings*. New York: Simon and Schuster, 1982.

———. *Five Seasons*: A Baseball Companion. New York: Simon and Schuster, 1977.

Baylor, Don, with Claire Smith. *Don Baylor*. New York: St. Martin's Press, 1989.

Bench, Johnny, and William Brashler. *Catch You Later*. New York: Harper and Row, 1979.

Berkow, Ira. *Pitchers Do Get Lonely*. New York: Atheneum, 1988.

Berra, Yogi, with Tom Hortin. *Yogi: It Ain't Over*. New York: McGraw-Hill, 1989.

Berry, Robert C., William B. Gould IV, and Paul D. Staudohar. *Labor Relations in Professional Sports*. Dover, Mass.: Auburn House, 1986.

Berry, Robert C., and Glenn M. Wong. *Law and Business of the Sports Industries*, Vol. 1. Dover, Mass.: Auburn House, 1986.

Boswell, Thomas M., and Richard B. McKeown. "From Trial by Law to Trial by Auction." *Journal of Contemporary Law* 4 (1978): 176–89.

Bouton, Bobbie, and Nancy Marshall. *Home Games*. New York: St. Martin's/Marek, 1983.

Bouton, Jim. *Ball Four*. New York: World Publishing, 1970.

Brenner, Marie. "Boss Steinbrenner." *New York Magazine* (April 13, 1981): 24–29.

Broeg, Bob, and Stan Musial. *The Man Stan: Musial, Then and Now*. St. Louis: Bethany Press, 1977.

Brosnan, Jim. *The Long Season*. New York: Harper and Brothers, 1969.

Bryan, Mike. *Baseball Lives*. New York: Pantheon Books, 1989.

Butler, Hal. *Al Kaline and the Detroit Tigers*. Chicago: Henry Regnery, 1973.

Campanella, Roy. *It's Good to Be Alive*. Boston: Little, Brown, 1959.

Carew, Rod, with Ira Berkow. *Carew*. New York: Simon and Schuster, 1979.

Carter, Gary, and John Hough, Jr. *A Dream Season*. New York: Harcourt, Brace, Jovanovich, 1987.

Chelius, James R., and James B. Dworkin. "Free Agency and Salary Determination in Baseball." *Labor Law Journal* 33 (August 1982): 539–45.

Clark, Tom. *Champagne and Baloney*. New York: Harper and Row, 1976.

Clemens, Roger, and Peter Gammons. *Rocket Man: The Roger Clemens Story*. Lexington, Mass.: Stephen Greene Press, 1987.

Connor, Anthony J. *Voices from Cooperstown*. New York: Collier Books, 1984.

Craig, Peter S. "Organized Baseball: An Industry Study of a $100 Million Spectator Sport." Bachelor of Arts Thesis, Oberlin College, 1950.

Creamer, Robert W. *Stengel: His Life and Times*. New York: Simon and Schuster, 1984.

————. *Babe*. New York: Simon and Schuster, 1976.

Crepeau, Richard C. *Baseball: America's Diamond Mind, 1919–1941*. Gainesville: University Presses of Florida, 1980.

Curtis C. Flood v. Bowie K. Kuhn, et al. (June 19, 1972). *U.S. Supreme Court Reporter*. 407 U.S. 2112.

Daly, George, and William J. Moore. "Externalities, Property Rights, and the Allocation of Resources in Major League Baseball." *Economic Inquiry* 19 (January 1981): 77–99.

DiMaggio, Joe. *Lucky to Be a Yankee*. New York: Rudolph Field, 1947.

Duren, Ryne, with Robert Drury. *The Comeback*. Dayton, Ohio: Lorenz Press, 1978.

Durocher, Leo. *Nice Guys Finish Last*. New York: Simon and Schuster, 1975.

Dworkin, James B. "Salary Arbitration in Baseball: An Impartial Assessment after Ten Years." *Arbitration Journal* 41 (March 1986):63–70.

————. *Owners versus Players*. Boston: Auburn House, 1981.

Dworkin, James B., and Thomas J. Bergmann. "Collective Bargaining and the Player Reservation Compensation System in Professional Sports." *Employee Relations Law Journal* 4 (Autumn 1978): 241–56.

Federal Baseball Club v. National League. 259 U.S. at 207 (1922).

Feller, Bob. "I'll Never Quit Baseball." *Look* (March 13, 1956): 56–59.

Fleming, G. H. *Murderers' Row*. New York: William Morrow, 1985.

Flood, Curt. *The Way It Is*. New York: Trident Press, 1971.

Ford, Whitey, and Phil Pepe. *Slick*. New York: William Morrow, 1987.

Frick, Ford C. *Games, Asterisks, and People.* New York: Crown Publishers, 1973.

Frommer, Harvey. *Baseball's Greatest Managers.* New York: Franklin Watts, 1985.

Gallner, Sheldon M. *Pro Sports: The Contract Game.* New York: Charles Scribner's Sons, 1974.

Garvey, Steve, with Skip Rozin. *Garvey.* New York: Times Books, 1986.

Gibson, Bob. *From Ghetto to Glory.* Englewood Cliffs, N.J.: Prentice-Hall, 1968.

Goldstein, L. "Arbitration of Grievance and Salary Disputes in Professional Baseball: Evolution of a System of Private Law." *Cornell Law Review* 60 (August 1975): 1049–74.

Golenbock, Peter. *Dynasty: The New York Yankees 1949–1964.* Englewood Cliffs, N.J.: Prentice-Hall, 1975.

Gordon, Alison. *Foul Ball.* New York: Dodd Mead, 1985.

Gould, Paul. "Unionism's Bid in Baseball." *New Republic* (August 5, 1946): 134–37.

Grebey, C. Raymond, Jr. "Another Look at Baseball's Salary Arbitration." *Arbitration Journal* 38 (December 1983): 24–30.

Gregory, Paul M. *The Baseball Player: An Economic Study.* Washington, D.C.: Public Affairs Press, 1956.

Gropman, Donald. *Say It Ain't So, Joe!* Boston: Little, Brown, 1979.

Guidry, Ron, and Peter Golenbock. *Guidry.* Englewood Cliffs, N.J.: Prentice-Hall, 1980.

Gwartney, James, and Charles Haworth. "Employer Costs and Discrimination: The Case of Baseball." *Journal of Political Economy* 82 (July–August 1974): 873–882.

Hall, Donald, with Dock Ellis. *Dock Ellis in the Country of Baseball.* New York: Coward McCann and Geoghegan, 1975.

Hernandez, Keith, and Mike Bryan. *If at First.* New York: McGraw-Hill, 1986.

Herzog, Whitey, and Kevin Horrigan. *White Rat.* New York: Harper and Row, 1987.

Hill, James. "The Threat of Free Agency and Exploitation in Professional Baseball: 1976–1979." *Quarterly Review of Economics and Business* 25 (Winter 1985):68–82.

Hill, James Richard, and William Spellman. "Pay Discrimination in Baseball: Data from the Seventies." *Industrial Relations* (Winter 1984): 103–12.

———. "Professional Baseball: The Reserve Clause and Salary Structure." *Industrial Relations* 22 (Winter 1983):1–19.

Holtzman, Jerome. *No Cheering in the Press Box.* New York: Holt, Rinehart, and Winston, 1974.

Honig, Donald. *The Man in the Dugout.* Chicago: Follett Publishing, 1977.

———. *Baseball When the Grass Was Real.* New York: Coward McCann and Geoghegan, 1975.

House, Tom. *The Jock's Itch.* Chicago: Contemporary Books, 1989.

Jackson, Reggie, with Bill Libby. *Reggie: A Season with a Superstar.* Chicago: Playboy Press, 1975.

Jackson, Reggie, with Mike Lupica. *Reggie.* New York: Villard Books, 1984.

Johnstone, Jay, and Rick Talley. *Over the Edge.* Chicago: Contemporary Books, 1987.

———. *Temporary Insanity.* Chicago: Contemporary Books, 1985.

Jones, Cleon, with Ed Hershey. *Cleon.* New York: Coward McCann, 1970.

Kahn, Roger. *Joe and Marilyn.* New York: William Morrow, 1987.

————. *The Boys of Summer*. New York: Harper and Row, 1971.

Koppett, Leonard. *A Thinking Man's Guide to Baseball*. New York: E. P. Dutton, 1967.

Koufax, Sandy, with Ed Linn. *Koufax*. New York: Viking Press, 1966.

Kowet, Dan. *The Rich Who Own Sports*. New York: Random House, 1977.

Krasnow, Erwin G., and Herman M. Levy. "Unionization and Professional Sports." *Georgetown Law Journal* 51 (1962–63):749–82.

Kuhn, Bowie. *Hardball*. New York: New York Times Books, 1987.

Lapchick, Richard E. *Broken Promises: Racism in American Sports*. New York: St. Martin's/Marek, 1984.

Lasorda, Tommy, and David Fisher. *The Artful D-O-D-G-E-R*. New York: Arkin House, 1985.

Lee, Bill, and Dick Lally. *The Wrong Stuff*. New York: Viking Press, 1984.

Lehman-Haupt, Christopher. *Me and DiMaggio*. New York: Simon and Schuster, 1986.

Lieb, Frederick G. *Connie Mack: Grand Old Man of Baseball*. New York: G. P. Putnam's Sons, 1945.

Lowell, C. M. "Collective Bargaining and the Professional Team Sport Industry." *Law and Contemporary Problems* 38 (Winter–Spring 1973): 3–41.

Lowenfish, Lee, and Tony Lupien. *The Imperfect Diamond*. New York: Stein and Day, 1980.

Lyle, Sparky, and Peter Golenbock. *The Bronx Zoo*. New York: Crown Publishers, 1979.

McCallum, John D. *Ty Cobb*. New York: Praeger Publishers, 1975.

McCarver, Tim, with Ray Robinson. *Oh Baby, I love It!* New York: Villard Books, 1987.

McGraw, John J. *My Thirty Years in Baseball*. New York: Boni and Liveright, 1928.

McLain, Denny, with Dave Diles. *Nobody's Perfect*. New York: Dial Press, 1975.

Major League Baseball Players Benefit Plan Annual Report, 1987.

Mann, Arthur. *Branch Rickey*. Cambridge, Mass.: Riverside Press, 1957.

Mantle, Mickey, and Herb Gluck. *The Mick*. New York: Doubleday, 1985.

Markham, Jesse W., and Paul V. Teplitz. *Baseball Economics and Public Policy*. Lexington, Mass.: Lexington Press, 1981.

Martin, Billy, and Peter Golenbock. *Number 1*. New York: Delacorte Press, 1980.

Martin, Billy, with Phil Pepe. *Billy Ball*. Garden City, N. Y.: Doubleday, 1987.

Martin, Philip L. "The Labor Controversy in Professional Baseball: The *Flood* Case." *Labor Law Journal* (September 1972): 567–71.

Mays, Willie, and Lou Sahadi. *Say Hey: The Autobiography of Willie Mays*. New York: Simon and Schuster, 1988.

Medoff, Marshall H. "On Monopolistic Exploitation in Baseball." *Quarterly Review of Economics* 16 (Summer 1976): 113–21.

————"A Reappraisal of Racial Discrimination against Blacks in Professional Baseball." *Review of Black Political Economy* (Spring 1975): 259–68.

Michelson, Herb. *Charlie O*. Indianapolis: Bobbs-Merrill, 1975.

Miller, Marvin J. "Arbitration of Baseball Salaries: Impartial Adjudication in Place of Management Fiat." *Arbitration Journal* 38 (December 1983):31–35.

Mogull, Robert G. "Salary Discrimination in Major League Baseball." *Review of Black Political Economy* (Spring 1975): 269–79.

Morris, John P. "In the Wake of the Flood." *Law and Contemporary Problems* (1973):85–98.

Munson, Thurman, with Martin Appel. *Thurman Munson.* New York: Coward McCann and Geoghegan, 1978.

Nicolau, George. Before the Major League Baseball Arbitration Panel: In the Matter of Arbitration between the Major League Baseball Players Association and the 26 Major League Baseball Clubs. Grievance No. 87–3, August 31, 1988.

Noll, Roger G. *Government and the Sports Business.* Washington, D.C.: Brookings Institution, 1974.

Paige, Satchel. *Maybe I'll Pitch Forever.* Garden City, N.Y.: Doubleday, 1962.

Parrott, Harold. *The Lords of Baseball.* New York: Praeger Publishers 1976.

Pascal, Anthony H., and Leonard A. Rapping. "The Economics of Racial Discrimination in Organized Baseball." In Anthony Pascal, ed. *Racial Discrimination in Economic Life.* Lexington, Mass.: Lexington Books, 1972: 119–56.

"Pete Rose." *60 Minutes, as Broadcast over the CBS Television Network.* Transcript. Vol. 11. No. 24 February 25, 1979.

Peterson, Robert. *Only the Ball Was White.* New York: McGraw-Hill, 1984.

Piniella, Lou, and Maury Allen. *Sweet Lou.* New York: G. P. Putnam's Sons, 1986.

Pluto, Terry, and Jeffrey Neuman. *A Baseball Winter.* New York: Macmillan, 1986.

Professional Baseball Clubs. 66LA114 (C.P. Seitz, 1975).

Raimundo, Henry J. "Free Agents' Impact on the Labor Market for Baseball Players." *Journal of Labor Research* (Spring, 1983): 183–94.

Ritter, Lawrence S. *The Glory of Their Times.* New York: William Morrow, 1984.

Ritter, Lawrence, and Donald Honig. *The Image of Their Greatness.* 2nd Ed. New York: Crown Publishers, 1984.

Roberts, Thomas T. "Sports Arbitration." *Industrial Relations Law Journal* 10:1 (1988):8–11.

———. Before the Major League Baseball Arbitration Panel: In the Matter of the Arbitration between Major League Baseball Players Association and the 26 Major League Baseball Clubs. Grievance No. 86–2. September 21, 1987.

Robinson, Frank, and Barry Stainbach. *Extra Innings.* New York: McGraw-Hill, 1988.

Robinson, Jackie, with Alfred Duckett. *I Never Had It Made.* New York: G. P. Putnam's Sons, 1972.

Rose, Pete, and Bob Hartzel. *Charlie Hustle.* Englewood Cliffs, N.J.: Prentice-Hall, 1975.

Roseboro, John, with Bill Libby. *Glory Days with the Dodgers and Other Days with Others.* New York: Atheneum, 1978.

Rosenblatt, Aaron. "Negroes in Baseball: The Failure of Success." *Transaction* 4 (September 1967):51–53.

Rosenthal, Harold. *The 10 Best Years of Baseball.* Chicago: Critegacy Books, 1979.

Roth, Alvin E. "Further Thoughts from the Power of Alternatives: An Example from Labor-Management Negotiations in Major League Baseball." *Negotiation Journal* (October 1985):359–62.

Rottenberg, Simon. "The Baseball Players' Labor Market." *Journal of Political Economy* 64 (June 1956):242–58.

Rowan, Carl T., with Jackie Robinson. *Wait till Next Year.* New York: Random House, 1960.

Ruth, Babe, with Bob Considine. *The Babe Ruth Story*. New York: E. P. Dutton, 1948.

Schaap, Dick. *Steinbrenner*. New York: G. P. Putnam's Sons, 1982.

Schneider, Russell S. *Frank Robinson: The Making of a Manager*. New York: Coward McCann and Geoghegan, 1976.

Scoville, James. "Has Collective Bargaining Altered the Salary Structure of Baseball?" *Monthly Labor Review* 100 (March 1977): 51–53.

Scully, Gerald W. "Pay and Performance in Major League Baseball." *American Economic Review* 64 (December 1974):915–31.

———. "Economic Discrimination in Professional Sports." *Law and Contemporary Problems* (Winter–Spring 1973):67–84.

Seitz, Peter. "Footnotes to Baseball Salary Arbitration." *Arbitration Journal* (June 1974):98–104.

Seymour, Harold R. *Baseball: The Early Years*. New York: Oxford University Press, 1960.

Shapiro, Paul W. "Monopsony Means Never Having to Say You're Sorry—A Look at Baseball's Minor Leagues." *Journal of Contemporary Law* 4 (1978): 191–208.

Smith, Red. *To Absent Friends*. New York: New American Library, 1982.

———. *Strawberries in the Winter Time*. New York: Quadrangle, 1974.

Snider, Duke, with Bill Gilbert. *The Duke of Flatbush*. New York: Kensington, 1988.

Sobel, Lionel S. *Professional Sports and the Law*. New York: Law-Arts Publishers, 1977.

Sommers, Paul M., and Noel Quinton. "Pay and Performance in Major League Baseball: The Case of the First Family of Free Agents." *Journal of Human Resources* (Summer 1982):426–36.

Stargell, Willie, and Tom Bird. *Willie Stargell*. New York: Harper and Row, 1984.

Staudohar, Paul D., and Edwin M. Smith. "The Impact of Free Agency on Baseball Salaries." *Compensation Review* (3 Quarter 1981): 46–55.

Stieb, Dave, with Kevin Boland. *Tomorrow I'll Be Perfect*. New York: Doubleday, 1986.

Stokes, Geoffrey. *Pinstripe Pandemonium*. New York: Harper and Row, 1984.

"Strike Two." *60 Minutes, as Broadcast over the CBS Television Network*. Transcript. Vol. 12. No. 29. March 30, 1980.

Thompson, Danny, with Bob Fowler. *E–6: The Diary of a Major League Shortstop*. Minneapolis: Dillon Press, 1975.

"The Threat of Free Agency and Exploitation in Professional Baseball, 1976–1977." *Quarterly Review of Economics and Business* 25 (Winter 1985):68–82.

Toolson v. New York Yankees, Inc. 346 U.S. 356 (1953).

Topkis, Jay. "Monopsony in Manpower: Organized Baseball Meets the Anti-trust Laws." *Yale Law Journal* 62 (March 1953):576–639.

Tullius, John. *I'd Rather Be a Yankee*. New York: Macmillan, 1986.

Tygiel, Jules. *Baseball's Great Experiment*. New York: Oxford University Press, 1983.

Underwood, John. *Spoiled Sport*. Boston: Little, Brown 1984.

U.S. Congress, House, "Inquiry into Professional Sports." Hearings. 94th Cong., 2nd Sess., 1976.

U.S. Congress, House, Subcommittee or Monopolies and Commercial Law, Committee on the Judiciary. "Antitrust Policy and Professional Sports." Oversight Hearings. 97th Cng., 2nd Sess., July 14, 15, 16, 1982.

U.S. Congress, House, Subcommittee on Study "Organized Baseball." Report Pursuant to H. R. Res. 95. 82nd Cong. 2nd Sess., May 27, 1952.

U.S. Congress, Senate, Subcommittee on Antitrust and Monopoly of the Committee on the Judiciary. "Professional Sports Antitrust Bill, 1964." Hearings. 88th Cong., January 30, 31, February 17, 18, 1964.

―――. "Organized Professional Team Sports." Hearings. 85th Cong., 2nd Sess., July 1958.

Veeck, Bill, and Ed Linn. *Veeck—As in Wreck*. New York: Bantam Books, 1963.

Voight, David Q. *America through Baseball*. Chicago: Nelson-Hall, 1976.

Ward, John. "Is the Ballplayer a Chattel?" *Lippincott's Monthly Magazine* (August 1887):310, 319.

Welch, Bob, and George Vescey. *Five O'Clock Comes Early*. New York: William Morrow, 1982.

Whitfield, Shelby. *Kiss It Goodbye*. New York: Abeland-Schuman, 1973.

"Who Says Baseball Is like Ballet?" *Forbes* 107 (April 1, 1971):24–26, 30, 31.

Williams, Ted, with John Underwood. *My Turn at Bat; The Story of My Life*. New York: Simon and Schuster, 1969.

Winfield, Dave, with Tom Parker. *Winfield: A Player's Life*. New York: W. W. Norton, 1988.

Wong, Glenn M. "A Survey of Grievance Arbitration Cases in Major League Baseball." *Arbitration Journal* 41 (March 1986): 42–62.

Index

About the Author

After receiving his Bachelor's degree from Knox College and Master's degree from the University of Illinois, *Ken Jennings* spent four years with Union Carbide in various industrial relations assignments. He then received a Ph.D. from the University of Illinois and has been with the University of North Florida for 16 years where he has written numerous articles and books.

A Chicago Cubs fan and dabbler in baseball cards ("Reds" and "Blues" are the first cards he remembers), he lives with his wife, Jackie, son, Bret, and daughter, Allison.